Anthony Trollope

The Land-Leaguers

Anthony Trollope

The Land-Leaguers

ISBN/EAN: 9783744709026

Printed in Europe, USA, Canada, Australia, Japan

Cover: Foto ©ninafisch / pixelio.de

More available books at **www.hansebooks.com**

THE
LAND-LEAGUERS

BY
ANTHONY TROLLOPE

A NEW EDITION

London
CHATTO & WINDUS, PICCADILLY
1884
[*All rights reserved*]

CONTENTS.

	PAGE
CHAPTER I.	
JONES OF CASTLE MORONY	1
CHAPTER II.	
MAN IN THE MASK	8
CHAPTER III.	
...R BROSNAN	15
CHAPTER IV.	
BLAKE OF CARNLOUGH	22
CHAPTER V.	
O'MAHONY AND HIS DAUGHTER	27
CHAPTER VI.	
...EL AND HER LOVERS	34
CHAPTER VII.	
...'S	40
CHAPTER VIII.	
...STMAS-DAY, 1880	48
CHAPTER IX.	
... DALY	52
CHAPTER X.	
...YTOWNGAL	59
CHAPTER XI.	
... .	64

CONTENTS.

PAGE

CHAPTER XII.
"DON'T HATE HIM, ADA" 70

CHAPTER XIII.
EDITH'S ELOQUENCE. 75

CHAPTER XIV.
RACHEL'S CORRESPONDENCE 79

CHAPTER XV.
CAPTAIN YORKE CLAYTON 85

CHAPTER XVI.
CAPTAIN CLAYTON COMES TO THE CASTLE . . . 92

CHAPTER XVII.
RACHEL IS FREE 98

CHAPTER XVIII.
FRANK JONES HAS CEASED TO EXIST 104

CHAPTER XIX.
FIFTH AVENUE AND NEWPORT 112

CHAPTER XX.
BOYCOTTING 117

CHAPTER XXI.
LAX, THE MURDERER 124

CHAPTER XXII.
MORONY CASTLE IS BOYCOTTED 129

CHAPTER XXIII.
TOM DALY IS BOYCOTTED 135

CHAPTER XXIV.
"FROM THE FULL HEART THE MOUTH SPEAKS" . . 141

CHAPTER XXV.
THE GALWAY BALL 149

CHAPTER XXVI.
LORD CASTLEWELL 155

CONTENTS.

CHAPTER XXVII.
... FUNDS WERE PROVIDED 163

CHAPTER XXVIII.
... WAS NOT DONE WITH THE FUNDS 170

CHAPTER XXIX.
... WAS DONE WITH THE FUNDS 176

CHAPTER XXX.
... ROAD TO BALLYGLUNIN 184

CHAPTER XXXI.
... GALWAY COURT HOUSE 189

CHAPTER XXXII.
... O'MAHONY AS MEMBER OF PARLIAMENT . . . 195

CHAPTER XXXIII.
CAPTAIN CLAYTON'S LOVE-MAKING 201

CHAPTER XXXIV.
LORD CASTLEWELL'S LOVE-MAKING 206

CHAPTER XXXV.
MR. O'MAHONY'S APOLOGY 214

CHAPTER XXXVI.
RACHEL WRITES ABOUT HER LOVERS 222

CHAPTER XXXVII.
RACHEL IS ILL 227

CHAPTER XXXVIII.
LORD CASTLEWELL IS MUCH TROUBLED 233

CHAPTER XXXIX.
CAPTAIN CLAYTON'S FIRST TRIUMPH 240

CHAPTER XL.
YORKE CLAYTON AGAIN MAKES LOVE 247

CHAPTER XLI.
THE STATE OF IRELAND 251

CONTENTS.

	PAGE
CHAPTER XLII.	
LORD CASTLEWELL'S FAREWELL	261
CHAPTER XLIII.	
MR. MOSS IS FINALLY ANSWERED	266
CHAPTER XLIV.	
FRANK JONES COMES BACK AGAIN	271
CHAPTER XLV.	
MR. ROBERT MORRIS	277
CHAPTER XLVI.	
CONG	283
CHAPTER XLVII.	
KERRYCULLION	290
CHAPTER XLVIII.	
THE NEW ARISTOCRACY FAILS	296
CHAPTER XLIX.	301

THE LAND-LEAGUERS.

CHAPTER I.

MR. JONES OF CASTLE MORONY.

IN the year 1850 the two estates of Ballintubber and Morony were sold to Mr. Philip Jones, under the Estates Court, which had then been established. They had been the property of two different owners, but lay conveniently so as to make one possession for one proprietor. They were in the County Galway, and lay to the right and left of the road which runs down from the little town of Headford to Lough Corrib. At the time when the purchase was made there was no quieter spot in all Ireland, or one in which the lawful requirements of a landlord were more readily performed by a poor and obedient tenantry. The people were all Roman Catholics, were for the most part uneducated, and it may be said of them that not only were their souls not their own, but that they were not ambitious even of possessing their own bodies. Circumstances have changed much with them since that date. Not only have they in part repudiated the power of the priest as to their souls, but, in compliance with teaching which has come to them from America, they claim to be masters also of their bodies. Never were a people less fitted to exercise such dominion without control. Generous, kindly, impulsive, and docile, they have been willing to follow any recognised leader. When Philip Jones bought the property that had belonged to the widow O'Dwyer—for Ballintubber had for the last hundred years been the property of the O'Dwyers—and Morony, which had been an outlying town-land belonging to the Hacketts for the last two centuries, he had at first been looked down upon as a new comer. But all that had passed by, and Mr. Jones was as much respected as though he had been an O'Jones from the time of Queen Elizabeth. But now the American teaching had come up, and things were different.

Mr. Jones had expended over £30,000 in purchasing the property, and was congratulated by all men on having done well with his money. There were some among his friends in England —and his friends were all English—who had told him that he was incurring a great risk in going into so distant and wild a country. But it was acknowledged that he could not in England have obtained so good a return in the way of rent. And it was soon found that the opportunities for improving the property were many and close at hand. At the end of ten years all men who knew Mr. Jones personally, or had seen the increasing comforts of Morony Castle, declared that, as he liked the kind of life, he had done uncommonly well for himself.

Nor had he done badly for his three married sisters, each of whom had left £4,000 in his hands. All the circumstances of the Miss Jones's as they had been, it will be here unnecessary to explain. Since Philip had become owner of Morony Castle, each of them had married, and the three brothers-in-law were equally well satisfied with the investment of their money. It will, however, thus be understood that the property did not belong entirely to Mr. Jones, and that the brothers-in-law and their wives were part owners. Mr. Jones, however, had been in possession of some other means, and had been able to use capital in improving the estate. But he was an aspiring man, and in addition to his money had borrowed something beyond. The sum borrowed, however, had been so small and so well expended, as to have created no sense of embarrassment in his mind.

When our story commences he was the father of four children. The elder and the younger were boys, and two girls came between them. In 1880, Frank, the elder, was two-and-twenty. The two girls who followed close after were twenty and nineteen, and the youngest boy, who was born after an interval of nearly ten years, was but ten years old. Some years after the mother had died, and Mr. Jones had since lived as a widower. It may be as well to state here that in 1880 he was fifty-five years old.

When his wife had died, the nature of the man had apparently been changed. Of all men he had been the most cheerful, the most eager, and the most easily pleased. He had worked hard at his property, and had loved his work. He knew every man and woman about the place, and always had a word to say to them. He had had a sailing boat on the lake, in which he had spent much of his time, but his wife had always been with him. Since her death he had hardly put his foot within the boat. He had lately become quick and short-tempered, but always with a visible attempt to be kind to those around him. But people said of him that since his wife had died he had shown an indifference to the affairs of the world. He was anxious—so it was said—to leave matters as much as possible to his son ; but, as has been already stated, his son was only twenty-two. He had formerly taken a great pleasure in attending the assizes at Galway. He had been named as a grand juror for the county, which he had indeed regarded as a great compliment; but since his wife's death he had not once attended.

People said of him that he had become indifferent to the work of his life, but in this they hardly spoke the truth. He had become indifferent rather to what had been its pleasures. To that which his conscience told him was its work, he applied himself with assiduity enough. There were two cares which sat near his heart: first, that no one should rob him; and secondly, that he should rob no one. It will often be the case that the first will look after itself, whereas the second will require careful watching. It was certainly the case with Philip Jones that he was most anxious to rob no one. He was, perhaps, a little too anxious that no one should rob him.

A few words must be said of his children. Frank, the eldest, was a good-looking, clever boy, who had been educated at the Queen's College, at Galway, and would have been better trained to meet the world had circumstances enabled him to be sent to a public school in England. As it was he thought himself, as heir to Morony Castle, to be a little god upon earth; and he thought also that it behoved his sisters and his brother, and the various dependants about the place, to treat him as though he were a god. To his father he was respectful, and fairly obedient in all matters, save one. As to that one matter, from which arose some trouble, much will have to be said as the story goes on.

The two girls were named Ada and Edith, and were, in form and figure, very unlike each other. Ada, the eldest, was tall, fair-haired, and very lovely. It was admitted in County Galway that among the Galway lasses no girl exceeded Ada Jones in brightness of beauty. She was sweet-tempered also, and gracious as she was lovely. But Edith did not share the gifts, which the fairy had bestowed upon her sister, in equal parts. She was, however, clever, and kind, and affectionate. In all matters, within the house, she was ready to accept a situation below her sister's; but this was not by her sister's doing. The demigod of the family seemed to assume this position, but on Ada's part there was no assumption. Edith, however, felt her infirmity. Among girls this is made to depend more on physical beauty than on other gifts, and there was no doubt that in this respect Edith was the inferior. She was dark, and small of stature, not ungraceful in her movements, or awkward in her person. She was black-haired, as had been her mother, and almost swarthy in her complexion, and there was a squareness about her chin which robbed her face of much of its feminine softness. But her eyes were very bright, and when she would laugh, or say something intended to make another laugh, her face would be brightened up with fun, good-humour, or wit, in a manner which enabled no one to call her plain.

Of the younger boy, Florian, much will be
goes on ; but what can be said of a boy who i
shall be descriptive and also interesting? He
age, but clever and sharp, and, since his mot
been his father's darling. He was beautiful to
all the children, except poor Edith, but the nei
that his education had been much neglect
intended to send him to college at Galway. A
for a short time flitted before the father's e
thought that he would have the boy prepared
but lately things had not gone quite so well a
and that idea had passed by. So that it wa
that Florian Jones would follow his brother to
Those who used to watch his ways would
professors of Galway College would have so
him.

While the mother had lived no family had
ruled than that of the Jones's, but since
irregularities had gone on. The father had m
the younger boy, and thereby had done mischief
too, had become proud of his position, and an
made to check him with a hard hand ; and
absolute working of the farm had been left to hi
had come, in which Mr. Jones would be sometin
sometimes too lenient. Of the girls it must
that they were to be blamed for no fault after
come. Everyone at Morony had felt that th
been the death of the mistress. But it must
other things had happened shortly afterwards
to create disturbance. One of the family ha
intended to become a Roman Catholic. The
Protestants, the father and mother having
England as Protestants. They were not,
Protestants, as those will know who best kno
had been no horror of a Catholic. According
way to heaven had been open to both Catho
only it had suited her to say her prayers a
fashion. The girls had been filled with no pio
Mr. Jones himself, some of the Protestan
neighbourhood of Tuam had declared that
hearted in the matter. An old clergyma
cathedral, and who had been chaplain to Bi
been heard to declare that he would rather h
avowed Papist.

But the one who had now declared hims
will say pervert if my readers wish it,—was
young friend Florian. He came in one da
sisters that he meant to be a Roman Cat

laughed at him, and told him that he did not know what he was talking about. "Don't I though?" said Florian. "I've had no end of an argument with Father Malachi, and he's got the best o' me. I'm not going to church any more." When his brother Frank was told, he threatened to "lick the young sinner." "That's about the best can be said for you Protestants," said the young imp. "You lick us when you're strong enough." But the father, when he heard the tidings, declared that he would not have his son molested. No doubt he would live to see his mistake. It was to be hoped that he would do so. But there should be no compulsion. So Master Florian remained for the present attached to his Catholic propensities, and duly went to mass at Ballintubber. This had taken place in the autumn of the year.

There had occurred a circumstance which may be called the beginning of our story. It must first be told that Mr. Jones kept about four hundred acres of the estate in his own hands, and had been held to have done very well with it. A tract of this land lay down on Lough Corrib, and had in former days produced almost nothing but rushes. By means of drains and sluices, which had not been brought into use without the expenditure of much capital, he had thoroughly fertilised some eighty acres, where he grew large crops of hay, which he sent across the lake to Galway, and fed his sheep on the after-grass with great profit. But the care of the sluices had been a great labour, and, latterly, a great trouble to Mr. Jones. He had looked for no evil at the hands of his workmen, or tenants, or neighbours. But he had been taught by experience to expect great carelessness. It was when the rain had fallen in heavy quantities, and when the lough was full that the evil was chiefly expected. Late in the autumn there came news up to the Castle, that the flood gates on the Ballintubber marshes had now been opened, and that the entire eighty acres were under water. Mr. Jones and his eldest son rushed down, and found that it was impossible to do anything. They could only wait till the waters had retreated, which would not take place for six months. The entire crop for the next year had been destroyed. Then Mr. Jones returned to the Castle stricken by a great blow, and was speechless for the rest of the day.

When the news had been brought, the family had been together at the breakfast table. The father and son had gone out together with the teller of the story. But Ada and Edith and Florian were left at the table. They all sat looking at each other till Edith was the first to speak.

"Flory, what do you know of all this?"

"What should I know?" said Flory. The two sisters looked at him, and each was aware that he did know something. Ada was not so quick as Edith, but even she was aroused. And from this moment Edith began to take the lead in managing her brother.

"You do," said Ada. "How was it done? Who did it—and why?"

"Sorrow a know, I know," said the boy.

"Flory, that is a lie," said Edith very solemnly, looking at him with all her eyes.

"You've no right to say that," said Florian. "It's just because I've turned Catholic, and it's all your spite." But the boy blushed ruby red, and the colour told its own story.

As soon as the news had been announced, Edith had seen the boy's countenance and had instantly watched him. His colour had not risen at once; but his lower jaw had fallen, and his eyes had glanced furtively round, and his whole frame had quivered. Then the rush of blood had flown to his face, and the story had been told so that Edith could read it. His first emotion had made it plain even to Ada. "Flory, you know all about it," said Ada.

Edith got up and went across the room and knelt down at the boy's side, leaning against his chair and looking up into his face. "Flory, you may lie with your voice, but you cannot stifle your heart within you. You have confessed the truth."

"I have not," said Flory; "I wasn't in it at all."

"Who says that you were in it? But you know."

"'Deed and I know nothin'." Now the boy began to cry. "You have no right to say I did it. Why should I do the likes of that?"

"Where were you at four o'clock yesterday afternoon?" asked Edith.

"I was just out, up at the lodge yonder."

"Flory, I know that you have seen this thing done. I am as certain of it as though I had been there myself."

"I haven't seen anything done—and I won't stay here to be questioned this way," said the boy, feeling that his blushes would betray him, and his incapacity to "lie square," as the Americans say.

Then the two sisters were left to talk over the matter together. "Did you not see it in his face?" said Edith.

"Yes, I saw something. But you don't mean to say that he knew it was to be done? That would make him a fiend."

"No; I don't think he knew it was to be done. But when Frank was teasing him the other day about his Catholic nonsense, and saying that he would not trust a Papist, Florian took the part of Pat Carroll. If there be a man about the place who would do a base turn to father, it's Pat Carroll. Now I know that Flory was down near the lough yesterday afternoon. Biddy Ryan saw him. If he went on he must have seen the water coming in."

"What shall we do?" asked Ada.

"Ah!—that's just it. What shall we do? If he could be made to tell the truth, that would be best. But as he denies it, father will believe him. Florian will say that we are spiting him because of his religion."

"But, Edith, we must tell father." At last it was decided that Edith should take the boy and talk to him. He was more prone to listen to Edith than to Ada. Edith did find her brother, and talked to him for an hour,—but in vain. He had managed to collect himself after his past breakdown, and was better able to bear the examination to which his sister put him, than at the first moment. He still blushed when he was questioned; till he became dogged and surly. The interview ended with repeated asseverations on Flory's part, that he knew nothing of the meadows.

Mr. Jones and his eldest son returned to the house, having been absent the entire day. "As sure as I am a living man, Pat Carroll has been at the doing of it," said Frank.

"He cannot have done it alone," said Ada.

"There have been others in it."

"That has been the worst of it," said the father. "Of course I have known since the beginning of the year, that that man would do any devil's turn of work against me. But one man cannot do much."

"Too much! too much!" said Edith.

"One man can murder me, of course. But we haven't yet come to such a state of things as that. Twelve months ago I thought there was not a man about the place who would raise his hand to do me an ill turn. I have done them many good turns in my time."

"You have, father," said Ada.

"Then this man came to me and said that because the tenants away in County Mayo were not paying their rents, he could not pay his. And he can sell his interest on his holding now for £150. When I endeavoured to explain this to him, and that it was at my cost his interest in the farm had been created, he became my enemy. I don't mind that; one has to look for that. But that others should be joined in it, and that there should be no one to say that they had seen it! There must have been five pairs of hands at work, and twenty pairs of eyes must have seen what the others were doing."

The two sisters looked at each other, but they said nothing. "I suppose we shall work it out of them some day," said Frank.

"I suppose nothing of the kind," said the father. "There are eighty acres of meadow lying under Lough Corrib this moment which will not give a ton of hay next summer, or food for a sheep next autumn. The pastures will be saturated, and sheep would perish with foot-rot and fluke. Then money must be laid out again upon it, just that Mr. Carroll may again wreak his vengeance." After that there was silence, for the children felt that not a word could be spoken which would comfort their father.

When they sat down to dinner, Mr. Jones asked after Florian. "He's not well," said Edith.

"Florian not well! So there's another misfortune."

"His ill-health is rather ill-humour. Biddy will take care of him, father."

"I do not choose that he should be looked after by Biddy in solitude. I suppose that somebody has been teasing him."

"No, father," said Edith, positively.

"Has anyone been speaking to him about his religion?"

"Not a word," said Edith. Then she told herself that to hold her tongue at the present moment would be cowardly. "Florian, father, has misbehaved himself, and has gone away cross. I would leave him, if I were you, till to-morrow."

"I know there is ill-will against him," said the father. All this was ill-judged on behalf of Mr. Jones. Peter, the old butler, who had lived in the family, was in the room. Peter, of course, was a Roman Catholic, and, though he was as true as steel, it could not but be felt that in this absurd contest he was on the side of the "young masther."

Down in the kitchen the conversion of the "young masther" to the true religion was a great affair, and Mr. Frank and the young ladies were looked upon as hard-hearted and cruel, because they stood in the way of this act of grace. Nothing more was said about Florian that night.

CHAPTER II.

THE MAN IN THE MASK.

EDITH, before she went to bed that night, crept up to her brother's bedroom and seated herself on the bedside. It was a little room which Florian occupied alone, and lay at the back of the house, next to that in which Peter slept. Here, as she sat on the bed, she could see by a glance that young Florian feigned to be asleep.

"Flory, you are pretending to be asleep." Flory uttered a short snore,—or rather snort, for he was not a good actor. "You may as well wake up, because otherwise I shall shake you."

"Why am I to be shaked up in bed?"

"Because I want to speak to you."

"Why am I to be made to speak when I want to sleep?"

"Papa has been talking about you downstairs. He has

come home from Ballintubber, very tired and very unhappy, and he thinks you have been made to go to bed without your supper because we have been attacking you about religion. I have told him that nobody has said a word to you."

"But you did."

"Not a word."

"You didn't tell him all that you told me—about letting in the water?" This was asked in a tone of great anxiety.

"Not a word,—not as yet."

"And you won't? Mind, I tell you it's all untrue. What do I know about letting in the water?"

"Who did it?"

"I'm not going to tell."

"You know, then?"

"No, I don't. But I'm not going to tell as though I knew it. You don't care about it in your religion, but we Catholics don't like telling lies."

"You saw nothing?"

"Whatever I saw I'm not to tell a lie about it."

"You've promised not, you mean?"

"Now, Edy, you're not going to trap me. You've got your own religion and I've got mine. It's a great thing in our religion to be able to hold your tongue. Father Malachi says it's one of the greatest trials which a man has to go through."

"Then, Flory, am I to gather that you will say nothing further to me?" Here the boy shook his head. "Because in that case I must tell father. At any rate, he must be told, and if you do not tell him I shall."

"What is there to be told?"

"I shall tell him exactly what I saw,—and Ada. I saw,—we saw,—that when the news came about the flood, you were conscious of it all. If you will go to father and tell him the truth he will be but very little angry with you I don't suppose you had a hand in it yourself."

"No!" shouted the boy.

"But I think you saw it, and that they made you swear an oath. Was that not so?"

"No!" whispered the boy.

"I am sure it was so." Then the boy again plucked up his courage, and declared with a loud voice, that it was not so.

That night before she retired to rest, Edith went to her father and told him all that she had to say. She took Ada with her, and together they used all their eloquence to make their father believe as they believed.

"No," said Edith, "he has not confessed. But words drop from him which make us sure that he knows who did it. I am certain that he saw it done. I don't mean to say that he saw the whole thing. The water, I suppose, was coming in all night."

"The whole night! While we were sleeping in our beds, the waters of the lough were ruining me," said the father.

"But he saw enough to be able to tell you who did it."

"I know who did it. It was that ruffian Carroll."

"But father, you will want evidence."

"Am I to bring up my own boy to swear that he was there, witnessing what was done, as the friend of my enemies? I do not believe that he was there at all."

"If you question him, he will probably own to it. It will be better to get at the truth and face it. He is only ten years old. You must tell me the story of his pretended conversion."

"Why should it be pretended?" asked the father.

"Well; of his conversion," said Edith.

"I don't see what it has to do with it. Am I to put myself forward as a bigoted Protestant? Florian has been foolish, but am I to say that I am angry, where I am not angry—not specially angry."

"It will show the influence under which he has taken up Carroll's side," said Edith.

"Or the influence under which he has been made to hold his tongue," said Ada.

"Just so," said Edith. "We do not think that he has made one with your enemies in the matter. But he has seen them at work and has been made to promise that he will hold his tongue. I don't suppose you mean to let the affair slip by without punishing anyone."

When the girls left him, Mr. Jones was by no means persuaded. As far as he could ascertain from examination of the persons about the locality, there was no one willing to state in evidence that he had seen anything. The injury had been done in November, on a wet, dreary, dull afternoon. He did learn that at half-past three the meadows were in their usual condition. As to the sluices, the gates of which had been pulled out and thrown away in twenty different places, he could learn nothing; no one had seen a sluice gate touched. As to Florian, and what Florian had been seen to do, he had asked no question, because Florian's name had not then been mentioned. But he had been struck by the awful silence of the people. There were women there, living on the spot, with whose families his family had been on the most kindly terms. When rheumatism was rife,—and rheumatism down on the lough side had often been rife,—they had all come up to the Castle for port wine and solace. He had refused them nothing,—he or his dear wife, who had gone, or his daughters; and, to give them their due, they had always been willing to work for him at a moment's notice. He would have declared that no man in Ireland was on better terms with his tenantry than he; and now, because there had been a quarrel between him and that pestilent fellow

Carroll,—whom he had been willing to buy out from his bit of land and let him go to America, so that they might all be at peace,—could they all have turned against him and taken Carroll's part? As far as he had been able to gather the feelings of the people, from conversations with them, they had all acknowledged Carroll to be wrong. He would have said that there was not one among them who was not his friend, rather than Carroll's. He was aware that there had been ill-feeling about in other parts of the country. There had been,—so he was told,—a few demagogues in Galway town, American chiefly, who had come thither to do what harm they could; and he had heard that there was discontent in parts of Mayo, about Ballyhaunis and Lough Glinn; but where he lived, round Lough Corrib, there had been no evil symptoms of such a nature. Now suddenly he found himself as though surrounded by a nest of hornets. There were eighty acres of his land under water, and no one would tell him how it was done, or by whom.

And now, to make the matter worse, there had come upon him this trouble with reference to his own boy. He would not believe the story which his daughters had told him; and yet he knew within his heart that they were infinitely the better worthy of credit. He believed in them. He knew them to be good and honest and zealous on his behalf; but how much better did he love poor Florian! And in this matter of the child's change of religion, in which he had foolishly taken the child's part, he could not but think that Father Malachi had been most unkind to him; not that he knew what Father Malachi had done in the matter, but Florian talked as though he had been supported all through by the priest. Father Malachi had, in truth, done very little. He had told the boy to go to his father. The boy had said that he had done so, and that his father had assented. "But Frank and the girls are totally against it. They have no sense of religion at all." Then Father Malachi told him to say his prayers, and come regularly to mass.

Mr. Jones agreed with his daughters that it behoved him to punish the culprit in this matter, but, nevertheless, he thought that it would be better for him to let it go unpunished than to bring his boy into collision with such a one as Pat Carroll. He twice talked the matter over with Florian, and twice did so to no effect. At first he threatened the young sinner, and frowned at him. But his frowns did no good. Florian, if he could stand firm against his sister Edith, was sure that he could do so against his father. Then Mr. Jones spoke him fair, and endeavoured to explain to him how sad a thing it would be if his boy were to turn against his own father and the interests of the family generally.

"But I haven't," said Florian confidently.

"You should tell me what you saw on that afternoon."

"I didn't see anything," said Florian sulkily.

"I don't believe he knew anything about it," said Mr. Jones to Edith afterwards. Edith could only receive this in silence, and kept her own opinion to herself. Ada was altogether of her mind, but Frank at last came round to his father's view. "It isn't probable," he said to his sisters, "that a boy of his age should be able to keep such a secret against four of us; and then it is most improbable that he should have seen anything of the occurrence and not have come at once to his father." But the girls held to their own opinion, till at last they were told by Frank that they were two pig-headed nincompoops.

Things were going on in this way, and Mr. Jones was still striving to find out evidence by which a case might be substantiated against Pat Carroll, when that gentleman, one winter afternoon, was using his eloquence upon Master Florian Jones. It was four o'clock, and the darkness of the night was now coming on very quickly. The scene was a cottage, almost in the town of Headford, and about two miles from the nearest part of the Morony estate. In this cottage Carroll was sitting at one side of a turf fire, while an old woman was standing by the doorway making a stocking. And in this cottage also was another man, whose face was concealed by an old crape mask, which covered his eyes and nose and mouth. He was standing on the other side of the fireplace, and Florian was seated on a stool in front of the fire. Ever and anon he turned his gaze round on the mysterious man in the mask, whom he did not at all know; and, in truth, he was frightened awfully through the whole interview by the man in the mask, who stood there by the fireside, almost close to Florian's elbow, without speaking a word; nor did the old woman say much, though it must be presumed that she heard all that was said.

"Faix, Mr. Flory, an' it's well for you you've come," said Carroll. "Jist you sit steady there, 'cause it won't do the laist good in life you're moving about where all the world'd see you." It was thus that the boy was addressed by him, whom we may now call his co-conspirator, and Carroll showed plainly, by his movements and by the glances which he cast around him, that he understood perfectly the dreadful nature of the business in which he was engaged. "You see that jintl'man there?" And Carroll pointed to the man in the mask.

"I see him," said poor Florian, almost in tears.

"You'd better mark him, that's all. If he cotches a hould o' ye he'd tear ye to tatthers, that's all. Not that he'd do ye the laist harum in life if ye'd just hould yer pace, and say nothin' to nobody."

"Not a word I'll say, Pat."

"Don't! That's all about it. Don't! We knows,—he knows, —what they're driving at down at the Castle. Sorra a word comes out of the mouth o' one on 'em, but that he knows it." Here the man in the mask shook his head and looked as horrible as a man in a mask can look. "They'll tell ye that the father who owns ye ought to know all about it. It's just him as shouldn't know."

"He don't," said Florian.

"Not a know;—an' if you main to keep yourself from being holed as they holed Muster Bingham the other day away at Hollymount." The boy understood perfectly well what was meant by the process of "holing." The Mr. Bingham, a small landlord, who had been acting as his own agent some twenty miles off, in the County of Mayo, had been frightfully murdered three months since. It was the first murder that had stained the quarrel which had now commenced in that part of the country. Mr. Bingham had been unpopular, but he had to deal with such a small property, that no one had imagined that an attack would be made on him. But he had been shot down as he was driving home from Hollymount, whither he had gone to receive rent. He had been shot down during daylight, and no one had as yet been brought to justice for the murder. "You mind's Muster Bingham, Muster Flory; eh? He's gone, and sorra a soul knows anything about it. It's I'd be sorry to think you'd be polished off that way." Again the man in the mask made signs that he was wide awake.

To tell the truth of Florian, he felt rather complimented in the midst of all his horrors in being thus threatened with the fate of Mr. Bingham. He had heard much about Mr. Bingham, and regarded him as a person of much importance since his death. He was raised to a level now with Mr. Bingham. And then his immediate position was very much better than Bingham's. He was alive, and up to the present moment,—as long as he held his tongue and told nothing,—he would be regarded with friendly eyes by that terrible man in the mask. But, through it all, there was the agonising feeling that he was betraying them all at home. His father and Edith and Frank would not murder him when they found him out, but they would despise him. And the boy knew something,—he knew much of what was due by him to his father. At this moment he was much in dread of Pat Carroll. He was in greater dread of the man in the mask. But as he sat there, terrified by them as they intended to terrify him, he was aware of all that courage would demand from him. If he could once escape from that horrid cabin, he thought that he might be able to make a clean breast and tell everything. "It's I that'd be awful sorry that anything like what happened Bingham, should happen to you, Muster Flory."

"Why wouldn't you; and I'd have done nothing against you?" said Florian. He did feel that his conduct up to the present moment deserved more of gratitude than of threats from Pat Carroll.

"You're to remimber your oath, Muster Flory. You're become one of us, as Father Brosnan was telling you. You're not to be one of us, and then go over among them schaming Prothestants."

"I haven't gone over among them,—only my father is one of them."

"What's yer father to do with it now you're a Catholic? Av you is ever false to a Catholic on behalf of them Prothestants, though he's twice yer own father, you'd go t' hell for it; that's where you'd be going. And it's not only that, but the jintl'man as is there will be sending you on the journey." Then Pat signified that he alluded to the man in the mask, and the gentleman in the mask clenched his fist and shook it,—and shook his head also. "You ask Father Brosnan also, whether you ain't to be thrue to us Catholics now you're one of us? It's a great favour as has been done you. You're mindful o' that—ain't you?" Poor Flory said that he was mindful.

Here they were joined by another conspirator, a man whom Florian had seen down by the sluices with Pat Carroll, and whom he thought he remembered to have noticed among the tenants from the other side of Ballintubber. "What's the chap up to now?" asked the stranger.

"He ain't up to nothin'," said Carroll. "We're only a cautioning of him."

"Not to be splitting on yourself?"

"Nor yet on you," said Carroll.

"Sorra a word he can say agin me," said the stranger. "I wasn't in it at all."

"But you was," said Florian. "I saw you pick the latch up and throw it away."

"You've sharp eyes, ain't you, to be seeing what warn't there to be seen at all? If you say you saw me in it, I'll have the tongue out of your mouth, you young liar."

"What's the good of frightening the boy, Michael? He's a good boy, and isn't agoing to peach upon any of us."

"But I ain't a liar. He's a liar." This Florian said, plucking up renewed courage from the kind words Pat Carroll had said in his favour.

"Never mind," said Pat, throwing oil on the troubled waters. "We're all frinds at present, and shall be as long as we don't split on nobody."

"It's the meanest thing out,—that splitting on a pal," said the man who had been called Michael. "It's twice worse when one does it to one's father. I wouldn't show a ha'porth of mercy to such a chap as that."

"And to a Catholic as peached to a Prothestant," said

Carroll, intending to signify his hatred of such a wretch by spitting on the ground.

"Or to a son as split because his father was in the question." Then Michael spat twice upon the floor, showing the extremity of the disgust which in such a case would overpower him.

"I suppose I may go now," said Florian. He was told by Pat Carroll that he might go. But just at that moment the man in the mask, who had not spoken a word, extemporised a cross out of two bits of burned wood from the hearth, and put it right before Florian's nose; one hand held one stick, and the other, the other. "Swear," said the man in the mask.

"Bedad! he's in the right of it. Another oath will make it all the stronger. 'That ye'll never say a word of this to mortial ears, whether father or sister or brother, let 'em say what they will to yer, s'help yer, the Blessed Virgin.'"

"I won't then," said Florian, struggling to get at the cross to kiss it.

"Stop a moment, me fine fellow," said Michael. "Nor yet to no one else—and you'll give yourself up to hell flames av you don't keep the blessed oath to the last day of your life. Now let me kiss it, Pat. I wouldn't be in his shoes for a ten pun note if he breaks that oath."

"Nor I neither," said Pat. "Oh laws, no." Then Florian was allowed to escape from the cabin. This he did, and going out into the dark, and looking about him to see that he was not watched, made his way in at the back door of a fairly large house which stood near, still in the outskirts of the town of Headford. It was a fairly large house in Headford; but Headford does not contain many large houses. It was that in which lived Father Giles, the old parish priest of Tuam;—and with Father Giles lived his curate, that Father Brosnan of whom mention has above been made.

CHAPTER III.

FATHER BROSNAN.

THERE has come a change among the priests in Ireland during the last fifty years, as has been natural. Among whom has there not come a change in half a century? In England, statesmen are different, and parsons, and judges, and peers. When an entire country has been left unmoved by the outside world, so as to seem to have been left asleep while others have been awake, the different classes will seem to be the same at the end of every half century. A village lawyer in Spain will be as was a village lawyer fifty years ago. But a parish priest in Ireland will be an altered personage, because the country generally has not been sleeping.

There used to be two distinct sorts of priests; of whom the elder, who had probably been abroad, was the better educated; whereas the younger, who was home-nurtured, had less to say for himself on general topics. He was generally the more zealous in his religious duties, but the elder was the better read in doctrinal theology. As to the political question of the day, they were both apt to be on the list against the Government, though not so with such violence as to make themselves often obnoxious to the laws. It was natural that they should be opposed to the Government, as long as the Protestant Church claimed an ascendency over them. But their feelings and aspirations were based then on their religious opinions. Now a set of men has risen up, with whom opposition to the rulers of the country is connected chiefly with political ideas. A dream of Home Rule has made them what they are, and thus they have been roused into waking life, by the American spirit, which has been imported into the country. There is still the old difference between the elder and the younger priests. The parish priest is not so frequently opposed to the law, as is his curate. The parish priest is willing that the landlord shall receive his rents, is not at least anxious, that he shall be dispossessed of his land. But the curate has ideas of peasant proprietors; is very hot for Home Rule, is less obedient to the authority of the bishops than he was of yore, and thinks more of the political, and less of the religious state of his country.

This variance of feeling might be seen in the three priests who have been already mentioned in our story. Father Giles was the parish pastor of Headford, in which position he had been for nearly forty years. He was a man seventy years of age, in full possession of all his faculties, very zealous in the well-being of his people, prone to teach them that if they would say their prayers, and do as they were bid by their betters, they would, in the long run, and after various phases of Catholic well or ill-being, go to heaven. But they would also have enough to eat in this world; which seemed to be almost more prominent in Father Giles's teaching than the happy bliss of heaven. But the older Father Giles became the more he thought of the good things of this world, on behalf of his people, and the less he liked being troubled with the political desires of his curate. He had gone so far as to forbid Father Brosnan to do this, or to do that on various occasions, to make a political speech here, or to attend a demonstration there;—in doing which, or in not doing it, the curate sometimes obeyed, but sometimes disobeyed the priest, thereby bringing Father Giles in his old age into infinite trouble.

But Father Malachi, in the neighbouring parish of Ballintubber, ran a course somewhat intermediate between these two.

He, at the present moment had no curate who interfered with his happiness. There was, indeed, a curate of Ballintubber—so named; but he lived away, not inhabiting the same house with Father Malachi, as is usual in Ireland; having a chapel to himself, and seldom making his way into our part of the country. Father Malachi was a strong-minded man, who knew the world. He, too, had an inclination for Home Rule, and still entertained a jealousy against the quasi-ascendancy of a Protestant bishop; but he had no sympathy whatever with Father Brosnan. Ireland for the Irish might be very well, but he did not at all want to have Ireland for the Americans. Father Giles and Father Malachi certainly agreed on one thing—that Brosnan was a great trouble.

If the conversion of Florian Jones was to be attributed to any clerical influence, Father Brosnan was entitled to claim the good or the evil done; but in truth very few polemical arguments had been used on the occasion. The boy's head had been filled with the idea of doing something remarkable, and he had himself gone to the priest. When a Protestant child does go to a priest on such a mission, what can the priest do but accept him? He is bound to look upon the suppliant as a brand to be saved from the burning. "You stupid young ass!" the priest may say to himself, apostrophising the boy; "why don't you remain as you are for the present? Why do you come to trouble me with a matter you can know nothing about?" But the priest must do as his Church directs him, and the brands have to be saved from the burning. Father Brosnan sent the boy to Father Malachi, and Father Malachi told the lad to go to his terrestrial father. It was this that Mr. Jones had expected, and there the boy was received as a Catholic.

But to Father Brosnan the matter was much more important in its political view. Father Brosnan knew the application as to his rent which had been made by Pat Carroll to his landlord. He was of opinion that no rent ought to be paid by any Irish tenant to any landlord—no rent, at least, to a Protestant landlord. Wrath boiled within his bosom when he heard of the answer which was given, as though Mr. Jones had robbed the man by his refusal. Mr. Brosnan thought that for the present a tenant was, as a matter of course, entitled to abatement in his rent, as in a short time he must be entitled to his land without paying any. He considered not at all the circumstances, whether, as had been the case on certain properties in Mayo, all money expended had been so expended by the tenant, or by the landlord, as had been the case with Pat Carroll's land. That was an injustice, according to Mr. Brosnan's theory; as is all property in accordance with the teaching of some political doctors who are not burdened with any.

It would have been unfair to Mr. Brosnan to say that he

sympathised with murderers, or that he agreed with those who
considered that midnight outrages were fair atonements; he demanded rights. He himself would have been hot with righteous
indignation, had such a charge been made against him. But
in the quarrel which was now beginning all his sympathies
were with the Carrolls at large, and not with the Jones's at
large. At every victory won by the British Parliament his
heart again boiled with indignation. At every triumphant note
that came over the water from America—which was generally
raised by the record of the dollars sent—he boiled, on the other
hand, with joy. He had gleams in his mind of a Republic. He
thought of a Saxon as an evil being. The Queen, he would say,
was very well, but she was better at a distance. The Lord-
Lieutenant was a British vanity, and English pomp, but the
Chief Secretary was a minister of the Evil One himself. He
believed that England was enriched by many millions a year
robbed from Ireland, and that Ireland was impoverished to the
same extent. He was a man thoroughly disloyal, and at the
same time thoroughly ignorant, altogether in the dark as to
the truth of things, a man who, whatever might be his
fitness for the duties of the priesthood, to which he had been
educated, had no capability of perceiving political facts, and no
honesty in teaching them. But it would have been unjust to
him to say that he was a murderer, or that he countenanced
murder.

To him it was that young Florian now betook himself, and
found him seated alone in the back parlour in Father Giles's
house. The old priest was out, and Father Brosnan was
engaged on some portion of clerical duties. To give him his
due, he performed those duties rigidly, and the more rigidly
when, in doing them, he obeyed the letter of the law rather
than the spirit. As Father Giles, in his idea of his duties,
took altogether the other side of the question, and, in thinking
of the spirit, had nearly altogether ignored the letter, it may be
imagined that the two men did not agree together very well. In
truth, Father Giles looked upon Father Brosnan as an ignorant,
impertinent puppy, whereas Father Brosnan returned the compliment by regarding Father Giles as half an infidel, and almost
as bad as a Protestant.

"Well, Master Florian," said the priest, "and how are things
going with you?"

"Oh! Father Brosnan, I'm in terrible throuble."

"What throuble's up now?"

"They're all agin me at home, and father's nearly as bad
as any of them. It's all along of my religion."

"I thought your father had given his consent?"

"So he has; but still he's agin me. And my two sisters are
dead agin me. What am I to do about Pat Carroll?"

" Just hould your tongue."

" They do be saying that because what Pat and the other boys did was agin father's interest, I am bound to tell."

" You've given a promise ? "

" I did give a promise."

" And you swore an oath ? " said the priest solemnly.

" I did swear an oath certainly."

" Then you must hould your tongue. In such a case as this I cannot absolve you from your word. I don't know what it is that Pat Carroll did." Here it must be admitted Father Brosnan did not stick to the absolute truth. He did know what Pat Carroll had done. All Headford knew that Mr. Jones's meadows had been flooded, and the priest must have known that the present cause of trouble at Castle Morony, was the injury thus done. Father Brosnan knew and approved of Pat Carroll's enmity to the Jones family. But he was able to justify the falsehood of his own heart, by stumbling over the degree of knowledge necessary. There was a sense in which he did not know it. He need not have sworn to it in a Court of Law. So he told himself, and so justified his conscience. "You need not tell me," he went on to say when the boy was proceeding to whisper the story, " I am not bound to know what it is that Pat Carroll does, and what it is that your father suffers. Do you go home, and keep your toe in your pump, as they say, and come to me for confession a day or two before Christmas. And if any of them say anything to you about your religion, just sit quiet and bear it."

The boy was then dismissed, and went home to his father's home, indifferent as to who might see him now, because he had come from the priest's house. But the terror of that man in the mask still clung to him; and mingled with that was the righteous fear, which still struck cold to his heart, of the wicked injury which he was doing his father. Boy though he was, he knew well what truth and loyalty, and the bonds which should bind a family together, demanded from him. He was miserable with a woe which he had not known how to explain to the priest as he thought of his terrible condition. At first Pat Carroll and his friends had recommended themselves to him. He had, in truth, only come on the scene of devastation down by the lough, by mere accident. But he had before heard that Pat was a grieved man, in reference to his rent, and had taken it into his boyish heart to sympathise with such sorrows. When Pat had got hold of him on the spot, and had first exacted the promise of secrecy, Florian had given it willingly. He had not expected to be questioned on the subject, and had not attributed the importance to it which it had afterwards assumed. He had since denied all knowledge of it, and was of course burdened with a boy's fear of having to acknowledge the falsehood. And now there had been added to it that awful scene in the cabin at Headford, and on the top of that had come the priest's injunction. " In such a case as this I cannot absolve you from your word." It was so that the priest had addressed him, and there was something in it that struck his young mind with awe. There was the man in the mask tendering to him the oath upon the cross ; and there had been Pat Carroll assuring him of that man's wrath. Then there had come the other stranger, speaking out angrily, and promising to him all evil, were he to divulge a word.

Nevertheless, his conscience was so strong within him, that when he reached the Castle he had almost made up his mind to tell his father everything. But just as he was about to enter the Lodge gate, he was touched on the arm by a female. " Master Florian," said the female, " we is all in your hands." It was now dark night, and he could not even see the woman's face. She seemed indeed to keep her face covered, and yet he could see the gleam of her eyes. " You're one of us now, Master Florian."

" I'm a Catholic, if you mean that."

" What else should I mane? Would ye be unthrue to your own people? Do ye know what would happen you if ye commit such a sin as that? I tould them up there that you'd never bring down hell fire upon yer head, by such a deed as that. It isn't what ye can do to him he'll mind, I said, but the anger o' the Blessed Virgin. Worn't it thrue for me what I said, Master Florian?" She held him in the dark, and he could see the glimmer of her eyes, and hear the whisper of her voice, and she frightened him with the fear of the world to come. As he made his way up to the hall door, it was not the dread of the man in the mask, so much as the fear inspired by this woman which made him resolve that, come what come might, he must stick to the lie which he had told.

After breakfast the next morning, his father summoned him into his room. "Now," said Flory to himself, as he followed his father trembling,—" now must I be true." By this he meant that he must be true to his co-conspirators. If he were false to them, he would have to incur the anger of the Blessed Virgin. How this should be made to fall upon him, he did not in the least understand ; but he did understand that the Virgin as he had thought her, should be kind, and mild, and gracious. He had never stopped to think whether the curse as uttered by the woman, might or might not be true. Of loyalty to his father he had thought much ; but now he believed that it behoved him to think more of loyalty to the Virgin, as defined by the woman in the dark.

He followed his father into the magistrates' room, leaving his brother and two sisters in the parlour. He was glad that none of them were invited to accompany him, for he felt that his father was more prone to believe him, than were either his sisters or even his brother. "Florian," said his father, "you know, do you not, the trouble to which I have been put about this man, Pat Carroll?"

"Yes, father; I know you have."

"And the terrible loss which I have incurred! Eighty acres are under water. I suppose the miscreant will have cost me between £400 and £500."

"As much as that?" said Florian, frightened by the magnitude of the sum named.

"Indeed he will. It is hard to calculate the extent of the malignity of a wicked man. Whether the barony will share the loss with me I cannot yet say; but in either case the wickedness will be the same. There is no word bad enough for it. It is altogether damnable; and this is done by a man who calls me in question because of my religion." Here the father paused, but Florian stood by without an answer. If Pat Carroll was right in his religion, his father must be wrong; and Florian thought that Pat Carroll was right. But he did not see how the two things were joined together,—the opening of the sluices, and the truth of Pat Carroll's religious convictions. "But bad as the matter is as regards Pat Carroll, it is all as nothing in reference to the accusation made against you." Here the father came up, and laying his two hands on the boy's shoulders looked sadly into his face. "I cannot believe that my own boy, my darling boy, has joined in this evil deed against me!" Here the father ceased and waited for his son to speak.

The son remembered the determination to which he had come, and resolved to adhere to it. "I didn't," he said after a pause.

"I cannot believe it of you; and yet, your sisters who are as true as steel, who are so good that I bless God morning and night that He in His mercy has left me such treasures,—they believe it."

"They are against me because of my religion."

"No, Florian, not so; they disapprove of your change in religion, but they are not brought to accuse you by such a feeling. They say that they see it in your face."

"How can they see all that in my face?"

"That though you are lying persistently, you cannot hide from them that you are lying. They are not only good girls, but they have very sharp wits. A cleverer girl than Edith, or one better able to read the truth of a boy's head, or even a man's, I have never known. I hardly dare to put my own judgment against hers."

"In this case she knows nothing about it."

"But to me it is of such vital importance! It is not simply that your evidence is needed to punish the man; I would let the man go and all the evil that he has done me. But not for any money that I could name would I entertain such an opinion of my son. Were I convinced at this moment that you are innocent, I should be a happy man."

"Then you may, father."

"But your manner is against you. You do not answer me with that appearance of frankness which I should have expected."

"Of course it all makes me very miserable. How can a fellow be frank when he's suspected like this?"

"Florian, do you give me your most solemn assurance that you saw nothing of this evil work while it was being perpetrated?"

"Yes, father."

"You saw nothing, and you knew nothing?"

"No, father."

"You have no reason to accuse Pat Carroll, except by what you have heard?"

"No, father."

"Nor anyone else?"

"No, father." Then Mr. Jones stood silent looking at his son. And the more he looked the more he doubted him. When the boy had uttered "No, father," for the last time Mr. Jones felt almost convinced — almost convinced that Edith was right. "You may go now, Florian," he said. And the boy departed, fully convinced that his father had disbelieved him.

CHAPTER IV.

MR. BLAKE OF CARNLOUGH.

THREE or four days after the occurrences narrated in the last chapter, Mr. Jones got on to his car and had himself driven down to Carnlough, the seat of Mr. Thomas Blake, a gentleman living about two miles the other side of Tuam. To reach Carnlough he had a journey to make of about ten miles, and as he seldom went, in these days, so far away from home, the fact of his going was known to all the household.

"Father is going to Carnlough," Florian said to Peter, the butler. "What is he going for?"

"'Deed, then, Master Flory, who can tell that? Mr. Blake is a very old friend of master's?"

"But why is he going now? It isn't often he goes to Carnlough; and when he does go, he is sure to say why."

"I shouldn't wonder af he's going to ax him as to how he shall get rid of the waters."

"He knows that better than Mr. Blake can tell him."

"Or maybe he's going to inquire how he shall cotch a hould of Pat Carroll."

It was evident, from the butler's answers, that all the world at Morony Castle felt that at present Mr. Jones could engage himself on no other subject than that of the flood.

"I wish father wouldn't think so much about the flood. After all, what's £500? It won't ruin a man like my father."

But the butler showed by his visage that he regarded £500 as a very serious matter, and that he was not at all astonished by the occupation which it gave to his master's thoughts.

Mr. Blake, of Carnlough, was the first Irishman with whom Mr. Jones had become acquainted in the County Galway. It was through his instance, indeed, that the Morony and Ballintubber properties had been bought, so that the acquaintance must have been well established before the purchase had been made. Mr. Blake was a man of good property, who, in former years, had always been regarded as popular in the county. He was a Protestant, but had not made himself odious to the Roman Catholics around him as an Orangeman, nor had he ever been considered to be hard as a landlord. He thought, perhaps, a little too much of popularity, and had prided himself a little perhaps, on managing "his boys"—as he called the tenants— with peculiar skill. Even still he could boast of his success, though there had arisen some little difficulties as to rent over at Carnlough; and, indeed, he was frightened lest some of the evil ways which had begun to prevail in the neighbouring parts of County Mayo, should make their way into County Galway.

Mr. Blake and Mr. Jones had been very intimate. It had been at Mr. Blake's instance that Mr. Jones had been brought on to the Grand Jury. But latterly they had not seen very much of each other. Mr. Jones, since the death of his wife, did not go frequently to Galway, and Carnlough was a long distance for a morning's drive. But on this occasion Mr. Jones drove himself over simply with the view of making a morning call. "Well, Jones, how are you;—and how are the girls, and how is Frank, and how is that young pickle, Master Florian?" These questions were answered by others of a similar nature. "How are the girls, and how is Mrs. Blake, and what is going on here at Carnlough?" There was no inquiry after the eldest son, for it was Mr. Blake's misfortune that he had no male child to inherit his property.

"Faith, then, things ain't going on a bit too well," said Mr. Blake. "Abatement, abatement, nothing but abatement! Nobody abates me anything. I have to pay all the family charges just the same as ever. What would they say if I was to take away my wife and girls, shut up Carnlough, and go and live in France? I could give them some abatement then and be a richer man. But how would they like to have Carnlough empty?"

"There's no danger of that, I think."

"Upon my word, I don't know. The girls are talking of it, and when they begin to talk of a thing, I am very likely to do it. And Mrs. Blake is quite ready."

"You wouldn't leave the country?"

"That's just it. I'll stay if they'll let me. If they'll pay me rent enough to enable me to live here comfortably, I'll not desert them. But if they think that I'm to keep up the place on borrowed money, they'll find their mistake. I didn't mind ten per cent. for the last two years, though I have taken to drinking whisky punch in my old age, instead of claret and sherry. And I don't mind ten per cent. for this year, though I am sorely in want of a young horse to carry me. But if the ten per cent. is to go on, or to become twenty per cent. as one blackguard hinted, I shall say good-bye to Carnlough. They may fight it out then with Terry Daly as they can." Now, Terry Daly was the well-known agent for the lands of Carnlough. "What has brought you over here to-day?" asked Mr. Blake. "I can see with half an eye that there is some fresh trouble."

"Indeed there is."

"I have heard what they did with your sluices. That's another trick they've learnt out of County Mayo. When a landlord is not rich enough to give them all that they want, they make the matter easier by doing the best they can to ruin him. I don't think anything of that kind has been done at Carnlough."

"There is worse than that," said Mr. Jones sorrowfully.

"The devil there is! They have not mutilated any of your cattle?"

"No, there is nothing of that kind. The only enemy I've got about the place, as far as I know, is one Pat Carroll. It was he and others, whom he paid to serve him, that have let the waters in upon the meadows. Eighty acres are under water at this moment. But I can bear that like a man. The worst of that is, that all the neighbours should have seen him do it, and not one of them have come forward to tell me."

"That is the worst," said Mr. Blake. "There must be some terrible understanding among them, some compact for evil, when twenty men are afraid to tell what one man has been seen to do. It's fearful to think that the priests should not put a stop to it. How is Master Florian getting on with his priest?"

"It's about him that I have come to speak to you," said Mr. Jones.

"About Florian?"

"Yes; indeed. When I tell you my story, I think you will understand that I would tell it to no one but yourself in County Galway. I fear that Florian saw the men at work upon the flood gates."

"And will he not tell the truth?"

"You must remember that I cannot say that I know anything. The boy declares that he saw nothing; that he knows nothing. "I have no evidence; but his sisters are sure that it is so. Edith says that he certainly was present when the gates were removed. She only judges from his manner and his countenance."

"What made her suspect him?" asked Mr. Blake.

"Only that she saw him when the news was brought to us. Edith is not ill-natured. She would not be prone to make a story against her brother."

"If Edith says so, it is so," said Mr. Blake, who among all Edith's admirers was one of the most ardent.

"I don't quite say that. I only mean to express my conviction that she intends to get at the truth."

"I'll wager my life upon her," said Mr. Blake. "As to the other;—well, you know, Jones, that he has turned Roman Catholic."

"That means nothing," said the distressed father. "He is only ten years old. Of course he's a fool for his pains; but he would not on that account do such a deed as this."

"I don't know. You must remember that he will be telling everything to the priests."

"We have two priests about us," said Mr. Jones, "and I would trust them in anything. There is Father Giles at Headford, and he is as fair a man as any clergyman of our own could be. You cannot imagine that he would give such advice to my boy?"

"Not Father Giles certainly," said the other man.

"Then down with us at Ballintubber there is Father Malachi."

"I know him too," said Mr. Blake. "He would not interfere with a boy like Florian. Is there no one else? What curate lives with Father Malachi?"

"There is none with him at Ballintubber. One Brosnan lives with Father Giles."

."That man is a firebrand," said Mr. Blake. "He is a wretched politician, always preaching up Home Rule."

"But I do not think that even he would teach a boy to deceive his own father in such a matter as this."

"I am not sure," said Blake. "It is very difficult to get at the vagaries of mind in such a man as Mr. Brosnan. But what do you intend to do?"

"I have come to you for advice. But remember this: in my present frame of mind, the suspicion that I feel as to poor Florian is ten times worse to me than the loss of all my meadows. If I could find out Edith to have been wrong, I should be at once relieved of the great trouble which sits heaviest at my heart."

"I fear that Edith is right," said Mr. Blake.

"You are prejudiced a little in her favour. Whatever she says you will think right."

"You must weigh that, and take it for what it's worth," said Mr. Blake. "We know that the boy has got himself into bad hands. You do not suspect him of a desire to injure you?"

"Oh, no!" said the father.

"But he has seen these men do it, and now refuses to tell you. They have terrified him."

"He is not a cowardly boy," said Mr. Jones, still standing up for his son.

"But they have made him swear an oath that he will not tell. There has been something of that sort. What does he say himself?"

"Simply that he knows nothing about it."

"But how does he say it? Does he look you in the face? A boy of that kind may lie. Boys do—and girls also. When people say they don't, they know nothing about it; but if it's worth one's while to look at them one can generally tell when they're lying. I'm not a bit afraid of a boy when he is lying,— but only of one who can lie as though he didn't lie."

"I think that Florian is lying," said Mr. Jones slowly; "he does not look me in the face, and he does not lie straightforward."

"Then Edith is right; and I am right when I swear by her."

"But what am I to do with him? If, as I suppose, he saw Pat Carroll do the mischief, he must have seen others with him. If we knew who were the lot, we could certainly get the truth out of some of them, so as to get evidence for a conviction."

"Can't he be made to speak?" asked Mr. Blake.

"How can I make him? It will be understood all about Morony that he has been lying. And I feel that it is thought that he has made himself a hero by sticking to his lie. If they should turn upon him?" Mr. Blake sat silent but made no immediate reply. "It would be better for me to let the whole thing slide. If they were to kill him!"

"They would not do that. Here in County Galway they have not come to that as yet. There is not a county in all Ireland in which such a deed could be done," said Mr. Blake, standing up for his country. "Are you to let this ruffian pass unpunished while you have the power of convicting him? I think that you are bound to punish him. For the sake of your country you are bound to do so."

"And the boy?" said Mr. Jones, hoarsely.

"He is but ten years old, and will soon live it down. And the disgrace of the lie will be drowned in the triumph of telling the truth at last. We should all feel,—I should feel,—that he would in such case deserve well, rather than ill, of his father and of me, and of all of us. Besides you had some idea of sending him to school in England." Here Mr. Jones shook his head, intending to indicate that no such expensive step as that would be possible after the loss incurred by the flooding of the eighty acres. "At any rate my advice to you is to make him declare the truth. I think little harm of a boy for lying, but I do think harm of those who allow a lie to pass unnoticed." So saying Mr. Blake ended the meeting, and took Mr. Jones away to see Mrs. Blake and the girls.

"I do suppose that father has gone to Carnlough, to consult with Mr. Blake about this affair of the flood." It was thus that Ada spoke to her brother Florian, when he came to her discussing the matter of their father's absence.

"What can Mr. Blake know about it?" said Florian.

"I suppose he means to ask about you. It is quite clear, Florian, that no one in the house believes you."

"Peter does."

"You mean that Peter thinks you are right to stand to the lie now you have told it. More shame for Peter if he does!"

"You wouldn't have a fellow go and put himself out of favour with all the boys through the country? There is a horrible man that wears a mask——" Then he remembered, and stopped himself. He was on closer terms with Ada than with Edith, but not on terms so close as to justify his whispering a word about the man in the mask.

"Where did you see the man in the mask?" asked Ada. "Who is the man in the mask?"

"I don't know."

"But you know where you saw him. You must know that. What did the man in the mask say to you?"

"I am not going to tell you anything about him," said the boy. "I am not going to have my secrets got out of me in that way. It isn't honest. Nobody but a Protestant would do it." So saying Florian left his sister, with the tale of the man in the mask only half told.

CHAPTER V.

MR. O'MAHONY AND HIS DAUGHTER.

WE must now turn to another personage in our story, and tell our readers something of the adventures and conditions of this gentleman;—something also of his daughter. The adventures of her early life will occupy much of our time and many of our pages; and though her father may not be so interesting as it is hoped that she will become, still he was so peculiar in his modes of thought, and so honest, though by no means wise, in his manner of thinking, as to make his story also perhaps worth the telling.

Gerald O'Mahony was at the time of the flooding of Mr. Jones's meadows not much more than forty years old. But he was already the father of a daughter nearly twenty. Where he was born, from what parents, or to what portion of Ireland his family belonged, no one knew. He himself had been heard to declare a suspicion that his father had come from County Kerry. But as he himself had been, according to his own statement, probably born in the United States, the county to which his father had belonged is not important. He had been bred up as a Roman Catholic, but had long since thrown over all the prejudices of his religion. He had married when he was quite young, and had soon lost his wife. But in talking of her now he always described her as an angel. But though he looked to be so young as to be his daughter's brother, rather than her father, he had never thought of marrying again. His daughter he declared was everything to him. But those who knew him well said that politics were dearer to him even than his daughter. Since he had been known in County Galway, he had passed and repassed nearly a dozen times between New York and Ireland; and his daughter had twice come with him. He had no declared means, but he had never been known to borrow a shilling, or to leave a bill unpaid. But he had frequently said aloud that he had no money left, and that unless he returned to his own country he and his daughter must be taken in by some poor-house. For Mr. O'Mahony, fond as he was of Ireland, allowed no one to say that he was an Irishman.

But his troubles were apparently no troubles to him. He was always good-humoured, and seemed always to be happy—except when in public, when he was engaged upon politics. Then he would work himself up into such a state of indignant anger as seemed to be altogether antagonistic to good-humour. The position he filled,—or had filled,—was that of lecturer on behalf of the United States. He had lectured at Manchester, at Glasgow, at Liverpool, and lately all over Ireland. But he had risen to such a height of wrath in advocating the doctrine of Republicanism that he had been stopped by the police. He had been held to have said things disrespectful of the Queen. This he loudly denied. He had always, he said, spoken of the Queen's virtues, her graces, and general fitness for her high office. He had declared,—and this was true,—that of all kings and queens of whom he had read in history she was the best. But, he had gone on to say there should be no king or queen. The practice was an absurdity. The reverence paid even to the high office was such as, in his idea, degraded a man. Even in America, the Kotooing which took place before the President's toe was to him an abomination. No man in accordance with his theory should worship another man. Titles should only be used as indicative of a man's trade or occupation. As one man was Mr. General Grant, another man should be Mr. Bricklayer Green. He could not do away with the Queen. But for the woman, he was quite disposed to worship her. All women were to be worshipped, and it was a privilege of a man to worship a woman. When a woman possessed so many virtues as did the Queen of England, it became a man's duty to worship them. But it was a woman whom he would worship, and not the Queen. This was carried to such a length, and he was so eloquent on the subject that the police were desired to interfere, and he was made to hold his tongue,—at any rate as far as England and Ireland were concerned.

He had made Galway a kind of centre home, attracted thither by the friendship which his daughter had made with Ada and Edith Jones. For though Ada and Edith were by no means Republican in their thoughts and feelings, it had come to pass that they dearly loved the American girl who was so. Rachel O'Mahony had frequently been at Morony Castle, as had also her father; and Mr. Jones had taken delight in controverting the arguments of the American, because, as he had said, the American had been unselfish and true. But since his lecturing had been stopped, it had become necessary that he should go elsewhere to look for means of livelihood, and he had now betaken himself to London for that purpose,—a circumstance which will be explained at greater length as the story progresses.

Republicanism was not the only matter in his political creed to which Gerald O'Mahony was devoted. Though he was no Irishman, as he delighted to intimate, his heart was Irish; and during his various visits to the country, he had filled his bosom with thoughts of Irish wrongs. No educated man was ever born and bred in more utter ignorance of all political truths than this amiable and philanthropic gentleman. In regard to Ireland his theory was that the land should be taken from the peasant proprietors, and divided among the peasants who tilled it. When asked what should be done with the present owners, he was quite ready with his answer: " Let them be paid for the property by the State!" He would have no man injured to the extent of a shilling. When asked where the State was to get the money, he declared that that was a mere detail. States did get money. As for the landlords themselves, with the money in their pockets, let them emigrate to the United States, if they were in want of something to do. As to the division of the land,—that, he said, would settle itself. One man would have ten acres, and another fifty; but that would be fair, because one man had been used to pay for ten, and another to pay for fifty. As for the men who got no land in the scramble he could see no injustice. The man who chanced to have been a tenant for the last twelve months, must take the benefit of his position. No doubt such man could sell his land immediately after he got it, because Freedom of Sale was one of the points of his charter. He could see the injustice of giving the land at a rent fixed by the State, because the State has no right to interfere in ordinary contracts between man and man. But if the land was to be given up without any rent, then he could see no injustice. Thus, and thus only, could Ireland be made to return to the beauty and the grace of her original simplicity. But on the wrongs arising from the want of Home Rule he was warmer even than on those which the land question had produced. Why should Ireland be governed by a British Parliament, a British Lord-Lieutenant, a British Chief-Secretary, a British Commander-in-Chief, and trodden under foot by a British soldiery? Why should Scotland be so governed, why should Wales, why should Yorkshire?" Mr. Jones would reply, "Repeal the Unions; restore the Heptarchy!" Mr. O'Mahony had but a confused idea of what the Heptarchy had been. But he was sure that it would be for the benefit of Ireland, that Irish knives should be made of Irish steel. "As undoubtedly would have been the case if the question of protection were to be left to an Irish Parliament to settle," said Mr. Jones. "Heaven help the man who would want to cut his mutton. His best chance would be that he would soon have no mutton to cut."

So the dispute was carried on with much warmth on one side, and with many arguments on the other, but without any quarrelling. It was impossible to quarrel with O'Mahony, who was thoroughly unselfish, and desirous of no violence. When he had heard what had been done in reference to Mr. Jones's meadows, and had been told of the suspected conduct of Pat Carroll, he was as indignant as though he had himself been a landed proprietor, or even an Orangeman. And on Mr. Jones's part there was a desire to do justice to all around him, which came within the capacity of O'Mahony's vision. He knew that Mr. Jones himself was a fair-dealing, honest gentleman, and he could not, therefore, quarrel with him.

There is a steamer running from the town of Galway, across Lough Corrib, to the little village of Cong, on the Mayo side of the lake, which stops and picks up passengers within a mile of Morony Castle. From this, passengers are landed, so that the means of transit between Galway and Mr. Jones's house are peculiarly easy. Up and down by this steamer Ada and Edith Jones had frequently gone to visit their friend, and as frequently that friend had come to visit them. But unfortunately the steamer had been open to others besides the young ladies, and Rachel O'Mahony had found a dearer friend than either of the girls at Morony Castle. It had come to pass that Frank Jones and Rachel O'Mahony had declared themselves to be engaged.

On no such ground as want of wealth, or want of family, or want of education, had Mr. Jones based his objection to the match; but there had been a peculiarity in the position of Rachel which had made him hesitate. It was not that she was an American, but such an American! It was not that he was a Republican, but such a Republican! And she was more anxious to carry Frank away with her to the United States, and to join him in a political partnership with her father, than to come and settle herself down at the Castle. Thus there had arisen an understanding on the part of the young people, that, though they were engaged, they were engaged without the consent of the young man's father. Rachel therefore was not to be brought to the Castle while Frank was there. To all this Rachel's father had assented, in a smiling indifferent manner, half intended to ridicule all who were concerned. As it was not a question of politics, Mr. O'Mahony could not work himself up to any anger, or apparently even to anxiety in the matter. "Your young people,"—here he meant English and Irish generally,—" are taught to think they should begin the world where we leave it off."

"Your young people are just as fond of what money will buy as are ours," said Mr. Jones.

"But they are fonder of one another, even, than of money. When they love one another they become engaged. Then they marry. And as a rule they don't starve. As a rule people with us seldom do starve. As for making out an income for a young man to start with, that with us is quite out of the question. Frank some day will have this property."

"That won't give him much of an income," said Mr. Jones, who since the affair of the flood had become very despondent in reference to the estate.

"Then he's as well off now as ever he will be, and might as well marry the girl." But all this was said with no eagerness.

"They are merely boy and girl as yet," said Mr. Jones.

"I was married, and Rachel was born before I was Frank's age." So saying, Mr. O'Mahony consented to come to Morony Castle, and bid them adieu, without bringing his girl with him. This was hard upon Ada and Edith, as Mr. Frank, of course, went into Galway as often as he pleased, and made his adieu after his own fashion.

And there had come up another cause which had created further objections to the marriage in Mr. Jones's mind. Mr. O'Mahony had declared that as his lecturing was brought to an end by the police, he must throw himself upon Rachel's capabilities for earning some money. Rachel's capabilities had been often discussed at the Castle, but with various feelings on the three sides into which the party had formed themselves. All the Jones's were on one side, and declared that the capability had better not be exercised. In this they were probably wrong;

—but it was their opinion. They had lived for many years away from London. The children had so lived all their lives; and they conceived that prejudices still existed which had now been banished or nearly banished from the world. Mr. O'Mahony, who formed another party, thought that the matter was one of supreme indifference. As long as he could earn money by lecturing it was well that he should earn it. It was always better that the men of a family should work than the women; but, if the man's talent was of no use, then it might be well to fall back upon the woman. He only laughed at the existence of a prejudice in the matter. He himself had no prejudices. He regarded all prejudices as the triumph of folly over education.

But Rachel, who was the third party in the discussion, had a very strong feeling of her own. She was of opinion that if the capability in question existed, it ought to be exercised. On that subject,—her possession of the capability,—she entertained, she said, strong doubts. But if the capability existed it certainly ought to be used. That was Rachel's opinion, expressed with all the vigour which she knew how to throw into the subject.

This capability had already been exercised in New York, where it had been efficacious, though the effect had not been great. She had been brought up to sing, and great things had been promised of her voice. An American manager had thought much of her performance, though she had hitherto, he said, been young, and had not come to the strength of her throat. But he had himself seen to her education, almost as a child, and had been sure that sooner or later she would do great things in the musical world. Mr. Mahomet M. Moss was the gentleman in question, and he at present was in London. That such a voice as Rachel O'Mahony's should be lost to the world, was to his thinking a profanity, an indecency, an iniquity, a wasting of God's choicest gifts, and an abomination not to be thought of; for Mr. Mahomet M. Moss was in the affairs of his own profession a most energetic gentleman. Rachel rather turned up her nose at Mr. Mahomet M. Moss; but she was very anxious to go to London and to take her chance, and to do something, as she said, laughing, just to keep her father's pot a little on the boil;—but for Mr. Mahomet M. Moss she did not care one straw. Mr. O'Mahony was therefore ready to start on the journey, and had now come to Morony Castle to say farewell to his friend Mr. Jones. "Are you sure about that fellow Moss?" said Mr. Jones.

"What do you call sure about him? He's as big a swindler, I guess, as you shall find from here to himself."

"And are you going to put Rachel into his hands?"

"Well, I think so;—after a sort of fashion. He'll swindle her out of three parts of what she earns;—but she'll get the fourth part. It's always the way with a young girl when she's first brought out."

"I don't mean about money. Will you leave her conduct in his hands?"

"He'll be a clever chap who'll undertake to look after Rachel's conduct. I guess she'll conduct herself mostly."

"You'll be there, to be sure," said Mr. Jones.

"Yes, I shall be there; and she'll conduct me too, very likely."

"But, Mr. O'Mahony,—as a father!"

"I know pretty well what you would be saying. Our young folk grow old quicker a long sight than yours do. Now your girls here are as sweet as primroses out of the wood. But Rachel is like a rose that has been brought up to stand firm on its own bush. I'm not a bit afraid of her. Nor yet is your son. She looks as though you might blow her away with the breath from your mouth. You try her, and you'll find that she'll want a deal of blowing."

"Does not a young girl lose something of the aroma of her youth by seeing too much of the world too soon?"

"How old do you expect her to be when she's to die?"

"Rachel! How can I tell? She is only as yet entering upon life, and her health seems to be quite confirmed."

"The best confirmed I ever knew in my life. She never has a day's illness. Taking all the chances one way and another, shall we say sixty?"

"More than that, I should think," said Mr. Jones.

"Say sixty. She may fall down a trap in the theatre, or be drowned in one of your Cunarders."

"The Cunard steamers never drown anybody," said Mr. Jones.

"Well, then, a White Star—or any cockle-shell you may please to name. We'll put her down for sixty as an average."

"I don't know what you are driving at," said Mr. Jones.

"She has lived a third of her life already, and you expect her to know nothing, so that the aroma may still cling to her. Aroma does very well for earls' daughters and young marchionesses, though as far as I can learn, it's going out of fashion with them. What has an American girl to do with aroma, who's got her bread to earn? She's got to look to her conduct, and to be sharp at the same time. Mr. Mahomet M. Moss will rob her of seventy-five cents out of every dollar for the next twelve months. In three years' time he'll rob her of nothing. Only that she knows what conduct means, he'd have to look very sharp to keep his own."

"It is not natural," said Mr. Jones.

"But it's American. Marvels are not natural, and we are marvellous people. I don't know much about aroma, but I think you'll find Rachel will come out of the washing without losing much colour in the process."

Then the two friends parted, and Mr. O'Mahony went back to Galway, preparatory to his journey to London.

CHAPTER VI.

RACHEL AND HER LOVERS.

On the day following that of O'Mahony's return to Galway, he, and his daughter, and Frank Jones were together at Galway Station preparatory to the departure of the O'Mahonys for Dublin and London. " I guess you two have got something to say to each other, so I'll leave you to yourselves," said the father.

" I guess we have," said Rachel, " so if you'll wait here we'll come to you when the cars are fixed." So saying, Rachel put her hand on her lover's arm and walked off with him along the platform. Rachel O'Mahony had not been badly described when her father said of her that she looked as though she might be blown away. She was very fair and small and frail to look at. Her father had also said of her that her health was remarkably good,—" the best confirmed that he had ever known in his life." But though this too, was true, she hardly looked it. No one could have pointed out any sign of malady about her; only one would have said that there was nothing of her. And the colour on her face was so evanescent that he who watched her was inclined to think that she herself was like her colour. And she moved as though she was always on the vanishing point. " I'm very fond of eating," she had been heard to say. " I know it's vulgar ; but it's true." No doubt she was fond of eating, but so is a sparrow. There was nothing she would not attempt to do in the way of taking exercise. She would undertake very long walks, and would then fail, and declare that she must be carried home ; but she would finally get through the day's work better than another woman who appeared to have double her strength. Her feet and hands were the tiniest little adjuncts to a grown human body that could be seen anywhere. They looked at least to be so. But they were in perfect symmetry with her legs and arms. " I wish I were bigger," she had once been heard to say, " because I could hit a man." The man to whom she alluded was Mr. Mahomet M. Moss. " I sometimes want to hit a woman, but that would be such a small triumph." And yet she had a pride in her little female fineries. " Now, Frank," she had once said, " I guess you won't get another woman in all Galway to put her foot into that boot ; nor yet in New York either."

" I don't think I could," said the enraptured Frank.

" You'd better take it to New York and try, and if you find the lady you can bring her back with you."

Frank refused the commission, saying something of course very pretty as to his mistress's foot. " Ten buttons ! These only have eight," she said, objecting to a present which her lover had just brought her. " If I had ten buttons, and the gloves to fit me, I'd cut my arm off and put it under a glass case. Lovers are sent out to do all possible and impossible things in order to deserve their lady-loves. You shall go and wander about till you find a glove with ten buttons to fit me, then I'll consent to be Mrs.——Jones." By all of which little manœuvres Frank was charmed and oppressed to the last degree. When she would call herself the "future Mrs.——Jones," he would almost feel inclined to abandon both the name and the property. "Why not be Mrs. Morony," Rachel would say, "or Mrs. Ballintubber? The Ballintubber, of Ballintubber, would sound exquisitely, and then I should always be called 'Madam.'"

Her beauty was all but perfect, as far as symmetry was concerned, only that there was not enough of it ; and for the perfection of female beauty a tone of colour is, methinks, needed somewhat darker than that which prevailed with Rachel O'Mahony. Her hair was so light that one felt it rather than saw it, as one feels the sunlight. It was soft and feathery, as is the under plumage on the wings of some small tropical birds. "A lock of my hair!" she had once said to Frank ; "but it will all go into nothing. You should have paid your vows to some girl who could give you a good lump of hair fit to stuff a pillow with. If you have mine you will think in a few weeks that the spiders have been there and have left their dust behind." But she gave him the lock of hair, and laid it on his lips with her own little hands.

There was not enough of her beauty. Even in touching her a lover could not but feel that he had to deal with a little child. In looking at her he could only look down upon her. It was not till she spoke, and that her words came to his assistance, that he found that he had to deal with one who was not altogether a child. "Mr. Mahomet M. Moss declares his opinion that I shall be seen above the gaslights. It was very civil and complimentary of Mahomet M. M. But I mean to make myself heard. Mahomet M. M. did not seem to think of this." Since Frank had known her she had taken every opportunity in her power of belittling Mahomet M. M., as she was wont to call Mr. Moss.

Frank Jones was, in truth, a handsome stalwart young man, clever enough for the world, who thought a good deal of himself, and who thought very much more of the girl whom he loved. It was chiefly because he was absolutely unlike an American that Rachel O'Mahony had come to love him. Who does not know the "got up" look of the gentleman from the other side of the water, who seems to know himself to be much better than his father, and infinitely superior to his grandfather ; who is always ready to make a speech on every occasion, and who feels himself to be fit company for a Prime Minister as soon as he has left school. Probably he is. Young Jones was not so; and it was on account of this deficiency that Rachel prized him. "I'm not like a young girl myself," she had said to her father, "but I do love a jolly nice boy. With us at sixteen, they are all but decrepit old men, and yet they are such little monkeys."

"For a little monkey, what do you think of yourself?" her father had replied. But the conversation then had not gone any further.

"I know you'll be after me before long," Rachel said to Frank, as they walked up and down the platform together.

"If I do, I shall ask you to marry me at once," he replied.

"I shall never do that without your father's leave."

"Is that the way they manage things in America?"

"It's the way I shall manage them here," said Rachel. "I'm in the unfortunate position of having three papas to whom I must attend. There is papa O'Mahony——"

"You will never be incommoded much by him," he replied.

"He is the least potent of the three, no doubt Then there is papa Jones. He is absolutely omnipotent in this matter. He would not let me come down to Castle Morony for fear I should contaminate you all. I obeyed without even daring to feel the slightest snub, and if I were married to-morrow, I should kiss his toe in token of respect, and with a great deal more affection than I should kiss your half-bearded lips, sir." Here Frank got a hold of her hand beneath his arm and gave it a squeeze. "He is the real old-fashioned father in the play, who is expected to come out at last with a hundred thousand dollars and his blessing."

"And who is the third papa?"

"Don't you know? Mahomet M. Moss. He is the third papa—if only he would consent to remain in that comparatively humble position." Here Frank listened to her words with sharp ears, but he said nothing at the moment. "Mahomet M. Moss is at any rate my lord and master for the present."

"Not whilst I am alive," said Frank.

"But he is. There is no use in rebelling. You are not my lord and master until you have gone through a certain ceremony. I wish you were. Will that satisfy you?"

"There is something in the name of lord and master which a girl shouldn't apply to anyone but to him who is to be her husband."

"Fiddlestick! Mr. Lord and Master that is to be, but is not as yet. But he is, in many respects. I don't think, Frank, you can imagine the horror I feel in reference to that vilest of human-beings. I shall carry a dagger with me, in order to have it ready for any occasion."

"What does he do? You shall not go to be subjected to such danger and such annoyance."

She turned round, and looked up into his face as with derision. "The annoyance no doubt will be mine, Frank, and must be endured; the danger will be his, I think. Nor shall I use the dagger that I spoke of. I can look at him, and I can make him hear my voice, in spite of the smallness of my stature. But there is no one in this world whom I detest as I do that greasy Jew. It is not for what he does, but that I simply detest him. He makes love to me."

"What!"

"Oh! he does. You needn't look like that. You needn't be a bit jealous."

"I shall come over at once."

"And knock him on the head! You had better not do that, because we want to make some money by his means. As a lover I can keep him at a distance. I wish I could do so to you, Mr. Jones."

"Why do you wish to keep me at a distance?"

"Because you know how to be troublesome. It is much harder to keep a lover at a distance when you really love him with all your heart"—here she looked up into his face and squeezed his arm, and nearly made him mad for the moment—"than a beast like that, who is no better than a toad to you. There, do you see that ugly old man there?" She pointed to a cross-looking old gentleman of sixty, who was scolding a porter violently. "Why aren't you jealous of that man?"

"You never saw him before."

"That's just the reason, He may be worth my affection, but I know that that Mahomet M. M. is not. You begin with the most bitter hatred on my part. I don't hate that old gentleman. I rather like him on the whole, though he was so cross. At any rate he's not a greasy Jew. Papa says that hating Jews is a prejudice. Loving you is a prejudice, I suppose."

"My darling!"

"You can't suppose you are the best man I ever saw, can you?"

"It's a sort of thing we are not to reason about."

"Then it's a prejudice. I'm prejudiced against Mahomet M. M. I'm equally prejudiced in favour of Mr. Jones, junior, of Ballintubber. It's horrible to be troubled by the one."

"Well!"

"Well! There's nothing more coming, Mr. Jones. Only don't you come over in any of your fits of jealousy, or you'll have to be sent back again. You're not my lord and master—yet."

"I wish I were."

"So do I. What more do you want than that? I don't believe there's another girl in New York would say as much to you,—nor yet in County Galway."

"But what does he say to you?"

"Well; just the kind of things that you never say. And he certainly never does the kind of things which you do; and that, Mr. Jones, is an improvement. But papa is in a hurry, and I shouldn't wonder if the train didn't go on in a quarter of an hour. I'll write to you about Mahomet M. M.; and if I behave very badly, such as prodding him with the dagger, or something of that sort, then I will let you know the details. You can't do it here, so you may as well go." So saying she jumped into the carriage, and the train had started before Frank Jones had begun to think whether he could do it there or no.

"He's a good fellow, take him all round," said Mr. O'Mahony, when the carriages had left the station.

"As good as the rest of them."

"I think he is better."

"Of course we all think so of our own. Why should he be better than any other young lady's Mr. Jones? I don't suppose he is better; but we'll endeavour to believe that he is up to the average."

"Is that all that you've got to say for him, Rachel?"

"What! To you? Not exactly—if I am to speak the solid truth; which I don't see why I should have to do, even to my own father. I do think him above the average. I think him so much above the average as to be the best of all. But why? Simply because I believe him when he says he wants to marry me, and make me his companion for life. And then there's an affinity between us which God certainly manages. Why should I trust him in every detail of life with a perfect faith, and not trust Mr. Mahomet M. Moss to the extent of half-a-crown? If he were to ask me for everything I have in the world, I should give it to him, without a thought except of his goodness in taking care of it for me. I wouldn't let Mahomet M. Moss have a dollar of mine without giving me his bond. Papa, there will be a row between me and Mr. Mahomet·M. Moss, and so it's well to put you on your guard."

"What sort of a row, my dear?"

"A very rowy row. I don't mean about dollars, for you'll have to manage that just at first. When we have got into the running, I think I shall have something to say on that subject too."

"What row do you mean?"

"He'll misbehave himself. He always does, more or less."

"The poor fellow can't open his mouth without your saying that he misbehaves himself."

"That's quite true; he can't. He can't brush his hair, or tie his cravat, or settle his pantaloons, without misbehaving himself. He certainly can't look out of his eye without gross misbehaviour."

"What is he to do then?" said Mr. O'Mahony. "Nature has imbued him with all these peculiarities, and you are fantastic to find fault with him."

"Perhaps so—but then I am fantastic. When you've got a dirty coat on, or Frank, I don't find fault with it; but when he's got a clean coat, I writhe at him in my disgust. Yet, upon the whole, I like men to have clean coats."

"But you haven't said how the row is to come."

"Because I don't know; but it will come. It won't be about his coat, nor yet his hat, unless he puts it close down under my nose. My time, as I understand, is to be at his disposal."

"There will be an agreement made as to all that."

"An agreement as to my performances. I quite understand that I must be present at fixed times at the theatre, and that he must fix them. That will not worry me; particularly if you will go to the theatre with me."

"Of course I will do that when you want it."

"But he is to come to me with his beastly lessons. Am I to have no relief from that?"

"The hours can be fixed."

"But they won't be fixed. There's no doubt that he understands his trade. He can make me open my mouth and keep it open. And he can tell me when I sing false or flat. Providence when she gave him that horrid head of hair, did give him also the peculiarity of a fine ear. I think it is the meanest thing out for a man to be proud of that. If you can run a straight furrow with a plough it is quite as great a gift."

"That is nonsense, my dear. Such an ear as Mr. Moss's is very rare."

"A man who can see exactly across an entire field is just as rare. I don't see the difference. Nor when a woman sings do I respect her especially because of her voice. When a man can write a poem like Homer, or rule a country like Washington, there is something to say for him. I shall tell him that I will devote one hour a day to practising and no more."

"That will settle the difficulty; if it be enough."

"But during that hour, there is to be no word spoken except what has to do with the lessons. You'll bear me out in that?"

"There must be some give-and-take in regard to ordinary conversation."

"You don't know what a beast he is, papa. What am I to do if he tells me to my face that I'm a beautiful young woman?"

"Tell him that you're quite aware of the fact, but that it is a matter you do not care to talk about."

"And then he'll simper. You do not know what a vile creature he can be. I can take care of myself. You needn't be a bit afraid about that. I fancy I could give him a slap on the face which would startle him a little. And if we came to blows, I do believe that he would not have a leg to stand upon. He is nearly fifty."

"My dear!"

"Say forty. But I do believe a good shove would knock him off his nasty little legs. I used to think he wore a wig; but no hairdresser could be such a disgrace to his profession to let such a wig as that go out of his shop."

"I always regarded him as a good-looking young man," said Mr. O'Mahony. Here Rachel shook her head, and made a terrible grimace. "It's all fancy, you know," continued he.

"I suppose it is. But if you hear that I have told him that I regard him as a disgusting monkey, you must not be surprised." This was the last conversation which Mr. O'Mahony and his daughter had respecting Mahomet M. Moss, till they reached London.

CHAPTER VII.

BROWN'S.

WHEN Mr. O'Mahony and his daughter stepped out of the train on the platform at Euston Square, they were at once encountered by Mr. Mahomet M. Moss. "Oh, dear!" ejaculated Miss O'Mahony, turning back upon her father. "Cannot you get rid of him?" Mr. O'Mahony, without a word of reply to his daughter, at once greeted Mr Moss most affectionately. "Yes, my bird is here—as you see. You have taken a great deal of trouble in coming to meet us." Mr. Moss begged that the trouble might be taken as being the greatest pleasure he had ever had in his life. "Nothing could be too much to do for Miss O'Mahony." He had had, he said, the wires at work, and had been taught to expect them by this train. Would Miss O'Mahony condescend to take a seat in the carriage which was waiting for her? She had not spoken a word, but had laid fast hold of her father's arm. "I had better look after the luggage," said the father, shaking the daughter off. "Perhaps Mr. Moss will go with you," said she;—and at the moment she looked anything but pleasant. Mr. Moss expressed his sense of the high honour which was done him by her command, but suggested that she should seat herself in the carriage. "I will stand here under this pillar," she said. And as she took her stand it would have required a man with more effrontery than Mr. Moss possessed to attempt to move her. We have seen Miss O'Mahony taking a few liberties with her lover, but still very affectionate. And we have seen her enjoying the badinage of perfect equality with her papa. There was nothing then of the ferocious young lady about her. Young ladies,—some young ladies,—can be very ferocious. Miss O'Mahony appeared to be one of them. As she stood under the iron post waiting till her father and Mr. Moss returned, with two porters carrying the luggage, the pretty little fair, fly-away Rachel looked as though she had in her hand the dagger of which she had once spoken, and was waiting for an opportunity to use it.

"Is your maid here, Miss O'Mahony?" asked Mr. Moss.

"I haven't got a maid," said Rachel, looking at him as though she intended to annihilate him.

They all seated themselves in the carriage with their small parcels, leaving their luggage to come after them in a cab which Mr. Moss had had allowed to him. But they, the O'Mahonys, knew nothing of their immediate destination. It had been clearly the father's business to ask; but he was a man possessed of no presence of mind. Suddenly the idea struck Rachel, and she called out with a loud voice, "Father, where on earth are we going?"

"I suppose Mr. Moss can tell us."

"You are going to apartments which I have secured for Miss O'Mahony at considerable trouble," said Mr. Moss. "The theatres are all stirring."

"But we are not going to live in a theatre."

"The ladies of the theatres find only one situation convenient. They must live somewhere in the neighbourhood of the Strand. I have secured two sitting-rooms and two bed-rooms on the first floor, overlooking the views at Brown's."

"Won't they cost money?" asked the father.

"Of course they will," said Rachel. "What fools we have been! We intended to go to some inn for one night till we could find a fitting place,—somewhere about Gower Street."

"Gower Street wouldn't do at all," said Mr. Moss. "The distance from everything would be very great." Two ideas passed at that moment through Rachel's mind. The first was that the distance might serve to keep Mr. Moss out of her sitting-room, and the second was that were she to succeed in doing this, she might be forced to go to his sitting-room. "I think Gower Street would be found to be inconvenient, Miss O'Mahony."

"Bloomsbury Square is very near. Here we are at the hotel. Now, father, before you have anything taken off the carriages, ask the prices."

Then Mr. Moss, still keeping his seat, made a little speech. "I think if Miss O'Mahony would allow me, I would counsel her against too rigid an economy. She will have heard of the old proverb,—'A penny wise and a pound foolish.'"

"'Cut your coat according to your cloth,' I have heard of that too; and I have heard of 'Burning a candle at both ends.'"

"'You shouldn't spoil your ship for a ha'porth of tar,'" said Mr. Moss with a smile, which showed his idea, that he had the best of the argument.

"It won't matter for one night," said Mr. O'Mahony, getting out of the carriage. Half the packages had been already taken off the cab.

Rachel followed her father, and without attending to Mr. Moss got hold of her father in the street. "I don't like the look of the house at all, father, you don't know what the people would be up to. I shall never go to sleep in this house." Mr. Moss, with his hat off, was standing in the doorway, suffused, as to his face, with a bland smile.

It may be as well to say at once that the house was all that an hotel ought to be, excepting, perhaps, that the prices were a little high. The two sitting-rooms and the two bed-rooms, with the maid's room which had also been taken, did seem to be very heavy to Rachel, who knew down to a shilling—or rather, to a dollar, as she would have said—how much her father had in his pocket. Indefinite promises of great wealth had been also made to herself; but according to a scale suggested by Mr. Moss, a pound a night, out of which she would have to keep herself, was the remuneration immediately promised. Then a sudden thought struck Miss O'Mahony. They were still standing discussing the price in one of the sitting-rooms, and Mr. Moss was also there. "Father," she said, "I'm sure that Frank would not approve."

"I don't think that he would feel himself bound to interfere," said Mr. O'Mahony.

"When a young woman is engaged to a young man it does make a difference," she replied, looking Mr. Moss full in the face.

"The happy man," said Mr. Moss, still bowing and smiling, "would not be so unreasonable as to interfere with the career of his fair *fiancée*."

"If we stay here very long," said Rachel still addressing her father, "I guess we should have to pawn our watches. But here we are for the present, and here we must remain. I am awfully tired now, and should so like to have a cup of tea—by ourselves." then Mr. Moss took his leave, promising to appear again upon the scene at eleven o'clock on the following day. "Thank you," said Rachel, "you are very kind, but I rather think I shall be out at eleven o'clock."

"What is the use of your carrying on like that with the man?" said her father.

"Because he's a beast."

"My dear, he's not a beast. He's not a beast that you ought to treat in that way. You'll be a beast too if you come to rise high in your profession. It is a kind of work which sharpens the intellect, but is apt to make men and women beasts. Did you ever hear of a prima donna who thought that another prima donna sang better than she did?"

"I guess that all the prima donnas sing better than I do."

"But you have not got to the position yet. Mr. Moss, I take it, was doing very well in New York, so as to have become a beast, as you call him. But he's very good-natured."

'He's a nasty, stuck-up, greasy Jew. A decent young woman is insulted by being spoken to by him."

"What made you tell him that you were engaged to Frank Jones?"

"I thought it might protect me—but it won't. I shall tell him next time that I am Frank's wife. But even that will not protect me."

"You will have to see him very often."

"And very often I shall have to be insulted. I guess he does the same kind of thing with all the singing girls who come into his hands."

"Give it up, Rachel."

"I don't mind being insulted so much as some girls do, you know. I can't fancy an English girl putting up with him— unless she liked to do as he pleased. I hate him;—but I think I can endure him. The only thing is, whether he would turn against me and rend me. Then we shall come utterly to the ground, here in London."

"Give it up."

"No! You can lecture and I can sing, and it's odd if we can't make one profession or the other pay. I think I shall have to fight with him, but I won't give it up. What I am afraid is that Frank should appear on the scene. And then, oh law! if Mr. Moss should get one blow in the eye!"

There she sat, sipping her tea and eating her toast, with her feet upon the fender, while Mr. O'Mahony ate his mutton chop and drank his whisky and water.

"Father, now I am coming back to my temper, I want something better than this buttered toast. Could they get me a veal cutlet, or a bit of cold chicken?"

A waiter was summoned.

"And you must give me a little bit of ham with the cold chicken. No, father; I won't have any wine because it would get into my head, and then I should kill Mr. Mahomet M. Moss."

"My dear," said her father when the man had left the room, "do you wish to declare all your animosities before the waiter?"

"Well, yes, I think I do. If we are to remain here it will be better that they should all know that I regard this man as my schoolmaster. I know what I'm about; I don't let a word go without thinking of it."

Then again they remained silent, and Mr. O'Mahony pretended to go to sleep—and eventually did do so. He devoted himself for the time to Home Rule, and got himself into a frame of mind in which he really thought of Ireland.

"The first flower of the earth, and first gem of the sea."

Why should she not be so? She had all the sentiment necessary, all the poetry, all the eloquence, all the wit. And then when he was beginning to think whether something more than sentiment and eloquence were not necessary, he went to sleep.

But Rachel was not sleeping. Her thoughts were less stationary than her father's, and her ideas more realistic. She had been told that she could sing, and she had sung at New York with great applause. And she had gone on studying, or rather practising, the art with great diligence. She had already become aware that practice was more needed than study. All, nearly all, this man could teach her was to open her mouth. Nature had given her an ear, and a voice, if she would work hard so as to use it. It was there before her. But it had seemed to her that her career was clogged with the necessary burden of Mr. Moss. Mr. Moss had got hold of her, and how should she get rid of him? He was the Old Man of the Sea, and how should she shake him off? And then there was present to her alone a vision of Frank Jones. To live at Morony Castle and be Frank Jones's wife, would not that be sweeter than to sing at a theatre under the care of Mr. Mahomet M. Moss? All the sweetness of a country life in a pleasant house by the lake side, and a husband with her who would endure all the little petulancy, and vagaries, and excesses of her wayward but affectionate temper, all these things were present to her mind. And to be Mistress Jones, who could look all the world in the face, this,—as compared with the gaslight of a theatre, which might mean failure, and could only mean gaslight—this, on the present occasion, did tempt her sorely. Her moods were very various. There were moments of her life when the gaslight had its charm, and in which she declared to herself that she was willing to run all the chances of failure for the hope of success. There were moments in which Mr. Moss loomed less odious before her eyes. Should she be afraid of Mr. Moss, and fly from her destiny because a man was greasy? And to this view of her circumstances she always came at last when her father's condition pressed itself upon her. The house beside the lake was not her own as yet, nor would it be her husband's when she was married.

Nor could there be a home for her father there as long as old Mr. Jones was alive, nor possibly when his son should come to the throne. For a time he must go to America, and she must go with him. She had declared to herself that she could not go back to the United States unless she could go back as a successful singer. For these reasons she resolved that she would face Mr. Moss bravely and all his horrors.

"If that gentleman comes here to-morrow at eleven, show him up here," she said to the waiter.

"Mr. Moss, ma'am?" the waiter asked.

"Yes, Mr. Moss," she answered in a loud voice, which told the man much of her story. "Where did that piano come from?" she asked brusquely.

"Mr. Moss had it sent in," said the man.

"And my father is paying separate rent for it?" she asked.

"What's that, my dear? What's that about rent?"

"We have got this piano to pay for. It's one of Erard's. Mr. Moss has sent it, and of course we must pay till we have sent it back again. That'll do."

Then the man went.

"It's my belief that he intends to get us into pecuniary difficulties. You have only got £62 left."

"But you are to have twenty shillings a day till Christmas."

"What's that?"

"According to what he says it will be increased after Christmas. He spoke of £2 a day."

"Yes; if my singing be approved of. But who is to be the judge? If the musical world choose to say that they must have Rachel O'Mahony, that will be all very well. Am I to sing at twenty shillings a day for just as long as Mr. Moss may want me? And are we to remain here, and run up a bill which we shall never be able to pay, till they put us out of the door and call us swindlers?"

"Frank Jones would help us at a pinch if we came to that difficulty," said the father.

"I wouldn't take a shilling from Frank Jones. Frank Jones is all the world to me, but he cannot help me till he has made me his wife. We must go out of this at the end of the first week, and send the piano back. As far as I can make it out, our expenses here will be about £17 10s. a week. What the piano will cost, I don't know; but we'll learn that from Mr. Moss. I'll make him understand that we can't stay here, having no more than twenty shillings a day. If he won't undertake to give me £2 a day immediately after Christmas, we must go back to New York while we've got money left to take us."

"Have it your own way," said Mr. O'Mahony.

"I don't mean to remain here and wake up some morning and find that I can't stir a step without asking Mahomet M. M. for some money favour. I know I can sing; I can sing at any rate, to the extent of forty shillings a day. For forty shillings a day I'll stay; but if I can't earn that at once let us go back to New York. It is not the poverty I mind so much, nor yet the debt, nor yet even your distress, you dear old father. You and I could weather it out together on a twopenny roll. Things would never be altogether bad with us as long as we are together; and as long as we have not put ourselves in the power of Mahomet M. M. Fancy owing Mr. Moss a sum of money which we couldn't pay! Mahomet's 'little bill!' I would say to a Christian : 'All right, Mr. Christian, you shall have your money in good time, and if you don't it won't hurt you.' He wouldn't be any more than an ordinary Christian, and would pull a long face; but he would have no little scheme ready, cut and dry, for getting my body and soul under his thumb."

"You are very unchristian yourself, my dear."

"I certainly have my own opinion of Mahomet M. M., and I shall tell him to-morrow morning that I don't mean to run the danger."

Then they went to bed and slept the sleep of the just. They ordered breakfast at nine, so that, as Rachel said, the heavy mutton chop might not be sticking in her throat as she attempted to show off before Mr. Moss on his arrival. But from eight till nine she passed her time in the double employment of brushing her hair and preparing the conversation as it was to take place between herself and Mr. Moss. When a young lady boasts that she doesn't "let a word go without thinking of it," she has to be careful in preparing her words. And she prepared them now.

"There will be two of them against me," she said to herself as she made the preparation. "There'll be the dear old governor, and the governor that isn't dear. If I were left quite to myself I think I could do it easier. But then it might come to sticking a knife into him."

"Father," she said, during breakfast, "I'm going to practise for half-an-hour before this man comes."

"That means that I'm to go away."

"Not in the least. I shall go into the next room where the piano lives, and you can come or not just as you please. I shall be squalling all the time, and as we do have the grandeur of two rooms for the present, you might as well use them. But when he comes we must take care and see that matters go right. You had better leave us alone at first, that I may sing to him. Then, when that's over, do you be in waiting to be called in. I mean to have a little bit of business with my trusted agent, manager, and parent in music, 'Mahomet M. M.'"

She went to the instrument, and practised there till half-past eleven, at which hour Mr. Moss presented himself. "You'll want to hear me sing of course," she said without getting up from the music-stool.

"Just a bar or two to know how you have improved. But it is hardly necessary. I see from the motion of your lips that you have been keeping your mouth open. And I hear from the tone of your voice, that it is all there. There is no doubt about you, if you have practised opening your mouth."

"At any rate you shall hear, and if you will stand there you shall see."

Then the music lesson began, and Mr. Moss proved himself to be an adept in his art. Rachel did not in the least doubt his skill, and obeyed him in everything as faithfully as she would have done, had he been personally a favourite with her. "Allow me to express my great delight and my strong admiration for the young débutante. As far as Miss O'Mahony is concerned the word failure may be struck out of the language. And no epithet should be used to qualify success, but one in the most superlative degree. Allow me to——" And he attempted to raise her hand to his lips, and to express his homage in a manner certainly not unusual with gentlemen of his profession.

"Mr. Moss," said the young lady starting up, "there need be nothing of that kind. There had better not. When a young woman is going to be married to a young man, she can't be too careful. You don't know perhaps, but I'm going to be Mrs. Jones. Mr. Jones is apt to dislike such things. If you'll wait half a moment, I'll bring papa in." So saying she ran out of the room, and in two minutes returned, followed by her father. The two men shook hands, and each of them looked as though he did not know what he was expected to say to the other. "Now then, father, you must arrange things with Mr. Moss."

Mr. Moss bowed. "I don't exactly know what I have got to arrange," said Mr. O'Mahony.

"We've got to arrange so that we shan't get into debt with Mr. Moss."

"There need not be the least fear in the world as to that," said Mr. Moss.

"Ah; but that's just what we do fear, and what we must fear."

"So unnecessary,—so altogether unnecessary," said Mr. Moss, expecting to be allowed to be the banker for the occasion. "If you will just draw on me for what you want."

"But that is just what we won't do." Then there was a pause, and Mr. Moss shrugged his shoulders. "It's as well to understand that at the beginning. Of course this place is too expensive for us, and we must get out of it as soon as possible."

"Why in such a hurry?" said Mr. Moss raising his two hands.

"And we must send back the piano. It was so good of you to think of it! But it must go back."

"No, no, no!" shouted Mr. Moss. "The piano is my affair. A piano more or less for a few months is nothing between me and Erard's people. They are only too happy."

"I do not in the least doubt it. Messrs. Erard's people are always glad to secure a lady who is about to come out as a singer. But they send the bill in at last."

"Not to you;—not to you."

"But to you. That would be a great deal worse, would it not, father? We might as well understand each other."

"Mr. O'Mahony and I will understand each other very well."

"But it is necessary that Miss O'Mahony and you should understand each other also. My father trusts me, and I cannot tell you how absolutely I obey him."

"Or he you," said Mr. Moss, laughing.

"At any rate we two know what we are about, sir. You will not find us differing. Now Mr. Moss, you are to pay me twenty shillings a day."

"Till Christmas;—twenty shillings a night till Christmas."

"Of course we cannot live here on twenty shillings a day. The rooms nearly take it all. We can't live on twenty shillings a day anyhow."

"Then make it forty shillings immediately after the Christmas holidays.

"I must have an agreement to that effect," said Rachel, "or we must go back to Ireland. I must have the agreement before Christmas, or we shall go back. We have a few pounds which will take us away."

"You must not speak of going away, really, Miss O'Mahony."

"Then I must have an agreement signed. You understand that. And we shall look for cheaper rooms to-day. There is a little street close by where we can manage it. But on the one thing we are determined;—we will not get into debt."

CHAPTER VIII.

CHRISTMAS-DAY, 1880.

ON Christmas-day Rachel O'Mahony wrote a letter to her lover at Morony Castle:—

"Cecil Street, Christmas-day, 1880,

"DEAREST FRANK,

"You do love me, don't you? What's the use of my loving you, and thinking that you are everything, only that you are to love me. I am quite content that it should be so. Only let it be so. You'll ask me what reason I have to be jealous. I am not jealous. I do think in my heart that you think that

I'm—just perfect. And when I tell myself that it is so, I lay myself back in my chair and kiss at you with my lips till I am tired of kissing the space where you ain't. But if I am wrong, and if you are having a good time of it with Miss Considine at Mrs. McKeon's ball, and are not thinking a bit of me and my kisses, what's the use? It's a very unfair bargain that a woman makes with a man. 'Yes; I do love you,' I say,—'but——' Then there's a sigh. 'Yes; I'll love you,' you say——'if——' Then there's a laugh. . If I tell a fib, and am not worth having, you can always recuperate. But we can't recuperate. I'm to go about the world and be laughed at, as the girl that Frank Jones made a fool of. Oh! Mr. Jones, if you treat me in that way, won't I punish you? I'll jump into the lough with a label round my neck telling the whole story. But I am not a bit jealous, because I know you are good.

"And now I must tell you a bit more of my history. We got rid of that lovely hotel, paying £6 10s., when that just earned £1. And I have brought the piano with me. The man at Erard's told me that I should have it for £2 10s. a month, frankly owning that he hoped to get my custom. 'But Mr. Moss is to pay nothing?' I asked. He swore that Mr. Moss would have to pay nothing, and leave what occurred between him and me. I don't think he will. £30 a year ought to be enough for the hire of a piano. So here we are established, at £10 a month —the first-floor, with father's bedroom behind the sitting-room. I have the room upstairs over the sitting-room. They are small stumpy little rooms,—'but mine own.' Who says—'But mine own?' Somebody does, and I repeat it. They are mine own, at any rate till next Saturday.

"And we have settled this terrible engagement and signed it. I'm to sing for Moss at 'The Embankment' for four months, at the rate of £600 a year. It was a Jew's bargain, for I really had filled the house for a fortnight. Fancy a theatre called 'The Embankment!' There is a nasty muddy rheumatic sound about it; but it's very prettily got up, and the exits and entrances are also good. Father goes with me every night, but I mean to let him off the terrible task soon. He smiles, and says he likes it. I only tell him he would be a child if he did. They want to change the piece, but I shall make them pay me for my dresses; I am not going to wear any other woman's old clothes. It's not the proper way to begin, you have to begin as a slave or as an empress. Of course, anybody prefers to do the empress. They try, and then they fail, and tumble down. I shall tumble down, no doubt; but I may as well have my chance.

"And now I'm going to make you say that I'm a beast. And so I am. I make a little use of Mahomet M. M.'s passion to achieve my throne instead of taking up at once with serfdom. But I do it without vouchsafing him even the first corner of a

E

smile. The harshest treatment is all that he gets. Men such
as Mahomet M. will live on harsh treatment for a while, looking
forward to revenge when their time comes. But I shall soon
have made sure of my throne, or shall have failed; and in
either case shall cease to care for Mahomet M. By bullying
him and by treating him as dust beneath my feet, I can do
something to show how proud I am, and how sure I am of
success. He offers me money—not paid money down, which
would have certain allurements. I shouldn't take it. I needn't
tell you that. I should like to have plenty of loose sovereigns,
so as to hire broughams from the yard, instead of walking, or
going in a 'bus about London, which is very upsetting to my
pride. Father and I go down to the theatre in a hansom, when
we feel ourselves quite smart. But it isn't money like that which
he offers. He wants to pay me a month in advance and suggests
that I shall get into debt, and come to him to get me out of it.
There was some talk of papa going to New York for a few weeks,
and he said he would come and look after me in his absence.
'Thank you, Mr. Moss,' I said, 'but I'm not sure I should
want any looking after, only for such as you.' Those are the
very words I spoke, and I looked him full in the face. 'Why,
what do you expect from me?' he said. 'Insult,' I replied, as
bold as brass. And then we are playing the two lovers at 'The
Embankment.' Isn't it a pretty family history? He said nothing
at the moment, but came back in half an hour to make some
unnecessary remarks about the part. 'Why did you say just
now that I insulted you?' he asked. 'Because you do,' I replied.
'Never, never!' he exclaimed, with most grotesque energy. 'I
have never insulted you.' You know, my dear, he has twenty
times endeavoured to kiss my hand, and once he saw fit to
stroke my hair. Beast! If you knew the sort of feeling I have
for him—such as you would have if you found a cockroach in
your dressing-case. Of course in our life young women have to
put up with this kind of thing, and some of them like it. But he
knows that I am going to be married, or at any rate am engaged,
Mr. Frank. I make constant use of your name, telling everybody that I am the future Mrs. Jones, putting such weight upon
the Jones. With me he knows that it is an insult; but I don't
want to quarrel with him if I can help it, and therefore I
softened it down. 'You hear me say, Mr. Moss, that I'm an
engaged young woman. Knowing that, you oughtn't to speak
to me as you do.' 'Why, what do I say?' You should have
seen his grin as he asked me; such a leer of triumph as though
he knew that he were getting the better of me. 'Mr. Jones
wouldn't approve if he were to see it.' 'But luckily he don't,'
said my admirer. Oh, if you knew how willingly I'd stand at a
tub and wash your shirts, while the very touch of his gloves
makes me creep all over with horror. 'Let us have peace for

the future,' I said. 'I dislike all those familiarities. If you will only give them up we shall go on like a house on fire.' Then the beast made an attempt to squeeze my hand as he went out of the room. I retreated, however, behind the table, and escaped untouched on that occasion.

"You are not to come over, whatever happens, until I tell you. You ought to know very well by this time that I can fight my battles by myself; and if you did come, there would be an end altogether to the £200 which I am earning. To give him his due, he's very punctual with his money, only that he wants to pay me in advance, which I will never have. He has been liberal about my dresses, telling me to order just what I want, and have the bill sent in to the costume manager. When I have worn them they become the property of the theatre. God help any poor young woman that will ever be expected to get into them. So now you know exactly how I am standing with Mahomet M. M.

"Poor father goes about to public meetings, but never is allowed to open his mouth for fear he should say something about the Queen. I don't mean that he is really watched, but he promised in Ireland not to lecture any more if they would let him go, and he wishes to keep his word. But I fear it makes him very unhappy. He has, at any rate, the comfort of coming home and giving me the lecture, which he ought to have delivered to more sympathetic ears. Not but what I do care about the people; only how am I to know whether they ought to be allowed to make their own petticoats, or why it is that they don't do so? He says it's the London Parliament; and that if they had members in College Green, the young women would go to work at once, and make petticoats for all the world. I don't understand it, and wish that he had someone else to lecture to.

"How are you getting on with all your own pet troubles? Is the little subsiding lake at Ballintubber still a lake? And what about poor Florian and his religion? Has he told up as yet? I fear, I fear, that poor Florian has been fibbing, and that there will be no peace for him or for your father till the truth has been told.

"Now, sir, I have told you everything, just as a young woman ought to tell her future lord and master. You say you ought to know what Moss is doing. You do know, exactly, as far as I can tell you. Of course you wouldn't like to see him, but then you have the comfort of knowing that I don't like it either. I suppose it is a comfort, eh, my bold young man? Of course you want me to hate the pig, and I do hate him. You may be sure that I will get rid of him as soon as I conveniently can. But for the present he is a necessary evil. If you had a home to give me, I would come to it—oh, so readily! There is something in the glitter of a theatre—what people call the boards, the gaslights, the music, the mock love-making, the pretence of being somebody, the feeling of mystery which is attached to you, and the feeling you have that you are generally unlike the world at large—which has its charms. Even your name, blazoned in a dirty play-bill, without any Mister or Mistress to guard you, so unlike the ways of ordinary life, does gratify one's vanity. I can't say why it should be so, but it is. I always feel a little prouder of myself when father is not with me. I am Miss O'Mahony, looking after myself, whereas other young ladies have to be watched. It has its attractions.

"But—but to be the wife of Frank Jones, and to look after Frank's little house, and to cook for him his chicken and his bacon, and to feel that I am all the world to him, and to think——! But, oh, Frank, I cannot tell you what things I think. I do feel, as I think them, that I have not been made to stand long before the glare of the gas, and that the time will certainly come when I shall walk about Ballintubber leaning on your arm, and hearing all your future troubles about rents not paid, and waters that have come in.

"Your own, own girl,
"RACHEL O'MAHONY."

CHAPTER IX.

BLACK DALY.

FRANK JONES received his letter just as he was about to leave Castle Morony for the meet at Ballytowngal, the seat, as everybody knows, of Sir Nicholas Bodkin. Ballytowngal is about two miles from Claregalway, on the road to Oranmore. Sir Nicholas is known all through the West of Ireland, as a sporting man, and is held in high esteem. But there is, I think, something different in the estimation which he now enjoys from that which he possessed twenty years ago. He was then, as now, a Roman Catholic,—as were also his wife and children; and, as a Roman Catholic, he was more popular with the lower classes, and with the priests, who are their natural friends, than with his brother grand-jurors of the country, who were, for the most part, Protestants.

Sir Nicholas is now sixty years old, and when he came to the title at thirty, he was regarded certainly as a poor man's friend. He always lived on the estate. He rarely went up to Dublin, except for a fortnight, when the hunting was over, and when he paid his respects to the Lord Lieutenant. The house at Ballytowngal was said, in those days, to be as well kept up as any mansion in County Galway. But the saying came probably from those who were not intimate in the more gloriously maintained mansions. Sir Nicholas had £5,000 a year, and though he did manage to pay his bills annually, spent every shilling of it. He preserved his foxes loyally, and was quite as keen about the fishing of a little river that he owned, and which ran down from his demesne into Lough Corrib. He was particular also about his snipe, and would boast that in a little spinney at Ballytowngal were to be met the earliest woodcock found in the West of Ireland. He was a thorough sportsman ;—but a Roman Catholic—and as a Roman Catholic he was hardly equal in standing to some of his Protestant neighbours. He voted for Major Stackpoole, when Major Stackpoole stood for the county on the Liberal interest, and was once requested to come forward himself, and stand for the City as a Roman Catholic. This he did not do, being a prudent man ; but at that period, from twenty to thirty years ago, he was certainly regarded as inferior to a Protestant by many of the Protestant gentlemen of the country.

But things are changed now. Sir Nicholas's neighbours, such of them at least that are Protestants, regard Sir Nicholas as equal to themselves. They do not care much for his religion, but they know that he is not a Home-Ruler, or latterly, since the Land-league sprang into existence, a Land-leaguer. He is, in fact, one of themselves as a county gentleman, and the question of religion has gone altogether into abeyance. Had you known the county thirty years ago, and had now heard Sir Nicholas talking of county matters, you would think that he was one of the old Protestants. It was so that the rich people regarded him,—and so also the poor. But Sir Nicholas had not varied at all. He liked to get his rents paid, and as long as his tenants would pay them, he was at one with them. They had begun now to have opinions of their own on the subject, and he was at one with them no longer.

Frank Jones had heard in Galway, that there was to be a difficulty about drawing the Ballytowngal coverts. The hounds were to be allowed to draw the demesne coverts, but beyond that they were to be interrupted. Foxes seldom broke from Ballytowngal, or if they did they ran to Moytubber. At Moytubber the hounds would probably change,—or would do so if allowed to continue their sport in peace. But at Moytubber the row would begin. Knowing this, Frank Jones was anxious to leave his home in time, as he was aware that the hounds would be carried on to Moytubber as quickly as possible. Black Daly had sworn a solemn oath that he would draw Moytubber in the teeth of every Home-Ruler and Land-leaguer in County Galway.

A word or two must be said descriptive of Black Daly, as he

was called, the master of the Galway hounds. They used to be called the Galway blazers, but the name had nearly dropped out of fashion since Black Daly had become their master, a quarter of a century since. Who Black Daly was, or whence he had come, many men, even in County Galway, did not know. It was not that he had no property, but that his property was so small, as to make it seem improbable that the owner of it should be the master of the county hounds. But in truth Black Daly lived at Daly's Bridge, in the neighbourhood of Castle Blakeney, when he was supposed to be at home. And the house in which he lived he had undoubtedly inherited from his father. But he was not often there, and kept his kennels at Ahaseragh, five miles away from Daly's Bridge. Much was not therefore known of Mr. Daly, in his own house.

But in the field no man was better known, or more popular, if thorough obedience is an element of popularity. The old gentry of the county could tell why Mr. Daly had been put into his present situation five-and-twenty years ago; but the manner of his election was not often talked about. He had no money, and very few acres of his own on which to preserve foxes. He had never done anything to earn a shilling since he had been born, unless he may have been said to have earned shillings by his present occupation. As he got his living out of it, he certainly may have been said to have done so. He never borrowed a shilling from any man, and certainly paid his way. But if he told a young man that he ought to buy a horse the young man certainly bought it. And if he told a young man that he must pay a certain price, the young man generally paid it. But if the young man were not ready with his money by the day fixed, that young man generally had a bad time of it. Young men have been known to be driven not only out of County Galway, but out of Ireland itself, by the tone of Mr. Daly's voice, and by the blackness of his frown. And yet it was said generally that neither young men nor old men were injured in their dealings with Mr. Daly. "That horse won't be much the worse for his splint, and he's worth £70 to you, because you can ride him ten stone. You had better give me £70 for him." Then the young man would promise the £70 in three months' time, and if he kept his word, would swear by Black Daly ever afterwards. In this way Mr. Daly sold a great many horses.

But he had been put into his present position because he hunted the hounds, during the illness of a distant cousin, who was the then master. The master had died, but the county had the best sport that winter that it had ever enjoyed. "I don't see why I should not do it as well as another," Tom Daly had said. He was then known as Tom Daly. "You've got no money," his cousin had said, the son of the old gentleman who was just dead. It was well understood that the cousin wished to have the hounds, but that he was thought not to have all the necessary attributes. " I suppose the county means to pay for all sport," said Tom. Then the hat went round, and an annual sum of £900 a year was voted. Since that the hounds have gone on, and the bills have been paid ; and Tom has raised the number of days' hunting to four a week, or has lowered it to two, according to the amount of money given. He makes no proposition now, but declares what he means to do. " Things are dearer," he said last year, " and you won't have above five days a fortnight, unless you can make the money up to £1,200. I want £400 a day, and £400 I must have." The county had then voted him the money in the plenitude of its power, and Daly had hunted seven days a fortnight. But all the Galway world felt that there was about to be a fall.

Black Daly was a man quite as dark as his sobriquet described him. He was tall, but very thin and bony, and seemed not to have an ounce of flesh about his face or body. He had large, black whiskers,—coarse and jet black,—which did not quite meet beneath his chin. And he wore no other beard, no tuft, no imperial, no moustachios ; but when he was seen before shaving on a morning, he would seem to be black all over, and his hair was black, short, and harsh ; and though black, round about his ears it was beginning to be tinged with grey. He was now over fifty years of age ; but the hair on his head was as thick as it had been when he first undertook the hounds. He had great dark eyes in his head, deep down, so that they seemed to glitter at you out of caverns. And above them were great, bushy eyebrows, every hair of which seemed to be black, and harsh, and hard. His nose was well formed and prominent ; but of cheeks he had apparently none. Between his whiskers and his nose, and the corners of his mouth there was nothing but two hollow cavities. He was somewhat over six feet high, but from his extraordinary thinness gave the appearance of much greater height. His arms were long, and the waistcoat which he wore was always long ; his breeches were very long ; and his boots seemed the longest thing about him—unless his spurs seemed longer. He had no flesh about him, and it was boasted of him that, in spite of his length, and in spite of his height, he could ride under twelve stone. Of himself and of his doings, he never talked. They were secrets of his own, of which he might have to make money. And no one had a right to ask him questions. He did not conceive that it would be necessary for a gentleman to declare his weight unless he were about to ride a race. Now it was understood that for the last ten years Black Daly had ridden no races.

He was a man of whom it might be said that he never joked. Though his life was devoted in a peculiar manner to sport, and there may be thought to be something akin between the amusements and the lightness of life, it was all serious to him. Though he was bitter over it, or happy; triumphant, or occasionally in despair—as when the money was not forthcoming—he never laughed. It was all serious to him, and apparently sad, from the first note of a hound in the early covert, down to the tidings that a poor fox had been found poisoned near his earth. He had much to do to find sport for the county on such limited means, and he was always doing it.

He not only knew every hound in his pack, but he knew their ages, their sires and their dams; and the sires and the dams of most of their sires and dams. He knew the constitution of each, and to what extent their noses were to be trusted. "It's a very heavy scent to-day," he would say, "because Gaylap carries it over the plough. It's only a catching scent because the drops don't hang on the bushes." His lore on all such matters was incredible, but he would never listen to any argument. A man had a right to his own opinion; but then the man who differed from him knew nothing. He gave out his little laws to favoured individuals; not by way of conversation, for which he cared nothing, but because it might be well that the favoured individual should know the truth on that occasion.

As a man to ride he was a complete master of his art. There was nothing which a horse could do with a man on his back, which Daly could not make him do; and when he had ridden a horse he would know exactly what was within his power. But there was no desire with him for the showing off of a horse. He often rode to sell a horse, but he never seemed to do so. He never rode at difficult places unless driven to do so by the exigencies of the moment. He was always quiet in the field, unless when driven to express himself as to the faults of some young man. Then he could blaze forth in his anger with great power. He was constantly to be seen trotting along a road when hounds were running, because he had no desire to achieve for himself a character for hard riding. But he was always with his hounds when he was wanted, and it was boasted of him that he had ridden four days a week through the season on three horses, and had never lamed one of them. He was rarely known to have a second horse out, and when he did so, it was for some purpose peculiar to the day's work. On such days he had generally a horse to sell.

It is hardly necessary to say that Black Daly was an unmarried man. No one who knew him could conceive that he should have had a wife. His hounds were his children, and he could have taught no wife to assist him in looking after them, with the constant attention and tender care which was given to them by Barney Smith, his huntsman. A wife, had she seen to the feeding of the numerous babies, would have given them too much to eat, and had she not undertaken this care, she would have been useless at Daly's Bridge. But Barney Smith was invaluable; double the amount of work got usually from a huntsman was done by him. There was no kennel man, no second horseman, no stud-groom at the Ahaseragh kennels. It may be said that Black Daly filled all these positions himself, and that in each Barney Smith was his first lieutenant. Circumstances had given him the use of the Ahaseragh kennels, which had been the property of his cousin, and circumstances had not enabled him to build others at Daly's Bridge. Gradually he had found it easier to move himself than the hounds. And so it had come to pass that two rooms had been prepared for him close to the kennels, and that Mr. Barney Smith gave him such attendance as was necessary. Of strictly personal attendance Black Daly wanted very little; but the discomforts of that home, while one pair of breeches were supposed to be at Daly's Bridge, and the others at Ahaseragh, were presumed by the world at large to be very grievous.

But the personal appearance of Mr. Daly on hunting mornings, was not a matter of indifference. It was not that he wore beautiful pink tops, or came out guarded from the dust by little aprons, or had his cravat just out of the bandbox, or his scarlet coat always new, and in the latest fashion, nor had his hat just come from the shop in Piccadilly with the newest twist to its rim. But there was something manly, and even powerful about his whole apparel. He was always the same, so that by men even in his own county, he would hardly have been known in other garments. The strong, broad-brimmed high hat, with the cord passing down his back beneath his coat, that had known the weather of various winters; the dark, red coat, with long swallow tails, which had grown nearly black under many storms; the dark, buff striped waistcoat, with the stripes running downwards, long, so as to come well down over his breeches; the breeches themselves, which were always of leather, but which had become nearly brown under the hands of Barney Smith or his wife, and the mahogany top-boots, of which the tops seemed to be a foot in length, could none of them have been worn by any but Black Daly. His very spurs must have surely been made for him, they were in length and weight, and general strength of leather, so peculiarly his own. He was unlike other masters of hounds in this, that he never carried a horn; but he spoke to his hounds in a loud, indistinct chirruping voice, which all County Galway believed to be understood to every hound in the park.

One other fact must be told respecting Mr. Daly. He was a Protestant—as opposed to a Roman Catholic. No one had ever known him go to church, or speak a word in reference to religion. He was equally civil or uncivil to priest and parson when priest or parson appeared in the field. But on no account would he speak to either of them if he could avoid it. But he had in his heart a thorough conviction that all Roman Catholics ought to be regarded as enemies by all Protestants, and that the feeling was one entirely independent of faith and prayerbooks, or crosses and masses. For him fox-hunting—fox-hunting for others—was the work of his life, and he did not care to meddle with what he did not understand. But he was a Protestant, and Sir Nicholas Bodkin was a Roman Catholic, and therefore an enemy—as a dog may be supposed to declare himself a dog, and a cat a cat, if called upon to explain the cause of the old family quarrel.

Now there had come a cloud over his spirit in reference to the state of his country. He could see that the quarrel was not entirely one between Protestant and Catholic as it used to be, but still he could not get it out of his mind, but that the old causes were producing in a different way their old effects. Whiteboys, Terryalts, Ribbonmen, Repeaters, Physical-Force-men, Fenians, Home-Rulers, Professors of Dynamite, and American-Irish, were, to his thinking, all the same. He never talked much about it, because he did not like to expose his ignorance; but his convictions were not the less formed. It was the business of a Protestant to take rent, and of a Roman Catholic to pay rent. There were certain deviations in this ordained rule of life, but they were only exceptions. The Roman Catholics had the worst of this position, and the Protestants the best. Therefore the Roman Catholics were of course quarrelling with it, and therefore the Roman Catholics must be kept down. Such had been Mr. Daly's general outlook into life. But now the advancing evil of the time was about to fall even upon himself, and upon his beneficent labours, done for the world at large. It was whispered in County Galway that the people were about to rise and interfere with fox-hunting! It may be imagined that on this special day Mr. Daly's heart was low beneath his black-striped waistcoat, as he rode on his way to draw the coverts at Ballytowngal.

At the cross-roads of Monivea he met Peter Bodkin, the eldest son of Sir Nicholas. Now Peter Bodkin had quarrelled long and very bitterly with his father. Every acre of the property at Ballytowngal was entailed upon him, and Peter had thought that under such circumstances his father was not doing enough for him. The quarrel had been made up, but still the evil rankled in Peter's bosom, who was driven to live with his wife and family on £500 a year; and had found himself hardly driven to keep himself out of the hands of the Jews. His father had wished him to follow some profession, but this had been contrary to Peter's idea of what was becoming. But though he had only £500 a year, and five children, he did manage to keep two horses, and saw a good deal of hunting.

And among all the hunting men in County Galway he was the one who lived on the closest terms of intimacy with Black Daly. For, though he was a Roman Catholic, his religion did not trouble him much ; and he was undoubtedly on the same side with Daly in the feuds that were coming on the country. Indeed, he and Daly had entertained the same feelings for some years ; for, in the quarrels which had been rife between the father and son, Mr. Daly had taken the son's part, as far as so silent a man can be said to have taken any part at all.

"Well, Peter." "Well, Daly," were the greetings, as the two men met ; and then they rode on together in silence for a mile. "Have you heard what the boys are going to do?" asked the master. Peter shook his head. "I suppose there's nothing in it ?"

"I fear there is."

"What will they do?" asked Mr. Daly.

"Just prevent your hunting."

"If they touch me, or either of the men, by God ! I'll shoot some of them." Then he put his hand into his pocket, as much as to explain a pistol was there. After that the two men rode on in silence till they came to the gates of Ballytowngal.

CHAPTER X.

BALLYTOWNGAL.

DALY, among other virtues, or vices, was famed for punctuality. He wore a large silver watch in his pocket which was as true as the sun, or at any rate was believed by its owner to be so. From Daly's watch on hunting mornings there was no appeal. He always reached the appointed meet at five minutes before eleven, by his watch, and by his watch the hounds were always moved from their haunches at five minutes past eleven. Though the Lord Lieutenant and the Chief Secretary and the Lord Chancellor had been there, there would have been no deviation. The interval of ten minutes he generally spent in whispered confabulations with the earth-warners, secrets into which no attendant horseman ever dived ; for Black Daly was a mysterious man, who did not choose to be inquired into as to his movements. On this occasion he said not a word to any earth-warner, though two were in attendance ; but he sat silent and more gloomy than ever on his big black horse, waiting for the minutes to pass by till he should be able to run his hounds through the Ballytowngal coverts, and then hurry on to Moytubber.

Mr. Daly's mind was, in truth, fixed upon Moytubber, and what would there be done this morning. He was a simple-minded man, who kept his thoughts fixed for the most part on one object. He knew that it was his privilege to draw the coverts of Moytubber, and to hunt the country around; and he felt also, after some gallant fashion, that it was his business to protect the rights of others in pursuit of their favourite amusement. No man could touch him or either of his servants in the way of violence without committing an offence which he would be bound to oppose by violence. He was no lawyer, and understood not at all the statutes as fixed upon the subject. If a man laid a hand upon him violently, and would not take his hand off again when desired, he would be entitled to shoot that man. Such was the law, as in his simplicity and manliness he believed it to exist. He was a man not given to pistols; but when he heard that he was to be stopped in his hunting on this morning, and stopped by dastardly, pernicious curs who called themselves Land-leaguers, he went into Ballinasloe, and bought himself a pistol. Black Daly was a sad, serious man, who could not put up with the frivolities of life; to whom the necessity of providing for that large family of children was very serious; but he was not of his nature a quarrelsome man. But now he was threatened on the tenderest point; and with much simpler thought had resolved that it would be his duty to quarrel.

But just when he had spoken the word on which Barney and the hounds were prepared to move, Sir Nicholas trotted up to him. Sir Nicholas and all the sporting gentlemen of County Galway were there, whispering with each other, having collected themselves in crowds much bigger than usual. There was much whispering, and many opinions had been given as to the steps which it would be well that the hunt should take if interrupted in their sport. But at last Peter Bodkin had singled out his father, and had communicated to him the fact of Black Daly's pistol. "He'll use it, as sure as eggs are eggs," said Peter whispering to his father.

"Then there'll be murder," said Sir Nicholas, who though a good hunting neighbour had never been on very friendly terms with Mr. Daly.

"When Tom Daly says he'll do a thing, he means to do it," said Peter. "He won't be stopped by my calling it murder." Then Sir Nicholas had quickly discussed the matter with sundry other sportsmen of the neighbourhood. There were Mr. Persse of Doneraile, and Mr. Blake of Letterkenny, and Lord Ardrahan, and Sir Jasper Lynch, of Bohernane. During the ten minutes that were allowed to them, they put their heads together, and with much forethought made Mr. Persse their spokesman. Lord Ardrahan and Sir Jasper might have seemed to take upon themselves an authority which Daly would not endure. And Blake of Letterkenny would have been too young to carry with him sufficient weight. Sir Nicholas himself was a Roman

Catholic, and was Peter's father, and Peter would have been in a scrape for having told the story of the pistol. So Mr. Persse put himself forward. "Daly," he said, trotting up to the master, "I'm afraid we're going to encounter a lot of these Land-leaguers at Moytubber."

"What do they want at Moytubber? Nobody is doing anything to them."

"Of course not; they are a set of miserable ruffians. I'm sorry to say that there are a lot of my tenants among them. But it's no use discussing that now."

"I can only go on," said Daly, "as though they were in bed," Then he put his hand into his pocket, and felt that the pistol was there.

Mr. Persse saw what he did, and knew that his hand was on the pistol. "We have only a minute now to decide," he said.

"To decide what?" asked Daly.

"There must be no violence on our side." Daly turned round his face upon him, and looked at him from the bottom of those two dark caverns. "Believe me when I say it; there must be no violence on our side."

"If they attempt to stop my horse?"

"There must be no violence on our side to bring us, or rather you, to further grief."

"By God! I'd shoot the man who did it," said Daly.

"No, no; let there be no shooting. Were you to do so, there can be no doubt that you would be tried by a jury and——"

"Hanged," said Daly. "May be so; I have got to look that in the face. It is an accursed country in which we are living."

"But you would not encounter the danger in carrying out a trifling amusement such as this?"

Daly again turned round and looked at him. Was this work of his life, this employment on which he was so conscientiously eager, to be called trifling? Did they know the thoughts which it cost him, the hard work by which it was achieved, the days and nights which were devoted to it? Trifling amusement! To him it was the work of his life. To those around him it was the best part of theirs.

"I will not interfere with them," Daly said.

He alluded here to the enemies of hunting generally. He had not hunted the country so long without having had many rows with many men. Farmers, angry with him for the moment, had endeavoured to stop him as he rode upon their land; and they had poisoned his foxes from revenge, or stolen them from cupidity. He had borne with such men, expressing the severity of his judgment chiefly by the look of his eyes; but he had never quarrelled with them violently. They had been contemptible people whom it would be better to look at than to shoot. But here were men coming, or were there now, prepared to fight with him for his rights. And he would fight with them, even though hanging should be the end of it.

"I will not interfere with them, unless they interfere with me."

"Have you a pistol with you, Daly?" said Persse.

"I have."

"Then give it me."

"Not so. If I want to use a pistol it will be better to have it in my own pocket than in yours. If I do not want to use it I can keep it myself, and no one will be the wiser."

"Listen to me, Daly."

"Well, Mr. Persse?"

"Do not call me 'Mr. Persse,' as though you were determined to quarrel with me. It will be well that you should take advice in this matter from those whom you have known all your life. There is Sir Nicholas Bodkin——"

"He may be one of them for all that I can tell," said Daly.

"Lord Ardrahan is not one of them. And Sir Jasper Lynch, and Blake of Letterkenny, they are all there, if you will speak to them. In such a matter as this it is not worth your while to get into serious trouble. To you and me hunting is of much importance; but the world at large will not regard it as one in which blood should be shed. They will come prepared to make themselves disagreeable, but if there be bloodshed it will simply be by your hands. And think what an injury you would do to your side of the question, and what a benefit to theirs!"

"How so?"

"We are regarded as the dominant party, as gentlemen who ought to do what is right, and support the laws."

"If I am attacked may I not defend myself?"

"No; not by a pistol carried loaded into a hunting-field. You would have all the world against you."

Then the two men rode on silently together. The hounds were drawing the woods of Ballytowngal, but had not found, and were prepared to go on to Moytubber. But, according to the Galway custom, Barney Smith was waiting for orders from his master. Daly now sat stock-still upon his horse for awhile, looking at the dark fringe of trees by which the park was surrounded. He was thinking, as well as he knew how to think, of the position in which he was placed. To be driven to go contrary to his fixed purpose by fear was a course intolerable to him. But to have done that which was clearly injurious to his party was as bad. And this Persse to whom he had shown his momentary anger by calling him Mr., was a man whom he greatly regarded. There was no one in the field whose word would go further with him in hunting matters. He had clearly been rightly chosen as a deputation. But Daly knew that as he had gone to bed the previous night, and as he had got up in the morning, and as he had trotted along by the Monivea cross-roads, and had met Peter Bodkin, every thought of his mind had been intent on the pistol within his pocket. To shoot a man who should lay hold of him or his horse, or endeavour to stop his horse, had seemed to him to be bare justice. But he had resolved that he would first give some spoken warning to the sinner. After that, God help the man; for he would find no help in Black Tom Daly.

But now his mind was shaken by the admonitions of Mr. Persse. He could not say of Mr. Persse as he had said, most unjustly, of Sir Nicholas, that he was one of them. Mr. Persse was well-known as a Tory and a Protestant, and an indefatigable opponent of Home-Rulers. To Sir Nicholas, in the minds of some men, there attached a slight stain of his religion. "I will keep the pistol in my pocket," said Tom Daly, without turning his eyes away from the belt of trees.

"Had you not better trust it with me?" said Mr. Persse.

"No, I am not such an idiot as to shoot a man when I do not intend it.'

"Seeing how moved you are, I thought that perhaps the pistol might be safer in my hands."

"No, the pistol shall remain with me." Then he turned round to join Barney Smith, who was waiting for him up by the gate out of the covert. But he turned again to say a word to Mr. Persse. "Thank you, Persse, I am obliged to you. It might be inconvenient being locked up before the season is over." Then a weird grin covered his face; which was the nearest approach to laughter ever seen with Black Tom Daly.

From Ballytowngal to Moytubber was about a mile and a half. Some few, during the conversation between Mr. Persse and the master, had gone on, so that they might be the first to see what was in store for them. But the crowd of horsemen had remained with their eyes fixed upon Daly. He rode up to them and passed on without speaking a word, except that he gave the necessary orders to Barney Smith. Then two or three clustered round Mr. Persse, asking him whispered questions. "It'll be all right," said Persse, nodding his head; and so the *cortège* passed on. But not a word was spoken by Daly himself, either then or afterwards, except a whispered order or two given to Barney Smith. Moytubber is a gorse covert lying about three hundred yards from the road, and through it the horsemen always passed, on other occasions it was locked. Now the gate had been taken off its hinges and thrown back upon the bank; and Daly, as he passed into the field, perceived that the covert was surrounded by a crowd.

CHAPTER XI

MOYTUBBER.

"WHAT'S all this about?" said Tom as he rode up the covert side, and addressing a man whose face he happened to know. He was one Kit Mooney, a baker from Claregalway, who in these latter days had turned Land-leaguer. But he was one who simply thought that his bread might be better buttered for him on that side of the question. He was not an ardent politician; but few local Irishmen were so. Had no stirring spirits been wafted across the waters from America to teach Irishmen that one man is as good as another, or generally better, Kit Mooney would never have found it out. Had not his zeal been awakened by the eloquence of Mr. O'Meagher, the member for Athlone, who had just made a grand speech to the people at Athenry, Kit Mooney would have gone on in his old ways, and would at this moment have been touching his hat to Tom Daly, and whispering to him of the fox that had lately been seen " staling away jist there, Mr. Daly, 'fore a'most yer very eyes." But Mr. O'Meagher had spent three glorious weeks in New York, and, having practised the art of speaking on board the steamer as he returned, had come to Athenry and filled the mind of Kit Mooney and sundry others with political truth of the deepest dye. But the gist of the truths so taught had been chiefly this :— that if a man did not pay his rent, but kept his money in his pocket, he manifestly did two good things ; he enriched himself, and he so far pauperised the landlord, who was naturally his enemy. What other teaching could be necessary to make Kit understand,—Kit Mooney who held twenty acres of meadow land convenient to the town of Claregalway,—that this was the way to thrive in the world? "Rent is not known in America, that great and glorious country. Every man owns the fields which he cultivates. Why should you here allow yourselves to be degraded by the unmanly name of tenants? The earth which supports you should be as free to you as the air you breathe." Such had been the eloquence of Mr. O'Meagher ; and it had stirred the mind of Kit Mooney and made him feel that life should be recommenced by him under new principles. Things had not quite gone swimmingly with him since, because Nicholas Bodkin's agent had caused a sheriff's bailiff to appear upon the scene, and the notion of keeping the landlord's rent in the pocket had been found to be surrounded by difficulties. But the great principle was there, and there had come another eloquent man, who had also been in America ; and Kit Mooney was now a confirmed Land-leaguer.

"Faix thin, yer honour, it isn't much hunting the quality

will see this day out of Moytubber; nor yet nowhere round, av the boys are as good as their word."

"Why should they not hunt at Moytubber?" said Mr. Daly, who, as he looked around saw indeed ample cause why there should be no hunting. He had thought as he trotted along the road that some individual Land-leaguer would hold his horse by the rein and cause him to stop him in the performance of his duty; but there were two hundred footmen there roaming at will through the sacred precincts of the gorse, and Daly knew well that no fox could have remained there with such a crowd around him.

"The boys are just taking their pleasure themselves this fine Christmas morning," said Kit, who had not moved from the bank on which he had been found sitting. "Begorra, you'll find 'em all out about the counthry, intirely, Mr. Daly. They're out to make your honour welcome. There is lashings of 'em across in Phil French's woods and all down to Peter Brown's, away at Oranmore. There is not a boy in the barony but what is out to bid yer honour welcome this morning."

Kit Mooney could not have given a more exact account of what was being done by "the boys" on that morning had he owned all those rich gifts of eloquence which Mr. O'Meagher possessed. Tom Daly at once saw that there was no need for shooting any culprit, and was thankful. The interruption to the sport of the county had become much more general than he had expected, and it was apparently so organised as to have spread itself over all that portion of County Galway, in which his hounds ran. "Bedad, Mr. Daly, what Kit says is thrue," said another man whom he did not know. "You'll find 'em out everywhere. Why ain't the boys to be having their fun?"

It was useless to allow a hound to go into the covert of Moytubber. The crowd around was waiting anxiously to see the attempt made, so that they might enjoy their triumph. To watch Black Tom drawing Moytubber without a fox would be nuts to them; and then to follow the hounds on to the next covert, and to the next, with the same result, would afford them an ample day's amusement. But the Bodkins, and the Blakes, and the Persses were quite alive to this, and so also was Tom Daly. A council of war was therefore held, in order that the line of conduct might be adopted which might be held to be most conclusive to the general dignity of the hunt.

"I should send the hounds home," said Lord Ardrahan. "If Mr. Daly would call at my place and lunch, as he goes by, I should be most happy."

Tom Daly, on hearing this, only shook his head. The shake was intended to signify that he did not like the advice tendered, nor the accompanying hospitable offer. To go home would be

F

to throw down their arms at once, and acknowledge themselves beaten. If beaten to-day, why should they not be beaten on another day, and then what would become of Tom Daly's employment? A sad idea came across his mind, as he shook his head, warning him that in this terrible affair of to-day, he might see the end of all his life's work. Such a thought had never occurred to him before. If a crowd of disloyal Roman Catholics chose to prevent the gentry in their hunting, undoubtedly they had the power. Daly was slow at thinking, but an idea when it had once come home to him, struck him forcibly. As he shook his head at that moment he bethought himself, what would become of Black Daly if the people of the county refused to allow his hounds to run? And a second idea struck him,—that he certainly would not lunch with Lord Ardrahan. Lord Ardrahan was, to his thinking, somewhat pompous, and had been felt by Tom to expect that he, Tom, should acknowledge the inferiority of his position by his demeanour. Now such an idea as this was altogether in opposition to Tom's mode of living. Even though the hounds were to be taken away from him, and he were left at Daly's Bridge with the £200 a year which had come to him from his father, he would make no such acknowledgment as that to any gentleman in County Galway. So he shook his head, and said not a word in answer to Lord Ardrahan.

"What do you propose to do, Daly?" demanded Mr. Persse.

"Go on and draw till night. There's a moon, and if we can find a fox before ten, Barney and I will manage to kill him. Those blackguards can't keep on with us." This was Daly's plan, spoken out within hearing of many of the blackguards.

"You had better take my offer, and come to Ardrahan Castle," said his lordship.

"No, my lord," said Daly, with the tone of authority which a master of hounds always knows how to assume. "I shall draw on. Barney, get the hounds together." Then he whispered to Barney Smith that the hounds should go on to Kilcornan. Now Kilcornan was a place much beloved by foxes, about ten miles distant from Moytubber. It was not among the coverts appointed to be drawn on that day, which all lay back towards Ahaseragh. At Kilcornan the earths would be found to open. But it would be better to trot off rapidly to some distant home for foxes, even though the day's sport might be lost. Daly was very anxious that it should not be said through the country that he had been driven home by a set of roughs from any one covert or another. The day's draw would be known— the line of the country, that is, which, in the ordinary course of things, he would follow on that day. But by going to Kilcornan he might throw them off his scent. So he started for Kilcornan, having whispered his orders to Barney Smith, but communicating his intentions to no one else.

"What will you do, Daly?" said Sir Jasper Lynch.

"Go on."

"But where will you go?" inquired the baronet. He was a man about Daly's age, with whom Daly was on comfortable terms. He had no cause for being crabbed with Sir Jasper as with Lord Ardrahan. But he did not want to declare his purpose to any man. There is no one in the ordinary work of his life so mysterious as a master of hounds. And among masters no one was more mysterious than Tom Daly. And this, too, was no ordinary day. Tom only shook his head and trotted on in advance. His secret had been told only to Barney Smith, and with Barney Smith he knew that it would be safe.

So they all trotted off at a pace much faster than usual. "What's up with Black Tom now?" asked Sir Nicholas of Sir Jasper. "What's Daly up to now?" asked Mr. Blake of Mr. Persse. They all shook their heads, and declared themselves willing to follow their leader without further inquiry. "I suppose he knows what he's about," said Mr. Persse; "but we, at any rate, must go and see." So they followed him; and in half an hour's time it became apparent that they were going to Kilcornan.

But at Kilcornan they found a crowd almost equal to that which had stopped them at Moytubber. Kilcornan is a large demesne, into which they would, in the ordinary course, have made their entrance through the lodge gate. At present they went at once to an outlying covert, which was supposed to be especially the abode of foxes; but even here, as Barney trotted up with his hounds, at a pace much quicker than usual, they found that the ground before them had been occupied by Landleaguers. "You'll not do much in the hunting way to-day, Muster Daly," said one of the intruders. "When we heard you were a-coming we had a little hunt of our own. There ain't a fox anywhere about the place now, Muster Daly." Tom Daly turned round and sat on his big black horse, frowning at the world before him; a sorrowful man. What shall we do next? It does not behove a master of hounds to seek counsel in difficulty from anyone. A man, if he is master, should be sufficient to himself in all emergencies. No man felt this more clearly than did Black Tom Daly. He had been ashamed of himself once this morning, because he had taken advice from Mr. Persse. But now he must think the matter out for himself and follow his own devices.

It was as yet only two o'clock, but he had come on at a great pace, taking much more out of his horse than was usual to him on such occasions. But, sitting there, he did make up his mind.

F 2

He would go on to Mr. Lambert's place at Clare, and would draw the coverts, going there as fast as the horse's legs would carry him. There he would borrow two horses if it were possible, but one, at least, for Barney Smith. Then he would draw back by impossible routes, to the kennels at Ahaseragh. Men might come with him or might go; but to none would he tell his mind. If Providence would only send him a fox on the route, all things, he thought, might still be well with him. It would be odd if he and Barney Smith, between them, were not able to give an account of that fox when they had done with him. But if he should find no such fox—if he, the master of the Galway hounds, should have ridden backwards and forwards across County Galway, and have been impeded altogether in his efforts by wretched Land-leaguers, then—as he thought—a final day would have to come for him.

He spoke no word to anyone, but he did go on just as he proposed to himself. He drew Clare, but drew it blank; and then, leaving his own horses, he borrowed two others for himself and Barney, and went on upon his route. Before the day was over—or rather, before the night was far advanced—he had borrowed three others, in his course about the country, for himself and his servants. Quick as lightning he went from covert to covert; but the conspiracy had been well arranged, and a holiday for the foxes in County Galway was established for that day. Some men were very stanch to him, going with him whither they knew not, so that "poor dear Tom" might not be left alone; but alone he was during the long evening of that day, as far as all conversation went. He spoke to no one except to Barney, and to him only a few words; giving him a direction as to where he should go next, and into what covert he should put the hounds. They, too, must have been much surprised and very weary, as they dragged their tired limbs to their kennel, at about eight o'clock. And Tom Daly's ride across the country will long be remembered, and the exertions which he made to find a fox on that day.

But it was all in vain. As Tom ate his solitary mutton-chop, and drank his cold whisky and water, and then took himself to bed, he was a melancholy man. The occupation of his life, he thought, was gone. These reprobates, whom he now hated worse than ever, having learned their powers to disturb the amusements of their betters, would never allow another day's hunting in the county. He was aware now, though he never had thought of it before, by how weak a hold his right of hunting the country was held. He and his hounds could go into any covert; but so also could any other man, with or without hounds. To disturb a fox, three or four men would suffice; one would suffice according to Tom's idea of a fox. The occupation of his life was over.

Tom Daly was by nature a melancholy man. All County Galway knew that. He was a man not given to many words, by no means devoted to sport in the ordinary sense. It was a hard business that he had undertaken. The work was in every sense hard, and the payment made was very small. In fact no payment was made, other than that of his being lifted into a position in which he was able to hold his head high among gentlemen of property. What should he do with himself during the remainder of his life, if hunting in County Galway was brought to an end? He was an intent, eager man, whom it was hard to teach that the occupations of his life were less worthy than those of other men. But there had come moments of doubt as he had sat alone in his little room at Ahaseragh and had meditated, whether the pursuit of vermin was worthy all the energy which he had given to it.

"You may sell those brutes of yours now, and then perhaps you'll be able to educate your children." So Sir Nicholas Bodkin had addressed his eldest son, as they rode home together on that occasion.

"Why so?" Peter had asked, thinking more of the "brutes" alluded to than of the children. He was accustomed to the tone of his father's remarks, and cared for them not more than the ordinary son cares for the expression of the ordinary father's ill-humour. But now he knew that some reference was intended to the interruption that had been made in their day's sport, and was anxious to learn what his father thought about it. "Why so?" he asked.

"Because you won't want them for this game any longer. Hunting is done with in these parts. When a blackguard like Kit Mooney is able to address such a one as Tom Daly after that fashion, anything that requires respect may be said to be over. Hunting has existed solely on respect. I had intended to buy that mare of French's, but I shan't now."

"What does all that mean, Lynch?" said Mr. Persse to Sir Jasper, as they rode home together.

"It means qurrelling to the knife."

"In a quarrel to the knife," said Mr. Persse, "all lighter things must be thrown away. Daly had brought a pistol in his pocket as you heard this morning. I have been thinking of it ever since, and, putting two and two together, it seems to me to be almost impossible that hunting should go on in County Galway."

CHAPTER XII.

"DON'T HATE HIM, ADA."

AMONG those who had gone as far as Mr. Lambert's, but had not proceeded further, had been Frank Jones. He had heard and seen what has been narrated, and was as much impressed as others with the condition of the country. The populace generally—for so it had seemed to be—had risen *en masse* to put down the amusement of the gentry, and there had been a secret conspiracy, so that they had been able to do the same thing in different parts of the county. Frank, as he rode back to Morony Castle, a long way from Mr. Lambert's covert, was very melancholy in his mind. The persecution of Mahomet M. Moss and of the Land-leaguers together was almost too much for him.

When he got home his father also was melancholy, and the girls were melancholy. "What sport have you had, Frank?" said the father. But he asked the question in a melancholy tone, simply as being one which the son expects on returning from hunting. In this expectation Mr. Jones gave way. Frank shook his head, but did not utter a word.

"What do you mean by that?" asked the father.

"The whole country is in arms." This, no doubt, was an exaggeration, as the only arms that had been brought to Moytubber on that occasion had been the pistol in Tom Daly's pocket.

"In arms?" said Philip Jones.

"Well, yes! I call it so. I call men in arms, when they are prepared to carry out any illegal purpose by violence, and these men have done that all through the County Galway."

"What have they done?"

"You know where the meet was; well, they drew Ballytowngal, and found no fox there. It was not expected, and nothing happened there. The people did not come into old Nick Bodkin's demesne, but we had heard by the time that we were there that we should come across a lot of Land-leaguers at Moytubber. There they were as thick as bees round the covert, and there was one man who had the impudence to tell Tom Daly that draw where he might, he would draw in vain for a fox to-day in County Galway."

"Do you mean that there was a crowd?" asked Mr. Jones.

"A crowd! Yes, all Claregalway seemed to have turned out. Claregalway is not much of a place, but every one was there from Oranmore and from Athenry, and half the town from Galway city." This certainly was an exaggeration on the part of Frank, but was excused by his desire to impress his father with the real truth in the matter. "I never saw half such a number of people by a covert side. But the truth was soon known. They had beat Moytubber, and kicked up such a row as the foxes in that gorse had never heard before. And they were not slow in obtaining their object."

"Their object was clear enough."

"They didn't intend that the hounds should hunt that day either at Moytubber or elsewhere. Daly did not put his hounds into the covert at all; but rode away as fast as his horse's legs could carry him to Kilcornan."

"That must be ten miles at least," said his father.

"Twenty, I should think. But we rode away at a hand-gallop leaving the crowd behind us." This again was an exaggeration. "But when we got to the covert at Kilcornan there was just the same sort of crowd, and just the same work had been on foot. The men there all told us that we need not expect to find a fox. A rumour had got about the field by this time that Tom Daly had a loaded pistol in his pocket. What he meant to do with it I don't know. He could have done no good without a regular massacre."

"Did he show his pistol?"

"I didn't see it; but I do believe it was there. Some of the old fogies were awfully solemn about it."

"What was the end of it all?" asked Edith, who together with her sister was now listening to Frank's narrative.

"You know Mr. Lambert's place on the road towards Gort. It's a long way off, and I'm a little out of my latitude there. But I went as far as that, and found a bigger crowd than ever. They said that all Gort was there; but Tom having drawn the covert, went on, and swore that he wouldn't leave a place in all County Galway untried. He borrowed fresh horses, and went on with Barney Smith as grim as death. He is still drawing his covert somewhere."

It was thus that Frank Jones told the story of that day's hunting. To his father's ears it sounded as being very ominous. He did not care much for hunting himself, nor would it much perplex him if the Land-leaguers would confine themselves to this mode of operations. But as he heard of the crowds surrounding the coverts through the county, he thought also of his many acres still under water, by the operation of a man who had taken upon himself to be his enemy. And the whole morning had been spent in fruitless endeavours to make Florian tell the truth. The boy had remained surly, sullen, and silent. "He will tell me at last," Edith had said to her father. But her father had said, that unless the truth were now told, he must allow the affair to go by. "The time for dealing with the matter will be gone," he had said. "Pat Carroll is going about the country as bold as brass, and says that he will fix his own rent; whereas I know, and all the tenants know, that he ought to be in Galway jail. There isn't a man on the estate who isn't certain but that it was he, with five or six others, who let the waters in upon the meadows."

"Then why on earth cannot you make them tell?"

"They say that they only think it," said Edith.

"The very best of them only think it," said Ada.

"And there is not one of them," said Mr. Jones, "whom you could trust to put into a witness-box. To tell the truth, I do not see what right I have to ask them to go there. If I was to select a man,—or two, how can I say to them, 'forget yourself, forget your wife and children, encounter possible murder, and probable ruin, in order that I may get my revenge on this man?'"

"It is not revenge but justice," said Frank.

"It would be revenge to their minds. And if it came to pass that there was a man who would thus sacrifice himself to me, what must I do with him afterwards? Were I to send him to America with money, and take his land into my own hand, see what horrible things would be said of me. The sort of witness I want to back up others, who would then be made to come, is Florian."

"What would they do to him?" asked Edith.

"I could send him to an English school for a couple of years, till all this should have passed by. I have thought of that."

"That, too, would cost money," said Ada.

"Of course it would cost money, but it would be forthcoming, rather than the boy should be in danger. But the feeling to me, as to the boy himself, comes uppermost. It is that he himself should have such a secret in his bosom, and keep it there, locked fast, in opposition to his own father. I want to get it out of him while he is yet a boy, so that his name shall not go abroad as one who, by such manifest falsehood, took part against his own father. It is the injury done to him, rather than the injury done to me."

"He has promised his priest that he will not tell," said Edith, making what excuse she could for her brother.

"He has not promised his priest," said Mr. Jones. "He has made no promise to Father Malachi, of Ballintubber. If he has promised at all it is to that pestilent fellow at Headford. The curate at Headford is not his priest, and why should a promise made to any priest be more sacred than one made to another, unless it were made in confession? I cannot understand Florian. It seems as though he were anxious to take part with these wretches against his country, against his religion, and against his father. It is unintelligible to me that a boy of his age should, at the same time, be so precocious and so stupid. I have told him that I know him to be a liar, and that until he will tell the truth he shall not come into my presence." Having so spoken the father sat silent, while Frank went off to dress.

It was felt by them all that a terrible decision had been come to in the family. A verdict had gone out and had pronounced Florian guilty. They had all gradually come to think that it was so. But now the judge had pronounced the doom. The lad was not to be allowed into his presence during the continuance of the present state of things. In the first place, how was he to be kept out of his father's presence? And the boy was one who would turn mutinous in spirit under such a command. The meaning of it was that he should not sit at table with his father. But, in accordance with the ways of the family, he had always done so. A separate breakfast must be provided for him, and a separate dinner. Then would there not be danger that he should be driven to look for his friends elsewhere? Would he not associate with Father Brosnan, or worse again with Pat Carroll? "Ada," said Edith that night as they sat together, "Florian must be made to confess."

"How make him?"

"You and I must do it."

"That's all very well," said Ada, "but how? You have been at him now for nine months, and have not moved him. He's the most obstinate boy, I think, that ever lived."

"Do you know, there is something in it all that makes me love him the better?" said Edith.

"Is there? There is something in it that almost makes me hate him."

"Don't hate him, Ada—if you can help it. He has got some religious idea into his head. It is all stupid."

"It is beastly," said Ada.

"You may call it as you please," said the other, "it is stupid and beastly. He is travelling altogether in a wrong direction, and is putting everybody concerned with him in immense trouble. It may be quite right that a person should be a Roman Catholic —or that he should be a Protestant; but before one turns from one to the other, one should be old enough to know something about it. It is very vexatious; but with Flory there is, I think, some idea of an idea. He has got it into his head that the Catholics are a downtrodden people, and therefore he will be one of them."

"That is such bosh," said Ada.

"It is so, to your thinking, but not to his. In loving him or hating him you've got to love him or hate him as a boy. Of course it's wicked that a boy should lie,—or a man, or a woman, or a girl; but they do. I don't see why we are to turn against a boy of our own, when we know that other boys lie. He has got a notion into his head that he is doing quite right, because the priest has told him."

"He is doing quite wrong," said Ada.

"And now what are we to do about his breakfast? Papa

says that he is not to be allowed to come into the room, and papa means it. You and I will have to breakfast with him and dine with him, first one and then the other."

"But papa will miss us."

"We must go through the ceremony of a second breakfast and a second dinner." This was the beginning of Edith's scheme. "Of course it's a bore; all things are bores. This about the flood is the most terrible bore I ever knew. But I'm not going to let Flory go to the devil without making an effort to save him. It would be going to the devil, if he were left alone in his present position."

"Papa will see that we don't eat anything."

"Of course he must be told. There never ought to be any secrets in anything. Of course he'll grow used to it, and won't expect us to sit there always and eat nothing. He thinks he's right, and perhaps he is. Flory will feel the weight of his displeasure; and if we talk to him we may persuade him."

This state of things at Morony Castle was allowed to go on with few other words said upon the subject. The father became more and more gloomy, as the floods held their own upon the broad meadows. Pat Carroll had been before the magistrates at Headford, and had been discharged, as all evidence was lacking to connect him with the occurrence. Further effort none was made, and Pat Carroll went on in his course, swearing that not a shilling of rent should be paid by him in next March. "The floods had done him a great injury," he said laughingly among his companions, "so that it was unreasonable to expect that he should pay." It was true he had owed a half-year's rent last November; but then it had become customary with Mr. Jones's tenants to be allowed the indulgence of six months. No more at any rate would be said about rent till March should come.

And now, superinduced upon this cause of misery, had come the tidings which had been spread everywhere through the county in regard to the Galway hunt. Tom Daly nad gone on regularly with his meets, and had not indeed been stopped everywhere. His heart had been gladdened by a wonderful run which he had had from Carnlough. The people had not interfered there, and the day had been altogether propitious. Tom had for the moment been in high good humour; but the interruption had come again, and had been so repeated as to make him feel that his occupation was in truth gone. The gentry of the county had then held a meeting at Ballinasloe, and had decided that the hounds should be withdrawn for the remainder of the season. No one who has not ridden with the hounds regularly can understand the effect of such an order. There was no old woman with a turkey in her possession who did not feel herself thereby entitled to destroy the fox who came lurking about her poultry-yard. Nor was there a gentleman who owned a pheasant who did not feel himself animated in some degree by the same feeling. "As there's to be an end of fox-hunting in County Galway, we can do what we like with our own coverts." "I shall go in for shooting," Sir Nicholas Bodkin had been heard to say.

But Black Tom Daly sat alone gloomily in his room at Ahaseragh, where it suited him still to be present and look after the hounds, and told himself that the occupation of his life was gone. Who would want to buy a horse even, now the chief object for horses was at an end?

CHAPTER XIII.

EDITH'S ELOQUENCE.

THUS they lived through the months of January and February, 1881, at Morony Castle, and Florian had not as yet told his secret. As a boy his nature had seemed to be entirely altered during the last six months. He was thoughtful, morose, and obstinate to a degree, which his father was unable to fathom. But during these last two months there had been no intercourse between them. It may almost be said that no word had been addressed by either to the other. No further kind of punishment had been inflicted. Indeed, the boy enjoyed a much wider liberty than had been given to him before, or than was good for him. For his father not only gave no orders to him, but seldom spoke concerning him. It was, however, a terrible trouble to his mind, the fact that his own son should be thus possessed of his own peculiar secret, and should continue from month to month hiding it within his own bosom. With Father Malachi Mr. Jones was on good terms, but to him he could say nothing on the subject. The absurdity of the conversion, or perversion, of the boy, in reference to his religion, made Mr. Jones unwilling to speak of him to any Roman Catholic priest. Father Malachi would no doubt have owned that the boy had been altogether unable to see, by his own light, the difference between the two religions. But he would have attributed the change to the direct interposition of God. He would not have declared in so many words that a miracle had been performed in the boy's favour, but this would have been the meaning of the argument he would have used. In fact, the gaining of a proselyte under any circumstances would have been an advantage too great to jeopardise by any arguments in the matter. The Protestant clergyman at Headford, in whose parish Morony Castle was supposed to have been situated, was a thin, bigoted Protestant, of that kind which used to be common in Ireland. Mr. Armstrong was a gentleman, who held it to be an established fact that a Roman Catholic must necessarily go to the devil. In all the moralities he was perfect. He was a married man with a wife and six children, all of whom he brought up and educated on £250 a year. He never was in debt; he performed all his duties—such as they were—and passed his time in making rude and unavailing attempts to convert his poorer neighbours. There was a union,—or poor-house—in the neighbourhood, to which he would carry morsels of meat in his pocket on Friday, thinking that the poor wretches who had flown in the face of their priest by eating the unhallowed morsels, would then have made a first step towards Protestantism. He was charitable with so little means for charity; he was very eager in his discourses, in the course of which he would preach to a dozen Protestants for three quarters of an hour, and would confine himself to one subject, the iniquities of the Roman Catholic religion. He had heard of Florian's perversion, and had made it the topic on which he had declaimed for two Sundays. He had attempted to argue with Father Brosnan, but had been like a babe in his hands. He ate and drank of the poorest, and clothed himself so as just to maintain his clerical aspect. All his aspirations were of such a nature as to entitle him to a crown of martyrdom. But they were certainly not of a nature to justify him in expecting any promotion on this earth. Such was Mr. Joseph Armstrong, of Headford, and from him no aid, or counsel, or pleasant friendship could be expected in this matter.

The trouble of Florian's education fell for the nonce into Edith's hands. He had hitherto worked under various preceptors; his father, his sister, and his brother; also a private school at Galway for a time had had the charge of him. But now Edith alone undertook the duty. Gradually the boy began to have a way of his own, and to tell himself that he was only bound to be obedient during certain hours of the morning. In this way the whole day after twelve o'clock was at his own disposal, and he never told any of the family what he then did. Peter, the butler, perhaps knew where he went, but even to Peter the butler, the knowledge was a trouble; for Peter, though a staunch Roman Catholic, was not inclined to side with anyone against his own master. Florian, in truth, did see more of Pat Carroll than he should have done; and, though it would be wrong to suppose that he took a part against his father, he no doubt discussed the questions which were of interest to Pat Carroll, in a manner that would have been very displeasing to his father. "Faix, Mr. Flory," Pat would say to him, "'av you're one of us, you've got to be one of us; you've had a glimmer of light, as Father Brosnan says, to see the errors of your way; but you've got to see the errors of your way on 'arth as well as above. Dragging the rint out o' the body and bones o' the people, like hair from a woman's head, isn't the way, and so you'll have to larn." Then Florian would endeavour to argue with his friend, and struggle to make him understand that in the present complicated state of things it was necessary that a certain amount of rent should go to Morony Castle to keep up the expenses there.

"We couldn't do, you know, without Peter; nor yet very well without the carriage and horses. It's all nonsense saying that there should be no rent; where are we to get our clothes from?" But these arguments, though very good of their kind, had no weight with Pat Carroll, whose great doctrine it was that rent was an evil *per se;* and that his world would certainly go on a great deal better if there were no rent.

"Haven't you got half the land of Ballintubber in your hands?" said Carroll. Here Florian in a whisper reminded Pat that the lands of Ballintubber were at this moment under water, and had been put so by his operation. "Why wouldn't he make me a statement when I asked for it?" said Carroll with a coarse grin, which almost frightened the boy.

"Flory," said Edith to the boy that afternoon, "you did see the men at work upon the sluices that afternoon?"

"I didn't," said Florian.

"We all believe that you did."

"But I didn't."

"You may as well listen to me this once. We all believe that you did—papa and I, and Frank and Ada; Peter believes it; there's not a servant about the place but what belives it. Everybody believes it at Headford. Mr. Blake at Carnlough and all the Blakes believe it."

"I don't care a bit about Mr. Blake," said the boy.

"But you do care about your own father. If you were to go up and down to Galway by the boat, you would find that everybody on board believes it. The country people would say that you had turned against your father because of your religion. Mr. Morris, from beyond Cong, was here the other day, and from what he said about the floods it was easy to see that he believed it."

"If you believe Mr. Morris better than you do me, you may go your own ways by yourself."

"I don't see that, Flory. I may believe Mr. Morris in this matter better than I do you, and yet not intend to go my own ways by myself. I don't believe you at all on this subject."

"Very well, then, don't."

"But I want to find out, if I can, what may be the cause of so terrible a falsehood on your part. It has come to that, that though you tell the lie, you almost admit that it is a lie."

"I don't admit it."

"It is as good as admitted. The position you assume is this: 'I saw the gates destroyed, but I am not going to say so in evidence, because it suits me to take part with Pat Carroll, and to go against my own father.'"

"You've no business to put words like that into my mouth."

"I'm telling you what everybody thinks. Would your father treat you as he does now without a cause? And are you to remain here, and to go down and down in the world till you become such a one as Pat Carroll? And you will have to live like Pat Carroll, with the knowledge in everyone's heart that you had been untrue to your father. They are becoming dishonest, false knaves, untrue to their promises, the very scum of the earth, because of their credulity and broken vows; but what am I to say of you? You will have been as false and perfidious and credulous as they. You will have thrown away everything good to gratify the ambition of some empty traitor. And you will have done it all against your own father." Here she paused and looked at him. They were roaming at the time round the demesne, and he walked on, but said nothing. "I know what you are thinking of, Flory."

"What am I thinking of?"

"You're thinking of your duty; you are thinking whether you can bring yourself to make a clean breast of it, and break the promises which you have made."

"Nobody should break a promise," said he.

"And nobody should tell a lie. When one finds oneself in the difficulty one has to go back and find out where the evil thing first began."

"I gave the promise first," said Florian.

"No such promise should ever have been given. Your first duty in the matter was to your father."

"I don't see that at all," said Florian. "My first duty is to my religion."

"Even to do evil for its sake? Go to Father Malachi, and ask him."

"Father Malachi isn't the man to whom I should like to tell everything. Father Brosnan is a much better sort of clergyman. He is my confessor, and I choose to go by what he tells me."

"Then you will be a traitor to your father."

"I am not a traitor," said Florian.

"And yet you admit that some promise has been given—some promise which you dare not own. You cannot but know in your own heart that I know the truth. You have seen that man Carroll doing the mischief, and have promised him to hold your tongue about it. You have not, then, understood at all the nature or extent of the evil done. You have not, then, known that it would be your father's duty to put down this turbulent ruffian. You have promised, and having promised, Father Brosnan has frightened you. He and Pat Carroll together have cowed the very heart within you. The consequence is that you are becoming one of them, and instead of moving as a gentleman on the face of the earth, you will be such as they are. Tell the truth, and your father will at once send you to some school in England, where you will be educated as becomes my brother."

The boy was now sobbing in tears. He lacked the resolution to continue his lie, but did not dare to tell the truth.

"I will," he whispered.

"What will you do?"

"I well tell all that I know about it."

"Tell me, then, now."

"No, Edith, not now," he said.

"Will you tell papa, then?" said Edith.

"Papa is so hard to me."

"Whom will you tell, and when?"

"I will tell you, but not now. I will first tell Father Brosnan that I am going to do it; I shall not then have told the lie absolutely to my priest."

On this occasion Edith could do nothing further with him; and, indeed, the nature of the confession which she expected him to make was such that it should be made to some person beyond herself. She could understand that it must be taken down in some form that would be presentable to a magistrate, and that evidence of the guilt of Pat Carroll and evidence as to the possible evidence of others must not be whispered simply into her own ears. But she had now brought him to such a condition that she did think that his story would be told.

CHAPTER XIV.

RACHEL'S CORRESPONDENCE.

THERE was another cause of trouble at Morony Castle, which at the present moment annoyed them much. Frank had received three or four letters from Rachel O'Mahony, the purport of them all being to explain her troubles with Mahomet M. M., as she called the man; but still so as to prevent Frank from attempting to interfere personally.

"No doubt the man is a brute," she had said, "if a young lady, without ceasing to be ladylike, may so describe so elegant a gentleman. If not so, still he is a brute, because I can't declare otherwise, even for the sake of being ladylike. But what you say about coming is out of the question. You can't meddle with my affairs till you've a title to meddle. Now, you know the truth. I'm going to stick to you, and I expect you to stick to me. For certain paternal reasons you want to put the marriage off. Very well. I'm agreeable, as the folks say. If you would say that you would be ready to marry me on the first of April, again I should be agreeable. You can nowhere find a more agreeable young woman than I am. But I must be one thing or the other."

Then he wrote to her the sort of love-letter which the reader can understand. It was full of kisses and vows and ecstatic hopes, but did not name a day. In fact Mr. Jones, in the middle of his troubles, was unable to promise an immediate union, and did not choose that his son should marry in order that he might be supported by a singing girl. But to this letter Frank added a request—or rather a command—that he should be allowed to come over at once and see Mr. Mahomet. It was no doubt true that his father was, for the minute, a little backward in the matter of his income ; but still he wanted to look after Mahomet, and he wanted to be kissed.

"You must not come at all, and I won't even see you if you do. You men are always so weak, and want such a lot of petting. Mahomet tried to kiss me last night when I was singing to him before going to dress. I have to practise with him. I gave him such a blow in the face that I don't think he'll repeat the experiment, and I had my eyes about me. You needn't be at all afraid of me but what I am quick enough. He was startled at the moment, and I merely laughed. I'm not going to give up £100 a month because he makes a beast of himself; and I'm not going to call in father as long as I can help it ; nor do I mean to call in your royal highness at all. I tell everybody that I'm going to marry your royal highness, king Jones ; there isn't a bit of a secret about it. I talk of my Mr. Jones just as if we were married, because it all comes easier to me in that way. You will see that I absolutely believe in you and I expect that you shall absolutely believe in me. Send you a kiss ! Of course I do ; I am not at all coy of my favours. You ask Mahomet also as to what he thinks of the strength of my right arm. I examined his face so minutely when I had to fall into his arms on the stage, and there I saw the round mark of my fist, and the swelling all around it. And I thought to myself as I was singing my devotion that he should have it next time in his eye. But, Frank, mark my words : I won't have you here till you can come to marry me."

Frank did not go over, even on this occasion, as he was detained, not only by his mistress's danger, but by his father's troubles. Florian had almost, but had not quite, told the entire truth. He had said that he had seen the sluices broken, but had not quite owned who had broken them. He had declared that Pat Carroll had done "mischief," but had not quite said of what nature was the mischief which Carroll had done. It was now March, and the hunting troubles were still going on. The whole gentry in County Galway had determined to take Black Tom Daly's part, and to carry him on through the contest. But the effect of taking Black Tom Daly's part was to take the part against which the Land-leaguers were determined to enrol themselves. For of all men in the county, Black Tom was the most unpopular. And of all men he was the most determined; with him it was literally a question between God and Mammon. A man could not serve both. In the simplicity of his heart, he thought that the Land-leaguers were children of Satan, and that to have any dealings with them, or the passage of any kindness, was in itself Satanic. He said very little, but he spent whole hours in thinking of the evil that they were doing. And among the evils was the unparalleled insolence which they displayed in entering coverts in County Galway. Now Frank Jones, who had not hitherto been very intimate with Tom, had taken up his part, and was fighting for him at this moment. Nevertheless the provocation to him to go to London was very great, and he had only put it off till the last coverts should be drawn on Saturday the 2nd of April. The hunt had determined to stop their proceedings earlier than usual; but still there was to be one day in April, for the sake of honour and glory.

But in the latter days of March there came a third letter from Rachel O'Mahony. Like the other letter it was cheerful, and high-spirited; but still it seemed to speak of impending dangers, which Frank, though he could not understand them, thought that he could perceive.

"My present engagement is to go on till the end of July, with an understanding that I am to have twenty guineas a night, for any evening that I may be required to sing in August. This your highness will perceive is a very considerable increase, and at three nights a week might afford an income on which your highness would perhaps condescend to come and eat a potato, in the honour of 'ould' Ireland till better times should come. That would be the happy potato which would be the first bought for such a purpose! But you must see that I cannot expect a continuance of my present engagement as the head of your royal highness' seraglio. I should have to look for another Chancellor of the Exchequer, and should probably find him. Mr. Mahomet M. Moss would hardly endure me as being part of the properties belonging to your royal highness.

"And now I must tell you my own little news. Beelzebub has taken a worse devil to himself, so that I am likely to be trodden down into the very middle of the pit. I choose to tell you because I won't have you think that I ever kept anything secret from you. If I describe the roars of Mrs. Beelzebub to you, and her red claws, and her forky tongue, and her fiery tail, it is not because I like her as a subject of poetry, but because this special subject comes uppermost ; and you shall never say to me, Why didn't you tell me when you were introduced to Beelzebub's wife? and assert, as men are apt to do, that you would not have allowed me to make her acquaintance. Mrs. Beelzebub appears on the stage as belonging to Mahomet, but how they have mixed it all up together among themselves, I do not quite know. I do not think that they're in love with one another, because she is not jealous of me. She is Madame Socani in the plot, and a genuine American from New York; but she can sing ; she has a delicious soprano voice, soft and powerful ; but she has also a temper and temperament such as no woman, nor yet no devil, ought to possess. Of Monsieur Socani, or Signor Socani, or Herr Socani, I never yet heard. But such men do not always make themselves troublesome. I have to sing with her, and a woman you may say would not be troublesome, but she and Mahomet between them consider themselves competent to get me under their thumb. I don't intend to be under their thumb. I intend to be under nobody's thumb but yours ; and the sooner the better. Now you know all about it ; but as you shall value the first squeeze which you shall get when you do come, don't come till your coming has been properly settled."

Then there was a fourth letter in which she described her troubles, still humorously, and with some attempt at absolute comedy. But she certainly wrote with a purpose of making him understand that she was subjected to very considerable annoyance. She was still determined not to call upon him for assistance ; and she warned him that any assistance whatever would be out of his power. A lover on the scene, who could not declare his purpose of speedy marriage, would be worse than useless. All that she saw plainly,—or at any rate declared that she saw plainly, though she was altogether unable to explain it to Frank Jones. "Mrs. Beelzebub is certainly the queen of the devils. I remember when you read 'Paradise Lost' to us at Morony Castle, which I thought very dull. Milton arranged the ranks in Pandemonium differently ; but there has been a revolution since that, and Mrs. Beelzebub has everything just as she pleases. I am beginning to pity Mahomet, and pity, they say, is akin to love. She urges him,—well, just to make love to me. What reason there is between them I don't know, but I am sure she wants him to get me altogether into his hands. I'm not sure but what she is Mahomet's own wife. This is a horrid kettle of fish, as you will see. But I think I'll turn out to be head cook yet. If God does not walk atop of the devils what's the use of running straight ? But I am sure He will, and the more so because there is in truth no temptation.

"She told me the other day to my face, that I was a fool. 'I know I am,' said I demurely, 'but why?' Then she came out with her demand. It was very simple, and did not in truth amount to much. I was to become—just mistress to Mr. Moss." Frank Jones, when he read this, crushed the paper up in his hand and went upstairs to his bedroom, determined to pack up immediately. But before he had progressed far, he got out the letter and read the remainder. "'You,' I said, 'are an intimate acquaintance of Mr. Moss.'

"'I am his particular friend,' she said with that peculiar New York aping of a foreign accent, which is the language that was, I am sure, generally used by the devils.

"'Ask him, with my best compliments,' I said, 'whether he remembers the blow I hit him in the face. Tell him I can hit much harder than that ; tell him that he will never find me unprepared, for a moment.'

"Now I have got another little bit of news for you. Some body has found out in New York that I am making money. It is true, in a limited way. £100 a month is something, and so they've asked papa to subscribe as largely as he can to a grand Home-Rule-anti-Protestant, hate-the-English, stars-and-stripes society. It is the most loyal and beneficent thing out, and dear papa thinks I can do nothing better with my wealth than bestow it upon these birds of freedom. I have no doubt they are all right, because I am an American-Irish, and have not the pleasure of knowing Black Tom Daly. I have given them £200, and am therefore, at this moment, nearly impecunious. On this account I do not choose to give up my engagement—£100 a month, with an additional possibility of twenty guineas a night when August shall be here. You will tell me that after the mild suggestion made by Mrs. Beelzebub, I ought to walk out of the house, and go back to County Galway immediately. I don't think so. I am learning every day how best to stand fast on my own feet. I am earning my money honestly, and men and women here in London are saying that in truth I can sing. A very nice old gentleman called on me the other day from Covent Garden, and, making me two low bows, asked whether I was my own mistress some time in October next. I thought at the moment that I was at any rate free from the further engagement proposed by Mrs. Beelzebub, and told him that I was free. Then he made me two lower bows, touched the tips of my fingers, and said that he would be proud to wait upon me in a few days with a definite proposal. This old gentleman may mean twenty guineas a night for the whole of next winter, or something like £250 a month. Think of that, Mr. Jones. But how am I to go on in my present impecunious position if I quarrel altogether with my bread and butter? So now you know all about it.

"Remember that I have told my father nothing as to Mrs. Beelzebub's proposition. It is better not ; he would disown it, and would declare that I had invented it from vanity. I do think that a woman in this country can look after herself if she be minded so to do. I know that I am stronger than Mr. Moss and Mrs. Beelzebub together. I do believe that he will pay me his money as he has always done, and I want to earn my money. I have some little precautions—just for a rainy day. I have told you everything—everything, because you are to be my husband. But you can do me no good by coming here, but may cause me a peck of troubles. Now, good-bye, and God bless you. A thousand kisses.

"Ever your own,
"R.

"Tell everybody that I'm to be Mrs. Jones some day."

Frank finished packing up, and then told his father that he was going off to Athenry at once, there to meet the night mail train up to Dublin.

"Why are you going at once, in this sudden manner?" asked his father.

Frank then remembered that he could not tell openly the story of Mrs. Beelzebub. Rachel had told him in pure simple-minded confidence, and though he was prepared to disobey her, he would not betray her. "She is on the stage," he said.

"I am aware of it," replied his father, intending to signify that his son's betrothed was not employed as he would have wished.

"At the Charing Cross Opera," said the son, endeavouring to make the best of it.

"Yes; at the Charing Cross Opera, if that makes a difference."

"She is earning her bread honestly."

"I believe so," said Mr. Jones, "I do believe so, I do think that Rachel O'Mahony is a thoroughly good girl."

"I am sure of it," said Ada and Edith almost in the same breath.

"But not the less on that account is the profession distasteful to me. You do not wish to see your sisters on the stage?"

"I have thought of all that, sir," said Frank, "I have quite made up my mind to make Rachel my wife, if it be possible."

"Do you mean to live on what she may earn as an actress?" Here Frank remained silent for a moment. "Because if you do, I must tell you that it will not become you as a gentleman to accept her income."

"You cannot give us an income on which we may live."

"Certainly not at this moment. With things as they are in Ireland now, I do not know how long I may have a shilling with which to bless myself. It seems to me that for the present it is your duty to stay at home, and not to trouble Rachel by going to her in London."

"At this moment I must go to her."

"You have given no reason for your going." Frank thought of it, and told himself that there was in truth no reason. His going would be a trouble to Rachel, and yet there were reasons which made it imperative for him to go. "Have you asked yourself what will be the expense?" said his father.

"It may cost I suppose twelve pounds, going and coming."

"And have you asked yourself how many twelve pounds will be likely to fall into your hands just at present? Is she in any trouble?"

"I had rather not talk about her affairs," said Frank.

"Is not her father with her?"

"I do not think he is the best man in the world to help a girl in such an emergency." But he had not described what was the emergency.

"You think that a young man, who certainly will be looked on as the young lady's lover, but by no means so certainly as the young lady's future husband, will be more successful?"

"I do," said Frank, getting up and walking out of the room. He was determined at any rate that nothing which his father could say should stop him, as he had resolved to disobey all the orders which Rachel had given him. At any rate, during that night and the following day he made his way up to London.

CHAPTER XV.

CAPTAIN YORKE CLAYTON.

AT this period of our story much had already been said in the outside world as to flooding the meadows of Ballintubber. Like other outrages of the same kind, it had not at first been noticed otherwise than in the immediate neighbourhood; and though a terrible injury had been inflicted, equal in value to the loss of five or six hundred pounds, it had seemed as though it would pass away unnoticed, simply because Mr. Jones had lacked evidence to bring it home to any guilty party. But gradually it had become known that Pat Carroll had been the sinner, and the causes also which had brought about the crime were known. It was known that Pat Carroll had joined the Land-leaguers in the neighbouring county of Mayo with great violence, and that he had made a threat that he would pay no further rent to his landlord. The days of the no-rent manifestation had not yet come, as the obnoxious Members of Parliament were not yet in prison; but no-rent was already firmly fixed in the minds of many men, about to lead in process of time to "Arrears Bills," and other abominations of injustice. And among those conspicuous in the West, who were ready to seize fortune by the forelock, was Mr. Pat Carroll. In this way his name had come forward, and inquiries were made of Mr. Jones which distressed him much. For though he was ready to sacrifice his meadows and his tenant, and his rent, he was most unwilling to do it if he should be called upon at the same time to sacrifice his boy's character for loyalty.

There had been a man stationed at Castlerea for some months past, who in celebrity had almost beaten the notorious Pat Carroll. This was one Captain Yorke Clayton, who, for nearly twelve months had been in the County Mayo. It was supposed that he had first shown himself there as a constabulary officer, and had then very suddenly been appointed resident magistrate. Why he was Captain nobody knew. It was the fact, indeed, that he had been employed as adjutant in a volunteer regiment in England, having gone over there from the police force in the north of Ireland. His title had gone with him by no fault or no virtue of his own, and he had blossomed forth to the world of Connaught as Captain Clayton before he knew why he was about to become famous. Famous, however, he did become.

He had two attributes which, if Fortune helps, may serve to make any man famous. They were recklessness of life and devotion to an idea. If Fortune do not help, recklessness of life amidst such dangers as those which surrounded Captain Clayton will soon bring a man to his end, so that there will be no question of fame. But we see men occasionally who seem to find it impossible to encounter death. It is not at all probable that this man wished to die. Life seemed to him to be pleasant enough: he was no forlorn lover; he had fairly good health and strength; people said of him that he had small but comfortable private means; he was remarkable among all men for his good looks; and he lacked nothing necessary to make life happy. But he appeared to be always in a hurry to leave it. A hundred men in Mayo had sworn that he should die. This was told to him very freely; but he had only laughed at it, and was generally called "the woodcock," as he rode about among his daily employments. The ordinary life of a woodcock calls upon him to be shot at; but yet a woodcock is not an easy bird to hit.

Then there was his devotion to an idea! I will not call it loyalty, lest I should seem to praise the man too vehemently for that which probably was simply an instinct in his own heart. He lived upon his hatred of a Land-leaguer. It was probably some conviction on his own part that the original Land-leaguer had come from New York, which produced this feeling. And it must be acknowledged of him with reference to the lower order of Land-leaguers that he did admit in his mind a possibility that they were curable. There were to him Land-leaguers and Land-leaguers ; but the Land-leaguer whom Captain Yorke Clayton hated with the bitterest prejudice was the Land-leaguing Member of Parliament. Some of his worst enemies believed that he might be detected in breaking out into illegal expressions of hatred, or, more unfortunately still, into illegal acts, and that so the Government might be compelled to dismiss him with disgrace. Others, his warmest friends, hoped that by such a process his life might be eventually saved. But for the present Captain Yorke Clayton had saved both his character and his neck, to the great surprise both of those who loved him and the reverse. He had lately been appointed Joint President Magistrate for Galway, Mayo, and Roscommon, and had removed his residence to Galway. To him also had Pat Carroll become intimately known, and to him the floods of Ballintubber were a peculiar case. It was one great desire of his heart to have Pat Carroll incarcerated as a penal felon. He did not very often express himself on this subject, but Pat Carroll knew well the nature of his wishes. "A thundering bloody rapparee" was the name by which Carroll delighted to call him. But Carroll was one who exercised none of that control over his own tongue for which Captain Clayton was said to be so conspicuous. During the last month Mr. Jones had seen Captain Clayton more than once at Galway, and on one occasion he had come down to Morony Castle attended by a man who was supposed to travel as his servant, but who was known by all the world to be a policeman in disguise. For Captain Clayton had been strictly forbidden by the authorities of the Castle to travel without such a companion ; and an attempt had already been made to have him dismissed for disobedience to these orders.

Captain Clayton, when he had been at Morony Castle, had treated Flory with great kindness, declining to cross-question him at all. "I would endeavour to save him from these gentlemen," he had said to his father. "I don't quite think that we understand what is going on within his mind ;" but this had been before the conversation last mentioned which had taken place between Flory and his sisters. Now he was to come again, and make further inquiry, and meet half-a-dozen policemen from the neighbourhood. But Florian had as yet but half confessed, and almost hoped that Captain Clayton would appear among them as his friend.

The girls, to tell the truth, had been much taken with the appearance of the gallant Captain. It seems to be almost a shame to tell the truth of what modest girls may think of any man whom they may chance to meet. They would never tell it to themselves. Even two sisters can hardly do so. And when the man comes before them, just for once or twice, to be judged and thought of at a single interview, the girl,—such as were these girls,—can hardly tell it to herself. "He is manly and brave, and has so much to say for himself, and is so good-looking, that what can any girl who has her heart at her own disposal wish for better than such a lover?" It would have been quite impossible that either of Mr. Jones's daughters could ever have so whispered to herself. But was it not natural that such an unwhispered thought should have passed through the mind of Ada—Ada the beautiful, Ada the sentimental, Ada the young lady who certainly was in want of a lover? "He is very nice, certainly," said Ada, allowing herself not another word, to her sister.

"But what is the good of a man being nice when he is a 'woodcock?'" said Edith. "Everybody says that his destiny is before him. I daresay he is nice, but what's the use?"

"You don't mean to say that you think he'll be killed?" said Ada.

"I do, and I mean to say that if I were a man, it might be that I should have to be killed too. A man has to run his chance, and if he falls into such a position as this, of course he must put up with it. I don't mean to say that I don't like him the better for it."

"Why does he not go away and leave the horrid country?" said Ada.

"Because the more brave men that go away the more horrid the country will become. And then I think a man is always the happier if he has something really to think of. Such a one as Captain Clayton does not want to go to balls."

"I suppose not," said Ada plaintively, as though she thought it a thousand pities that Captain Clayton should not want to go to balls.

"Such a man," said Edith with an air of firmness, "finds a woman when he wants to marry who will suit him,—and then he marries her. There is no necessity for any balls there."

"Then he ought not to dance at all. Such a man ought not to want to get married."

"Not if he means to be killed out of hand," said Edith. "The possible young woman must be left to judge of that. I shouldn't like to marry a 'woodcock,' however much I might admire him. I do think it well that there should be such men as Captain Clayton. I feel that if I were a man I ought to wish to be one myself. But I am sure I should feel that I oughtn't to ask a girl to share the world with me. Fancy marrying a man merely to be left a sorrowing widow! It is part of the horror of his business that he shouldn't even venture to dance, lest some poor female should be captivated."

"A girl might be captivated without dancing," said Ada.

"I don't mean to say that such a man should absolutely tie himself up in a bag so that no poor female should run any possible danger, but he oughtn't to encourage such risks. To tell the truth, I don't think that Captain Clayton does."

Ada that afternoon thought a great deal of the position,—not, of course, in reference to herself. Was it proper that such a man as Captain Yorke Clayton should abstain from falling in love with a girl, or even from allowing a girl to fall in love with him because he was in danger of being shot? It was certainly a difficult question. Was any man to be debarred from the pleasures, and incidents, and natural excitements of a man's life because of the possible dangers which might possibly happen to a possible young woman? Looking at the matter all round, Ada did not see that the man could help himself unless he were to be shut up in a bag, as Edith had said, so as to prevent a young woman from falling in love with him. Although he were a "woodcock," the thing must go on in its own natural course. If misfortunes did come, why misfortunes must come. It was the same thing with any soldier or any sailor. If she were to fall in love with some officer,—for the supposition in its vague, undefined form was admissible even to poor Ada's imagination,—she would not be debarred from marrying him merely by the fact that he would have to go to the wars. Of course, as regarded Captain Yorke Clayton, this was merely a speculation. He might be engaged to some other girl already for anything she knew;—"or cared," as she told herself with more or less of truth.

Captain Yorke Clayton came down by the boat that afternoon to Morony Castle, Frank Jones having started for London two or three days before. He reached the pier at about four o'clock, accompanied by his faithful follower, and was there met by Mr. Jones himself, who walked up with him to the Castle. There was a short cut across the fields to Mr. Jones's house; and as they left the road about a furlong up from the pier, they were surrounded by the waters which Mr. Carroll had let in upon the Ballintubber meadows.

"You won't mind my fellow coming with us?" said Captain Clayton.

"'Your fellow,' as you call him, is more than welcome. I came across this way because some of Pat Carroll's friends may be out on the high road. If they fire half-a-dozen rifles from behind a wall at your luggage, they won't do so much harm as if they shot at yourself."

"There won't be any shooting here," said Clayton, shaking his head, "he's not had time to get a stranger down and pay him. They always require two or three days' notice for that work; and there isn't a wall about the place. You're not giving Mr. Pat Carroll a fair chance for his friends. I could dodge them always with perfect security by myself, only the beaks up in Dublin have given a strict order. As they pay for the pistols I am bound to carry them." Then he lifted up the lappets of his coat and waistcoat, and showed half-a-dozen pistols stuck into his girdle. "Our friend there has got as many more."

"I have a couple myself," said Mr. Jones, indicating their whereabouts, and showing that he was not as yet so used to carry them, as to have provided himself with a belt for the purpose.

Then they walked on, chatting indifferently about the Land-leaguers till they reached the Castle. "The people are not cowards," Captain Clayton had said. "I believe that men do become cowards when they are tempted to become liars by getting into Parliament. An Irishman of a certain class does at any rate. But those fellows, if they were put into a regiment, would fight like grim death. That man there," and he pointed back over his shoulder, "is as brave a fellow as I ever came across in my life. I don't think that he would hesitate a moment in attacking three or four men armed with revolvers. And gold wouldn't induce him to be false to me. But if Mr. Pat Carroll had by chance got hold of him before he had come my way, he might have been the very man to shoot you or me from behind a wall, with a bit of black crape on his face. What's the reason of it? I love that man as my brother, but I might have hated him as the very devil."

"The force of example, sir," said Mr. Jones, as he led the way into the quiet, modern residence which rejoiced to call itself Morony Castle.

"What are we to do about this boy?" said Mr. Jones, when they had seated themselves in his study.

"Are you friends with him yet?"

"No; I declared to his sister that I would not sit down to table with him till he had told the truth, and I have kept my word."

"How does he bear it?"

"But badly," said the father. "It has told upon him very much. He complains to his sister that I have utterly cast him off."

"It is the oddest case I ever heard of in my life," said the Captain. "I suppose his change of religion has been at the bottom of it—that and the machinations of the priest down at Headford. When we recollect that there must have been quite a crowd of people looking on all the while, it does seem odd that we should be unable to get a single witness to tell the truth, knowing as we do, that this lad was there. If he would only name two who were certainly there, and who certainly saw the deed done, that would be enough; for the people are not, in themselves, hostile to you."

"You know he has owned that he did see it," said the

father. "And he has acknowledged that Pat Carroll was there, though he has never mentioned the man's name. His sisters have told him that I will not be satisfied unless I hear him declare that Pat Carroll was one of the offenders."

"Let us have him in, sir, if you don't mind."

"Just as he is?"

"I should say so. Or let the young ladies come with him, if you do not object. Which of them has been most with him since your edict went forth?"

Mr. Jones declared that Edith had been most with her brother, and the order went forth that Edith and Florian should be summoned into the apartment.

Ada and Edith were together when the order came. Edith was to go down and present herself before Captain Yorke Clayton.

"Mercy me," said Edith, jumping up, "I hope they won't shoot at him through the window whilst I am there."

"Oh! Edith, how can you think of such a thing?"

"It would be very unpleasant if some assassin were to take my back hair for Captain Clayton's brown head. They're very nearly the same colour."

And Edith prepared to leave the room, hearing her brother's slow, heavy step as he passed before the door.

"Won't you go first and brush your hair?" said Ada; "and do put a ribbon on your neck."

"I'll do nothing of the kind. It would be a sheer manœuvring to entrap a man who ought to be safeguarded against all such female wiles. Besides, I don't believe a bit that Captain Clayton would know the difference between a young lady with or without a ribbon. What evidence can I give?—that's the question."

So saying, Edith descended to her father's room.

She found Florian with his hand upon the door, and they both entered the room. I have said that Captain Clayton was a remarkably good-looking man, and I ought, perhaps to give some explanation of the term when first introducing him to the reader in the presence of a lady who is intended to become the heroine of this story; but it must suffice that I have declared him to be good-looking, and that I add to that the fact that though he was thirty-five years old, he did not look to be more than five-and-twenty. The two peculiarities of his face were very light blue eyes, and very long moustachios. "Florian and I have come to see the latter-day hero," said Edith, laughing as she entered the room; "though I know that you are so done up with pistols that no peaceable young woman ought to come near you." To this he made some sportive reply, and then before a minute had passed over their heads he had taken Florian by the hand.

CHAPTER XVI.

CAPTAIN CLAYTON COMES TO THE CASTLE.

"WELL, my boy, how are you?" asked the Captain.

"There's nothing particularly the matter with me," said Florian.

"I suppose all this is troubling you?"

"All what? You mean about Pat Carroll. Of course it's troubling me. Nobody will believe a word that I say."

"But they do believe you now that you are telling the truth," said Edith.

"Do you hold your tongue, miss," said the boy, "I don't see why you should have so much to say about it."

"She has been your best friend from first to last," said the father. "If it had not been for Edith I would have turned you out of the house. It is terrible to me to think that a boy of mine should refuse to say what he saw in such a matter as this. You are putting yourself on a par with the enemies of your own family. You do not know it, but you are nearly sending me to the grave." Then there was a long pause, during which the Captain kept his eyes fixed on the boy's face. And Edith had moved round so as to seat herself close to her brother, and had taken his hand in hers.

"Don't, Edith," said the boy. "Leave me alone, I don't want to be meddled with," and he withdrew his hand.

"Oh, Florian!" said the girl, "try to tell the truth and be a gentleman: whether it be for you or against you, tell the truth."

"I'm not to mind a bit about my religion then?"

"Does your religion bid you tell a lie?" asked the Captain.

"I'm not telling a lie, I am just holding my tongue. A Catholic has a right to hold his tongue when he is among Protestants."

"Even to the ruin of his father?" suggested the Captain.

"I don't want to ruin papa. He said he was going to turn—to turn me out of the house. I would go and drown myself in the lake if he did, or in one of those big dykes which divide the meadows. I am miserable among them—quite miserable. Edith never gives me any peace, day or night. She comes and sits in my bedroom, begging me to tell the truth. It ought to be enough when I say that I will hold my tongue. Papa can turn me out to drown myself if he pleases. Edith goes on cheating the words out of me till I don't know what I'm saying. If I am to be brought up to tell it all before the judge I shan't know what I have said before, or what I have not said."

"*Nil conscire tibi*," said the father, who had already taught his son so much Latin as that.

"But you did see the sluice gates torn down, and thrown back into the water?" said the Captain. Here Florian shook his head mournfully. "I understood you to acknowledge that you had seen the gates destroyed."

"I never said as much to you," said the boy.

"But you did to me," said Edith.

"If a fellow says a word to you, it is repeated to all the world. I never would have you joined with me in a secret. You are a great deal worse than——, well, those fellows that you abuse me about. They never tell anything that they have heard among themselves, to people outside."

"Pat Carroll, you mean?" asked the Captain.

"He isn't the only one. There's more in it than him."

"Oh yes; we know that. There were many others in it besides Pat Carroll, when they let the waters in through the dyke gates. There must have been twenty there."

"No, there weren't—not that I saw."

"A dozen, perhaps!"

"You are laying a trap for me, but I am not going to be caught. I was there, and I did see it. You may make the most of that. Though you have me up before the judge, I needn't say a word more than I please."

"He is more obstinate," said his father, "than any rebel that you can meet."

"But so mistaken," said the Captain, "because he can refuse to answer us who are treating him with such tenderness and affection, who did not even want to wound his feelings more than we can help, he thinks that he can hold his peace in the same fashion, before the entire court; and that he can do so, although he has owned that he knows the men."

"I have never owned that," said the boy.

"Not to your sister?"

"I only owned to one."

"Pat Carroll?" said the Captain; but giving the name merely as a hint to help the boy's memory.

But the boy was too sharp for him. "That's another of your traps, Captain Clayton. If she says Pat Carroll, I can say it was Tim Brady. A boy's word will be as good as a girl's, I suppose."

"A lie can never be as good as the truth, whether from a boy or a girl," said the Captain, endeavouring to look him through and through. The boy quavered beneath his gaze, and the Captain went on with his questioning. "I suppose we may take it for granted that Pat Carroll was there, and that you did see him?"

"You may take anything for granted."

"You would have to swear before a jury that Pat Carroll was there."

Then there was another pause, but at last, with a long sigh, the boy spoke out. "He was there, and I did see him." Then he burst into tears and threw himself down on the ground, and hid his face in his sister's lap.

"Dear Flory," said she. "My own brother! I knew that you would struggle to be a gentleman at last."

"It will all come right with him now," said the Captain. But the father frowned and shook his head. "How many were there with him?" asked the Captain, intent on the main business.

But Florian, feeling that it would be as good to be hung for a sheep as a lamb, and feeling also that he had at last cast aside all the bonds which bound him to Pat Carroll and Father Brosnan,—feeling that there was nothing left for him but the internecine enmity of his old friends,—got up from the floor, and wiping away the tears from his face, spoke out boldly the whole truth as he knew it. "It was dark, and I didn't see them all. There were only six whom I could see, though I know that there were many others round about among the meadows whose names I had heard, though I do not remember them."

"We will confine ourselves to the six whom you did see," said the Captain, preparing to listen quietly to the boy's story. The father took out a pen and ink, but soon pushed it on one side. Edith again got hold of the boy's hand, and held it within her own till his story was finished.

"I didn't see the six all at once. The first whom I did see was Pat Carroll, and his brother Terry, and Tim Brady. They were up there just where the lane has turned down from the steamboat road. I had gone down to the big sluice gates before anyone had noticed me, and there were Tim and Terry smashing away at the gate hinges, up to their middles in mud; and Pat Carroll was handing them down a big crowbar. Terry, when he saw me, fell flat forward into the water, and had to be picked out again."

"Did they say anything to threaten you?" said the Captain.

"Tim Brady said that I was all right, and was a great friend of Father Brosnan's. Then they whispered together, and I heard Terry say that he wouldn't go against anything that Father Brosnan might say. Then Pat Carroll came and stood over me with the crowbar."

"Did he threaten you?"

"He didn't do it in a threatening way; but only asked me to be hand and glove with them."

"Had you been intimate with this man before?" asked the Captain.

"He had been very intimate with him," said the father. "All this calamity has come of his intimacy. He has changed his religion and ceased to be a gentleman." Here the boy again sobbed, but Edith still squeezed his hand.

"What did you say," asked the Captain, "when he bade you be hand and glove with him?"

"I said that I would. Then they made the sign of a cross, and swore me on it. And they swore me specially to say nothing up here. And they swore me again when they met down at Tim Rafferty's house in Headford. I intended to keep my word, and I think that you ought to have let me keep it."

"But there were three others whom you saw," urged the Captain.

"There was Con Heffernan, and a man they call Lax, who had come from Lough Conn beyond Castlebar."

"He's not a man of this county."

"I think not, though I had seen him here before. He has had something to do with the Land-leaguers up about Foxford."

"I think I have a speaking acquaintance with that Mr. Lax," said the Captain; and everybody could perceive that the tone of his voice was altered as he spoke about Mr. Lax. "And who was the sixth?"

"There was that old man, papa, whom they call Terry. But he wasn't doing anything in particular."

"He is the greatest blackguard on the estate," said the father.

"But we will confine ourselves to the five," said the Captain, "not forgetting Mr. Lax. What was Mr. Lax doing?"

"I can't remember what they were all doing. How is a fellow to remember them all? There were those two at the hinges, and Pat Carroll was there pulling his brother out of the water."

"Terry was Pat's brother?"

"They are brothers," said the father.

"And then they went on, and took no notice of me for a time. Lax came up and scowled at me, and told me that if a word was said I should never draw the breath of life again."

"But he didn't do anything?" asked the Captain.

"I don't remember. How is a fellow to remember after so many months?"

"Why didn't you tell the truth at the time?" said his father angrily. Another tear stood in each of the poor boy's eyes, and Edith got closer to him, and threw her left arm round his waist. "You are spoiling him by being so soft with him," said the father.

"He is doing the best he can, Mr. Jones," said the Captain. "Don't be harsh with him now. Well, Florian, what came next?"

"They bade me go away, and again made me swear another oath. It was nearly dark then, and it was quite dark night before I got up to the house. But before I went I saw that there were many others standing idle about the place."

"Do you remember any particularly?"

"Well, there was another of the Carrolls, a nephew of Pat's; and there was Tony Brady, Tim's brother. I can't at this moment say who else there were."

"It would be as well to have as many as we do know, not to prosecute them, but to ask them for their evidence. Three or four men will often contradict each other, and then they will break down. I think we have enough now. But you must remember that I have only questioned you as your friend and as your father's friend. I have not taken down a word that you have said. My object has been simply that we might all act together to punish a vindictive and infamous outrage. Pat Carroll has had nothing to get by flooding your father's meadows. But because your father has not chosen to forgive him his rent, he has thought fit to do him all the injury in his power. I fear that there are others in it, who are more to blame even than Pat Carroll. But if we can get hold of this gentleman, and also of his friend Mr. Lax, we shall have done much."

Then the meeting was over for that evening, and Captain Clayton retired to his own room. "You needn't mind following me here, Hunter," he said to the policeman.

"I wouldn't be too sure, sir."

"You may be sure in Mr. Jones's house. And no one in the country has any idea of committing murder on his own behalf. I am safe till they would have had time to send for someone out of another county. But we shall be back in Galway to-morrow." So saying, Hunter left his master alone, and the Captain sat down to write an account of the scene which had just taken place. In this he gave every name as the boy had given it, with accuracy; but, nevertheless, he added to his little story the fact that it had been related from memory.

Edith took her brother away into her own room, and there covered him with kisses. "Why is papa so hard to me?" said the boy, sobbing. Then she explained to him as gently as she could, the grounds which had existed for hardness on his father's part. She bade him consider how terrible a thing it must be to a father, to have to think that his own son should have turned against him, while the country was in such a condition.

"It is not the flood, Flory, nor the loss of the meadows being under water. It is not the injury that Pat Carroll has done him, or any of the men whom Pat Carroll has talked into enmity. That, indeed, is very dreadful. To these very men he has been their best friend for many years. And now they would help in his ruin, and turn us and him out as beggars upon the world, because he has not chosen to obey the unjust bidding of one of them." Here the boy hung down his head, and turned away his face. "But it is not that. All that has had no effect in nigh breaking his heart. Money is but money. No one can bear its loss better than our papa. Though he might have to starve, he would starve like a gallant man ; and we could starve with him. You and I, Frank and Ada, would bear all that he could bear. But——" The boy looked up into her face again, as though imploring her to spare him, but she went on with her speech. "But that a son of his should cease to feel as a gentleman should feel,—and a Christian ! It is that which moves him to be hard, as you call it. But he is not hard ; he is a man, and he cannot kiss you as a woman does ;—as your sister does ;" here she almost smothered the boy with kisses, "but, Florian, it is not too late ; it is never too late while you still see that truth is god-like, and that a lie is of all things the most devilish. It is never too late while you feel what duty calls you to do." And again she covered him with kisses, and then allowed him to go away to his own room.

When Edith was alone she sat back in an easy-chair, with her feet on the fender before the turf fire, and began to consider how things might go with her poor brother. "If they should get hold of him, and murder him !" she said to herself. The thought was very dreadful, but she comforted herself with reflecting that he might be sent out of the country, before the knowledge of what he had done should get abroad. And then by means of that current of thought, which always runs where it listeth, independent of the will of the thinker, her ideas flew off to Captain Yorke Clayton. In her imagination she had put down Captain Clayton as a possible lover for her sister. She possessed a girlish intuition into her sister's mind which made her feel that her sister would not dislike such an arrangement. Ada was the beauty of the family, and was supposed, at any rate by Edith, to be the most susceptible of the two sisters. She had always called herself a violent old maid, who was determined to have her own way. But no one had ever heard Ada speak of herself as an old maid. And then as to that danger of which Ada had spoken, Edith knew that such perils must be overlooked altogether among the incidents of life. If it came to her would she refuse her hand to a man because his courage led him into special perils. She knew that it would only be an additional ground for her love. And of Ada, in that respect, she judged as she did of herself. She knew that Ada thought much of manly beauty, and her eyes told her that Captain Yorke Clayton was very handsome. "If he were as black as Beelzebub," she said to herself, "I should like him the better for it ; but Ada would prefer a man to be beautiful." She went to work to make a match in her own mind between Ada and Captain Clayton ; but the more she made it, the more she continued to think—on her own behalf— that of all men she had ever seen, this man had pleased her fancy most. "But Captain Yorke Clayton, you were never more mistaken in all your life if you think that Edith Jones has taken a fancy to your handsome physiognomy." This she said in almost audible words. "But nevertheless, I do think that you are a hero. For myself, I don't want a hero—and if I did, I shouldn't get one." But the arrangements made in the house that night were those which are customary for a favoured young man's reception when such matters are left to the favouring young lady in the family.

When Mr. Jones found himself alone in his study, he began to think of the confession which Florian had made. It had gradually come to pass that he had been sure of the truth for some months, though he had never before heard it declared by his son's lips. Since the day on which he had called on Mr. Blake at Carnlough, he had been quite sure that Edith was right. He was almost sure before. Now the truth was declared exactly as she had surmised it. And what should he do with the boy? He could not merely put him forward as a witness in this case. Some reason must be given, why the truth had not been told during the last six months. As he thought of this, he felt that the boy had disgraced himself for ever.

And he thought of the boy's danger. He had rashly promised that the boy should be sent to England out of harm's way; but he now told himself that the means of doing so were further from him than ever; and that he was daily becoming a poorer, if not a ruined man. Of the rents then due to him, not a penny would, he feared, be paid.

CHAPTER XVII.

RACHEL IS FREE.

RACHEL O'MAHONY found her position to be very embarrassing. She had though it out to the best of her ability, and had told herself that it would be better for her not to acquaint her father with all the circumstances. Had he been told the nature of the offer made to her by Madame Socani, he would at once, she thought, have taken her away from the theatre. She would have to abandon the theatre, at which she was earning her money. This would have been very bad. There would have been some lawsuit with Mahomet Moss, as to which she could not have defended herself by putting Madame Socani into the witness-box. There had been no third person present, and any possible amount of lying would have been very easy to Madame Socani. Rachel was quick enough, and could see at a moment all that lying could do against her. "But he tried to kiss me," she would have had to say. Then she could see how, with a shrug of his shoulders, her enemy would have ruined her. From such a contest a man like Moss comes forth without even a scratch that can injure him. But Rachel felt that she would have been utterly annihilated. She must tell someone, but that someone must be he whom she intended to marry.

And she, too, had not been quite prudent in all respects since she had come to London. It had been whispered to her that a singer of such pretensions should be brought to the theatre and carried home in her private brougham. Therefore, she had spent more money than was compatible with the assistance given to her father, and was something in debt. It was indispensable to her that she should go on with her engagement.

But she told her father that it was absolutely necessary that he should go with her to the theatre every night that she sang. It was but three nights a week, and the hours of her work were only from eight till ten. He had, however, unfortunately made another engagement for himself. There was a debating society, dramatic in its manner of carrying on its business, at which three or four Irish Home-Rulers were accustomed to argue among themselves, before a mixed audience of Englishmen and Irishmen, as to the futility of English government. Here Mr. O'Mahony was popular among the debaters, and was paid for his services. Not many knew that the eloquent Irishman was the father of the singer who, in truth, was achieving for herself a grand reputation. But such was the case. A stop had been put upon his lecturings at Galway; but no policeman in London seemed to be aware that the Galway incendiary and the London debater were one and the same person. So there came to him an opening for picking up a few pounds towards their joint expenses.

"But why should you want me now, more than for the last fortnight?" he said, contending for the use of his own time.

"Mr. Moss is disagreeable."

"Has he done anything new?" he asked.

"He is always doing things new—that is more beastly—one day than the day before."

"He doesn't come and sing with you now at your own rooms."

"No; I have got through that, thank Heaven! To tell the truth, father, I am not in the least afraid of Mr. Moss. Before he should touch me you may be sure that he would have the worst of it."

"Of course I will do what you want," said her father; "but only if it be not necessary——"

"It is necessary. Of course, I do not wish to be dragged up

to the police-court for sticking Mr. Moss in the abdomen. That's what it would come to if we were left together."

"Do you mean to say that you require my presence to prevent anything so disagreeable as that?"

"If they know, or if he knows that you're in the house, there will be nothing of the kind. Can't you arrange your debates for the other nights?"

So it was, in fact, settled. Everybody about the theatre seemed to be aware that something was wrong. Mr. O'Mahony had not come back to be constantly on the watch, like a Newfoundland dog, without an object. To himself it was an intolerable nuisance. He suspected his daughter not at all. He was so far from suspecting her that he imagined her to be safe, though half-a-dozen Mosses should surround her. He could only stand idle behind the scenes, or sit in her dressing-room and yawn. But still he did it, and asked no further questions.

Then while all this was going on, the polite old gentleman from Covent Garden had called at her lodgings in Cecil Street and had found both her and her father at home.

"Oh, M. Le Gros," she had said, "I am so glad that you should meet my father here."

Then there was a multiplicity of bowing, and M. Le Gros had declared that he had never had so much honour done him as in being introduced to him who was about to become the father of the undoubted prima donna of the day. At all which Mr. O'Mahony made many bows, and Rachel laughed very heartily; but in the end an engagement was proposed and thankfully accepted, which was to commence in the next October. It did not take two minutes in the making. It was an engagement only for a couple of months; but, as M. Le Gros observed, such an engagement would undoubtedly lead to one for all time. If Covent Garden could only secure the permanent aid of Mademoiselle O'Mahony, Covent Garden's fortune would be as good as made. M. Le Gros had quite felt the dishonesty of even suggesting a longer engagement to mademoiselle. The rate of payment would be very much higher, ve-ry, ve-ry, ve-ry much higher when mademoiselle's voice should have once been heard on the boards of a true operatic theatre. M. Le Gros had done himself the honour of being present on one or two occasions at the Charing Cross little playhouse. He did believe himself to have some small critical judgment in musical matters. He thought he might venture—he really did think that he might venture—to bespeak a brilliant career for mademoiselle. Then, with a great many more bowings and scrapings, M. Le Gros, having done his business, took his leave.

"I like him better than Mahomet M.," said Rachel to her father.

"They're both very civil," said Mr. O'Mahony.

"One has all the courtesy of hell! With the other it is—well, not quite the manners of heaven. I can imagine something brighter even than M. Le Gros; but it does very well for earth. M. Le Gros knows that a young woman should be treated as a human being; and even his blandishments are pleasant enough as they are to take the shape of golden guineas. As for me, M. Le Gros is quite good enough for my idea of this world."

But on the next day, a misfortune took place which well-nigh obliterated all the joy which M. Le Gros had produced. It was not singing night, and Mr. O'Mahony had just taken up his hat to go away to his debating society, when Frank Jones was announced. "Frank, what on earth did you come here for?" These were the words with which the lover was greeted. He had endeavoured to take the girl in his arms, but she had receded from his embrace.

"Why, Rachel!" he exclaimed.

"I told you not to come. I told you especially that you were not to come."

"Why did you tell him so?" said Mr. O'Mahony; "and why has he come?"

"Not one kiss, Rachel?" said the lover.

"Oh, kisses, yes! If I didn't kiss you father would think that we had already quarrelled. But it may be that we must do so. When I had told you everything, that you should rush up to London to look after me—as though you suspected me!"

"What is there to suspect?" said the father.

"Nothing—I suspect nothing," said Frank. "But there were things which made it impossible that I should not wish to be nearer. She was insulted."

"Who insulted her?"

"The devil in the shape of a woman," said Rachel. "He takes that shape as often as the other."

"Rachel should not be left in such hands," said Frank.

"My dear Mr. Jones, you have no right to say in what hands I shall be left. My father and I have got to look after that between us. I have told you over and over again what are my intentions in the matter They have been made in utter disregard of myself, and with the most perfect confidence in you. You tell me that you cannot marry me."

"Not quite at present."

"Very well; I have been satisfied to remain as engaged to you; but I am not satisfied to be subject to your interference."

"Interference!" he said.

"Well now; I'm going." This came from Mr. O'Mahony. "I've got to see if I can earn a few shillings, and tell a few truths. I will leave you to fight out your battles among you."

"There will be no battles," said Frank.

"I hope not, but I feel that I can do no good. I have such

absolute trust in Rachel, that you may be quite sure that I shall back her up in whatever she says. Now, good-night," and with that he took his leave.

"I am glad he has gone, because he would do us no good," said Rachel. "You were angry with me just now because I spoke of interference. I meant it. I will not admit of any interference from you." Then she sat with her two hands on her knees, looking him full in the face. "I love you with all my heart, and am ready to tell everyone that I am to become your wife. They have a joke about it in the theatre, calling me Mrs. Jones; and because nobody believes what anybody says they think you're a myth. I suppose it is queer that a singing girl should marry Mr. Jones. I'm to go in the autumn to Covent Garden, and get ever so much more money, and I shall still talk about Mr. Jones,—unless you and I agree to break it off."

"Certainly not that," said he.

"But it is by no means certain. Will you go back to Ireland to-morrow morning, and undertake not to see me again until you come prepared to marry me? If not, we must break it off."

"I can hardly do that."

"Then," said she, rising from her chair, "it is broken off, and I will not call myself Mrs. Jones any more." He too rose from his chair and frowned at her by way of an answer. "I have one other suggestion to make," she said. "I shall receive next October what will be quite sufficient for both of us, and for father too. Come and bear the rough and the smooth together with us."

"And live upon you?"

"I should live upon you without scruple if you had got it. And then I shall bear your interference without a word of complaint. Nay, I shall thank you for it. I shall come to you for advice in everything. What you say will be my law. You shall knock down all the Mosses for me;—or lock them up, which would be so much better. But you must be my husband."

"Not yet. You should not ask me as yet. Think of my father's position. Let this one sad year pass by."

"Two—three, if there are to be two or three sad years! I will wait for you till you are as grey as old Peter, and I have not a note left in my throat. I will stick to you like beeswax. But I will not have you here hanging about me. Do you think that it would not be pleasant for me to have a lover to congratulate me every day on my little triumphs? Do you think that I should not be proud to be seen leaning always on your arm, with the consciousness that Mr. Moss would be annihilated at his very first word? But when a year had passed by, where should I be? No, Frank, it will not do. If you were at Morony Castle things would go on very well. As you choose to assume to yourself the right of interference, we must part."

"When you tell me of such a proposition as that made to you by the woman, am I to say nothing?"

"Not a word;—unless it be by letter from Morony Castle, and then only to me. I will not have you here meddling with my affairs. I told you, though I didn't tell my father, because I would tell you everything."

"And I am to leave you,—without another word?"

"Yes, without another word. And remember that from this moment I am free to marry any man that may come the way."

"Rachel!"

"I am free to marry any man that may come the way. I don't say I shall do so. It may take me some little time to forget you. But I am free. When that has been understood between us I am sure you will interfere no longer; you will not be so unkind as to force upon me the necessity of telling the truth to all the people about the theatre. Let us understand each other."

"I understand," said he, with the air of a much injured man.

"I quite know your position. Trusting to your own prospects, you cannot marry me at present, and you do not choose to accept such income as I can give you. I respect and even approve your motives. I am living a life before the public as a singer, in which it is necessary that I should encounter certain dangers. I can do so without fear, if I be left alone. You won't leave me alone. You won't marry me, and yet you won't leave me to my own devices; therefore, we had better part." He took her by the hand sorrowfully, as though preparing to embrace her. "No, Mr. Jones," she said, "that is all done. I kissed you when my father was here, because I was then engaged to be your wife. That is over now, and I can only say good-bye." So saying, she retired, leaving him standing there in her sitting-room.

He remained for awhile meditating on his position, till he began to think that it would be useless for him to remain there. She certainly would not come down; and he, though he were to wait for her father's return, would get no more favourable reply from him. He, as he had promised, would certainly "back up" his daughter in all that she had said. As he went down out of the room with that feeling of insult which clings to a man when he has been forced to quit a house without any farewell ceremony, he certainly did feel that he had been ill-used. But he could not but acknowledge that she was justified. There was a certain imperiousness about her which wounded his feelings as a man. He ought to have been allowed to be dominant. But then he knew that he could not live upon her income. His father would not speak to him had he gone back to Morony Castle expressing his intention of doing so.

CHAPTER XVIII.

FRANK JONES HAS CEASED TO EXIST.

To tell the truth, Rachel had a thorough good cry before she went to bed that night. Though there was something hard, fixed, imperious, almost manlike about her manner, still she was as soft-hearted as any other girl. We may best describe her by saying that she was an American and an actress. It was impossible to doubt her. No one who had once known her could believe her to be other than she had declared herself. She was loyal, affectionate, and dutiful. But there was missing to her a feminine weakness, which of all her gifts is the most valuable to an English woman, till she makes the mistake of bartering it away for women's rights. We can imagine, however, that the stanchest woman's-right lady should cry for her lost lover. And Rachel O'Mahony cried bitterly for hers. "It had to be done," she said, jumping up at last in her bedroom, and clenching her fist as she walked about the chamber. "It had to be done. A girl situated as I am cannot look too close after herself. Father is more like my son than my father; he has no idea that I want anything done for me. Nor do I want much," she said, as she went on rapidly taking the short course of the room. "No one could say a word about me till I brought my lover forward and showed him to the theatre. I think they did believe him to be a myth; but a myth in that direction does no harm till he appears in the flesh. They think that I have made an empty boast about my Mr. Jones. The ugliest girl that ever came out may do the same thing, and nobody ever thinks anything of it. A lover in the clouds never does any harm, and now my lover is in the clouds. I know that he has gone, and will never come to earth again. How much better I love him because he would not take my offer. Then there would have been a little contempt. And how could I expect him to yield to me in everything, with this brute Moss insulting me at every turn? I do not think he had the courage to send me that message, but still! What could I do but tell Frank? And then what could Frank do but come? I would have come, let any girl have bade me to stay away!" Here she had imagined herself to be the lover, and not the girl who was loved. "But it only shows that we are better apart. He cannot marry me, and I cannot marry him. The Squire is at his wit's end with grief." By "the Squire" Mr. Jones had been signified. "It is better as it is. Father and the Squire ought never to have been brought together,—nor ought I and Frank. I suppose I must tell them all at the theatre that Mr. Jones belongs to me no longer. Only if I did so, they would think that I was holding out a lure to Mahomet M. There's papa. I'll go down and tell him all that need be told about it." So saying, she ascended to their sitting-room.

"Well, my dear, what did you do with Frank?"

"He has gone back to Ireland under the name of Mr. Jones."

"Then there was a quarrel?"

"Oh dear yes! there was safe to be a quarrel."

"Does it suit your book upon the whole?"

"Not in the least. You see before you the most wretched heroine that ever appeared on the boards of any theatre. You may laugh, but it's true. I don't know what I've got to say to Mr. Moss now. If he comes forward in a proper manner, and can prove to me that Madame Socani is not Madame Mahomet M. Moss, I don't know what I can do but accept him. The Adriatic is free to wed another." Then she walked about the room, laughing to prevent her tears.

"Did you hear anything about Castle Morony?"

"Not a word."

"Or the boy Florian?"

"Not a syllable;—though I was most anxious to ask the question. When you are intent upon any matter, it does not do to go away to other things. I should have never made him believe that he was to leave me in earnest, had I allowed him to talk about Florian and the girls. He has gone now. Well; —good-night, father. You and I, father, are all in all to each other now. Not but what somebody else will come, I suppose."

"Do you wish that somebody else should come, as you say?"

"I suppose so. Do not look so surprised, father. Girls very seldom have to say what they really wish. I have done with him now. I had him because I really loved him,—like a fool as I was. I have got to go in for being a singing girl. A singing woman is better than a singing girl. If they don't have husbands, they are supposed to have lovers. I hope to have one or the other, and I prefer the husband. Mr. Jones has gone. Who knows but what the Marquis de Carabas may come next?"

"Could you change so soon?"

"Yes;—immediately. I don't say I should love the Marquis, but I should treat him well. Don't looked so shocked, dear father. I never shall treat a man badly,—unless I stick a knife into Mahomet M. Moss. It would be best perhaps to get a singing Marquis, so that the two of us might go walking about the world together, till we had got money enough to buy a castle. I am beginning to believe M. Le Gros. I think I can sing. Don't you think, father, that I can sing?"

"They all say so."

"It is very good to have one about me, like you, who are not enthusiastic. But I can sing, and I am pretty too;—pretty enough along with my singing to get some fool to care for me. Yes; you may look astonished. Over there in Galway I was fool enough to fall in love. What has come of it? The man tells me that he cannot marry me. And it is true. If he were to marry me what would become of you?"

"Never mind me," said her father.

"And what would become of him? And what would become of me? And what would become of the dreadful little impediments which might follow? Of course to me Frank Jones is the best of men. I can't have him; and that is just all about it. I am not going to give up the world because Frank Jones is lost. Love is not to be lord of all with me. I shall steer my little boat among the shiny waters of the London theatres, and may perhaps venture among the waves of Paris and New York; but I shall do so always with my eyes open. Gas is the atmosphere in which I am destined to glitter; and if a Marquis comes in the way,—why, I shall do the best I can with the Marquis. I won't bring you to trouble if I can help it, or anyone else with whom I have to do. So good-night, father." Then she kissed his forehead, and went up to bed leaving him to wonder at the intricacies of his position.

He had that night been specially eloquent and awfully indignant as to the wrongs done to Ireland by England. He had dealt with millions of which Great Britain was supposed by him to have robbed her poor sister. He was not a good financier, but he did in truth believe in the millions. He had not much capacity for looking into questions of political economy, but he had great capacity for arguing about them and for believing his own arguments. The British Parliament was to him an abomination. He read the papers daily, and he saw that the number of votes on his side fell from sixty to forty, and thirty, and twenty; and he found also that the twenty were men despised by their own countrymen as well as Englishmen; that they were men trained to play a false game in order to achieve their objects;—and yet he believed in the twenty against all the world, and threw in his lot without a scruple and without a doubt. Nor did he understand at all the strength of his own words. He had been silenced in Ireland and had rigorously obeyed the pledge that he had given. For he was a man to whom personally his word was a bond. Now he had come over to London, and being under no promise, had begun again to use the words which came to him without an effort. As he would sweep back his long hair from his brows, and send sparks of fire out of his eyes, he would look to be the spirit of patriotic indignation; but he did not know that he was thus powerful. To tell the truth,—and as he had said to earn a few shillings,—

was the object of his ambition. But now, on this evening, three London policemen in their full police uniform, with their fearful police helmets on, had appeared in the room in which his dramatic associates had on this evening given way to Gerald O'Mahony's eloquence. Nothing had been said to him; but as he came home he was aware that two policemen had watched him. And he was aware also that his words had been taken down in shorthand. Then he had encountered his daughter, and all her love troubles. He had heard her expound her views as to life, and had listened as she had expressed her desire to meet with some Marquis de Carabas. She had said nothing with which he could find fault; but her whole views of life were absolutely different from his. According to his ideas, there should be no Marquises, no singing girls making huge fortunes—only singing girls in receipt of modest sums of money; and that when dire necessity compelled them. There should be no gorgeous theatres flaring with gas, and certainly no policemen to take down men's words. Everything in the world was wrong,—except those twenty Members of Parliament.

Three or four days after this, Rachel found that a report was abroad at the theatre that she had dissolved her engagement with Mr. Jones. At this time the three policemen had already expressed their opinion about Mr. O'Mahony; but they, for the present, may be left in obscurity. "*Est-il vrai que M. Jones n'existe plus?*" These words were whispered to her, as she was dressing, by Madame Socani, while Mr. O'Mahony had gone out to say a word to a police detective, who had called to see him at the theatre. As Madame Socani was an American woman, there was no reason why she should not have asked the question in English—were it not that as it referred to an affair of love it may be thought that French was the proper language.

"Mr. Jones isn't any more, as far as I am concerned," said Rachel, passing on.

"Oh, he has gone!" said Madame Socani, following her into the slips. They were both going on to the stage, but two minutes were allowed to them, while Mahomet M. Moss declared in piteous accents, the woe which awaited him because Alberta,—who was personated by Rachel,—had preferred the rustic Trullo to him who was by birth a Prince of the Empire.

"Yes, Mr. Jones has gone, Madame,—as you are so anxious to know."

"But why? Can it be that there was no Mr. Jones?" Then Rachel flashed round upon the woman. "I suppose there was no Mr. Jones."

"*O, mio tesor.*" These last three words were sung in a delicious contralto voice by Elmira,—the Madame Socani of the occasion,—and were addressed to the Prince of the Empire,

who, for the last six weeks, had been neglecting her charms.
Rachel was furious at the attack made upon her, but in the
midst of her fury she rushed on to the stage, and kneeling
at the feet of Elmira, declared her purpose of surrendering the
Prince altogether. The rustic Trullo was quite sufficient for
her. "Go, fond girl. Trullo is there, tying up the odoriferous
rose." Then they all four broke out into that grand quartette,
in the performance of which M. Le Gros had formed that
opinion which had induced him to hold out such golden hopes
to Rachel. Rachel looked up during one of her grand shakes
and saw Frank Jones seated far back among the boxes. "Oh,
he hasn't left London yet," she said to herself, as she prepared
for another shake.

"Your papa desires me to say with his kindest love, that he
has had to leave the theatre." This came from Mr. Moss when
the piece was ended.

He was dressed as princes of the empire generally do dress
on the stage, and she as the daughter of the keeper of the king's
garden.

"So they tell me; very well, I will go home. I suppose he
has had business."

"A policeman, I fear. Some little pecuniary embarrassment." A rumour had got about the theatre that Mr.
O'Mahony was overwhelmed with money difficulties. Mr.
Moss had probably overheard the rumour.

"I don't believe that at all. It is something political, more
likely."

"Very likely, I don't know, I will see you to your house."
And Mahomet M. looked as though he were going to jump
into the brougham in the garments of the imperial prince.

"Mr. Moss, I can go very well alone." And she turned
round upon him and stood in the doorway so as to oppose his
coming out, and frowned upon him with that look of anger
which she knew so well how to assume.

"I have that to say to you which has to be said at once."

"You drive about London with me in that dress? It would
be absurd. You are painted all round your eyes. I wouldn't
get into a carriage with you on any account."

"In five minutes I will have dressed myself."

"Whether dressed or undressed it does not signify. You
know very well that I would on no account get into a carriage
with you. You are taking advantage of me because my father
is not here. If you accompany me I will call for a policeman
directly we get into the street."

"Ah, you do not know," said Mr. Moss. And he looked at
her exactly as he had looked about an hour ago when he was
making love to her as Trullo's betrothed.

"Here is my father," she said; for at that moment Mr.

O'Mahony appeared within the theatre, having made his way up from the door in time to take his daughter home.

"Mr. O'Mahony," said Mr. Moss, "I shall do myself the honour of calling to-morrow and seeing your daughter at her apartments in Gower Street."

"You will see father too," said Rachel.

"I shall be delighted," said Moss. "It will give me the greatest pleasure on earth to see Mr. O'Mahony on this occasion." So saying the imperial prince made a low bow, paint and all, and allowed the two to go down into the street, and get into the brougham.

Mr. O'Mahony at once began with his own story. The policeman who had called for him had led him away round the corner into Scotland Yard, and had there treated him with the utmost deference. Nothing could be more civil to him than had been the officer. But the officer had suggested to him that he had been the man who had said some rough words about the Queen in Galway, and had promised to abstain in future from lecturing. "To this I replied," said he, "that I had said nothing rough about the Queen. I had said that the Queen was as nearly an angel on earth as a woman could be. I had merely doubted whether there should be Queens. Thereupon the policeman shook his head and declared that he could not admit any doubt on that question. 'But you wouldn't expect me to allow it in New York,' said I. 'You've got to allow it here,' said he. 'But my pledge was made as to Ireland,' said I. 'It is all written down in some magistrate's book, and you'll find it if you send over there.' Then I told him that I wouldn't break my word for him or his Queen either. Upon that he thanked me very much for my civility, and told me that if I would hurry back to the theatre I should be in time to take you home. If it was necessary he would let me hear from him again. 'You will know where to find me,' said I, and I gave him our address in Farringdon Street, and told him I should be there to-morrow at half-past eight. He shook hands with me as though I had been his brother;—and so here I am."

Then she began to tell her story, but there did not seem to be much of interest in it. "I suppose he'll come?" said Mr. O'Mahony.

"Oh, yes, he'll come."

"It's something about M. Le Gros," said he. "You'll find that he'll abuse that poor Frenchman."

"He may save himself the trouble," said Rachel. Then they reached Gower Street, and went to bed, having eaten two mutton chops apiece.

On the next morning at eleven o'clock tidings were brought up to Rachel in her bedroom that Mr. Moss was in the sitting-room downstairs.

"Father is there?" exclaimed Rachel.

Then the girl, who had learned to understand that Mr. Moss was not regarded as a welcome visitor, assured her that he was at the moment entertained by Mr. O'Mahony. "He's a-telling of what the perlice said to him in the City, but I don't think as the Jew gentleman minds him much." From which it may be gathered that Rachel had not been discreet in speaking of her admirer before the lodging-house servant.

She dressed herself, not in a very great hurry. Her father, she knew, had no other occupation at this hour in the morning, and she did not in the least regard how Mr. Moss might waste his time. And she had to think of many things before she could go down to meet him. Meditating upon it all, she was inclined to think that the interview was intended as hostile to M. Le Gros. M. Le Gros would be represented, no doubt, as a Jew twice more Jewish than Mr. Moss himself. But Rachel had a strong idea that M. Le Gros was a very nice old French gentleman. When he had uttered all those "ve-rys," one after another with still increasing emphasis, Rachel had no doubt believed them all. And she was taking great trouble with herself, practising every day for two hours together, with a looking-glass before her on the pianoforte, as Mr. Moss had made her quite understand that the opening of her mouth wide was the chief qualification necessary to her, beyond that which Nature had done for her. Rachel did think it possible that she might become the undoubted prima donna of the day, as M. Le Gros had called her; and she thought it much more probable that she should do so under the auspices of M. Le Gros, than those of Mr. Moss. When, therefore, she went down at last to the sitting-room, she did so, determined to oppose Mr. Moss, as bidding for her voice, rather than as a candidate for her love. When she entered the room, she could not help beginning with something of an apology, in that she had kept the man waiting; but Mr. Moss soon stopped her. "It does not signify the least in the world," he said, laying his hand upon his waistcoat. "If only I can get this opportunity of speaking to you while your father is present." Then, when she looked at the brilliance of his garments, and heard the tones of his voice, she was sure that the attack on this occasion was not to be made on M. Le Gros. She remained silent, and sat square on her chair, looking at him. A man must be well versed in feminine wiles, who could decipher under Rachel's manners her determination to look as ugly as possible on the occasion. In a moment she had flattened every jaunty twist and turn out of her habiliments, and had given to herself an air of absolute dowdyism. Her father sat by without saying a word. "Miss O'Mahony, if I may venture to ask a question, I trust you may not be offended."

"I suppose not as my father is present," she replied.

"Am I right in believing the engagement to be over which bound you to Mr.——Jones?"

"You are," said Rachel, quite out loud, giving another quite unnecessary twist to her gown.

"That obstacle is then removed?"

"Mr. Jones is removed, and has gone to Ireland." Then Mr. Moss sighed deeply. "I can manage my singing very well without Mr.——Jones."

"Not a doubt. Not a doubt. And I have heard that you have made an engagement in all respects beneficial with M. Le Gros, of Covent Garden. M. Le Gros is a gentleman for whom I have a most profound respect."

"So have I."

"Had I been at your elbow, it is possible that something better might have been done; but two months;—they run by— oh, so quickly!"

"Quite so. If I can do any good I shall quickly get another engagement."

"You will no doubt do a great deal of good. But Mr. Jones is now at an end."

"Mr. Jones is at an end," said Rachel, with another blow at her gown. "A singing girl like me does better without a lover, —especially if she has got a father to look after her."

"That's as may be," said Mr. O'Mahony.

"That's as may be," said Mr. Moss, again laying his hand upon his heart. The tone in which Mr. Moss repeated Mr. O'Mahony's words was indicative of the feeling and poetry within him. "If you had a lover such as is your faithful Moss," the words seemed to say, "no father could look after you half so well."

"I believe I could do very well with no one to look after me."

"Of course you and I have misunderstood each other hitherto."

"Not at all," said Rachel.

"I was unaware at first that Mr. Jones was an absolute reality. You must excuse me, but the name misled me."

"Why shouldn't a girl be engaged to a man named Jones? Jones is as good a name as Moss, at any rate; and a deal more——" She had been going to remark that Jones was the more Christian of the two, but stopped herself.

"At any rate you are now free?" he said.

"No, I am not. Yes, I am. I am free, and I mean to remain so. Why don't you tell him, father?"

"I have got nothing to tell him, my dear. You are so much better able to tell him everything yourself."

"If you would only listen to me, Miss O'Mahony."

"You had better listen to him, Rachel."

"Very well; I will listen. Now go on." Then she again

thumped herself. And she had thumped her hair, and thumped herself all round till she was as limp and dowdy as the elder sister of a Low Church clergyman of forty.

"I wish you to believe, Miss O'Mahony, that my attachment to you is most devoted." She pursed her lips together and looked straight out of her eyes at the wall opposite. "We belong to the same class of life, and our careers lie in the same groove." Hereupon she crossed her hands before her on her lap, while her father sat speculating whether she might not have done better to come out on the comic stage. "I wish you to believe that I am quite sincere in the expression which I make of a most ardent affection." Here again he slapped his waist-coat and threw himself into an attitude. He was by no means an ill-looking man, and though he was forty years old, he did not appear to be so much. He had been a public singer all his life, and was known by Rachel to have been connected for many years with theatres both in London and New York. She had heard many stories of his amorous adventures, but knew nothing against his character in money matters. He had, in truth, always behaved well to her in whatever pecuniary transactions there had been between them. But he had ventured to make love to her, and had done so in a manner which had altogether disgusted her. She now waited till he paused for a moment in his eloquence, and then she spoke a word.

"What about Madame Socani?"

CHAPTER XIX.

FIFTH AVENUE AND NEWPORT.

"WHAT about Madame Socani?" Rachel, as she said this, abandoned for the moment her look against the wall, and shook herself instantly free of all her dowdiness. She flashed fire at him from her eyes, and jumping up from her seat, took hold of her father by his shoulder. He encircled her waist with his arm, but otherwise sat silent, looking Mr. Moss full in the face. It must be acknowledged on the part of Rachel that she was prepared to make her accusation against Mr. Moss on perhaps insufficient grounds. She had heard among the people at the theatre, who did not pretend to know much of Mr. Moss and his antecedents, that there was a belief that Madame Socani was his wife. There was something in this which offended her more grossly than ever,—and a wickedness which horrified her. But she certainly knew nothing about it; and Madame Socani's proposition to herself had come to her from Madame Socani, and not from Mr. Moss. All she knew of Madame Socani was that she had been on the boards in New York, and had there made for herself a reputation. Rachel had on one occasion sung with her, but it had been when she was little more than a child.

"What is Madame Socani to me?" said Mr. Moss.

"I believe her to be your wife."

"Oh, heavens! My wife! I never had a wife, Miss O'Mahony;—not yet! Why do you say things so cruel to me?"

He, at any rate, she was sure, had sent her that message. She thought that she was sure of his villainous misconduct to her in that respect. She believed that she did know him to be a devil, whether he was a married man or not.

"What message did you send to me by Madame Socani?"

"What message? None!" and again he laid his hand upon his waistcoat.

"He asked me to be——" But she could not tell her father of what nature was the message, "Father, he is a reptile! If you knew all, you would be unable to keep your hands from his throat. And now he dares to come here and talk to me of his affection. You had better bid him leave the room and have done with him."

"You hear what my daughter says, Mr. Moss."

"Yes, I hear her," answered the poor, innocent-looking tenor. "But what does she mean? Why is she so fierce?"

"He knows, father," said Rachel. "Have nothing further to say to him."

"I don't think that I do quite know," said Mr. O'Mahony. "But you can see, at any rate, Mr. Moss, that she does not return your feeling."

"I would make her my wife to-morrow," said Mr. Moss, slapping his waistcoat once more. "And do you, as the young lady's papa, think of what we two might do together. I know myself, I know my power. Madame Socani is a jealous woman. She would wish to be taken into partnership with me,—not a partnership of hearts, but of theatres. She has come with some insolent message, but not from me;—ah, not from me!"

"You never tried to kiss me? You did not make two attempts?"

"I would make two thousand if I were to consult my own heart."

"When you knew that I was engaged to Mr. Jones!"

"What was Mr. Jones to me? Now I ask your respectable parent, is Miss Rachel unreasonable? When a gentleman has lost his heart in true love, is he to be reproached because he endeavours to seize one little kiss? Did not Mr. Jones do the same?"

"Bother Mr. Jones!" said Rachel, overcome by the absurdity of the occasion. "As you observed just now, Mr. Jones and I are two. Things have not turned out happily, though I am not obliged to explain all that to you. But Mr. Jones is to me all that a man should be; you, Mr. Moss, are not. Now, father, had he not better go?"

"I don't think any good is to be done, I really don't," said Mr. O'Mahony.

"Why am I to be treated in this way?"

"Because you come here persevering when you know it's no good."

"I think of what you and I might do together with Moss's theatre between us."

"Oh, heavens!"

"You should be called the O'Mahony. Your respectable papa should keep an eye to your pecuniary interest."

"I could keep an eye myself for that."

"You would be my own wife, of course—my own wife."

"I wouldn't be anything of the kind."

"Ah, but listen!" continued Mr. Moss. "You do not know how the profits run away into the pockets of *impresarios* and lessees and money-lenders. We should have it all ourselves. I have £30,000 of my own, and my respectable parent in New York has as much more. It would all be the same as ours. Only think! Before long we would have a house on the Fifth Avenue so furnished that all the world should wonder; and another at Newport, where the world should not be admitted to wonder. Only think!"

"And Madame Socani to look after the furniture!" said Rachel.

"Madame Socani should be nowheres."

"And I also will be nowheres. Pray remember that in making all your little domestic plans. If you live in the Fifth Avenue, I will live in 350 Street; or perhaps I should like it better to have a little house here in Albert Place. Father, don't you think Mr. Moss might go away?"

"I think you have said all that there is to be said." Then Mr. O'Mahony got up from his chair as though to show Mr. Moss out of the room.

"Not quite, Mr. O'Mahony. Allow me for one moment. As the young lady's papa you are bound to look to these things. Though the theatre would be a joint affair, Miss O'Mahony would have her fixed salary; that is to say, Mrs. Moss would."

"I won't stand it," said Rachel getting up. "I won't allow any man to call me by so abominable a name,—or any woman." Then she bounced out of the room.

"It's no good, you see," said Mr. O'Mahony.

"I by no means see that so certain. Of course a young lady like your daughter knows her own value, and does not yield all at once."

"I tell you it's no good. I know my own daughter."

"Excuse me, Mr. O'Mahony, but I doubt whether you know the sex."

The two men were very nearly of an age; but O'Mahony assumed the manners of an old man, and Mr. Moss of a young one.

"Perhaps not," said Mr. O'Mahony.

"They have been my study up from my cradle," said Mr. Moss.

"No doubt."

"And I think that I have carried on the battle not without some little *éclat*."

"I am quite sure of it."

"I still hope that I may succeed with your sweet daughter."

"Here the battle is of a different kind," not without a touch of satire in the tone of his voice, whatever there might be in the words which he used. "In tournaments of love, you have, I do not doubt, been very successful; but here it seems to me that the struggle is for money."

"That is only an accident."

"But the accident rises above everything. It does not matter in the least which comes first. Whether it be for love or money my daughter will certainly have a will of her own. You may take my word that she is not to be talked out of her mind."

"But Mr. Jones is gone?" asked Moss.

"But she is not on that account ready to transfer her affections at a moment's notice. To her view of the matter there seems to be something a little indelicate in the idea."

"Bah!" said Mr. Moss.

"You cannot make her change her mind by saying bah."

"Professional interests have to be considered," said Mr. Moss.

"No doubt; my daughter does consider her professional interests every day when she practises for two hours."

"That is excellent,—and with such glorious effects! She has only now got the full use of her voice. My G——! what could she not do if she had the full run of Moss's Theatre! She might choose whatever operas would suit her best; and she would have me to guide her judgment! I do know my profession, Mr. O'Mahony. A lady in her line should always marry a gentleman in mine; that is, if she cares about matrimony."

"Of course she did intend to be married to Mr. Jones."

"Oh! Mr. Jones, Mr. Jones! I am sick of Mr. Jones. What could Mr. Jones do? He is only a poor ruined Irishman. You must feel that Mr. Jones was only in the way. I am offering her all that professional experience and capital can do. What are her allurements?"

"I don't in the least know, Mr. Moss."

"Only her beauty."

"I thought, perhaps it was her singing."

"That joined," said Mr. Moss. "No doubt her voice and her beauty joined together. Madame Socani's voice is as valuable,—almost as valuable."

"I would marry Madame Socani if I were you."

"No! Madame Socani is,—well a leetle past her prime. Madame Socani and I have known each other for twenty years. Madame Socani is aware that I am attached to your daughter. Well; I do not mind telling you the truth. Madame Socani and I have been on very intimate terms. I did offer once to make Madame Socani my wife. She did not see her way in money matters. She was making an income greater than mine. Things have changed since that. Madame Socani is very well, but she is a jealous woman. Madame Socani hates your daughter. Oh, heavens, yes! But she was never my wife. Oh, no! A woman at this profession grows old quicker than a man. And she has never succeeded in getting a theatre of her own. She did try her hand at it in New York, but that came to nothing. If Miss Rachel will venture along with me, we will have 500,000 dollars before five years are gone. She shall have everything that the world can offer—jewels, furniture, hangings! She shall keep the best table in New York, and shall have her own banker's account. There's no such success to be found anywhere for a young woman. If you will only just turn it in your mind, Mr. O'Mahony." Then Mr. Moss brushed his hat with the sleeve of his coat and took his leave.

He had nearly told the entire truth to Mr. O'Mahony. He had never married Madame Socani. As far as Madame Socani knew, her veritable husband, Socani, was still alive. And it was not true that Mr. Moss had sent that abominable message to Rachel. The message, no doubt, had expressed a former wish on his part; but that wish was now in abeyance. Miss O'Mahony's voice had proved itself to him to be worth matrimony;—that and her beauty together. In former days, when he had tried to kiss her, he had valued her less highly. Now, as he left the room, he was fully content with the bargain he had suggested. Mr. Jones was out of the way, and her voice had proved itself to his judgment to be worth the price he had offered.

When her father saw her again he began meekly to plead for Mr. Moss.

"Do you mean to say, father," she exclaimed, "that you have joined yourself to him?"

"I am only telling you what he says."

"Tell me nothing at all. You ought to know that he is an abomination. Though he had the whole Fifth Avenue to offer to me I would not touch him with a pair of tongs."

But she, in the midst of her singing, had been much touched by seeing Frank Jones among the listeners in the back of one of the boxes. When the piece was over there had come upon her a desire to go to him and tell him that, in spite of all she had said, she would wait for him if only he would profess himself ready to wait for her. There was not much in it,—that a man should wait in town for two or three days, and should return to the theatre to see the girl whom he professed to regard. It was only that, but it had again stirred her love. She had endeavoured to send to him when the piece was over; but he was gone, and she saw him no more.

CHAPTER XX.

BOYCOTTING.

FRANK JONES went back to County Galway, having caught a last glimpse of his lady-love. But his lady-love could not very well make herself known to him from the stage as she was occupied at the moment with Trullo. And as he had left the theatre before her message had been brought round, he did so with a bitter conviction that everything between them was over. He felt very angry with her,—no doubt unreasonably. The lady was about to make a pocketful of money; and had offered to share it with him. He refused to take any part of it, and declined altogether to incur any of the responsibilities of marriage for the present. His father's circumstances too were of such a nature as to make him almost hopeless for the future. What would he have had her do? Nevertheless he was very angry with her.

As he made his way westward through Ireland he heard more and more of the troubles of the country. He had not in fact been gone much more than a week, but during that week sad things had happened. Boycotting had commenced, and had already become very prevalent. To boycott a man, or a house, or a firm, or a class of men, or a trade, or a flock of sheep, or a drove of oxen, or unfortunately a county hunt, had become an exact science, and was exactly obeyed. It must be acknowledged that throughout the south and west of Ireland the quickness and perfection with which this science was understood and practised was very much to the credit of the intelligence of the people. We can understand that boycotting should be studied in Yorkshire, and practised,—after an experience of many years. Laying on one side for the moment all ideas as to the honesty and expediency of the measure, we think that Yorkshire might in half a century learn how to boycott its neighbours. A Yorkshire man might boycott a Lancashire man, or Lincoln might boycott Nottingham. It would require much teaching ;—many books would have to be written, and an infinite amount of heavy slow imperfect practice would follow. But County Mayo and County Galway rose to the requirements of the art almost in a night! Gradually we Englishmen learned to know in a dull glimmering way what they were about ; but at the first whisper of the word all Ireland knew how to ruin itself. This was done readily by people of the poorer class,—without any gifts of education, and certainly the immoderate practice of the science displays great national intelligence.

As Frank Jones passed through Dublin he learned that Morony Castle had been boycotted ; and he was enough of an Irishman to know immediately what was meant. And he heard, too, while in the train that the kennels at Ahaseragh had been boycotted. He knew that with the kennels would be included Black Daly, and with Morony Castle his unfortunate father. According to the laws on which the practice was carried on nothing was to be bought from the land of Morony Castle, and nothing sold to the owners of it. No service was to be done for the inhabitants, as far as the laws of boycotting might be made to prevail. He learned from a newspaper he bought in Dublin that the farm-servants had all left the place, and that the maids had been given to understand that they would encounter the wrath of the new lords in the land if they made a bed for any Jones to lie upon.

As he went on upon his journey his imagination went to work to picture to himself the state of his father's life under these circumstances. But his imagination was soon outstripped by the information which reached him from fellow-travellers. "Did ye hear what happened to old Phil Jones down at Morony?" said a passenger, who got in at Moate, to another who had joined them at Athlone.

"Divil a hear thin."

"Old Phil wanted to get across from Ballyglunin to his own place. He had been down to Athenry. There was that chap who is always there with a car. Divil a foot would he stir for Phil. Phil has had some row with the boys there about his meadows, and he's trying to prosecute. More fool he. A quiet, aisy-going fellow he used to be. But it seems he has been stirred now. He has got some man in Galway jail, and all the country is agin him. Anyways he had to foot it from Ballyglunin to Headford, and then to send home to Morony for his own car." In this way did Frank learn that his father had in truth incurred boycotting severity. He knew well the old man who had attended the Ballyglunin station with almost a hopeless desire of getting a fare, and was sure that nothing short of an imperious edict from the great Land-leaguing authorities in the district, would have driven him to the necessity of repudiating a passenger.

But when he had reached the further station of Ballinasloe he learned sadder tidings in regard to his friend Tom Daly. Tom Daly had put no man in prison, and yet the kennels at Ahaseragh had been burned to the ground. This had occurred only on the preceding day; and he got the account of what had happened from a hunting man he knew well. "The hounds were out, you know, last Saturday week as a finish, and poor Tom did hope that we might get through without any further trouble. We met at Ballinamona, and we drew Blake's coverts without a word. We killed our fox too and then went away to Pulhaddin gorse. I'll be blest if all the county weren't there. I never saw the boys swarm about a place so thick. Pulhaddin is the best gorse in the county. Of course it was no use drawing it; but as we were going away on the road to Loughrea the crowd was so thick that there was no riding among them. Ever so many horsemen got into the fields to be away from the crowd. But Tom wouldn't allow Barney and the hounds to be driven from the road. I never saw a man look so angry in my life. You could see the passion that was on him. He never spoke a word, nor raised a hand, nor touched his horse with his spur; but he got blacker and blacker, and would go on whether the crowd moved asunder or not. And he told Barney to follow him with the hounds, which Barney did, looking back ever and anon at the poor brutes, and giving his instructions to the whips to see well after that they did not wander. They threatened Barney scores of times with their sticks, but he came on, funking awfully, but still doing whatever Tom told him. I was riding just behind him among the hounds so that I could see all that took place. At last a ruffian with his shillelagh struck Barney over the thigh. I had not time to get to him; indeed I doubt whether I should have done so, but Tom, ——; by George, he saw out of the back of his head. He turned round, and, without touching his horse with spur or whip, rode right at the ruffian. If they had struck himself, I think he would have borne it more easily."

"How did it end?"

"They said that the blackguard was hurt, but I saw him escape and get away over the fence. Then they all set upon Tom, but by G—— it was glorious to see the way in which he held his own. Out came that cross of his, four foot and a half long, with a thong as heavy as a flail. He soon had the road clear around him, and the big black horse you remember, stood as steady as a statue till he was bidden to move on. Then when he had the hounds, and Barney Smith and the whips to himself, —and I was there—we all rode off at a fast trot to Loughrea."

"And then?"

"We could do nothing but go home; the whole county seemed to be in a ferment. At Loughrea we went away in our own directions, and poor Tom with Barney Smith rode home to Ahaseragh. But not a word did he speak to anyone, even to Barney; nor did Barney dare to speak a word to him. He trotted all the way to Ahaseragh in moody silence, thinking of the terrible ill that had been done him. I have known Tom for twenty years, and I think that if he loves any man he loves me. But he parted from me that day without a word."

"And then the kennels were set on fire?"

"Before I left Loughrea I heard the report, spread about everywhere, that Tom Daly had recklessly ridden down three or four more poor countrymen on the road. I knew then that some mischief would be in hand. It was altogether untrue that he had hurt anyone. And he was bound to interfere on behalf of his own servant. But when I heard this morning that a score of men had been there in the night and had burned the kennels to the ground, I was not surprised." Such was the story that Frank Jones heard as to Tom Daly before he got home.

On reaching Ballyglunin he looked out for the carman, but he was not there. Perhaps the interference with his task had banished him. Frank went on to Tuam, which increased slightly the distance by road to Morony. But at Tuam he found that Morony had in truth been boycotted. He could not get a car for love or money. There were many cars there, and the men would not explain to him their reasons for declining to take him home; but they all refused. "We can't do it, Mr. Frank," said one man; and that was the nearest approach to an explanation that was forthcoming. He walked into town and called at various houses; but it was to no purpose. It was with difficulty that he found himself allowed to leave his baggage at a grocer's shop, so strict was the boycotting exacted. And then he too had to walk home through Headford to Morony Castle.

When he reached the house he first encountered Peter, the butler. "Faix thin, Mr. Frank," said Peter, "throubles niver comed in 'arnest till now. Why didn't they allow Mr. Flory just to hould his pace and say nothing about it to no one?"

"Why has all this been done?" demanded Frank.

"It's that born divil, Pat Carroll," whispered Peter. "I wouldn't be saying it so that any of the boys or girls should hear me,—not for my throat's sake. I am the only one of 'em," he added, whispering still lower than before, "that's doing a ha'porth for the masther. There are the two young ladies a-working their very fingers off down to the knuckles. As for me, I've got it all on my shoulders." No doubt Peter was true to his master in adversity, but he did not allow the multiplicity of his occupations to interfere with his eloquence.

Then Frank went in and found his father seated alone in his magistrate's room. "This is bad, father," said Frank, taking him by the hand.

"Bad! yes, you may call it bad. I am ruined, I suppose. There are twenty heifers ready for market next week, and I am told that not a butcher in County Galway will look at one of them."

"Then you must send them on to Westmeath; I suppose the Mullingar butchers won't boycott you?"

"It's just what they will do."

"Then send them on to Dublin."

"Who's to take them to Dublin?" said the father, in his distress.

"I will if there be no one else. We are not going to be knocked out of time for want of two or three pairs of hands."

"There are two policemen here to watch the herd at night. They'd cut the tails off them otherwise as they did over at Ballinrobe last autumn. To whom am I to consign 'em in Dublin? While I am making new arrangements of that kind their time will have gone by. There are five cows should be milked morning and night. Who is to milk them?"

"Who is milking them?"

"Your sisters are doing it, with the aid of an old woman who has come from Galway. She says she has not long to live, and with the help of half-a-crown a day cares nothing for the Land-leaguers. I wish someone would pay me half-a-crown a day, and perhaps I should not care."

Then Frank passed on through the house to find his sisters, or Flory as it might be. He had said not a word to his father in regard to Florian, fearing to touch upon a subject which, as he well knew, must be very sore. Had Florian told the truth when the deed was done, Pat Carroll would have been tried at once, and, whether convicted or acquitted, the matter would have been over long ago. In those days Pat Carroll had not become a national or even a county hero. But now he was able to secure the boycotting of his enemy even as far distant as Ballyglunin or Tuam. In the kitchen he found Ada and Edith, who had no comfort in these perilous days except when they could do everything together. At the present moment they were roasting a leg of mutton and boiling potatoes, which Frank knew were intended especially for his own eating.

"Well, my girls, you are busy here," he said.

"Oh, yes, busy!" said Ada, who had put up her face to be kissed so as not to spoil her brother's coat by touching it with her hands. "How is Rachel?"

"Rachel is pretty well, I believe. We will not talk of Rachel just at present."

"Is anything wrong?" asked Edith.

"We will not talk about her, not now. What is all this that has happened here?"

"We are just boycotted," said Ada; "that's all."

"And you think that it's the best joke in the world?"

"Think it a joke!" said Edith.

"Why, we have to be up every morning at five o'clock," said Ada; "and at six we are out with the cows."

"It is no joke," said Edith, very seriously. "Papa is broken-hearted about it. Your coming will be of the greatest comfort to us, if only because of the pair of hands you bring. And poor Flory!"

"How has it gone with Flory?" he asked. Then Edith told the tale as it had to be told of Florian, and of what had happened because of the evidence he had given. He had come forward under the hands of Captain Yorke Clayton and repeated his whole story, giving it in testimony before the magistrates. He declared it all exactly as he had done before in the presence of his father and his sister and Captain Clayton. And he had sworn to it, and had had his deposition read to him. He was sharp enough, and understood well what he was doing. The other two men were brought up to support him,—the old man Terry and Con Heffernan. They of course had not been present at the examination of Flory, and were asked,—first one and then the other,—what they knew of the transactions of the afternoon on which the waters had been let in on the meadows of Ballintubber. They knew nothing at all, they said. They "disremembered" whether they had been there on the occasion, "at all, at all." Yes; they knew that the waters had been in upon the meadows, and they believed that they were in again still. They didn't think that the meadows were of much good for this year. They didn't know who had done it, "at all, at all." People did be saying that Mr. Florian had done it himself, so as to spite his father because he had turned Catholic. They couldn't say whether Mr. Florian could do it alone or not. They thought Mr. Florian and Peter, the butler, and perhaps one other, might do it amongst them. They thought that Yorke Clayton might perhaps have been the man to help him. They didn't know that Yorke Clayton hadn't been in the county at that time. They wished with all their hearts that he wasn't there now, because he was the biggest blackguard they had ever heard tell of.

Such was the story which was now told to Frank of the examination which took place in consequence of Florian's confession. The results were that Pat Carroll was in Galway jail, committed to take his trial at the next assizes in August for the offence which he had committed; and that Florian had been bound over to give evidence. "What does Florian do with himself?" his brother asked.

"I'm afraid he is frightened," said Ada.

"Of course he is frightened," said her sister. "How should he not be frightened? These men have been telling him for the last six months that they would surely murder him if he turned round and gave evidence against them. Oh, Frank, I fear that I have been wrong in persuading him to tell the truth."

"Not though his life were sacrificed to-morrow. To have kept the counsels of such a ruffian as that against his own father would have been a disgrace to him for ever. Does not my father think of sending him to England?"

"He says that he has not the money," said Edith.

"Is it so bad as that with him?"

"I am afraid it is very bad,—bad at any rate, for the time coming. He has not had a shilling of rent for this spring, and he has to pay the money to Mrs. Pulteney and the others. Poor papa is sorely vexed, and we do not like to press him. He suggested himself that he would send Florian over to Mr. Blake's; but we think that Carnlough is not far enough, and that it would be unfair to impose such a trouble on another man."

"Could he not send him to Mrs. Pulteney?" Now Mrs. Pulteney was a sister of Mr. Jones.

"He does not like to ask her," said Edith. "He thinks that Mrs. Pulteney has not shown herself very kind of late. We are waiting till you speak to him about it."

"But what does Florian do with himself?" he asked.

"You will see. He does little or nothing, but roams about the house and talks to Peter. He did not even go to mass last Sunday. He says that the whole congregation would accuse him of being a liar."

"Does he not know that he has done his duty by the lie he has told?"

"But to go alone among these people!" said Ada.

"And to hear their damnable taunts!" said Edith. "It is very hard upon him. I think it is papa's idea to keep him here till after the trial in August, and then, if possible, to send him to England. There would be the double journey else, and papa thinks that there would be no real danger till his evidence had been given."

Then Frank went out of the house and walked round the demesne, so that he might think at his ease of all the troubles of his family.

CHAPTER XXI.

LAX, THE MURDERER.

FRANK JONES found his brother Florian alone in the butler's pantry, and was told that Peter was engaged in feeding the horses and cleaning out the stables. "He's mostly engaged in that kind of work now," said Florian.

"Who lays the tablecloth?" asked Frank.

"I do; or Edith; sometimes we don't have any tablecloth, or any clean knives and forks. Perhaps they'll have one to-day because you have come."

"I wouldn't give them increased trouble," said Frank.

"Papa told them to put their best foot forward because you are here. I don't think he minds at all about himself. I think papa is very unhappy."

"Of course he's unhappy, because they have boycotted him. How should he not be unhappy?"

"It's worse than that," whispered Florian.

"What can be worse?"

"If you'll come with me I'll tell you. I don't want to say it here, because the girls will hear me,—and that old Peter will know everything that's said."

"Come out into the grounds, and take a turn before dinner." At this Florian shook his head. "Why not, Flory?"

"There are fellows about," said Flory.

"What fellows?"

"The very fellows that said they'd kill me. Do you know that fellow Lax? He's the worst of them."

"But he doesn't live here."

"All the same, I saw him yesterday."

"You were out then, yesterday?"

"Not to say out," said Flory. "I was in the orchard just behind the stables; and I could see across into the ten-acre piece. There, at the further side of the field, I saw a fellow who I am sure was Lax. Nobody walks like him, he's got that quick, suspicious way of going. It was just nearly dark; it was well-nigh seven, and I had been with Peter in the stables, helping to make up the horses, and I am sure it was Lax."

"He won't come near you and me on the broad walk," said Frank.

"Won't he? You don't know him. There are half-a-dozen places there where he could hit us from behind the wall. Come up into your room, and I'll tell you what it is that makes papa unhappy." Then Frank led the way upstairs to his bedroom, and Florian followed him. When inside he shut the door, and seated himself on the bed close to his brother. "Now I'll tell you," said he.

"What is it ails him?"

"He's frightened," said Florian, "because he doesn't wish me to be—murdered."

"My poor boy! Who could wish it?" Here Florian shook his head. "Of course he doesn't wish it."

"He made me tell about the meadow gates."

"You had to tell that, Flory."

"But it will bring them to murder me. If you had heard them make me promise and had seen their looks! Papa never thought about that till the man had come and worked it all out of me."

"What man?"

"The head of the policemen, Yorke Clayton. Papa was so fierce upon me then, that he made me do it."

"You had to do it," said Frank. "Let things go as they might, you had to do it. You would not have it said of you that you had joined these ruffians against your father."

"I had sworn to Father Brosnan not to tell. But you care nothing for the priest, of course."

"Nothing in the least."

"Nor does father. But when I had told it all at his bidding, and had gone before the magistrates, and they had written it down, and that man Clayton had read it all and I had signed it, and papa had seen the look which Pat Carroll had turned upon me, then he became frightened. I knew that that man Lax was in the room at the moment. I did not see him, but I felt that he was there. Now I don't go out at all, except just into the orchard and front garden. I won't go even there, as I saw Lax about the place yesterday. I know that they mean to murder me."

"There will be no danger," said Frank, "unless Carroll be convicted. In that case your father will have you sent to a school in England."

"Papa hasn't got the money; I heard him tell Edith so. And they wouldn't know how to carry me to the station at Ballyglunin. Those boys from Ballintubber would shoot at me on the road. It's that that makes papa so unhappy."

Then they all went to dinner with a cloth laid fair on the table, for Frank, who was as it were a stranger. And there were many inquiries made after Rachel and her theatrical performances. Tidings as to her success had already reached Morony, and wonderful accounts of the pecuniary results. They had seen stories in the newspapers of the close friendship which existed between her and Mr. Moss, and hints had been given for a closer tie. "I don't think it is likely," said Frank.

"But is anything the matter between you and Rachel?" asked Edith.

At that moment Peter was walking off with the leg of mutton, and Ada had run into the kitchen to fetch the rice pudding, which she had made to celebrate her brother's return. Edith winked at her brother to show that all questions as to the tender subject should be postponed for the moment.

"But is it true," said Ada, "that Rachel is making a lot of money?"

"That is true, certainly," said her brother.

"And that she sings gloriously?"

"She always did sing gloriously," said Edith. "I was sure that Rachel was intended for a success."

"I wonder what Captain Yorke Clayton would think about her," said Ada. "He does understand music, and is very fond of young ladies who can sing. I heard him say that the Miss Ormesbys of Castlebar sang beautifully; and he sings himself, I know."

"Captain Clayton has something else to do at present than to watch the career of Miss O'Mahony in London." This was said by their father, and was the first word he had spoken since they had sat down to dinner. It was felt to convey some reproach as to Rachel; but why a reproach was necessary was not explained.

Peter was now out of the room, and the door was shut.

"Rachel and I have come to uuderstand each other," said Frank. "She is to have the spending of her money by herself, and I by myself am to enjoy life at Morony Castle."

"Is this her decision?" asked Edith.

It was on Frank's lips to declare that it was so; but he remembered himself, and swallowed down the falsehood unspoken.

"No," he said; "it was not her decision. She offered to share it all with me."

"And you?" said his father.

"Well, I didn't consent; and so we arranged that matters should be brought to an end between us."

"I knew what she would do," said Ada.

"Just what she ought," said Edith. "Rachel is a fine girl. Nothing else was to be expected from her."

"And nothing else was possible with you," said their father. And so that conversation was brought to an end.

On the next day Captain Clayton came up the lake from Galway, and was again engaged,—or pretended to be engaged,—in looking up for evidence in reference to the trial of Pat Carroll. Or it might be that he wanted to sun himself again in the bright eyes of Ada Jones. Again he brought Hunter, his double, with him, and boldly walked from Morony Castle into Headford, disregarding altogether the loaded guns of Pat Carroll's friends. In company with Frank he paid a visit to Tom Lafferty in his own house at Headford. But as he went there he insisted that Frank should carry a brace of pistols in his trousers' pockets. "It's as well to do it, though you should never use them, or a great deal better that you should never use them. You don't want to get into all the muck of shooting a wretched, cowardly Land-leaguer. If all the leaders had but one life among them there would be something worth going in for. But it is well that they should believe that you have got them. They are such cowards that if they know you've got a pistol with you they will be afraid to get near enough to shoot you with a rifle. If you are in a room with fellows who see that you have your hand in your trousers' pocket, they will be in such a funk that you cow half-a-dozen of them. They look upon Hunter and me as though we were an armed company of policemen." So Frank carried the pistols.

"Well, Mr. Lafferty, how are things going with you to-day?"

"'Deed, then, Captain Clayton, it ain't much as I'm able to say for myself. I've the decentry that bad in my innards as I'm all in the twitters."

"I'm sorry for that, Mr. Lafferty. Are you well enough to tell me where did Mr. Lax go when he left you this morning?"

"Who's Mr. Lax? I don't know no such person."

"Don't you, 'now? I thought that Mr. Lax was as well known in Headford as the parish priest. Why, he's first cousin to your second cousin, Pat Carroll."

"'Deed and he ain't then;—not that I ever heard tell of."

"I've no doubt you know what relations he's got in these parts."

"I don't know nothin' about Terry Lax."

"Except that his name is Terry," said the Captain.

"I don't know nothin' about him, and I won't tell nothin' either."

"But he was here this morning, Mr. Lafferty?"

"Not that I know of. I won't say nothin' more about him. It's as bad as lying you are with that d——d artful way of entrapping a fellow."

Here Terry Carroll, Pat's brother, entered the cabin, and took off his hat with an air of great courtesy. "More power to you, Mr. Frank," he said, "it's I that am glad to see you back from London. These are bad tidings they got up at the Castle. To think of Mr. Flory having such a story to tell as that."

"It's a true story at any rate," said Frank.

"Musha thin, not one o' us rightly knows. It's a long time ago, and if I were there at all, I disremember it. Maybe I was, though I wasn't doing anything on me own account. If Pat was to bid me, I'd do that or any other mortal thing at Pat's bidding."

"If you are so good a brother as that, your complaisance is likely to bring you into trouble, Mr. Carroll. Come along,

Jones, I've got pretty nearly what I wanted from them." Then when they were in the street, he continued speaking to Frank. "Your brother is right though, I wouldn't have believed it on any other testimony than one of themselves. That man Lax was here in the county yesterday. A more murderous fellow than he is not to be found in Connaught; and he's twice worse than any of the fellows about here. They will do it for revenge, or party purposes. He has a regular tariff for cutting throats. I should not wonder if he has come here for the sake of carrying out the threats which they made against your poor brother."

"Do you mean that he will be murdered?"

"We must not let it come to that. We must have Lax up before the magistrate for having been present when they broke the flood gates."

"Have you got evidence of that?"

"We can make the evidence serve its purpose for a time. If we can keep him locked up till after the trial we shall have done much. By heavens, there he is!"

As he spoke the flash of a shot glimmered across their eyes, and seemed to have been fired almost within a yard of them; but they were neither of them hit. Frank turned round and fired in the direction from whence the attack had come, but it was in vain. Clayton did bring his revolver from out his pocket, but held his fire. They were walking in a lane just out of the town that would carry them by a field-path to Morony Castle, and Clayton had chosen the path in order that he might be away from the public road. It was still daylight though it was evening, and the aggressor might have been seen had he attempted to cross their path. The lane was, as it were, built up on both sides with cabins, which had become ruins, each one of which might serve as a hiding-place. Hunter was standing close to them before another word was spoken.

"Did you see him?" demanded Clayton.

"Not a glimpse; but I heard him through there, where the dead leaves are lying." There are a lot of dead leaves strewed about, some of which were in sight, within an enclosure separated from them by a low ruined wall. On leaving this the Captain was over it in a moment, but he was over it in vain. "For God's sake, sir, don't go after him in that way," said Hunter, who followed close upon his track. "It's no more than to throw your life away."

"I'd give the world to have one shot at him," said Clayton. "I don't think I would miss him within ten paces."

"But he'd have had you, Captain, within three, had he waited for you."

"He never would have waited. A man who fires at you from behind a wall never will wait. Where on earth has he taken himself?" And Clayton, with the open pistol in his hand, began to search the neighbouring hovels.

"He's away out of that by this time," said Hunter.

"I heard the bullet pass by my ears," said Frank.

"No doubt you did, but a miss is as good as a mile any day. That a fellow like that who is used to shooting shouldn't do better is a disgrace to the craft. It's that fellow Lax, and as I'm standing on the ground this moment I'll have his life before I've done with him."

Nothing further came from this incident till the three started on their walk back to Morony Castle. But they did not do this till they had thoroughly investigated the ruins. "Do you know anything of the man?" said Frank, "as to his whereabouts? or where he comes from?" Then Clayton gave some short account of the hero. He had first come across him in the neighbourhood of Foxford near Lough Conn, and had there run him very hard, as the Captain said, in reference to an agrarian murder. He knew, he said, that the man had received thirty shillings for killing an old man who had taken a farm from which a tenant had been evicted. But he had on that occasion been tried and acquitted. He had since that lived on the spoils acquired after the same fashion. He was supposed to have come originally from Kilkenny, and whether his real name was or was not Lax, Captain Clayton did not pretend to say.

"But he had a fair shot at me," said Captain Clayton, "and it shall go hard with me but I shall have as fair a one at him. I think it was Urlingford gave the fellow his birth. I doubt whether he will ever see Urlingford again."

So they walked back, and by the time they had reached the Castle were quite animated and lively with the little incident. "It may be possible," said the Captain to Mr. Jones, "that he expected my going to Headford. It certainly was known in Galway yesterday, that I was to come across the lake this morning, and the tidings may have come up by some fellow-traveller. He would drop word with some of the boys at Ballintubber as he passed by. And they might have thought it likely that I should go to Headford. They have had their chance on this occasion, and they have not done any good with it."

CHAPTER XXII.

MORONY CASTLE IS BOYCOTTED.

THE men seemed to make a good joke of the afternoon's employment, but not so the young ladies. In the evening they had a little music, and Captain Clayton declared that the Miss

Ormesbys were grand performers. "And I am told that they are lovely girls," said Ada.

"Well, yes; lovely is a very strong word."

"I'd rather be called lovely than anything," said Ada.

"Now, Captain Clayton," said Edith, "if you wish for my respect, don't fall into the trap which Ada has so openly laid for you."

"I meant nothing of the kind," said Ada. "I hope that Captain Clayton knows me better. But, Captain Clayton, you don't mean that you'll walk down to the boat to-morrow?"

"Why not? He'll never have the pluck to fire at me two days running. And I doubt whether he'll allow me so fair a chance of seeing him."

"I wonder how you can sleep at night, knowing that such a man as this is always after your life."

"I wonder whether he sleeps at night, when he thinks such a man as I am after his life. And I allow him, to boot, all his walks and hiding-places." Then Ada began to implore him not to be too rash. She endeavoured to teach him that no good could come from such foolhardiness. If his life was of no value to himself, it was of great value to others;—to his mother, for instance, and to his sister. "A man's life is of no real value," said the Captain, "until he has got a wife and family—or at any rate, a wife."

"You don't think the wife that is to be need mind it?" said Edith.

"The wife that is to be must be in the clouds, and in all probability, will never come any nearer. I cannot allow that a man can be justified in neglecting his duties for the sake of a cloudy wife."

"Not in neglecting absolute duties," said Ada, sadly.

"A man in my position neglects his duty if he leaves a stone unturned in pursuit of such a blackguard as this. And when a man is used to it, he likes it. There's your brother quite enjoyed being shot at, just as though he were resident magistrate; at any rate, he looked as though he did."

So the conversation went on through the evening, during the whole of which poor Florian made one of the party. He said very little, but sat close to his sister Edith, who frequently had his hand in her own. The Captain constantly had his eye upon him without seeming to watch him, but still was thinking of him as the minutes flew by. It was not that the boy was in danger; for the Captain thought the danger to be small, and that it was reduced almost to nothing as long as he remained in the house,—but what would be the effect of fear on the boy's mind? And if he were thus harassed could he be expected to give his evidence in a clear manner? Mr. Jones was not present after dinner, having retired at once to his own room. But just as the girls had risen to go to bed, and as Florian was preparing to accompany them, Peter brought a message saying that Mr. Jones would be glad to see Captain Clayton before he went for the night. Then the Captain got up, and bidding them all farewell, followed Peter to Mr. Jones's room. "I shall go on by the early boat," he said as he was leaving the room.

"You'll have breakfast first, at any rate," said Ada. The Captain swore that he wouldn't, and the girls swore that he should. "We never let anybody go without breakfast," said Ada.

"And particularly not a man," said Edith, "who has just been shot at on our behalf." But the Captain explained that it might be as well that he should be down waiting for the boat half an hour at any rate before it started.

"I and Hunter," said he, "would have a fair look-out around us there, so that no one could get within rifle shot of us without our seeing them, and they won't look out for us so early. I don't think much of Mr. Lax's courage, but it may be as well to keep a watch when it can be so easily done." Then Ada went off to her bed, resolving that the breakfast should be ready, though it was an hour before the boat time. The boat called at the wharf at eight in the morning, and the wharf was three miles distant from the house. She could manage to have breakfast ready at half-past six.

"Ada, my girl," said Edith, as they departed together, "don't you make a fool of that young man."

"What do you mean by that?"

"Didn't you tell me that a man who has to be shot at ought not to be married; and didn't he say that he would leave his future wife up among the clouds?"

"He may leave her where he likes for me," said Ada. "When a man is doing so much for us oughtn't he to have his breakfast ready for him at half-past six o'clock?" There was no more then said between them on that subject; but Edith resolved that as far as boiling the water was concerned, she would be up as soon as Ada.

When the Captain went into Mr. Jones's room he was asked to sit down, and had a cigar offered to him. "Thanks, no; I don't think I'll smoke. Smoking may have some sort of effect on a fellow's hand. There's a gentleman in these parts who I should be sorry should owe his life to any little indulgence of that sort on my behalf."

"You are thinking of the man who fired at you?"

"Well, yes; I am. Not that I shall have any chance at him just at present. He won't come near me again this visit. The next that I shall hear from him will be from round some corner in the neighbourhood of Galway. I think I know every turn in that blackguard's mind."

"Have you been speaking to Florian about him, Captain Clayton?"

"Not a word."

"Nor has his brother?"

"I think not."

"What am I to do about the poor boy?" said the anxious father.

"Because of his fear about this very man?"

"He is only a boy, you know."

"Of course he is only a boy. You've no right to expect from him the pluck of a man. When he is as old as his brother he'll have his brother's nerve. I like to see a man plucky under fire when he is not used to it. When you've got into the way of it, it means nothing."

"What am I to do about Florian? There are four months before the assizes. He cannot remain in the house for four months."

"What would he be at the end of it?" said the Captain. "That is what we have to think of."

"Would it alter him?"

"I suppose it would,—if he were here with his sister, talking of nothing but this wretched man, who seems to haunt him. We have to remember, Mr. Jones, how long it was before he came forward with his story."

"I think he will be firm with it now."

"No doubt,—if he had to tell it out in direct evidence. When he is there in the court telling it, he will not think much of Mr. Lax, nor even of Pat Carroll, who will be in the dock glaring at him; nor would he think much of anything but his direct story, while a friendly barrister is drawing it out of him; but when it comes to his cross-examination, it will be different. He will want all his pluck then, and all the simplicity which he can master. You must remember that a skilful man will have been turned loose on him with all the ferocity of a bloodhound; a man will have all the cruelty of Lax, but will have nothing to fear; a man who will be serving his purpose all round if he can only dumbfound that poor boy by his words and his looks. A man, when he has taken up the cause of these ruffians, learns to sympathise with them. If they hate the Queen, hate the laws, hate all justice, these men learn to hate them too. When they get hold of me, and I look into the eyes of such a one, I see there my bitterest enemy. He holds Captain Yorke Clayton up to the hatred of the whole court, as though he were a brute unworthy of the slightest mercy,—a venomous reptile, against whom the whole country should rise to tear him in pieces. And I look round and see the same feeling written in the eyes of them all. I found it more hard to get used to that than to the snap of a pistol; but I have got used to it. Poor Florian will have had no such experience. And there will be no mercy shown to him because he is only a boy. Neither sex nor age is supposed to render any such feeling necessary to a lawyer. A lawyer in defending the worst ruffian that ever committed a crime will know that he is called upon to spare nothing that is tender. He is absolved from all the laws common to humanity. And then poor Florian has lied." A gloomy look of sad, dull pain came across the father's brow as he heard these words. "We must look it in the face, Mr. Jones."

"Yes, look it all in the face."

"He has repeated the lie again and again for six months. He has been in close friendship with these men. It will be made out that he has been present at all their secret meetings. He has been present at some of them. It will be very hard to get a jury to convict on his evidence if it be unsupported."

"Shall we withdraw him?" asked Mr. Jones.

"You cannot do it. His deposition has been sworn and put forward in the proper course. Besides it is his duty and yours, —and mine," he added. "He must tell his story once again, and must endure whatever torment the law-rebels of the court have in store for him. Only it will be well to think what course of treatment may best prepare him for the trial. You should treat him with the greatest kindness."

"He is treated kindly."

"But you, I think, and his sisters and his brother should endeavour to make him feel that you do not think harshly of him because of the falsehoods he has told. Go out with him occasionally." Here Mr. Jones raised his eyebrows as feeling surprised at the kind of counsel given. "Put some constraint on yourself so as to make him feel by the time he has to go into court with you that he has a friend with him."

"I trust that he always feels that," said Mr. Jones.

They went on discussing the matter till late at night, and Captain Clayton made the father understand what it was that he intended. He meant that the boy should be made to know that his father was to him as are other fathers, in spite of the lie which he had told, and of the terrible trouble which he had caused by telling it. But Mr. Jones felt that the task imposed upon him would be almost impossible. He was heavy at heart, and unable to recall to himself his old spirits. He had been thoroughly ashamed of his son, and was not possessed of that agility of heart which is able to leap into good humour at once. Florian had been restored to his old manner of life; sitting at table with his father and occasionally spoken to by him. He had been so far forgiven; but the father was still aware that there was still a dismal gap between himself and his younger boy, as regarded that affectionate intercourse which Captain Clayton recommended. And yet he knew that it was needed, and resolved that he would do his best, however imperfectly it might be done.

On the next morning the Captain went his way, and did ample homage to the kindly exertions made on his behalf by the two girls. "Now I know you must have been up all night, for you couldn't have done it all without a servant in the house."

"How dare you belittle our establishment!" said Ada. 'What do you think of Peter? Is Peter nobody? And, it was poor Florian who boiled the kettle. I really don't know whether we should not get on better altogether without servants than with them." The breakfast was eaten both by the Captain in the parlour and by Hunter in the kitchen in great good humour. "Now, my fine fellow," said the former, "have you got your pistols ready? I don't think we shall want them this morning, but it's as well not to give these fellows a chance." Hunter was pleased by being thus called into council before the young ladies, and they both started in the highest good humour. Captain Clayton, as he went, told himself that Ada Jones was the prettiest girl of his acquaintance. His last sentimental affinity with the youngest Miss Ormesby waxed feeble and insipid as he thought of Ada. Perhaps Edith, he said to himself, is the sharpest of the two, but in good looks she can't hold a candle to her sister. So he passed on, and with his myrmidon reached Galway, without incurring any impediment from Mr. Lax.

In the course of the morning, Mr. Jones sent for Florian, and proposed to walk out with him about the demesne. "I don't think there will be any danger," he said. "Captain Clayton went this morning, and the people don't know yet whether he has gone. I think it is better that you should get accustomed to it, and not give way to idle fears." The boy apparently agreed to this, and got his hat. But he did not leave the shelter of the house without sundry misgivings. Mr. Jones had determined to act at once upon the Captain's advice, and had bethought himself that he could best do so by telling the whole truth to the boy. "Now, Florian, I think it would be as well that you and I should understand each other." Florian looked up at him with fearful eyes, but made no reply. "Of course I was angry with you while you were hesitating about those ruffians."

"Yes; you were," said Florian.

"I can quite understand that you have felt a difficulty."

"Yes, I did," said Florian.

"But that is all over now."

"If they don't fire at me it is over, I suppose, till August."

"They shan't fire at you. Don't be afraid. If they fire at you, they must fire at me too." The father was walking with his arm about the boy's neck. "You, at any rate, shall incur no danger which I do not share. You will understand—won't you—that my anger against you is passed and gone?"

"I don't know," said the boy.

"It is so,—altogether. I hope to be able to send you to school in England very soon after the trial is over. You shall go to Mr. Monro at first, and to Winchester afterwards, if I can manage it. But we won't think of Winchester just at present. We must do the best we can to get a good place for you on your first going into the school."

"I am not afraid about that," said Florian, thinking that at the time when the school should have come all the evils of the trials would have been passed away and gone.

"All the same you might come and read with me every morning for an hour, and then for an hour with each of your sisters. You will want something to do to make up your time. And remember, Florian, that all my anger has passed away. We will be the best of friends, as in former days, so that when the time shall have come for you to go into court, you may be quite sure that you have a friend with you there."

To all this Florian made very little reply; but Mr. Jones remembered that he could not expect to do much at a first attempt. Weary as the task would be he would persevere. For the task would be weary even with his own son. He was a man who could do nothing graciously which he could not do *con amore*. And he felt that all immediate warm liking for the poor boy had perished in his heart. The boy had made himself the friend of such a one as Pat Carroll, and in his friendship for him had lied grossly. Mr. Jones had told himself that it was his duty to forgive him, and had struggled to perform his duty. For the performance of any deed necessary for the boy's security, he could count upon himself. But he could not be happy in his company as he was with Edith. The boy had been foully untrue to him—but still he would do his best.

CHAPTER XXIII.

TOM DALY IS BOYCOTTED.

WHEN the time came round, Frank Jones started for Ballinasloe, with his father's cattle and with Peter to help him. They did succeed in getting a boy to go with them, who had been seduced by a heavy bribe to come down for the purpose from Ballinasloe to Morony Castle. As he had been used to cattle, Peter's ignorance and Frank's also were of less account. They drove the cattle to Tuam, and there got them on the railway, the railway with its servants being beyond the power of the boycotters. At Ballinasloe they could not sell the cattle, as the name of Mr. Jones of Morony had become terribly notorious throughout County Galway. But arrangements had been made to send them to a salesman up in Dublin, and from Ballinasloe they had gone under the custody of Peter and the boy. No attempt was made absolutely to harm the beasts, or even to stop them in the streets. But throughout the town it seemed to be perfectly understood that they were the property of Philip Jones of Morony Castle, and that Philip Jones had been boycotted by the League. The poor beasts were sent on to Dublin without a truss of hay among them, and even Frank himself was refused a meal at the first inn at which he had called. He did afterwards procure accommodation; but he heard while in the house, that the innkeeper was threatened for what he had done. Had it not been that Peter had brought with him a large basket of provisions for himself and the boy, they, too, would have been forced to go on dinnerless and supperless to Dublin.

Frank, on his way back home, resolved that he would call on Mr. Daly at Daly's Bridge, near Castle Blakeney. It was Daly's wont to live at Daly's Bridge when the hounds were not hunting, though he would generally go four or five times a week from Daly's Bridge to the kennels. To Castle Blakeney a public car was running, and the public car did not dare or probably did not wish, to boycott anyone. He walked up to the open door at Daly's Bridge and soon found himself in the presence of Black Tom Daly. "So you are boycotted?" said Tom.

"Horse, foot, and dragoons," said Frank.

"What's to come of it, I wonder?" Tom as he said this was sitting at an open window making up some horse's drug to which was attached some very strong odour. "I am boycotted too, and the poor hounds, which have given hours of amusement to many of these wretches, for which they have not been called upon to pay a shilling. I shall have to sell the pack, I'm afraid," said Tom, sadly.

"Not yet, I hope, Mr. Daly."

"What do you mean by that? Who's to keep them without any subscription? And who's to subscribe without any prospect of hunting? For the matter of that who's to feed the poor dumb brutes? One pack will be boycotted after another till not a pack of hounds will be wanted in all Ireland."

"Has the same thing happened to any other pack?" asked Frank.

"Certainly it has. They turned out against the Muskerry; and there's been a row in Kildare. We are only at the beginning of it yet."

"I don't suppose it will go on for ever," said Frank.

"Why don't you suppose so? What's to be the end of it all? Do you see any way out of it?—for I do not. Does your father see his way to bringing those meadows back into his hands? I'm told that some of those fellows shot at Clayton the other day down at Headford. How are we to expect a man like Clayton to come foward and be shot at in that fashion? As far as I can see there will be no possibility for anyone to live in this country again. Of course it's all over with me. I haven't got any rents to speak of, and the only property I possess is now useless."

"What property?" asked Frank.

"What property?" rejoined Tom in a voice of anger. "What property? Ain't the hounds property, or were property a few weeks ago? Who'll subscribe for next year? We had a meeting in February, you know, and the fellows put down their names the same as ever. But they can't be expected to pay when there will be no coverts for them to draw. The country can do nothing to put a stop to this blackguardism. When they've passed this Coercion Bill they're going to have some sort of Land Bill,—just a law to give away the land to somebody. What's to come of the poor country with such men as Mr. Gladstone and Mr. Bright to govern it? They're the two very worst men in the whole empire for governing a country. Martial law with a regiment in each county, and a strong colonel to carry it out,—that is the only way of governing left us. I don't pretend to understand politics, but every child can see that. And you should do away with the constituencies, at any rate for the next five years. What are you to expect with such a set of men as that in Parliament,—men whom no one would speak to if they were to attempt to ride to hounds in County Galway? It makes me sick when I hear of it."

Such were Tom Daly's sad outlooks into the world. And sad as they were, they seemed to be justified by circumstances as they operated upon him. There could be no hunting in County Galway next session unless things were to change very much for the better. And there was no prospect of any such change. "It's nonsense talking of a poor devil like me being ruined. You ask me what property I have got."

"I don't think I ever asked that," said Frank.

"It don't matter. You're quite welcome. You'll find eight or nine pair of leather breeches in that press in there. And round about the room somewhere there are over a dozen pair of top-boots. They are the only available property I have got. They are paid for, and I can do what I please with them. The four or five hundred acres over there on the road to Tuam are mostly bog, and are strictly entailed so that I cannot touch them. As there is not a tenant will pay the rent since I've been boycotted it doesn't make much matter. I have not had a shilling from them for more than twelve months; and I don't suppose I ever shall see another. The poor hounds are eating their heads off; as fine a pack of hounds as any man ever owned, as far as their number goes. I can't keep them, and who'll buy them? They tell me I must send them over to Tattersall's. But as things are now I don't suppose they'll pay the expense. I don't care who knows it, but I haven't three hundred pounds in the world. And I'm over fifty years of age. What do you think of that as the condition for a man to be brought to?"

Frank Jones had never heard Daly speak at such length before, nor had he given him credit for so much eloquence. Nor, indeed, had anyone in the County of Galway heard him speak so many words till this misfortune had fallen upon him. And he would still be silent and reserved with all except a few hunting men whom he believed to be strongly influenced by the same political feeling as he was himself. Here was he boycotted most cruelly, but not more cruelly than was Mr. Jones of Morony Castle. The story of Florian Jones had got about the county, and had caused Mr. Jones to be pitied greatly by such men as Tom Daly. "His own boy to turn against him!" Tom had said. "And to become a Papist! A boy of ten years old to call himself a Papist, as if he would know anything about it. And then to lie,—to lie like that! I feel that his case is almost worse than mine." Therefore he had burst out with his sudden eloquence to Frank Jones, whom he had liked. "Oh, yes! I can send you over to Woodlawn Station. I have got a horse and car left about the place. Here's William Persse of Galway. He's the stanchest man we have in the county, but even he can do nothing."

Then Mr. Persse rode into the yard,—that Mr. Persse who, when the hounds met at Ballytowngal, had so strongly dissuaded Daly from using his pistol. He was a man who was reputed to have a good income, or at any rate a large estate,—though the two things at the present moment were likely to have a very various meaning. But he was a man less despondent in his temperament than Tom Daly, and one that was likely to prevail with Tom by the strength of his character. "Well, Tom," said Persse, as he walked into the house, "how are things using you now? How are you, Jones? I'm afraid your father is getting it rather hot at Morony Castle."

"They've boycotted us, that's all."

"So I understand. Is it not odd that some self-appointed individual should send out an edict, and that suddenly all organised modes of living among people should be put a stop to! Here's Tom not allowed to get a packet of greaves into his establishment unless he sends to Dublin for it."

"Nor to have it sent over here," said Tom, "unless I'll send my own horse and cart to fetch it. And every man and boy I have about the place is desired to leave me at the command of some d——d O'Toole, whose father kept a tinker's shop somewhere in County Mayo, and whose mother took in washing."

There was a depth of scorn intended to be conveyed by all this, because in Daly's estimation County Mayo was but a poor county to live in, as it had not for many a year possessed an advertised pack of foxhounds. And the O'Tooles were not one of the tribes of Galway, or a clan especially esteemed in that most aristocratic of the western counties.

"Have all the helpers gone?"

"I haven't asked them to stay; but unless they have stayed of their own accord I have just shaken hands with them. It's all that one gentleman can do to another when he meets him."

"Mr. Daly is talking of selling the hounds," said Frank Jones.

"Not quite yet, Tom," said Mr. Persse. "You mustn't do anything in a hurry."

"They'll have to starve if they remain here," said the master of hounds.

"I have come over here to say a word about them. I don't suppose this kind of thing will last for ever, you know."

"Can you see any end to it?" said the other.

"Not as yet I can't, except that troubles when they come generally do have an end. We always think that evils will last for ever,—and blessings too. When two-year-old ewes went up to three pound ten at Ballinasloe, we thought that we were to get that price for ever, but they were soon down to two seventeen six; and when we had had two years of the potato famine, we thought that there would never be another potato in County Galway. For the last five years we've had them as fine at Doneraile as ever I saw them. Nobody is ever quite ruined, or quite has his fortune made."

"I am very near the ruin," said Tom Daly.

"I would struggle to hold on a little longer yet," said the other. "How many horses have you got here and at Ahaseragh?"

"There are something over a dozen," said Tom. "There may be fifteen in all. I was thinking of sending a draught over to Tattersall's next week. There are some of them would not be worth a five-and-twenty pound note when you got them there!"

"Well, now I'll tell you what I propose. You shall send over four or five to be summered at Doneraile. There is grass enough there, and though I can't pay my debts, my credit is good at the corn-chandler's." Black Tom, as he heard this, sat still looking blacker than ever. He was a man who hated to have a favour offered to him. But he could bear the insult better from Persse of Doneraile than from anyone else in the county. "I've talked the matter over with Lynch——"

"D—— Lynch," said Daly. He didn't dislike Sir Jasper, but Sir Jasper did not stand quite so high in his favour as did Mr. Persse of Doneraile.

"You needn't d—— anybody; but just listen to me. Sir Jasper says that he will take three, and Nicholas Bodkin will do the same."

"They are both baronets," said Daly. "I hate a man with a handle to his name; he always seems to me to be stuck-up, as though he demanded something more than other people. There is that Lord Ardrahan——"

"A very good fellow too. Don't you be an ass. Lord Ardrahan has offered to take three more."

"I knew it," said Tom.

"It's not as though any favour were offered or received. Though the horses are your own property, they are kept for the services of the hunt. We all understand very well how things are circumstanced at present."

"How do you think I am to feed my hounds if you take away the horses which they would eat?" said Daly, with an attempt at a grim joke. But after the joke Tom became sad again, almost to tears, and he allowed his friend to make almost what arrangements he pleased for distributing both hounds and horses among the gentry of the hunt. "And when they are gone," said he, "I am to sit here alone with nothing on earth to do. What on earth is to become of me when I have not a hound left to give a dose of physic to?"

"We'll not leave you in such a sad strait as that," said Mr. Persse.

"It will be sad enough. If you had had a pack of hounds to look after for thirty summers, you wouldn't like to get rid of them in a hurry. I'm like an old nurse who is sending her babies out, or some mother, rather, who is putting her children into the workhouse because she cannot feed them herself. It is sad, though you don't see it in that light."

Frank Jones got home to Castle Morony that night full of sorrow and trouble. The cattle had been got off to Dublin in their starved condition, but he, as he had come back, had been boycotted every yard of the way. He could get in no car, nor yet in all Tuam could he secure the services of a boy to carry his bag for him. He learned in the town that the girls had sent over to purchase a joint of meat, but had been refused at every shop. "Is trade so plentiful," asked Frank, "that you can afford to do without it?"

"We can't afford to do with it," said the butcher, "if it's to come from Morony Castle."

CHAPTER XXIV.

"FROM THE FULL HEART THE MOUTH SPEAKS."

ADA was making the beds upstairs, and Edith was churning the butter down below in the dairy, when a little bare-footed boy came in with a letter.

"Please, miss, it's from the Captain, and he says I'm not to stir out of this till I come back with an answer."

The letter was delivered to Edith at the dairy door, and she saw that it was addressed to herself. She had never before seen the Captain's handwriting, and she looked at it somewhat curiously. "If he's to write to one of us it should be to Ada," she said to herself, laughing. Then she opened the envelope, which enclosed a large square stout letter. It contained a card and a written note, and on the card was an invitation, as follows: "The Colonel and Officers of the West Bromwich Regiment request the pleasure of the company of Mr. Jones, the Misses Jones, and Mr. Francis Jones to a dance at the Galway Barracks, on the 20th of May, 1881. Dancing to commence at ten o'clock."

Then there was the note, which Edith read before she took the card upstairs.

"My dear Miss Jones," the letter began. Edith again looked at the envelope and perceived that the despatch had been certainly addressed to herself—Miss Edith Jones; but between herself and her sister there could be no jealousy as to the opening of a letter. Letters for one were generally intended for the other also. "I hope you will both come. You ought to do so to show the county that, though you are boycotted, you are not smashed, and to let them understand that you are not afraid to come out of the house although certain persons have made themselves terrible. I send this to you instead of to your sister, because perhaps you have a little higher pluck. But do tell your father from me that I think he ought, as a matter of policy, to insist on your both coming. You could come down by the boat one day and return the next; and I'll meet you, for fear your brother should not be there.—Yours very faithfully,

"YORKE CLAYTON.

"I have got the fellows of the West Bromwich to entrust the card to me, and have undertaken to see it duly delivered. I hope you'll approve of my Mercury. Hunter says he doesn't care how often he's shot at."

It was, in the first place, necessary to provide for the Mercury because even a god cannot be sent away after the performance of such a journey without some provisions; and Edith, to tell the truth, wanted to look at the ball all round before she ventured to express an opinion to her sister and father. Her father, of course, would not go; but should he be left alone at Morony Castle to the tender mercies of Peter? And should Florian be left also without any woman's hands to take charge of him? And the butter, too, was on the point of coming, which was a matter of importance. But at last, having pulled off her butter-making apron and having duly patted the roll of butter, she went upstairs to her sister.

"Ada," she said, "here is such a letter;" and she held up the letter and the card.

"Who is it from?"

"You must guess," said Edith.

"I am bad at guessing, I cannot guess. Is it Mr. Blake of Carnlough?"

"A great deal more interesting than that."

"It can't be Captain Clayton," said Ada.

"Out of the full heart the mouth speaks. It is Captain Clayton."

"What does he say, and what is the card? Give it me. It looks like an invitation."

"Then it tells no story, because it is an invitation. It is from the officers of the West Bromwich regiment; and it asks us to a dance on the 20th of May."

"But that's not from Captain Clayton."

"Captain Clayton has written,—to me and not to you at all. You will be awfully jealous; and he says that I have twice as much courage as you."

"That's true, at any rate," said Ada, in a melancholy tone.

"Yes; and as the officers want all the girls at the ball to be at any rate as brave as themselves, that's a matter of great importance. He has asked me to go with a pair of pistols in my belt; but he is afraid that you would not shoot anybody."

"May I not look at his letter?"

"Oh, no! That would not be at all proper. The letter is addressed to me, Miss Edith Jones. And as it has come from such a very dashing young man, and pays me particular compliments as to my courage, I don't think I shall let anybody else see it. It doesn't say anything special about beauty, which I think uncivil. If he had been writing to you, it would have all been about feminine loveliness of course."

"What nonsense you do talk, Edith!"

"Well, there it is. As you will read it you must. You'll be awfully disappointed, because there is not a word about you in it."

Then Ada read the letter. "He says he hopes we shall both come."

"Well, yes! Your existence is certainly implied in those words."

"He explains why he writes to you instead of me."

"Another actual reference to yourself, no doubt. But then he goes on to talk of my pluck."

"He says it's a little higher than mine," said Ada, who was determined to extract from the Captain's words as much good as was possible, and as little evil to herself.

"So it is; only a little higher pluck! Of course he means that I can't come near himself."

"You wouldn't pretend to?" asked Ada.

"What! to be shot at like him, and to like it. I don't know any girl that can come quite up to that. Only if one becomes quite cock-sure, as he is, that one won't be hit, I don't see the courage."

"Oh, I do."

"But now about this ball?" said Edith. "Here we are, lone damsels, making butter in our father's halls, and turning down the beds in the lady's chamber, unable to buy anything because we are boycotted, and with no money to buy it if we were not. And we can't stir out of the house lest we should be shot, and I don't suppose that such a thing as a pair of gloves is to be got anywhere."

"I've got gloves for both of us," said Ada.

"Put by for a rainy day. What a girl you are for providing for difficulties! And you've got silk stockings too, I shouldn't wonder."

"Of course I have."

"And two ball dresses, quite new?"

"Not quite new. They are those we wore at Hacketstown before the flood."

"Good gracious! how were Noah's daughters dressed? Or were they dressed at all?"

"You always turn everything into nonsense," said Ada, petulantly.

"To be told I'm to wear a dress that had touched the heart of a patriarch, and had perhaps gone well-nigh to make me a patriarch's bride! But taking it for granted that the ball dresses with all their appurtenances are here, fit to win the heart of a modern Captain instead of an old patriarch, is there no other reason why we should not go?"

"What reason?" asked Ada, in a melancholy tone.

"There are reasons. You go to papa, and see whether he has not reasons. He will tell you that every shilling should be saved for Florian's school."

"It won't take many shillings to go to Galway. We couldn't well write to Captain Clayton and tell him that we can't afford it."

"People keep those reasons in the background," said Edith, "though people understand them. And then papa will say that in our condition we ought to be ashamed to show our faces."

"What have we done amiss?"

"Not you or I perhaps," said Edith; "but poor Florian. I am determined,—and so are you,—to take Florian to our very hearts, and to forgive him as though this thing had never been done. He is to us the same darling boy, as though he had never been present at the flood-gates; as though he had had no hand in bringing these evils to Morony Castle. You and I have been angry, but we have forgiven him. To us he is as dear as ever he was. But they know in the county what it was that was done by Florian Jones, and they talk about it among themselves, and they speak of you and me as Florian's sisters. And they speak of papa as Florian's father. I think it may well be that papa should not wish us to go to this ball."

Then there came a look of disappointment over Ada's face, as though her doom had already been spoken. A ball to Ada, and especially a ball at Galway,—a coming ball,—was a promise of infinite enjoyment; but a ball with Captain Yorke Clayton would be heaven on earth. And by the way in which this invitation had come he had been secured as a partner for the evening. He could not write to them, and especially call upon them to come without doing all he could to make the evening pleasant for them. She included Edith in all these promises of pleasantness. But Edith, if the thing was to be done at all, would do it all for Ada. As for the danger in which the man passed his life, that must be left in the hands of God. Looking at it with great seriousness, as in the midst of her joking she did look at these things, she told herself that Ada was very lovely, and that this man was certainly lovable. And she had taken it into her imagination that Captain Clayton was certainly in the road to fall in love with Ada. Why should not Ada have her chance? And why should not the Captain have his? Why should she not have her chance of having a gallant lovable gentleman for a brother-in-law? Edith was not at all prepared to give the world up for lost, because Pat Carroll had made himself a brute, and because the neighbours were idiots and had boycotted them. It must all depend upon their father, whether they should or should not go to the ball. And she had not thought it prudent to appear too full of hope when talking of it to Ada; but for herself she quite agreed with the Captain that policy required them to go.

"I suppose you would like it?" she said to her sister.

"I always was fond of dancing," replied Ada.

"Especially with heroes."

"Of course you laugh at me, but Captain Clayton won't be there as an officer; he's only a resident magistrate."

"He's the best of all the officers," said Edith with enthusiasm. "I won't have our hero run down. I believe him to have twice as much in him as any of the officers. He's the gallantest fellow I know. I think we ought to go, if it's only because he wants it."

"I don't want not to go," said Ada.

"I daresay not; but papa will be the difficulty."

"He'll think more of you than of me, Edith. Suppose you go and talk to him."

So it was decided; and Edith went away to her father, leaving Ada still among the beds. Of Frank not a word had been spoken. Frank would go as a matter of course if Mr. Jones consented. But Ada, though she was left among the beds, did not at once go on with her work; but sat down on that special bed by which her attention was needed, and thought of the circumstances which surrounded her. Was it a fact that she was in love with the Captain? To be in love to her was a very serious thing,—but so delightful. She had been already once,—well, not in love, but preoccupied just a little in thinking of one young man. The one young man was an officer, but was now in India, and Ada had not ventured even to mention his name in her father's presence. Edith had of course known the secret, but Edith had frowned upon it. She had said that Lieutenant Talbot was no better than a stick, although he had £400 a year of his own. "He'd give you nothing to talk about," said Edith, "but his £400 a year." Therefore when Lieutenant Talbot went to India, Ada Jones did not break her heart. But now Edith called Captain Clayton a hero, and seemed in all respects to approve of him; and Edith seemed to think that he certainly admired Ada. It was a dreadful thing to have to fall in love with a woodcock. Ada felt that if, as things went on, the woodcock should become her woodcock, the bullet which reached his heart would certainly pierce her own bosom also. But such was the way of the world. Edith had seemed to think that the man was entitled to have a lady of his own to love; and if so, Ada seemed to think that the place would be one very well suited to herself. Therefore she was anxious for the ball; and at the present moment thought only of the difficulties to be incurred by Edith in discussing the matter with her father.

"Papa, Captain Clayton wants us to go to a ball at Galway:" it was thus that Edith began her task.

"Wants you to go to a ball! What has Captain Clayton to do with you two?"

"Nothing on earth;—at any rate not with me. Here is his letter, which speaks for itself. He seems to think that we should show ourselves to everybody around, to let them know that we are not crushed by what such a one as Pat Carroll can do to us."

"Who says that we are crushed?"

L

"It is the people who are crushed that generally say so of themselves. There would be nothing unusual under ordinary circumstances in your daughter going to a ball at Galway."

"That's as may be."

"We can stay the night at Mrs. D'Arcy's, and she will be delighted to have us. If we never show ourselves it would be as though we acknowledged ourselves to be crushed. And to tell the truth, papa, I don't think it is quite fair to Ada to keep her here always. She is very beautiful, and at the same time fond of society. She is doing her duty here bravely; there is nothing about the house that she will not put her hand to. She is better than any servant for the way she does her work. I think you ought to let her go; it is but for the one night."

"And you?" asked the father.

"I must go with her, I suppose, to keep her company."

"And are not you fond of society?"

"No;—not as she is. I like the rattle very well just for a few minutes."

"And are not you beautiful?" he asked.

"Good gracious, no! Don't be such a goose, papa."

"To me you are quite as lovely as is Ada."

"Because you are only a stupid, old papa," but she kissed him as she said it. "You have no right to expect to have two beauties in the family. If I were a beauty I should go away and leave you, as will Ada. It's her destiny to be carried off by someone. Why not by some of these gallant fellows at Galway? It's my destiny to remain at home; and so you may know what you have got to expect."

"If it should turn out to be so, there will be one immeasurable comfort for me in the midst of all my troubles."

"It shall be so," said she, whispering into his ear. "But, papa, you will let us go to this ball in Galway, will you not? Ada has set her heart upon it." So the matter was settled.

The answer to Captain Clayton, sent by Edith, was as follows; but it was not sent till the boy aad been allowed to stuff himself with buttered toast and tea, which, to such a boy, is the acme of all happiness.

"Morony Castle, 8th of May, 1881.

"Dear Captain Clayton,

"We will both come, of course, and are infinitely obliged to you for the trouble you have taken on our behalf. Papa will not come, of course. Frank will, no doubt; but he is out after a salmon in the Hacketstown river. I hope he will get one, as we are badly off for provisions. If he cannot find a salmon, I hope he will find a trout, or we shall have nothing for three days running. Ada and I think we can manage a leg of mutton between us, as far as the cooking goes, but we haven't had a chance of trying our hands yet. Frank, however, will write to the officers by post. We shall sleep the night at Mrs. D'Arcy's, and can get there very well by ourselves. All the same, we shall be delighted to see you, if you will come down to the boat.

"Yours very truly,
"EDITH JONES.

"I must tell you what Ada said about our dresses, only pray don't tell any of the officers. Of course we had to have a consultation about our frocks, because everything in the shops is boycotted for us. 'Oh,' said Ada, 'there are the gauze dresses we wore at Hacketstown *before the flood!*' Only think of Ada and I·at a ball with the Miss Noahs, four or five thousand years ago."

Frank consented to go of course, but not without some little difficulty. He didn't think it was a time for balls. According to his view of things ginger should be no longer hot in the mouth.

"But why not?" said Edith. "If a ball at any time is a good thing, why should it be bad now? Are we all to go into mourning, because Mr. Carroll has so decreed? For myself I don't care twopence for the ball. I don't think it is worth the ten shillings which it will cost. But I am all for showing that we don't care so much for Mr. Carroll."

"Carroll is in prison," said Frank.

"Nor yet for Terry Lax, or Tim Brady, or Terry Carroll, or Tony Brady. The world is not to be turned away from its proper course by such a scum of men as that. Of course you'll do as a brother should do, and come with us."

To this Frank assented, and on the next day went out for another salmon, thinking no more about the party at Galway.

But the party at Galway was a matter of infinite trouble and infinite interest to the two girls. Those dresses which had been put by from before the flood were brought forth, and ironed, and re-ribboned, and re-designed, as though the fate of heroes and heroines depended upon them. And it was clearly intended that the fate of one hero and of one heroine should depend on them, though nothing absolutely to that effect was said at present between the sisters. It was not said, but it was understood by both of them that it was so; and each understood what was in the heart of the other. "Dear, dear Edith," said Ada. "Let them boycott us as they will," said Edith, "but my pet shall be as bright as any of them." There was a ribbon that had not been tossed, a false flower that had on it something of the bloom of newness. A faint offer was made by Ada to abandon some of these prettinesses to her sister, but Edith would have none of them. Edith pooh-poohed the idea as though it were monstrous. "Don't be a goose, Ada," she said; "of course this is to be your night. What does it signify what I wear?"

"Oh, but it does;—just the same as for me. I don't see why you are not to be just as nice as myself."

"That's not true, my dear."

"Why not true? There is quite as much depends on your good fortune as on mine. And then you are so much the cleverer of the two."

Then when the day for the ball drew near, there came to be some more serious conversation between them.

"Ada, love, you mean to enjoy yourself, don't you?"

"If I can I will. When I go to these things I never know whether they will lead to enjoyment or the reverse. Some little thing happens so often, and every thing seems to go wrong."

"They shouldn't go wrong with you, my pet."

"Why not with me as well as with others?"

"Because you are so beautiful to look at. You are made to be queen of a ball-room; not a London ball-room, where everything, I take it, is flash and faded, painted and stale, and worn out; but down here in the country, where there is some life among us, and where a girl may be supposed to be excited over her dancing. It is in such rooms as this that hearts are won and lost; a bid made for diamonds is all that is done in London."

"I never was at a London ball," said Ada.

"Nor I either; but one reads of them. I can fancy a man really caring for a girl down in Galway. Can you fancy a man caring for a girl?"

"I don't know," said Ada.

"For yourself, now?"

"I don't think anybody will ever care much for me."

"Oh, Ada, what a fib! It is all very pretty, your mock modesty, but it is so untrue. A man not love you! Why, I can fancy a man thinking that the gods could not allow him a greater grace than the privilege of taking you in his arms."

"Isn't anyone to take you in his arms, then?"

"No, no one. I am not a thing to be looked at in that light. I mean eventually to take to women's rights, and to make myself generally odious. Only I have promised to stick to papa, and I have got to do that first. You;——who will you stick to?"

"I don't know," said Ada.

"If I were to suggest Captain Yorke Clayton? If I were to suppose that he is the man who is to have the privilege?"

"Don't, Edith."

"He is my hero, and you are my pet, and I want to bring

you two together. I want to have my share in the hero; and still to keep a share in my pet. Is not that rational?"

"I don't know that there is anything rational in it all," said Ada. But still she went to bed well pleased that night.

CHAPTER XXV.

THE GALWAY BALL.

WHEN the 20th of May came, the three started off together for Galway, happy in spite of their boycotting. The girls at least were happy, though Frank was still somewhat sombre as he thought of the edict which Rachel O'Mahony had pronounced against him. When the boat arrived at the quay at Galway, Captain Clayton, with one of the officers of the West Bromwich, was there to meet it. "He is a wise man," whispered Edith to Ada, "he takes care to provide for number one."

"I don't see that at all," said Ada.

"That brave little warrior, who is four feet and a half high, is intended for my escort. Two is company and three is none. I quite agree as to that." Then they left the boat, and Edith so arranged the party that she was to walk between the small warrior and her brother, whereas Ada followed with Captain Clayton. In such straits of circumstances a man always has to do what he is told. Presence of mind and readiness is needful, but the readiness of a man is never equal to that of a woman. So they went off to Mrs. D'Arcy's house, and Ada enjoyed all the little preliminary sweets of the Captain's conversation. The words that were spoken all had reference to Edith herself; but they came from the Captain and were assuredly sweet.

"And it's really true that you are boycotted!" Mrs. D'Arcy asked.

"Certainly it's true."

"And what do they do to you? Do all the servants leave you?"

"Unless there be any like Peter who make up their minds to face the wrath of Land-leaguers. Peter has lived with us a long time, and has to ask himself whether it will be best for him to stay or go."

"And he stays? What a noble fellow!" said Mrs. D'Arcy.

"What would he do with himself if he didn't stay?" said Edith. "I don't suppose they'd shoot him, and he gets plenty to eat. The girls who were in the house and the young men about the place had friends of their own living near them, so they thought it better to go. Everybody of course does what is best for himself. And Peter, though he has suited himself, is already making a favour of it. Papa told him only yesterday that he might go himself if he pleased. Only think, we had to send all the horses last week into Galway to be shod ;—and then they wouldn't do it, except one man who made a tremendous favour of it, and after doing it charged double."

"But won't they sell you anything at Tuam?"

"Not a ha'porth. We couldn't get so much as soap for house-washing, unless Mrs. Blake had stood by us and let us have her soap. Ada and I have to do every bit of washing about the place. I do think well of Peter because he insists on washing his own shirts and stockings. Unfortunately we haven't got a mangle, and we have to iron the sheets if we want them to look at all nice. Ada's sheets and mine, and Florian's, are only just rough-pressed. Of course we get tea and those things down from Dublin. Only think of the way in which the tradespeople are ruining themselves. Everything has to go to Dublin to be sold; potatoes and cattle, and now butter. Papa says that they won't pay for the carriage. When you come to think of it, this boycotting is the most ruinous invention on both sides. When poor Florian declared that he would go to Mass after he had first told the story about Pat Carroll, they swore they would boycott the chapel if he entered the door. Not a single person would stay to receive the Mass. So he wouldn't go. It was not long after that when he became afraid to show his face outside the hall-door."

"And yet you can come here to this ball?" said Mrs. D'Arcy.

"Exactly so. I will go where I please till they boycott the very roads from under my feet. I expect to hear soon that they have boycotted Ada and me, so that no young man shall come and marry us. Of course, I don't understand such things, but it seems to me that the Government should interfere to defend us."

When the evening came, and the witching hour was there, Ada and Edith appeared at the barracks as bright as their second-hand finery could make them. They had awarded to them something of especial glory as being boycotted heroines, and were regarded with a certain amount of envy by the Miss Blakes, Miss Bodkins, Miss Lamberts, Miss Ffrenchs, and Miss Parsons of the neighbourhood. They had, none of them, as yet achieved the full honours of boycotting, though some of them were half-way to it. The Miss Ffrenchs told them how their father's sheep had been boycotted, the shepherd having been made to leave his place. The Miss Blakes had been boycotted because their brother had been refused a car. And the Bodkins of Ballytowngal were held to have been boycotted *en masse* because of the doings at Moytubber gorse. But none of them had been boycotted as had been the Miss Jones'; and therefore the Miss Jones' were the heroines of the evening.

"I declare it is very nice," Ada said to her sister that night, when they got home to Mrs. D'Arcy's, "because it got for us the pick of all the partners."

"It got for you one partner, at any rate," said Edith, "either the boycotting or something else." Edith had determined that it should be so; or had determined at any rate that it should seem to be so. In her resolution that the hero of the day should fall in love with her sister, she had almost taught herself to think that the process had already taken place. It was so natural that the bravest man should fall in love with the fairest lady, that Edith took it for granted that it already was so. She too in some sort was in love with her own sister. Ada to her was so fair, so soft, so innocent, so feminine and so lovable, that her very heart was in the project,—and the project that Ada should have the hero of the hour to herself. And yet she too had a heart of her own, and had told herself in so many words, that she herself would have loved the man,—had it been fitting that she should burden him with such a love. She had rejected the idea as unfitting, impossible, and almost unfeminine. There was nothing in her to attract the man. The idea had sprung up but for a moment, and had been cast out as being monstrous. There was Ada, the very queen of beauty. And the gallant hero was languishing in her smiles. It was thus that her imagination carried her on, after the notion had once been entertained. At the ball Edith did in fact dance with Captain Clayton quite as often as did Ada herself, but she danced with him, she said, as the darling sister of his supposed bride. All her talk had been about Ada,—because Edith had so chosen the subject. But with Ada the conversation had all been about Edith, because the Captain had selected the subject.

We all know how a little party is made up on such occasions. Though the party dance also with other people on occasions, they are there especially to dance with each other. An interloper or two now and again is very useful, so as to keep up appearances. The little warrior whom Edith had ill-naturedly declared to be four feet and a half high, but who was in truth five feet and a half, made up the former. Frank did not do much dancing, devoting himself to thinking of Rachel O'Mahony. The little man, who was a distinguished officer named Captain Butler, of the West Bromwich, had a very good time of it, dancing with Ada when Captain Clayton was not doing so. "The greatest brick I ever saw in my life!"—it was thus Captain Butler afterwards spoke of Edith, "but Ada is the girl for me, you know." Had Edith heard this, which she could not do, because she was then on the boat going back to Morony Castle, she would have informed Captain Butler that Ada was not the girl for him; but Captain Clayton, who heard the announcement made, did not seem to be much disturbed by it.

"It was a very nice party, Mrs. D'Arcy," said Edith the next morning.

"Was there a supper?"

"There was plenty to eat and drink, if you mean that, but we did not waste our time sitting down. I hate having to sit down opposite to a great ham when I am in the full tide of my emotions."

"There were emotions then?"

"Of course there were. What's the good of a ball without them? Fancy Captain Butler and no emotions, or Captain Clayton! Ask Ada if there were not. But as far as we were concerned, it was I who had the best of it. Captain Butler was my special man for the evening, and he had on a beautiful red jacket with gold buttons. You never saw anything so lovely. But Captain Clayton had just a simple black coat. That is so ugly, you know."

"Is Captain Clayton Ada's special young man?"

"Most particularly special, is he not, Ada?"

"What nonsense you do talk, Edith! He is not my special young man at all. I'm afraid he won't be any young woman's special young man very long, if he goes on as he does at present. Do you hear what he did over at Ardfry? There was some cattle to be seized for rent, and all the people on that side of the country were there. Ever so many shots were fired, and poor Hunter got wounded in his shoulder."

"He just had his skin raised," said Edith.

"And Captain Clayton got terribly mauled in the crowd. But he wouldn't fire a pistol at any of them. He brought some ringleader away prisoner,—he and two policemen. But they got all the cattle, and the tenants had to buy them back and pay their rent. When we try to seize cattle at Ballintubber they are always driven away to County Mayo. I do think that Captain Clayton is a real hero."

"Of course he is, my dear; that's given up to him long ago,—and to you."

In the afternoon they went home by boat, and Frank made himself disagreeable by croaking. "Upon my word," he said, "I think that this is hardly a fit time for giving balls."

"Ginger should not be hot in the mouth," said Edith.

"You may put it in what language you like, but that is about what I mean. The people who go to the balls cannot in truth afford it."

"That's the officers' look-out."

"And they are here on a very sad occasion. Everything is going to ruin in the country."

"I won't be put down by Pat Carroll," said Edith. "He

shall not be able to boast to himself that he has changed the natural course of my life."

"He has changed it altogether."

"You know what I mean. I am not going to yield to him or to any of them. I mean to hold my own against it as far as I can do so. I'll go to church, and to balls, and I'll visit my friends, and I'll eat my dinner every day of my life just as though Pat Carroll didn't exist. He's in prison just at present, and therefore so far we have got the best of him."

"But we can't sell a head of cattle without sending it up to Dublin. And we can't find a man to take charge of it on the journey. We can't get a shilling of rent, and we hardly dare to walk about the place in the broad light of day lest we should be shot at. While things are in this condition it is no time for dancing at balls. I am so broken-hearted at the present moment that but for my father and for you I would cut the place and go to America."

"Taking Rachel with you?" said Edith.

"Rachel just now is as prosperous as we are the reverse. Rachel would not go. It is all very well for Rachel, as things are prosperous with her. But here we have the reverse of prosperity, and according to my feelings there should be no gaiety. Do you ever realise to yourself what it is to think that your father is ruined?"

"We ought not to have gone," said Ada.

"Never say die," said Edith, slapping her little hand down on the gunwale of the boat. "Morony Castle and Ballintubber belong to papa, and I will never admit that he is ruined because a few dishonest tenants refuse to pay their rents for a time. A man such as Pat Carroll can do him an injury, but papa is big enough to rise above that in the long run. At any rate I will live as becomes papa's daughter, as long as he approves and I have the power." Discussing these matters they reached the quay near Morony Castle, and Edith as she jumped ashore felt something of triumph in her bosom. She had at any rate succeeded in her object. "I am sure we were right to go," she whispered to Ada.

Their father received them with but very few words; nor had Florian much to say as to the glories of the ball. His mind was devoted at present to the coming trial. And indeed, in a more open and energetic manner, so was the mind of Captain Clayton. "This will be the last holiday for me," he had said to Edith at the ball, "before the great day comes off for Patrick Carroll, Esq. It's all very well for a man once in a way, but there should not be too much of it."

"You have not to complain deeply of yourself on that head."

"I have had my share of fun in the world," he said; "but it grows less as I grow older. It is always so with a man as he gets into his work. I think my hair will grow grey very soon, if I do not succeed in having Mr. Carroll locked up for his life."

"Do you think they will convict him?"

"I think they will? I do think they will. We have got one of the men who is ready to swear that he assisted him in pulling down the gates."

"Which of the men?" she asked.

"I will tell you because I trust you as my very soul. His own brother, Terry, is the man. Pat, it seems, is a terrible tyrant among his own friends, and Terry is willing to turn against him, on condition that a passage to America be provided for him. Of course he is to have a free pardon for himself. We do want one man to corroborate your brother's evidence. Your brother no doubt was not quite straight at first."

"He lied," said Edith. "When you and I talk about it together, we should tell the simple truth. We have pardoned him his lie;—but he lied."

"We have now the one man necessary to confirm his testimony."

"But he is the brother."

"No doubt. But in such a case as this anything is fair to get at the truth. And we shall employ no falsehoods. This younger Carroll was instigated by his brother to assist him in the deed. And he was seen by your brother to be one of those who assisted. It seems to me to be quite right."

"It is very terrible," Edith said.

"Yes; it is terrible. A brother will have to swear against a brother, and will be bribed to do it. I know what will be said to me very well. They have tried to shoot me down like a rat; but I mean to get the better of them. And when I shall have succeeded in removing Mr. Pat Carroll from his present sphere of life, I shall have a second object of ambition before me. Mr. Lax is another gentleman whom I wish to remove. Three times he has shot at me, but he has not hit me yet."

From that time forth there had certainly been no more dances for Captain Clayton. His mind had been altogether devoted to his work, and amidst that work the trial of Pat Carroll had stood prominent. "He and I are equally eager, or at any rate equally anxious;" he had said to Edith, speaking of her brother, when he had met her subsequent to the ball. "But the time is coming soon, and we shall know all about it in another six weeks." This was said in June, and the trial was to take place in August.

CHAPTER XXVI.

LORD CASTLEWELL.

THE spring and early summer had worn themselves away in London, and Rachel O'Mahony was still singing at the Embankment Theatre. She and her father were still living in Cecil Street. The glorious day of October, which had been fixed at last for the 24th, on which Rachel was to appear on the Covent Garden boards, was yet still distant, and she was performing under Mr. Moss's behests at a weekly stipend of £15, to which there would be some addition when the last weeks of the season had come about, the end of July and beginning of August. But, alas! Rachel hardly knew what she would do to support herself during the dead months from August to October.

"Fashionable people always go out of town, father," she said.

"Then let us be fashionable."

"Fashionable people go to Scotland, but they won't take one in there without money. We shan't have £50 left when our debts are paid. And £50 would do nothing for us."

"They've stopped me altogether," said Mr. O'Mahony. "At any rate they have stopped the money-making part of the business. They have threatened to take the man's licence away, and therefore that place is shut up."

"Isn't that unjust, father?"

"Unjust! Everything done in England as to Ireland is unjust. They carried an Act of Parliament the other day, when in accordance with the ancient privileges of members it was within the power of a dozen stalwart Irishmen to stop it. The dozen stalwart Irishmen were there, but they were silenced by a brutal majority. The dozen Irishmen were turned out of the House, one after the other, in direct opposition to the ancient privileges; and so a Bill was passed robbing five million Irishmen of their liberties. So gross an injustice was never before perpetrated—not even when the bribed members sold their country and effected the accursed Union."

"I know that was very bad, father, but the bribes were taken by Irishmen. Be that as it may, what are we to do with ourselves next autumn?"

"The only thing for us is to seek for assistance in the United States."

"They won't lend us £100."

"We must overrun this country by the force of true liberal opinion. The people themselves will rise when they have the Americans to lead them. What is wanted now are the voices of true patriots loud enough to reach the people."

"And £100," said she, speaking into his ear, " to keep us alive from the middle of August to the end of October."

"For myself, I have been invited to come into Parliament. The County of Cavan will be vacant."

"Is there a salary attached?"

"One or two leading Irish members are speaking of it," said Mr. O'Mahony, carried away by the grandeur of the idea, " but the amount has not been fixed yet. And they seem to think that it is wanted chiefly for the parliamentary session. I have not promised, because I do not quite see my way. And to tell the truth, I am not sure that it is in Parliament that an honest Irishman will shine the best. What's the good when you can be silenced at a moment's notice by the word of some mock Speaker, who upsets all the rules of his office to put a gag upon a dozen men? When America has come to understand what it is that the lawless tyrant did on that night when the Irishmen were turned out of the House, will she not rise in her wrath, and declare that such things shall no longer be?" All this occurred in Cecil Street, and Rachel, who well understood her father's wrath, allowed him to expend in words the anger which would last hardly longer than the sound of them.

"But you won't be in Parliament for County Cavan before next August?" she asked.

"I suppose not."

"Nor will the United States have risen in their wrath so as to have settled the entire question before that time?"

"Perhaps not," said Mr. O'Mahony.

"And if they did I don't see what good it would do to us as to finding for us the money that we want."

"I am so full of Ireland's wrongs at this moment, and with the manner in which these policemen interfered with me, that I can hardly bring myself to think of your autumn plans."

"What are yours?" she asked.

"I suppose we should always have money enough to go to America. In America a man can at any rate open his mouth."

"Or a woman either. But according to what M. Le Gros says, in England they pay better at the present moment. Mr. Moss has offered to lend me the money ; but for myself I would sooner go into an English workhouse than accept money from Mr. Moss which I had not earned."

In truth, Rachel had been very foolish with her money, spending it as though there were no end to the source from which it had come, and her father had not been more prudent. He was utterly reckless in regard to such considerations, and would simply declare that he was altogether indifferent to his dinner, or to the new hat he had proposed to buy for himself when the subject was brought under his notice. He had latterly become more eager than ever as to politics, and was supremely happy as long as he was at liberty to speak before any audience those angry words which had however been, unfortunately for him, declared to be treasonable. He had, till lately, been taught to understand that the House of Commons was the only arena on which such permission would be freely granted,—and could be granted of course only to members of the House. Therefore the idea had entered his head that it would suit him to become a member,—more especially as there had arisen a grand scheme of a salary for certain Irish members of which he would be one. But even here the brutality of England had at last interfered, and men were not to be allowed to say what they pleased any longer even in the House of Commons. Therefore Mr. O'Mahony was much disturbed ; and although he was anxious to quarrel with no one individually, not even the policemen who arrested him, he was full of indignant wrath against the tyranny of England generally.

Rachel, when she could get no good advice from her father with regard to her future funds, went back again to her singing. It was necessary, at any rate, that she should carry out her present arrangement with Mr. Moss, and she was sure at least of receiving from him the money which she earned. But, alas ! she could not practise the economy which she knew to be necessary. The people at the theatre had talked her into hiring a one-horse open carriage in which she delighted to drive about, and in which, to tell the truth, her father delighted to accompany her. She had thought that she could allow herself this indulgence out of her £15 a week. And though she paid for the indulgence monthly, that and their joint living nearly consumed the stipend. And now, as her father's advice did not get beyond the very doubtful salary which might accrue to him as the future member for the County Cavan, her mind naturally turned itself to other sources. From M. Le Gros, or from M. Le Gros' employers, she was to receive £300 for singing in the two months before Christmas, with an assurance of a greatly increased though hitherto unfixed stipend afterwards. Personally she as yet knew no one connected with her future theatrical home but M. Le Gros. Of M. Le Gros all her thoughts had been favourable. Should she ask M. Le Gros to lend her some small sum of money in advance for the uses of the autumn ? Mr. Moss had made to her a fixed proposition on the subject, which she had altogether declined. She had declined it with scorn, as she was wont to do all favours proffered by Mr. Moss. Mr. Moss had still been gracious, and had smiled, and had ventured to express " a renewed hope," as he called it, that Miss O'Mahony would even yet condescend to look with regard on the sincere affection of her most humble servant. And then he had again expatiated on the immense success in theatrical life which would attend a partnership entered into between the skill and beauty and power of voice of Miss O'Mahony on the one side, and the energy, devotion, and capital of Mr. Moss on the other. "Psha!" had been Rachel's only reply; and so that interview had been brought to an end. But Rachel, when she came to think of M. Le Gros, and the money she was desirous of borrowing, was afflicted by certain qualms. That she should have borrowed from Mr. Moss, considering the length of their acquaintance might not have been unnatural; but of M. Le Gros she knew nothing but his civility. Nor had she any reason for supposing that M. Le Gros had money of his own at his disposal; nor did she know where M. Le Gros lived. She could go to Covent Garden and ask for him there; but that was all.

So she dressed herself prettily—neatly, as she called it—and had herself driven to the theatre. There, as chance would have it, she found M. Le Gros standing under the portico with a gentleman whom she represented to herself as an elderly old buck. M. Le Gros saw her and came down into the street at once with his hat in his hand.

"M. Le Gros," said she, "I want you to do me a great favour, but I have hardly the impudence to ask it. Can you lend me some money this autumn—say £100?" Thereupon M. Le Gros' face fell, and his cheeks were elongated, and his eyes were very sorrowful. "Ah, then, I see you can't," she said. "I will not put you to the pain of saying so. I ought not to have suggested it. My dealings with you have seemed to be so pleasant, and they have not been quite of the same nature down at 'The Embankment.'"

"My dear young lady——"

"Not another word; and I beg your pardon most heartily for having given you this moment's annoyance."

"There is one of the lessees there," said M. Le Gros, pointing back to the gentleman on the top of the steps, "who has been to hear you and to look at you this two times—this three times at 'The Embankment.' He do think you will become the grand singer of the age."

"Who is the judicious gentleman?" asked Rachel, whispering to M. Le Gros out of the carriage.

"He is Lord Castlewell. He is the eldest son of the Marquis of Beaulieu. He have—oh!—lots of money. He was saying—ah! I must not tell you what his lordship was saying of you because it will make you vain."

"Nothing that any lord can say of me will make me vain," said Rachel, chucking up her head. Then his lordship, thinking that he had been kept long enough standing on the top of the theatre steps, lifted his hat and came down to the carriage, the occupant of which he had recognised.

"May I have the extreme honour of introducing Mademoiselle O'Mahony to Lord Castlewell?" and M. Le Gros again pulled off his hat as he made the introduction. Miss O'Mahony found that she had become Mademoiselle as soon as she had drawn up her carriage at the front door of the genuine Italian Opera.

"This is a pleasure indeed," said Lord Castlewell. "I am delighted—more than delighted, to find that my friend Le Gros has engaged the services of Mademoiselle O'Mahony for our theatre."

"But our engagement does not commence quite yet, I am sorry to say," replied Rachel. Then she prepared herself to be driven away, not caring much for the combination of lord and lessee who stood in the street speaking to her. A lessee should be a lessee, she thought, and a lord a lord.

"May I do myself the honour of waiting upon you some day at 'The Embankment'?" said the lord, again pulling off his hat.

"Oh! certainly," said Rachel; "I should be delighted to see you." Then she was driven away, and did not know whether to be angry or not in having given Lord Castlewell so warm a welcome. As a mere stray lord there was no possible reason why he should call upon her; nor for her why she should receive him. Though Frank Jones had been dismissed, and though she felt herself to be free to accept any eligible lover who might present himself, she still felt herself bound on his behalf to keep herself free from all elderly theatrical hangers-on, especially from such men when she heard that they were also lords. But as she was driven away, she took another glance at the lord, and thought that he did not look so old as when she had seen him at a greater distance.

But she had failed altogether in her purpose of borrowing money from M. Le Gros. And for his sake she regretted much that the attempt had been made. She had already learned one or two details with reference to M. Le Gros. Though his manners and appearance were so pleasant, he was only a subaltern about the theatre; and he was a subaltern whom this lord and lessee called simply Le Gros. And from the melancholy nature of his face when the application for money was made to him, she had learned that he was both good-natured and impecunious. Of herself, in regard to the money, she thought very little at the present moment. There were still six weeks to run, and Rachel's nature was such that she could not distress herself six weeks in advance of any misfortune. She was determined that she would not tell her father of her failure. As for him, he would not probably say a word further of their want of money till the time should come. He confined his prudence to keeping a sum in his pocket sufficient to take them back to New York.

As the days went on which were to bring her engagement at "The Embankment" to an end, Rachel heard a further rumour about herself. Rumours did spring up at "The Embankment" to which she paid very little attention. She had heard the same sort of things said as to other ladies at the theatre, and took them all as a matter of course. Had she been asked, she would have attributed them all to Madame Socani; because Madame Socani was the one person whom, next to Mr. Moss, she hated the most. The rumour in this case simply stated that she had already been married to Mr. Jones, and had separated from her husband. "Why do they care about such a matter as that?" she said to the female from whom she heard the rumour. "It can't matter to me as a singer whether I have five husbands."

"But it is so interesting," said the female, "when a lady has a husband and doesn't own him; or when she owns him and hasn't really got him; it adds a piquancy to life, especially to theatrical life, which does want these little assistances."

Then one evening Lord Castlewell did call upon her at "The Embankment." Her father was not with her, and she was constrained by the circumstances of the moment to see his lordship alone.

"I do feel, you know, Miss O'Mahony," he said, thus coming back for the moment into everyday life, "that I am entitled to take an interest in you."

"Your lordship is very kind."

"I suppose you never heard of me before?"

"Not a word, my lord. I'm an American girl, and I know very little about English lords."

"I hope that you may come to know more. My special *métier* in life brings me among the theatres. I am very fond of music, and perhaps a little fond of beauty also."

"I am glad you have the sense, my lord, to put music the first."

"I don't know about that. In regard to you I cannot say which predominates."

"You are at liberty at any rate to talk about the one, as you are bidding for it at your own theatre. As to the other, you will excuse me for saying that it is a matter between me and my friends."

"Among whom I trust before long I may be allowed to be counted."

The little dialogue had been carried on with smiles and good humour, and Rachel now did not choose to interfere with them. After all she was only a public singer, and as such was hardly entitled to the full consideration of a gentlewoman. It was thus that she argued with herself. Nevertheless she had uttered her little reprimand and had intended him to take it as such.

"You are coming to us, you know, after the holidays."

"And will bring my voice with me, such as it is."

"But not your smiles, you mean to say."

"They are sure to come with me, for I am always laughing,—unless I am roused to terrible wrath. I am sure that will not be the case at Covent Garden."

"I hope not. You will find that you have come among a set who are quite prepared to accept you as a friend." Here she made a little curtsy. "And now I have to offer my sincere apologies for the little proposition I am about to make." It immediately occurred to her that M. Le Gros had betrayed her. He was a very civil-spoken, affable, kind old man; but he had betrayed her. "M. Le Gros happened to mention that you were anxious to draw in advance for some portion of the salary coming to you for the next two months." M. Le Gros had at any rate betrayed her in the most courteous terms.

"Well, yes; M. Le Gros explained that the proposition was not *selon les regles*, and it does not matter the least in the world."

"M. Le Gros has explained that? I did not know that M. Le Gros had explained anything."

"Well, then, he looked it," said Rachel.

"His looks must be wonderfully expressive. He did not look it to me at all. He simply told me, as one of the managers of the theatre, I was to let you have whatever money you wanted. And he did whisper to me,—may I tell you what he whispered?"

"I suppose you may. He seems to me to be a very good-natured kind of man."

"Poor old Le Gros! A good-natured man, I should say. He doesn't carry the house, that's all."

"You do that." Then she remembered that the man was a lord. "I ought to have said 'my lord,'" she thought; "but I forgot, I hope you'll excuse me—my lord."

"We are not very particular about that in theatrical matters; or, rather, I am particular with some and not with others. You'll learn all about it in process of time. M. Le Gros whispered that he thought there was not the pleasantest understanding in the world between you and the people here."

"Well, no; there is not,—my lord."

"Bother the lord,—just now."

"With all my heart," said Rachel, who could not avoid the little bit of fun which was here implied. "Not but what the—the people here—would find me any amount of money I chose to ask for. There are people, you see, one does not wish to borrow money from. I take my salary here, but nothing more. The fact is, I have not only taken it, but spent it, and to tell the truth, I have not a shilling to amuse myself with during the dull season. Mr. Moss knows all about it, and has simply asked how much I wanted. 'Nothing,' I replied, 'nothing at all; nothing at all.' And that's how I am situated."

"No debts?"

"Not a dollar. Beyond that I shouldn't have a dollar left to get out of London with." Then she remembered herself,— that it was expedient that she should tell this man something about herself. "I have got a father, you know, and he has to be paid for as well as me. He is the sweetest, kindest, most generous father that a girl ever had, and he could make lots of money for himself, only the police won't let him."

"What do the police do to him?" said Lord Castlewell.

"He is not a burglar, you know, or anything of that kind."

"He is an Irish politician, isn't he?"

"He is very much of a politician; but he is not an Irishman."

"Irish name," suggested the lord.

"Irish name, yes; so are half the names in my country. My father comes from the United States. And he is strongly impressed with the necessity of putting down the horrid injustice with which the poor Irish are treated by the monstrous tyranny of you English aristocrats. You are very nice to look at."

"Thank you, Miss O'Mahony."

"But you are very bad to go. You are not the kind of horses I care to drive at all. Thieves, traitors, murderers, liars."

"Goodness gracious me!" exclaimed the lord.

"I don't say anything for myself, because I am only a singing girl, and understand nothing about politics. But these are the very lightest words which he has at his tongue's end when he talks about you. He is the most good-tempered fellow in the world, and you would like him very much. Here is Mr. Moss." Mr. Moss had opened the door and had entered the room.

The greeting between the two men was closely observed by Rachel, who, though she was very imprudent in much that she did and much that she said, never allowed anything to pass by her unobserved. Mr. Moss, though he affected an intimacy with the lord, was beyond measure servile. Lord Castlewell accepted the intimacy without repudiating it, but accepted also the servility. "Well, Moss, how are you getting on in this little house?"

"Ah, my lord, you are going to rob us of our one attraction," and having bowed to the lord he turned round and bowed to the lady.

"You have no right to keep such a treasure in a little place like this."

"We can afford to pay for it, you know, my lord. M. Le Gros came here a little behind my back, and carried her off."

"Much to her advantage, I should say."

"We can pay," said Mr. Moss.

"To such a singer as Mademoiselle O'Mahony paying is not everything. An audience large enough, and sufficiently intelligent to appreciate her, is something more than mere money."

"We have the most intelligent audience in all London," Mr. Moss said in defence of his own theatre.

"No doubt," said the lord. He had, during this little intercourse of compliments, managed to write a word or two on a slip of paper, which he now handed to Rachel—"Will £200 do?" This he put into her hand, and then left her, saying that he would do himself the honour of calling upon her again at her own lodgings, "where I shall hope," he said, "to make the acquaintance of the most good-tempered fellow in the world." Then he took his leave.

CHAPTER XXVII.

HOW FUNDS WERE PROVIDED.

MR. MOSS at this interview again pressed his loan of money upon poor Rachel.

"You cannot get on, my dear young lady, in this world without money. If you have spent your income hitherto, what do you mean to do till the end of November? At Covent Garden the salaries are all paid monthly."

There was something so ineffably low and greasy in his tone of addressing her, that it was impossible to be surprised at the disgust which she expressed for him.

"Mr. Moss, I am not your dear young lady," she said.

"Would that you were! We should be as happy as the day is long. There would be no money troubles then." She could not fail to make comparisons between him and the English nobleman who had just left her, which left the Englishman infinitely superior; although, with the few thoughts she had given to him, she had already begun to doubt whether Lord Castlewell's morality stood very high. "What will you do for money for the next three months? You cannot do without money," said Mr. Moss.

"I have already found a friend," said Rachel most imprudently.

"What! his lordship there?"

"I am not bound to answer any such questions."

"But I know; I can see the game is all up if it has come to that. I am a fellow-workman, and there have been, and perhaps will be, many relations between us. A hundred pounds advanced here or there must be brought into the accounts sooner or later. That is honest; that will bear daylight; no young lady need be ashamed of that; even if you were Mrs. Jones you need not be ashamed of such a transaction."

"I am not Mrs. Jones," said Rachel in great anger.

"But if you were, Mr. Jones would have no ground of complaint, unless indeed on the score of extravagance. But a present from this lord!"

"It is no present. It does not come from the lord; it comes from the funds of the theatre."

"Ha, ha, ha!" laughed Mr. Moss. "Is that the little game with which he attempts to cajole you? How has he got his hand into the treasury of the theatre, so that he may be able to help you so conveniently? You have not got the money yet, I suppose?"

"I have not got his money—which may be dangerous, or yours—which would certainly be more so. Though from neither of you could the bare money hurt me, if it were taken with an innocent heart. From you it would be a distress, an annoyance, a blister. From him it would be simply a loan either from himself or from the theatre with which he is connected. I may be mistaken, but I have imagined that it would come from the theatre; I will ascertain, and if it be not so, I will decline the loan."

"Do you not know his character, nor his mode of living, nor his dealing with actresses? You will not at any rate get credit for such innocence when you tell the story. Why;—— he has come here to call upon you, and of course it is all over the theatre already that you are his mistress. I came in here to endeavour to save you; but I fear it is too late."

"Impudent scoundrel!" said Rachel, jumping up and glaring at him.

"That is all very well, but I have endeavoured to save you. I would believe none of them when they told me that you would not be my wife because you were married to Mr. Jones. Nor would I believe them when they have told me since that you were not fit to be the wife of anyone." Rachel's hand went in among the folds of her dress, and returned with a dagger in it. Words had been said to her now which she swore to herself were unbearable. "Yes; you are in a passion now;" and as he said so, he contrived to get the round table with which the room was garnished between himself and her.

"It is true," she said, "your words have been so base that I am no doubt angry."

"But if you knew it, I am endeavouring to save you. Imprudent as you have been I still wish to make you my wife." Here Rachel in her indignation spat upon the floor. "Yes; I am anxious to make you an honest woman."

"You can make no woman honest. It is altogether beyond your power."

"It will be so when you have taken this lord's money."

"I have not at any rate taken yours. It is that which would disgrace me. Between this lord and me there has been no word that could do so."

"Will he make you his wife?"

"Wife! No. He is married for aught I know. He has spoken to me no word except about my profession. Nor shall you. Cannot a woman sing without being wife to any man?"

"Ha, ha, yes indeed!"

She understood the scorn intended to be thrown on her line of life by his words, and was wretched to think that he was getting the better of her in conversation. "I can sing, and I need no husband."

"It is common with the friends of the lord that they do not generally rank very high in their profession. I have endeavoured to save you from this kind of thing, and see the return that I get! You will, however, soon have left us, and you will then find that to fill first place at 'The Embankment' is better than a second or a third at Covent Garden."

During these hot words on both sides she had been standing at a pier-glass, arranging something in her dress intended to suit Moss's fancy upon the stage,—Moss who was about to enact her princely lover—and then she walked off without another word. She went through her part with all her usual vigour and charm, and so did he. Elmira also was more pathetic than ever, as the night was supposed to be something special, because a royal duke and his young bride were in the stage box. The plaudits given would have been tremendous only that the building was so small, and the grand quartette became such a masterpiece that there was ha'f a column concerning it in the musical corner of the next morning's *Daily Telephone*. "If that girl would only go as I'd have her," said Mr. Moss to the most confidential of his theatrical friends, "I'd make her Mrs. Moss to-morrow, and her fame should be blazoned all over the world before twelve months had gone as Madame Moussa."

But Rachel, though she was enabled so to overcome her rage as to remember only her theatrical passion when she was on the stage, spent the whole of the subsequent night in thinking over the difficulty into which she had brought herself by her imprudence. She understood to the full the meaning of all those innuendoes which Mr. Moss had provided for her; and she knew that though there was in them not a spark of truth as regarded herself, still they were so truth-like as to meet with acceptance, at any rate from all theatrical personages. She had gone to M. Le Gros for the money clearly as one of the theatrical company with which she was about to connect herself. M. Le Gros had, to her intelligence, distinctly though very courteously declined her request. It might be well that the company would

accede to no such request ; but M. Le Gros, in his questionable
civility, had told the whole story to Lord Castlewell, who had
immediately offered her a loan of £200 out of his own pocket.
It had not occurred to her in the moment in which she had first
read the words in the presence of Mahomet M. M. that such
must necessarily be the case. Was it probable that Lord
Castlewell should on his own behalf recover from the treasury
of the theatre the sum of £200 ? And then the nature of this
lord's character opened itself to her eyes in all the forms which
Mr. Moss had intended that it should wear. A man did not
lend a young lady £200 without meaning to secure for himself
some reward. And as she thought of it all she remembered the
kind of language in which she had spoken of her father. She
had described him as an American in words which might so
probably give this noble old *roué* a false impression as to his
character. And yet she liked the noble old *roué*—liked him so
infinitely better than she did Mr. Moss. M. Le Gros had
betrayed her, or had, perhaps, said words leading to her betrayal ;
but still she greatly preferred M. Le Gros to Mr. Moss.

She was safe as yet with this lord. Not a sparkle of his gold
had she received. No doubt the story about the money would
be spread about from her own telling of it. People would believe
it because she herself had said so. But it was still within her
power to take care that it should not be true. She did what
was usual on such occasions. She abused the ill-feeling of the
world which by the malignity of its suspicions would not scruple
to drag her into the depths of misfortune, forgetting probably
that her estimation of others was the same as others of her.
She did not bethink herself that had another young lady at
another theatre accepted a loan from an unmarried lord of such
a character, she would have thought ill of that young lady. The
world ought to be perfectly innocent in regard to her because
she believed herself to be innocent ; and Mr. Moss, in expressing
the opinions of others, and exposing to her the position in which
she had placed herself, had simply proved himself to be the
blackest of human beings.

But it was necessary that she should at once do something
to whitewash her own character in her own esteem. This lord
had declared that he himself would call, and she was at first
minded to wait till he did so, and then to hand back to him the
cheque which she believed that he would bring, and to assure
him that under altered circumstances it would not be wanted.
But she felt that it would best become her to write to him
openly, and to explain the circumstances which had led to his
offering the loan. " There is nothing like being straightforward,"
she said to herself, " and if he does not choose to believe me,
that is his fault." So she took up her pen, and wrote quickly,
to the following effect :

"MY DEAR LORD CASTLEWELL,

"I want to tell you that I do not wish to have the £200 which you were good enough to say that you would lend me. Indeed I cannot take it under any circumstances. I must explain to you all about it, if your lordship pleases. I had intended to ask M. Le Gros to get the theatre people to advance me some small sum on my future engagement, and I had not thought how impossible it was that they should do so, as of course I might die before I had sung a single note. I never dreamed of coming to you, whose lordship's name I had not even heard in my ignorance. Then M. Le Gros spoke to you, and you came and made your proposition in the most good-natured way in the world. I was such a fool as not to see that the money must of course come from yourself.

"Mr. Moss has enlightened me, and has made me understand that no respectable young woman would accept a loan of money from you without blemish to her character. Mr. Moss, whom I do not in the least like, has been right in this. I should be very sorry if you should be taught to think evil of me before I go to your theatre; or indeed if I do not go at all. I am not up to all these things, and I suppose I ought to have consulted my father the moment I got your little note. Pray do not take any further notice of it.

"I am, very faithfully,
"Your lordship's humble servant,
"RACHEL O'MAHONY."

Then there was added a postscript: "Your note has just come and I return the cheque." As chance would have it the cheque had come just as Rachel had finished her letter, and with the cheque there had been a short scrawl as follows: "I send the money as settled, and will call to-morrow."

Whatever may have been Lord Castlewell's general sins among actresses and actors, his feelings hitherto in regard to Miss O'Mahony had not done him discredit. He had already heard her name frequently when he had seen her in her little carriage before the steps of Covent Garden Theatre, and had heard her sing at "The Embankment." Her voice and tone and feeling had enchanted him as he had wont to be enchanted by new singers of high quality, and he had been greatly struck by the brightness of her beauty. When M. Le Gros had told him of her little wants, he had perceived at once her innocence, and had determined to relieve her wants. Then, when she had told him of her father, and had explained to him the kind of terms on which they lived together, he was sure that she was pure as snow. But she was very lovely, and he could not undertake to answer for what feelings might spring up in her bosom. Now he had received this letter, and every word of it spoke to him in her favour. He took, therefore, a little trouble; and calling upon her the next morning at her lodgings, found her seated with Mr. O'Mahony.

"Father," she said, when the lord was ushered into the room, "this is Lord Castlewell. Lord Castlewell, this is my father."

Then she sat down, leaving the two to begin the conversation as they might best please. She had told her father nothing about the money, simply explaining that on the steps of the theatre she had met the lord, who was one of its proprietors.

"Lord Castlewell," said Mr. O'Mahony, "I am very proud," then he bowed. "I know very little about stage affairs, but I am confident that my daughter will do her duty to the best of her ability."

"Not more so than I am," said Lord Castlewell, upon which Mr. O'Mahony bowed again. "You have heard about this little *contretemps* about the money."

"Not a word," said Mr. O'Mahony, shaking his head.

"Nor of the terrible character which has been given you by your daughter."

"That I can well understand," said Mr. O'Mahony.

"She says that you wish to abolish all the English aristocracy."

"Most of them," said Mr. O'Mahony. "Peradventure ten shall be found honest, and I will not destroy them for ten's sake; but I doubt whether there be one."

"I should be grieved to think that you were the judge."

"And so should I," said Mr. O'Mahony. "It is so easy to utter curses when no power accompanies the utterances. The Lord must have found it uncomfortable in regard to Sodom. I can spit out all my fury against English vices and British greed without suffering one pang at my heart. What is this that you were saying about Rachel and her money?"

"She is in a little trouble about cash at the present moment."

"Not a doubt about it."

"And I have offered to lend her a trifle—£200 or so, just till she can work it off up at the theatre there."

"Then there is one of the ten at any rate," said Mr. O'Mahony.

"Meaning me?" asked the lord.

"Just so. Lending us £200, when neither of us have a shilling in our pocket, is a very good deed. Don't you think so, Rachel?"

"No," said Rachel. "Lord Castlewell is not a fit person to lend me £200 out of his pocket, and I will not have it."

"I did not know," said Mr. O'Mahony.

"You never know anything, you are such a dear, innocent old father."

"There's an end of it then," said he, addressing himself to the lord. He did not look in the least annoyed because his daughter had refused to take the loan, nor had he shown the slightest feeling of any impropriety when there was a question as to her accepting it.

"Of course I cannot force it upon you," said Lord Castlewell.

"No; a lord cannot do that, even in this country, where lords go for so much. But we are not a whit the less obliged to your lordship. There are proprieties and improprieties which I don't understand. Rachel knows all about them. Such a knowledge comes to a girl naturally, and she chooses either the one or the other, according to her nature. Rachel is a dragon of propriety."

"Father, you are a goose," said Rachel.

"I am telling his lordship the truth. There is some reason why you should not take the money, and you won't take it. I think it very hard that I should not have been allowed to earn it."

"Why were you not allowed?" asked the lord.

"Lest the people should be persuaded to rise up against you lords,—which they very soon would do,—and will do. You are right in your generation. The people were paying twenty-five cents a night to come and hear me, and so I was informed that I must not speak to them any more. I had been silenced in Galway before; but then I had spoken about your Queen."

"We can't endure that, you know."

"So I learn. She's a holy of holies. But I promised to say nothing further about her, and I haven't. I was talking about your Speaker of the House of Commons."

"That's nearly as bad," said Lord Castlewell, shaking his head.

"A second-rate holy of holies. When I said that he ought to obey certain rules which had been laid down for his guidance, I was told to walk out. 'What may I talk about?' I asked. Then the policeman told me 'the weather.' Even an Englishman is not stupid enough to pay twenty-five cents for that. I am only telling you this to explain why we are so impecunious."

"The policeman won't prevent my lending you £200."

"Won't he now? There is no knowing what a policeman can't do in this country. They are very good-natured, all the same."

Then Lord Castlewell turned to Rachel, and asked her whether her suspicions would go so far as to interfere between him and her father. "It is because I am a pretty girl that you are going to do it," she said, frowning, "or because you pretend to think so." Here the father broke out into a laugh, and the lord followed him. "You had better keep your money to yourself, my lord. You never can have used it with less chance of getting any return." This interview, however, was ended by the acceptance of a cheque from Lord Castlewell for £200, payable to the order of Gerald O'Mahony.

CHAPTER XXVIII.

WHAT WAS NOT DONE WITH THE FUNDS.

" SHE has taken his money all the same." This was said some weeks after the transaction as described in the last chapter, and was spoken by Madame Socani to Mr. Moss.

"How do you know?"

"I know very well. You are so infatuated by that young woman that you will believe nothing against her."

"I am infatuated with her voice; I know what she is going to do in the world. Old Barytone told me that he had never heard such a voice from a woman's mouth since the days of Malibran; and if there is a man who knows one voice from another, it is Barytone. He can taste the richness of the instrument down to its lowest tinkling sound."

"And you would marry such a one as she for her voice."

"And she can act. Ah! if you could have acted as she does it might have been different."

"She has got a husband just the same as me."

"I don't believe it; but never mind, I would risk all that. And I will do it yet. If you will only keep your toe in your pump, we will have such a company as nothing that Le Gros can do will be able to cut us down."

"And she is taking money from that lord."

"They all take money from lords," he replied. "What does it matter? And she is as stout a piece of goods as ever you came across. She has given me more impudence in the last eight months than ever I took from any of them. And by Jupiter I never so much as got a kiss from her."

"A kiss!" said Madame Socani with great contempt.

"And she has hit me a box on the cheek which I have had to put up with. She has always got a dagger about her somewhere, to give a fellow a prod in her passion." Here Mr. Moss laughed or affected to laugh at the idea of the dagger. "I tell you that she would have it into a fellow in no time."

"Then why don't you leave her alone? A little wizened monkey like that!" It was thus that Madame Socani expressed her opinion of her rival. "A creature without an ounce of flesh on her bones. Her voice won't last long. It never does with those little mean apes. There was Grisi and Tietjens,—they had something of a body for a voice to come out of. And here is this girl that you think so much of, taking money hand over hand from the very first lord she comes across."

"I don't believe a word of it," said the faithful Moss.

"You'll find that it is true. She will go away to some

watering-place in the autumn, and he'll be after her. Did you ever know him spare one of them? Or one of them, poor little creatures, that wouldn't rise to his bait?"

"She has got her father with her."

"Her father! What is the good of fathers? He'll take some of the money, that's all. I'll tell you what it is, Moss, if you don't drop her you and I will be two."

"With all my heart, Madame Socani," said Moss. "I have not the slightest intention of dropping her. And as for you and me, we can get on very well apart."

But Madame Socani, though she would be roused by jealousy to make this threat once a month, knew very well that she could not afford to sever herself from Mr. Moss; and she knew also that Mr. Moss was bound to show her some observance, or, at any rate, to find employment for her as long as she could sing.

But Mr. Moss was anxious to find out whether any money arrangements did or did not exist between Miss O'Mahony and the lord, and was resolved to ask the question in a straightforward manner. He had already found out that his old pupil had no power of keeping a secret to herself when thus asked. She would sternly refuse to give any reply; but she would make her refusal in such a manner as to tell the whole truth. In fact, Rachel, among her accomplishments, had not the power of telling a lie in such language as to make herself believed. It was not that she would scruple in the least to declare to Mr. Moss the very opposite to the truth in a matter in which he had, she thought, no business to be inquisitive; but when she did so she had no power to look the lie. You might say of her frequently that she was a downright liar. But of all human beings whom you could meet she was the least sly. "My dear child," the father used to say to her, "words to you are worth nothing, unless it be to sing them. You can make no impression with them in any other way." Therefore it was that Mr. Moss felt that he could learn the truth from simply questioning his pupil.

"Miss O'Mahony, may I say a few words to you?" So said Mr. Moss, having knocked at the door of Rachel's sitting-room. He had some months ago fallen into the habit of announcing himself, when he had come to give her lessons, and would inform the servant that he would take up his own name. Rachel had done what she could do to put an end to the practice, but it still prevailed.

"Certainly, Mr. Moss. Was not the girl there to show you up?"

"No doubt she was. But such ceremony between us is hardly necessary."

"I should prefer to be warned of the coming of my master.

I will see to that in future. Such little ceremonies do have their uses."

"Shall I go down and make her say that I am here, and then come up again?"

"It shall not be necessary, but you take a chair and begin!" Then Mr. Moss considered how he had better do so. He knew well that the girl would not answer kindly to such a question as he was desirous of asking. And it might be that she would be very uncivil. He was by no means a coward, but he had a vivid recollection of the gleam of her dagger. He smiled, and she looked at him more suspiciously because of his smile. He was sitting on a sofa opposite to her as she sat on a music-stool which she had turned round, so as to face him, and he fancied that he could see her right hand hide itself among the folds of her dress. "Is it about the theatre?"

"Well, it is;—and yet it isn't."

"I wish it were something about the theatre. It always seems to come more natural between you and me."

"I want you to tell me what you did at last about Lord Castlewell's money."

"Why am I to tell you what I did?"

"For friendship."

"I do not feel any."

"That's an uncivil word to say, mademoiselle."

"But it's true. You have no business to ask me about the lord's money, and I won't be questioned."

"It will be so deleterious to you if you accept it."

"I can take care of myself," she said, jumping off the chair. "I shall have left this place now in another month, and shall utterly disregard the words which anyone at your theatre may say of me. I shall not tell you whether the lord has lent me money or not."

"I know he has."

"Very well. Then leave the room Knowing as you do that I am living here with my own father, your interference is grossly impertinent."

"Your father is not going with you, I am afraid." She rushed at the bell and pulled it till the bell rope came down from the wire, but nobody answered the bell. "Can it be possible that you should not be anxious to begin your new career under respectable auspices?"

"I will not stand this. Leave the room, sir. This apartment is my own."

"Miss O'Mahony, you see my hand; with this I am ready to offer at once to place you in a position in which the world would look up to you."

"You have done so before, Mr. Moss, and your doing so again is an insult. It would not be done to any young lady unless she were on the stage, and were thought on that account to be open to any man about the theatre to say what he pleased to her."

"Any gentleman is at liberty to make any lady an offer."

"I have answered it. Now leave the room."

"I cannot do so until I have heard that you have not taken money from this reprobate."

At the moment the door opened, and the reprobate entered the room.

"Your servant told me that Mr. Moss was here, and therefore I walked up at once," said the reprobate.

"I am so much obliged to you," said Rachel. "Oh, Lord Castlewell! I am so much obliged to you. He tells me in the first place that you are a reprobate."

"Never mind me," said the lord.

"I don't mind what he says of you. He declares that my character will be gone for ever because you have lent my father some money."

"So it will," said Moss, who was not afraid to stand up to his guns.

"And how if she had accepted your offer?"

"No one would have thought of it. Come, my lord, you know the difference. I am anxious only to save her."

"It is to her father I have lent the money, who explained to me the somewhat cruel treatment he had received at the hands of the police. I think you are making an ass of yourself, Mr. Moss."

"Very well, my lord; very well," said Mr. Moss. "All the world no doubt will know that you have lent the money to the Irish Land-leaguer because of your political sympathy with him, and will not think for a minute that you have been attracted by our pretty young friend here. It will not suspect that it is she who has paid for the loan!"

"Mr. Moss, you are a brute!" said the lord.

"Can't he be turned out of the room?" asked Rachel.

"Well, yes; it is possible," said the lord, who slowly prepared to walk up and take some steps towards expelling Mr. Moss.

"It shall not be necessary," said Mahomet M. M. "You could not get me out, but there would be a terrible row in the house, which could not fail to be disagreeable to Miss O'Mahony. I leave her in your hands, and I do not think I could possibly leave her in worse. I have wished to make her an honest woman; what you want of her you can explain to herself." In saying this Mr. Moss walked downstairs and left the house, feeling, as he went, that he had got the better both of the lord and of the lady.

With Mr. Moss there was a double motive, neither of which

was very bright, but both of which he followed with considerable
energy. He had at first been attracted by her good looks,
which he had desired to make his own—at the cheapest price at
which they might be had in the market. If marriage were
necessary, so be it, but it might be that the young lady would not
be so *exigeant*. It was probably the expression of some such
feelings in the early days of their acquaintance which had made
him so odious to her. Then Frank Jones had come forward;
and like any good honest girl, in a position so public, she had
at once let the fact of Mr. Jones be made known, so as to
protect her. But it had not protected her, and Mr. Moss had
been doubly odious. Then, by degrees, he had become aware
of the value of her voice, and he perceived the charms that
there were in what he pictured to himself as a professional
partnership as well as a marriage. Various ideas floated
through his mind, down even to the creation of fresh names,
grand married names, for his wife. And if she could be got to
see it in the light he saw it, what a stroke of business they
might do! He was aware that she expressed personal dislike
to him; but he did not think much of that. He did not in the
least understand the nature of such dislike as she exhibited.
He thought himself to be a very good-looking man. He was
one of a profession to which she also belonged. He had no
idea that he was not a gentleman, but that she was a lady. He
did not know that there were such things. Madame Socani
told him that this young woman was already married to Mr.
Jones, but had left that gentleman because he had no money.
He did not believe this; but in any case he would be willing to
risk it. The peril would be hers and not his. It was his object
to establish the partnership, and he did not even yet see any
fatal impediment to it.

This lord who had been trapped by her beauty, by that and
by her theatrical standing, was an impediment, but could be
removed. He had known Lord Castlewell to be in love with a
dozen singers, partly because he thought himself to be a judge
of music, and partly simply because he had liked their looks.
The lord had now taken a fancy to Miss O'Mahony, and had
begun by lending her money. That the father should take
the money instead of the daughter, was quite natural to his
thinking. But he might still succeed in looking after Miss
O'Mahony, and rescuing the singer from the lord. By keeping
a close watch on her he must make it impossible for the lord to
hold her. Therefore, when he went away, leaving the lord and
singer together, he thought that for the present he had got the
better of both.

"Why did he tell you that I was a reprobate?" said the lord,
when he found himself alone with the lady.

"Well, perhaps it was because you are one, my lord," said

Rachel, laughing. She would constantly remember herself, and tell herself that as long as she called him by his title, she was protecting himself from that familiarity which would be dangerous.

"I hope you don't think so."

"Gentlemen generally are reprobates, I believe. It is not disgraceful for a gentleman to be a reprobate, but it is pleasant. The young women I daresay find it pleasant, but then it is disgraceful. I do not mean to disgrace myself, Lord Castlewell."

"I am sure you will not."

"I want you to be sure of it, quite sure. I am a singing girl; but I don't mean to be any man's mistress." He stared at her as she said this. "And I don't mean to be any man's wife, unless I downright love him. Now you may keep out of my way, if you please. I daresay you are a reprobate, my lord; but with that I have got nothing to do. Touching this money, I suppose father has not got it yet?"

"I have sent it."

"You are to get nothing for it, but simply to have it returned, without interest, as soon as I have earned it. You have only to say the word and I will take care that father shall send it you back again."

Lord Castlewell felt that the girl was very unlike others whom he had known, and who had either rejected his offers with scorn or had accepted them with delight. This young lady did neither. She apparently accepted the proffered friendship, and simply desired him to carry his reprobate qualities elsewhere. There was a frankness about her which pleased him much, though it hardly tended to make him in love with her. One thing he did resolve on the spur of the moment, that he would never say a word to her which her father might not hear. It was quite a new sensation to him, this of simple friendship with a singer, with a singer whom he had met in the doubtful custody of Mr. Moss; but he did believe her to be a good girl,—a good girl who could speak out her mind freely; and as such he both respected and liked her. "Of course I shan't take back the money till it becomes due. You'll have to work hard for it before I get it."

"I shall be quite contented to do that, my lord." Then the interview was over, and his lordship left the room.

But Lord Castlewell felt as he went home that this girl was worth more than other girls. She laughed at him for being a lord, but she could accept a favour from him, and then tell him to his face that he should do her no harm because she had accepted it. He had met some terrible rebuffs in his career, the memory of which had been unpleasant to him; and he had been greeted with many smiles, all of which had been insipid. What should he do with this girl so as to make the best of her? The only thing that occurred to him was to marry her! And yet such a marriage would be altogether out of his line of life.

CHAPTER XXIX.

WHAT WAS DONE WITH THE FUNDS.

The £200 was not spent in a manner of which Lord Castlewell would have altogether approved. About the end of August Mr. O'Mahony was summoned back to Ireland, and was induced, at a meeting held at the Rotunda, to give certain pledges which justified the advanced Irish party in putting him forward as a new member for the County of Cavan. The advanced Irish party had no doubt been attracted by the eloquence he had exhibited both in Galway and in London, and by the patriotic sentiments which he had displayed. He was known to be a Republican, and to look for the formation of a Republic to American aid. He had expressed most sincere scorn for everything English, and professed ideas as to Irish property generally in regard to which he was altogether ignorant of their meaning. As he was a sincerely honest man, he did think that something good for his old country would be achieved by Home Rule; though how the Home-Rulers would set to work when Home Rule should be the law of the land, he had not the remotest conception. There were many reasons, therefore, why he should be a fit member for an Irish county. But it must be admitted that he would not have been so unanimously selected had all the peculiarities of his mind been known. It might be probable that he would run riot under the lash of his leader, as others have done both before and since, when he should come to see all the wiles of that strategy which he would be called upon to support. And in such case the quarrel with him would be more internecine than with other foes, such as English members, Scotch members, Conservative Irish members, and Liberal Irish members not sworn to follow certain leaders. A recreant one out of twenty friends would be regarded with more bitter hatred than perhaps six hundred and thirty ordinary enemies. It might be, therefore, that a time of tribulation was in store for Mr. O'Mahony, but he did not consider these matters very deeply when the cheers rang loud in the hall of the Rotunda; nor did he then reflect that he was about to spend in an injudicious manner the money which must be earned by Rachel's future work.

When Rachel had completed her engagement with Mr. Moss, it had been intended that they should go down to Ambleside and there spend Lord Castlewell's money in the humble innocent enjoyment of nature. There had at that moment been nothing decided as to the County of Cavan. A pork-butcher possessed of some small means and unlimited impudence had put himself forward. But The Twenty had managed to put him through his facings, and had found him to be very ignorant in his use of the Queen's English. Now of late there had come up a notion that the small party required to make up for the thinness of their members by the strength of their eloquence. Practice makes perfect, and it is not to be wondered at therefore if a large proportion of The Twenty had become fluent. But more were wanted, and of our friend O'Mahony's fluency there could be no doubt. Therefore he was sent for, and on the very day of his arrival he proved to the patriotic spirits of Dublin that he was the man for Cavan. Three days afterwards he went down, and Cavan obediently accepted its man. With her father went Rachel, and was carried through the towns of Virginia, Baily-borough, and Ballyjamesduff, in great triumph on a one-horse car.

This occurred about the end of August, and Lord Castlewell's £200 was very soon spent. She had not thought much about it, but had been quite willing to be the daughter of a Member of Parliament if a constituency could be found willing to select her father. She did not think much of the duties of Parliament, if they came within the reach of her father's ability. She did not in truth think that he could under any circumstances do half a day's work. She had known what it was to practise, and, having determined to succeed, she had worked as only a singer can work who determines that she will succeed. Hour after hour she had gone on before the looking-glass, and even Mr. Moss had expressed his approval. But during the years that she had been so at work, she had never seen her father do anything. She knew that he talked what she called patriotic buncombe. It might be that he would become a very fitting member of Parliament, but Rachel had her doubt. She could see, however, that the £200 quickly vanished during their triumphant journeyings on the one-horse car. Everybody in County Cavan seemed to know that there was £200 and no more to be spent by the new member. There he was, however, Member of Parliament for the County of Cavan, and his breast was filled with new aspirations. Enmity, the bitterest enmity to everything English, was the one lesson taught him. But he himself had other feelings. What if he could talk over that Speaker, and that Prime Minister, that Government generally, and all the House of Commons, and all the House of Lords! Why should not England go her way and Ireland hers,— England have her monarchy and Ireland her republic, but still with some kind of union between them, as to the nature of which Mr. O'Mahony had no fixed idea in his brain whatsoever. But he knew that he could talk, and he knew also that he must now talk on an arena for admission to which the public would not pay twenty-five cents or more. His breast was much disturbed by the consideration that for all the work which he proposed to do no wages were to be forthcoming.

But while Mr. O'Mahony was being elected Member of Parliament for County Cavan, things were going on very sadly in County Galway. Wednesday, the 31st of August, had been the day fixed for the trial of Pat Carroll; and the month of August was quickly wearing itself away. But during the month of August Captain Clayton found occasion more than once to come into the neighbourhood of Headford. And though Mr. Jones was of an opinion that his presence there was adequately accounted for by the details of the coming trial, the two girls evidently thought that some other cause might be added to that which Pat Carroll had produced.

It must be explained that at this period Frank Jones was absent from Morony Castle, looking out for emergency men who could be brought down to the neighbourhood of Headford, in sufficient number to save the crop on Mr. Jones's farm. And with him was Tom Daly, who had some scheme in his own head with reference to his horses and his hounds. Mr. Persse and Sir Jasper Lynch had been threatened with a wide system of boycotting, unless they would give up Tom Daly's animals. A decree had gone forth in the county, that nothing belonging to the hunt should be allowed to live within its precincts. All the bitterness and the cruelty and the horror arising from this order are beyond the limit of this story. But it may be well to explain that at the present moment Frank Jones was away from Castle Morony, working hard on his father's behalf.

And so were the girls working hard;—making the butter, and cooking the meat, and attending to the bed-rooms. And Peter was busy with them as their lieutenant. It might be thought that the present was no time for love-making, and that Captain Clayton could not have been in the mood. But it may be observed that at any period of special toil in a family, when infinitely more has to be done than at any other time, love-making will go on with more than ordinary energy. Edith was generally to be found with her hair tucked tight off her face and enveloped in a coarse dairymaid's apron, and Ada, when she ran downstairs, would do so with a house-maid's dusting-brush at her girdle, and they were neither of them, when so attired, in the least afraid of encountering Captain Clayton as he would come out from their father's room. All the world knew that they were being boycotted, and very happy the girls were during the process. "Poor papa" did not like it so well. Poor papa thought of his banker's account, or rather of that bank at which there was, so to say, no longer any account. But the girls were light of heart, and in the pride of their youth. But, alas! they had both of them blundered frightfully. It was Edith, Edith the prudent, Edith the wise,

Edith, who was supposed to know everything, who had first gone astray in her blundering, and had taken Ada with her; but the story with its details must be told.

"My pet," she said to her elder sister, as they were standing together at the kitchen dresser, "I know he means to speak to you to-day."

"What nonsense, Edith!"

"It has to be done, some day, you know. And he is just the man to come upon one in the time of one's dire distress. Of course we haven't got a halfpenny now belonging to us. I was thinking only the other day how comfortable it is that we never go out of the house because we haven't the means to buy boots. Now Captain Clayton is just the man to be doubly attracted by such penury."

"I don't know why a man is to make an offer to a girl just because he finds her working like a housemaid."

"I do. I can see it all. He is just the man to take you in his arms because he found you peeling potatoes."

"I beg he will do nothing of the kind," said Ada. "He has never said a word to me, or I to him, to justify such a proceeding. I should at once hit him over the head with my brush."

"Here he comes, and now we will see how far I understand such matters."

"Don't go, Edith," said Ada. "Pray don't go. If you go I shall go with you. These things ought always to come naturally, —that is, if they come at all."

It did not "come" at that moment, for Edith was so far mistaken that Captain Clayton, after saying a few words to the girls, passed on out of the back-door, intent on special business. "What a wretched individual he is," said Edith. "Fancy pinning one's character on the doings of such a man as that. However, he will be back again to dinner, and you will not be so hard upon him then with your dusting-brush."

Before dinner the Captain did return, and found himself alone with Edith in the kitchen. It was her turn on this occasion to send up whatever meal in the shape of dinner Castle Morony could afford. "There you have it, sir," she said, pointing to a boiled neck of mutton, which had been cut from the remains of a sheep sent in to supply the family wants.

"I see," said he. "It will make a very good dinner,—or a very bad one, according to circumstances, as they may fall out before the dinner leaves the kitchen."

"Then they will have to fall out very quickly," said Edith. But the colour had flown to her face, and in that moment she had learned to suspect the truth. And her mind flew back rapidly over all her doings and sayings for the last three months. If it was so, she could never forgive herself. If it

was so, Ada would never forgive her. If it was so, they two
and Captain Yorke Clayton must be separated for ever.
"Well; what is it?" she said, roughly. The joint of meat had
fallen from her hands, and she looked up at Captain Clayton
with all the anger she could bring into her face.

"Edith," he said, "you surely know that I love you."

"I know nothing of the kind. There can be no reason why
I should know it,—why I should guess it. It cannot be so
without grievous wrong on your part."

"What wrong?"

"Base wrong done to my sister," she answered. Then she
remembered that she had betrayed her sister, and she remembered too how much of the supposed love-making had been
done by her own words, and not by any spoken by Captain
Clayton. And there came upon her at that moment a remembrance also of that other moment in which she had acknowledged to herself that she had loved this man, and had told
herself that the love was vain, and had sworn to herself that
she would never stand in Ada's way, and had promised to herself that all things should be happy to her as this man's sister-in-law. Acting then on this idea merely because Ada had been
beautiful she had gone to work,—and this had come of it! In
that minute that was allowed to her as the boiled mutton was
cooling on the dresser beneath her hand, all this passed through
her mind.

"Wrong done by me to Ada!" said the Captain.

"I have said it; but if you are a gentleman you will forget
it. I know that you are a gentleman,—a gallant man, such as
few I think exist anywhere. Captain Clayton, there are but
two of us. Take the best; take the fairest; take the sweetest.
Let all this be as though it had never been spoken. I will be
such a sister to you as no man ever won for himself. And Ada
will be as loving a wife as ever graced a man's home. Let it
be so, and I will bless every day of your life."

"No," he said slowly, "I cannot let it be like that. I have
learned to love you and you only, and I thought that you had
known it."

"Never!"

"I had thought so. It cannot be as you propose. I shall
never speak of your sister to a living man. I shall never
whisper a word of her regard even here in her own family.
But I cannot change my heart as you propose. Your sister is
beautiful, and sweet, and good; but she is not the girl who has
crept into my heart, and made a lasting home for herself there,
—if the girl who has done so would but accept it. Ada is not
the girl whose brightness, whose bravery, whose wit and ready
spirit have won me. These things go, I think, without any
effort. I have known that there has been no attempt on your

part; but the thing has been done and I had hoped that you were aware of it. It cannot now be undone. I cannot be passed on to another. Here, here, here is what I want," and he put his two hands upon her shoulders. "There is no other girl in all Ireland that can supply her place if she be lost to me."

He had spoken very solemnly, and she had stood there in solemn mood listening to him. By degrees the conviction had come upon her that he was in earnest, and was not to be changed in his purpose by anything that she could say to him. She had blundered, had blundered awfully. She had thought that with a man beauty would be everything; but with this man beauty had been nothing; nor had good temper and a sense of duty availed anything. She rushed into the dining-room carrying the boiled mutton with her, and he followed. What should she do now? Ada would yield—would give him up—would retire into the background, and would declare that Edith should be made happy, but would never lift up her head again. And she—she herself—could also give him up, and would lift up her head again. She knew that she had a power of bearing sorrow, and going on with the work of the world, in spite of all troubles, which Ada did not possess. It might, therefore, have all been settled, but that the man was stubborn, and would not be changed. "Of course, he is a man," said Edith to herself, as she put the mutton down. "Of course he must have it all to please himself. Of course he will be selfish."

"I thought you were never coming with our morsel of dinner," said Mr. Jones.

"Here is the morsel of dinner; but I could have dished it in half the time if Captain Clayton had not been there."

"Of course I am the offender," said he, as he sat down. "And now I have forgotten to bring the potatoes." So he started off, and met Florian at the door coming in with them. Mr. Jones carved the mutton, and Captain Clayton was helped first. In a boycotted house you will always find that the gentlemen are helped before the ladies. It is a part of the principle of boycotting that women shall subject themselves.

Captain Clayton, after his first little stir about the potatoes, ate his dinner in perfect silence. That which had taken place upset him more completely than the rifles of two or three Landleaguers. Mr. Jones was also silent. He was a man at the present moment nearly overwhelmed by his cares. And Ada, too, was silent. As Edith looked at her furtively she began to fear that her pet suspected something. There was a look of suffering in her face which Edith could read, though it was not plainly enough written there to be legible to others. Her father and Florian had no key by which to read it, and Captain Clayton never allowed his eyes to turn towards Ada's face. But it was imperative on both that they should not all fall into

some feeling of special sorrow through their silence. " It is just
one week more," she said, " before you men must be at
Galway."

"Only one week," said Florian.

" It will be much better to have it over," said the father. " I
do not think you need come back at all, but start at once from
Galway. Your sisters can bring what things you want, and say
good-bye at Athenry."

" My poor Florian ! " said Edith.

" I shan't mind it so much when I get to England," said the
boy. " I suppose I shall come home for the Christmas
holidays."

" I don't know about that," said the father. " It will depend
upon the state of the country."

" You will come and meet him, Ada ? " asked Edith.

" I suppose so," said Ada. And her sister knew from the
tone of her voice that some evil was already suspected.

There was nothing more said that night till Edith and Ada
were together. Mr. Jones lingered with his daughters, and the
Captain took Florian out about the orchard, thinking it well to
make him used to whatever danger might come to him from
being out of the house. " They will never come where they will
be sure to be known," said the Captain ; " and known by various
witnesses. And they won't come for the chance of a pop-shot.
I am getting to know their ways as well as though I had lived
there all my life. They count on the acquittal of Pat Carroll as
a certainty. Whatever I may be, you are tolerably safe as long
as that is the case."

" They may shoot me in mistake for you," said the boy.

" Well, yes ; that is so. Let us go back to the house. But I
don't think there would be any danger to-night any way." Then
they returned, and found Mr. Jones alone in the dining-room.
He was very melancholy in these days, as a man must be whom
ruin stares in the face.

Edith had followed Ada upstairs to the bed-rooms, and had
crept after her into that which had been prepared for Captain
Clayton. She could see now by the lingering light of an August
evening that a tear had fallen from each eye, and had slowly
run down her sister's cheeks. " Oh, Ada, dear Ada, what is
troubling you ? "

" Nothing,—much."

" My girl, my beauty, my darling ! Much or little, what is
it ? Cannot you tell me ? "

" He cares nothing for me," said Ada, laying her hand upon
the pillow, thus indicating the " he " whom she intended. Edith
answered not a word, but pressed her arm tight round her
sister's waist. " It is so," said Ada, turning round upon her
sister as though to rebuke her. " You know that it is so."

"My beauty, my own one," said Edith, kissing her.

"You know it is so. He has told you. It is not me that he loves; it is you. You are his chosen one. I am nothing to him,—nothing, nothing." Then she flung herself down upon the bed which her own hands had prepared for him.

It was all true. As the assertions had come from her one by one, Edith had found herself unable to deny a tittle of what was said. "Ada, if you knew my heart to you."

"What good is it? Why did you teach me to believe a falsehood?"

"Oh! you will kill me if you accuse me. I have been so true to you." Then Ada turned round upon the bed, and hid her face for a few minutes upon the pillow. "Ada, have I not been true to you?"

"But that you should have been so much mistaken;—you, who know everything."

"I have not known him," said Edith.

"But you will," said Ada. "You will be his wife."

"Never!" ejaculated the other.

Then slowly, Ada got up from the bed and shook her hair from off her face and wiped her eyes with her handkerchief. "It must be so," she said. "Of course it must, as he wishes it. He must have all that he desires."

"No, not so. He shall never have this."

"Yes, Edith, he must and he shall. Do you not know that you loved him before you ever bade me to do so? But why, oh, why did you ever make that great mistake? And why was I so foolish as to have believed you? Come," she said, "I must make his bed for him once again. He will be here soon now and we must be away." Then she did obliterate the traces of her form which her figure had made upon the bed, and smoothed the pillow, and wiped away the mark of her tear which had fallen on it. "Come, Edith, come," said she, "let us go and understand each other. He knows, for you have told him, but no one else need know. He shall be your husband, and I will be his sister, and all shall be bright between you."

"Never," said Edith. "Never! He will never be married if he waits for me."

"My dear one, you shall be his wife," said Ada. Such were the last words which passed between them on that night.

CHAPTER XXX.

THE ROAD TO BALLYGLUNIN.

THE days ran on for the trial of Pat Carroll, but Edith did not again see Captain Clayton. There came tidings to Morony Castle of the new honours which Mr. O'Mahony had achieved.

"I don't know that the country will be much the wiser for his services," said Captain Clayton. "He will go altogether with those wretched Land-leaguers."

"He will be the best of the lot," said Mr. Jones.

"It is saying very little for him," said Captain Clayton.

"He is an honest man, and I take him to be the only honest man among them."

"He won't remain a Land-leaguer long if he is honest. But what about his daughter?"

"Frank has seen her down in Cavan, and declares that she is about to make any amount of money at the London theatres."

"I take it they will find it quite a new thing to have a Member of Parliament among their number with an income," said Clayton. "But I'll bet any man a new hat that there is a split between him and them before the next Parliament is half over."

This took place during one of the visits which Captain Clayton had made to Morony Castle in reference to the coming trial. Florian had been already sent on to Mr. Blake's of Carnlough, and was to be picked up there on that very afternoon by Mr. Jones, and driven to Ballyglunin, so as to be taken from thence to the assize town by train. This was thought to be most expedient, as the boy would not be on the road for above half an hour.

After Captain Clayton had gone, Mr. Jones asked after Edith, and was told that she was away in Headford. She had walked into town to call on Mrs. Armstrong, with a view of getting a few articles which Mrs. Armstrong had promised to buy for her. Such was the story as given to Mr. Jones, and fully believed by him; but the reader may be permitted to think that the young lady was not anxious to meet the young gentleman.

"Ada," said Mr. Jones suddenly, "is there anything between Edith and Captain Clayton?"

"What makes you ask, papa?"

"Because Peter has hinted it. I do not care to have such things told me of my own family by the servant."

"Yes, there is, papa," said Ada boldly. "Captain Clayton is in love with Edith."

"This is no time for marrying or giving in marriage."

Ada made no reply, but thought that it must at the same time be a very good time for becoming engaged. It would have been so for her had such been her luck. But of herself she said nothing. She had made her statement openly and bravely to her sister, so that there should be no departing from it. Mr. Jones said nothing further at the moment, but before the girls had separated for the night Ada had told Edith what had occurred.

At that time they were in the house alone together,—alone as regarded the family, though they still had the protection of Peter. Mr. Jones had started on his journey to Galway.

"Papa," said Ada, "knows all about Yorke."

"Knows what?" demanded Edith.

"That you and he are engaged together."

"He knows more than I do, then. He knows more than I ever shall know. Ada, you should not have said so. It will have to be all unsaid."

"Not at all, dear."

"It will all have to be unsaid. Have you been speaking to Captain Clayton on the subject?"

"Not a word. Indeed it was not I who told papa. It was Peter. Peter said that there was something between you and him, and papa asked me. I told papa that he was in love with you. That was true at any rate. You won't deny that?"

"I will deny anything that connects my name with that of Captain Yorke Clayton."

But Ada had determined how that matter should arrange itself. Since the blow had first fallen on her, she had had time to think of it,—and she had thought of it. Edith had done her best for her (presuming that this brave Captain was the best) and she in return would do her best for Edith. No one knew the whole story but they two. They were to be to her the dearest friends of her future life, and she would not let the knowledge of such a story stand in her way or theirs.

The train was to start from the Ballyglunin station for Athenry at 4.20 p.m. It would then have left Tuam for Athenry, where it would fall into the day mail-train from Dublin to Galway. It was something out of the way for Mr. Jones to call at Carnlough; but Carnlough was not three miles from Ballyglunin, and Mr. Jones made his arrangements accordingly. He called at Carnlough, and there took up the boy on his outside car. Peter had come with him, so as to take back the car to Morony Castle. But Peter had made himself of late somewhat disagreeable, and Mr. Jones had in truth been sulky.

"Look here, Peter," he had said, speaking from one side of the car to the other, "if you are afraid to come to Ballyglunin with me and Master Flory, say so, and get down."

"I'm not afeared, Mr. Jones."

"Then don't say so. I don't believe you are afeared, as you call it."

"Then why do you be talking at me like that, sir?"

"I don't think you are a coward; but you are anxious to make the most of your services on my behalf. You are telling everyone that something special is due to you for staying in a boycotted house. It's a kind of service for which I am grateful, but I can't be grateful and pay too."

"Why do you talk to a poor boy in that way?"

"So that the poor boy may understand me. You are willing, I believe, to stick to your old master,—from sheer good heart. But you like to talk about it. Now I don't like to hear about it." After that Peter drove on in silence till they came to Carnlough.

The car had been seen coming up the avenue, and Mr. Blake, with his wife and Florian, were standing on the doorsteps. "Now do take care of the poor dear boy," said Mrs. Blake. "There are such dreadful stories of horrible men about the country."

"Don't mention such nonsense, Winifred," said her husband, "trying to frighten the boy. There isn't a human being between this and Ballyglunin for whom I won't be responsible. Till you come to a mile of the station it's all my own property."

"But they can shoot——" Then Mrs. Blake left the rest of her sentence unspoken, having been checked by her husband's eye. The boy, however, had heard it and trembled.

"Come along, Florian," said the father. "Get up along with Peter." The attempt which he had made to live with his son on affectionate paternal relations had hardly been successful. The boy had been told so much of murderers that he had been made to fear. Peter,—and other Peters about the country,—had filled his mind with sad foreboding. And there had always been something timid, something almost unmanly in his nature. He had seemed to prefer to shrink and cower and be mysterious with the Carrolls to coming forward boldly with such a man as Yorke Clayton. The girls had seen this, and had declared that he was no more than a boy; but his father had seen it and had made no such allowance. And now he saw that he trembled. But Florian got up on the car, and Peter drove them off to Ballyglunin.

Carnlough was not above three Irish miles from Ballyglunin; and Mr. Jones started on the little journey without a misgiving. He sat alone on the near side of the car, and Florian sat on the other, together with Peter who was driving. The horse was a heavy, slow-going animal, rough and hairy in its coat, but trustworthy and an old servant. There had been a time when Mr. Jones kept a carriage, but that had been before the bad

times had begun. The carriage horses had been sold after the
flood,—as Ada had called the memorable incident ; and now
there were but three cart horses at Morony Castle, of which this
one animal alone was habitually driven in the car. The floods,
indeed, had now retreated from the lands of Ballintubber and
the flood gates were mended ; but there would be no crop of hay
on all those eighty acres this year, and Mr. Jones was in no
condition to replace his private stud. As he went along on this
present journey he was thinking bitterly of the injury which had
been done him. He had lost over two hundred tons of hay, and
each ton of hay would have been worth three pounds ten
shillings. He had been unable to get a sluice gate mended till
men had been brought together from Monaghan and parts of
Cavan to mend them for him, and he had even to send these
men into Limerick to buy the material, as not a piece of timber
could be procured in Galway for the use of a household so well
boycotted as was Morony Castle. There had been also various
calls on Mr. Jones from those relatives whose money had been
left as mortgages on his property. And no rent had as yet come
in, although various tenants had been necessarily evicted.
Every man's hand was against him ; so that there was no money
in his coffers. He who had chiefly sinned against him,—who
was the first to sin,—was the sinner whom he was about to
prosecute at Galway. It must be supposed, therefore, that he
was not in a good humour as he was driven along the road to
Ballyglunin.

They had not yet passed the boundary fence between
Carnlough and the property of one of the numerous race of
Bodkins, when Mr. Jones saw a mask, which he supposed
to be a mask worn by a man, through a hole in the wall
just in front of him, but high above his head. And at the
same moment he could see the muzzles of a double-barrelled
rifle presented through the hole in the wall. What he saw he
saw but for a few seconds ; but he could see it plainly. He saw
it so plainly as to be able afterwards to swear to a black mask,
and to a double-barrelled gun. Then a trigger was pulled, and
one bullet—the second—went through the collar of his own coat,
while the first had had a more fatal and truer aim. The father
jumped up and turning round saw that his boy had fallen to the
ground. "Oh, my God!" said Peter, and he stopped the horse
suddenly. The place was one where the commencement had
been made of a cutting in the road during the potato failure of
1846 ; so that the wall and the rifle which had been passed
through it were about four or five feet above the car. Mr. Jones
rushed up the elevation, and clambered, he did not know how,
into the field. There he saw the back of a man speeding along
from the wall, and in the man's hand there was a gun. Mr.
Jones looked around but there was no one nigh him but Peter,

the old servant, and his dying boy. He could see, however, that the man who ran was short of stature.

But though his rage had sufficed to carry him up from the road into the field, the idea that his son had been shot caused him to pause as he ran, and to return to the road. When he got there he found two girls about seventeen and eighteen years of age, one sitting on the road with Florian's head on her lap, and the other kneeling and holding the boy's hands. "Oh, yer honour! sorrow a taste in life do we know about it," said the kneeling girl.

"Not a sight did we see, or a sound did we hear," said the other, "only the going off of the blunderbuss. Oh, wirra shure! oh, musha, musha! and it's dead he is, the darling boy." Mr. Jones came round and picked up poor Florian and laid him on the car. The bullet had gone true to its mark and had buried itself in his brain. There was the end of poor Florian Jones and all his troubles. The father did not say a word, not even in reply to Peter's wailings or to the girls' easy sorrow; but, taking the rein in his own hands, drove the car with the body on it back to Carnlough.

We can hardly analyse the father's mind as he went. Not a tear came to his relief. Nor during this half hour can he hardly have been said to sorrow. An intensity of wrath filled his breast. He had spent his time for many a long year in doing all in his power for those around him, and now they had brought him to this. They had robbed him of his boy's heart. They had taught his boy to be one of them, and to be untrue to his own people. And now, because he had yielded to better teachings, they had murdered him. They had taught his boy to be a coward; for even in his bereavement he remembered poor Florian's failing. The accursed Papist people were all cowards down to their backbones. So he said of them in his rage. There was not one of them who could look any peril in the face as did Yorke Clayton or his son Frank. But they were terribly powerful in their wretched want of manliness. They could murder, and were protected in their bloodthirstiness one by another. He did not doubt but that those two girls who were wailing on the road knew well enough who was the murderer, but no one would tell in this accursed, unhallowed, godless country. The honour and honesty of one man did not, in these days, prompt another to abstain from vice. The only heroism left in the country was the heroism of mystery, of secret bloodshed, and of hidden attacks.

He had driven back methodically to Carnlough gates, but he hesitated to carry his burden up to the hall-door. Would it not be better for him at once to go home, and there to endure the suffering that was in store for him? But he remembered that it would behove him to take what steps might be possible for tracing the murderer. That by no steps could anything be done, he was sure; but still the attempt was necessary. He had, however, paused a minute or two at the open gate when he was rebuked by Peter. "Shure yer honour is going up to the house to get the constables to scour the counthry."

"Scour the country!" said the father. "All the country will turn out to defend the murderer of my boy." But he drove up to the front, and Peter knocked at the door.

"Good heaven, Jones!" said Mr. Blake, as he looked at the car and its occupant. The poor boy's head was supported on the pillow behind the driver's seat on which no one sat. Peter held him by both his feet, and Mr. Jones had his hand within his grasp.

"So it is," said the father. "You know where they have cut the road just where your property meres with Bodkin's. There was a man above there who had loop-holed the wall. I saw his face wearing a mask as plain as I can see yours. And he had a double-barrelled gun. He fired the two shots, and my boy was killed by the first."

"They have struck you too on the collar of your coat."

"I got into the field with the murderer, and I could have caught the man had I been younger. But what would have been the use? No jury would have found him guilty. What am I to do? Oh, God! what am I to do?" Mrs. Blake and her daughter were now out upon the steps, and were filling the hall with their wailings. "Tell me, Blake, what had I better do?" Then Mr. Blake decided that the body should remain there that night, and Mr. Jones also, and that the police should be sent for to do whatever might seem fitting to the policemen's mind. Peter was sent off to Morony Castle with such a letter as Miss Blake was able to write to the two Jones girls. The police came from Tuam, but the result of their enquiries on that night need not be told here.

CHAPTER XXXI.

THE GALWAY COURT HOUSE.

THERE was a feeling very general in the county that the murder had been committed by the man named Lax, who was known to have been in the neighbourhood lately, and was declared by his friends at Headford to be now in Galway, waiting for the trial of Pat Carroll. But there seemed to be a feeling about the country that Florian Jones had deserved his fate. He had, it was said, been untrue to his religion. He had given a solemn promise to Father Brosnan,—of what nature was not generally known,—and had broken it. "The bittherness of the Orange feud was in his blood," said Father Brosnan. But neither did he explain the meaning of what he said, as none of the Jones family had ever been Orangemen. But the idea was common about Tuam and Headford that Pat Carroll was a martyr, and that Florian had been persuaded to turn Protestant in order that he might give false evidence against him. The reader, however, must understand that Florian still professed the Catholic religion at the moment of his death, and that all Headford was aware that Pat Carroll had broken the sluice gate at Ballintubber.

After an interval of two days the trial was about to go on at Galway in spite of the murder. It was quite true that by nothing could the breath of life be restored to Florian Jones. His evidence, such as it was, could now be taken only from his deposition. And such evidence was regarded as being very unfair both on one side and on the other. As given against Pat Carroll it was regarded as unfair, as being incapable of subjection to cross-examination. The boy's evidence had been extracted from him by his parents and by Captain Yorke Clayton, in opposition to the statements which had been made scores of times by himself on the other side, and which, if true, would all tend to exonerate the prisoner. It had been the intention of Mr. O'Donnell, the senior counsel employed to defend Carroll, to insist, with the greatest severity, on the lies told by the poor boy. It was this treatment which Florian had especially feared. There could be no such treatment now ; but Mr. O'Donnell would know well how to insist on the injustice of the deposition, in which no allusion would be made to the falsehood previously told. But on the other side it was said that the witness had been removed so that his evidence should not be given. They must now depend solely on the statement of Terry Carroll, Pat's brother, and who also had lied terribly before he told the truth. And he, too, was condemned more bitterly, even by Mr. Jones and his friends, in that he was giving evidence against his brother, than had he continued to lie on his behalf. The circumstances being such as they were, it was felt to be almost impossible to secure the conviction of Pat Carroll for the offence he had committed. And yet there were certainly a dozen persons who had seen that offence committed in the light of day, and many other dozens who knew by whom the offence had been committed.

And, indeed, the feeling had become common through the country that all the lawyers and judges in Ireland,—the lawyers and judges, that is, who were opposed to the Land-league,— could not secure a conviction of any kind against prisoners whom the Land-league was bound to support. It had come to

be whispered about, that there were men in the County of
Galway,—and men also in other counties,—too strong for the
Government, men who could beat the Government on any point,
men whom no jury could be brought to convict by any evidence;
men who boasted of the possession of certain secret powers,—
which generally meant murder. It came to be believed that
these men were possessed of certain mysterious capabilities
which the police could not handle, nor the magistrates touch.
And the danger to be feared from these men arose chiefly from
the belief in them which had become common. It was not that
they could do anything special if left to their own devices, but
that the crowds by whom they were surrounded trembled at
their existence. The man living next to you, ignorant, and a
Roman Catholic, inspired with some mysterious awe, would wish
in his heart that the country was rid of such firebrands. He
knew well that the country, and he as part of the country, had
more to get from law and order than from murder and misrule.
But murder and misrule had so raised their heads for the present
as to make themselves appear to him more powerful than law
and order. Mr. Lax, and others like him, were keenly alive to
the necessity of maintaining this belief in their mysterious
power.

The trial came on, having been delayed two days by the
murder of poor Florian Jones. His body had, in the meantime,
been taken home, and the only visitor received at Morony
Castle had been Yorke Clayton. On his coming he had been
at first closeted with Mr. Jones, and had then gone out and seen
the two girls together. He had taken Ada's hand first and then
Edith's, but he had held Edith's the longer. The girls had
known that it was so, but neither of them had said a word to
rebuke him. "Who was it?" asked Ada.

Clayton shook his head and ground his teeth. "Do you
know, or have you an idea? You know so much about the
country," said Edith.

"To you two, but to you only, I do know. He and I cannot
exist together. The man's name is Lax."

It may be imagined that the trial was not commenced at
Galway without the expression of much sympathy for Mr. Jones
and the family at Morony Castle. It is hard to explain the
different feelings which existed, feelings exactly opposed to
each other, but which still were both in their way general
and true. He was "poor Mr. Jones," who had lost his son,
and, worse still, his eighty acres of grass, and he was, also
"that fellow Jones," that enemy to the Land-league, whom
it behoved all patriotic Irishmen to get the better of and to
conquer. Florian had been murdered on the 30th of August,
which was a Tuesday, and the trial had been postponed until
Friday, the 2nd of September. It was understood that the boy was

to be buried at Headford, on Saturday, the 3rd; but, nevertheless, the father was in the assize town on the Friday. He was in the town, and at eleven o'clock he took his place in the Crown Court. He was a man who was still continually summoned as a grand juror, and as such had no difficulty in securing for himself a place. To the right of the judge sat the twelve jurors who had been summoned to try the case, and to the left was the grand jurors' box, in which Mr. Jones took his seat early in the day. And Frank was also in the court, and had been stopped by no one when he accompanied his father into the grand jurors' box.

But the court was crowded in a wonderful manner, so that they who understood the ways of criminal courts in Ireland knew that something special was boded. As soon as Mr. Justice Parry took his seat, it was seen that the court was much more than ordinarily filled, and was filled by men who did not make themselves amenable to the police. Many were the instructions given by the judge who had been selected with a special view to this trial. Judge Parry was a Roman Catholic, who had sat in the House of Commons as a strong Liberal, had been Attorney-General to a Liberal Government, and had been suspected of holding Home-Rule sentiments. But men, when they become judges, are apt to change their ideas. And Judge Parry was now known to be a firm man, whom nothing would turn from the execution of his duty. There had been many Judge Parrys in Ireland, who have all gone the same gait, and have followed the same course when they have accepted the ermine. A man is at liberty to indulge what vagaries he pleases, as long as he is simply a Member of Parliament. But a judge is not at liberty. He now gave special instructions to the officers of the court to keep quiet and to preserve order. But the court was full, densely crowded; and the noise which arose from the crowd was only the noise as of people whispering loudly among themselves.

The jury was quickly sworn and the trial was set on foot. Pat Carroll was made to stand up in the dock, and Mr. Jones looked at the face of the man who had been the first on his property to show his hostility to the idea of paying rent. He and Lax had been great friends, and it was known that Lax had sworn that in a short time not a shilling of rent should be paid in the County Mayo. From that assurance all these troubles had come.

Then the Attorney-General opened the case, and to tell the truth, he made a speech which, though very eloquent, was longer than necessary. He spoke of the dreadful state of the country, a matter which he might have left to the judge, and almost burst into tears when he alluded to the condition of Mr. Jones, the gentleman who sat opposite to him. And he spoke at full length of the evidence of the poor boy whose deposition he held in his hand, which he told the jury he would read to them later on in the day. No doubt the lad had deceived his father since the offence had been committed. He had long declared that he knew nothing of the perpetrators. The boy had seemed to entertain in his mind certain ideas friendly to the Land-league, and had made promises on behalf of Land-leaguers to which he had long adhered. But his father had at last succeeded, and the truth had been forthcoming. His lordship would instruct them how far the boy's deposition could be accepted as evidence, and how far it must fail. And so at last the Attorney-General brought his eloquent speech to an end.

And now there arose a murmuring sound in the court, and a stirring of feet and a moving of shoulders, louder than that which had been heard before. The judge, there on his bench, looking out from under his bushy eyebrows, could see that the people before him were all of one class. And he could see also that the half-dozen policemen who were kept close among the crowd, were so pressed as to be hardly masters of their own actions. He called out a word even from the bench in which there was something as to clearing the court; but no attempt to clear the court was made or was apparently possible. The first witness was summoned, and an attempt was made to bring him up through the dock into the witness-box. This witness was Terry Carroll, the brother of Pat, and was known to be there that he might swear away his brother's liberty. His head no sooner appeared, as about to leave the dock, than the whole court was filled with a yell of hatred. There were two policemen standing between the two brothers, but Pat only turned round and looked at the traitor with scorn. But the voices through the court sounded louder and more venomous as Terry Carroll stepped out of the dock among the policemen who were to make an avenue for him up to the witness-box.

It was the last step he ever made. At that moment the flash of a pistol was seen in the court; of a pistol close at the man's ear, and Terry Carroll was a dead man. The pistol had touched his head as it had been fired, so that there had been no chance of escape. In this way was the other witness removed, who had been brought thither by the Crown to give evidence as to the demolition of Mr. Jones's flood gates. And it was said afterwards,—for weeks afterwards,—that such should be the fate of all witnesses who appeared in the west of Ireland to obey the behests of the Crown.

Then was seen the reason why the special crowd had been gathered there, and of what nature were the men who had swarmed into court. Clayton, who had been sitting at the end of the row of barristers, jumped up over the back of the bench and rushed in among the people, who now tried simply to hold their own places, and appeared neither to be anxious to go in or out. "Tear an' ages, Musther Clayton, what are you after jumping on to a fellow in that way?" This was said by a brawny Milesian, on to whose shoulders our friend had leaped, meaning to get down among the crowd. But the Milesian had struck him hard, and would have knocked him down had there been room enough for him on which to fall. But Clayton had minded the blow not at all, and had minded the judge as little, making his way through the crowd over the dead body of Terry Carroll. He had been aware that Lax was in the court, and had seated himself opposite to the place where the man had stood. But Lax had moved himself during the Attorney-General's speech, either with the view of avoiding the Captain's eyes,—or if he were to be the murderer, of finding the best place from which the deed could be done. If this had been his object, certainly the place had been well selected. It was afterwards stated, that though fifty people at the judge's end of the court had seen the pistol, no eyes had seen the face of him who held it. Many faces had been seen, but nobody could connect a single face with the pistol. And it was proved also that the ball had entered the head just under the ear, with a slant upwards towards the brain, as though the weapon had been used by someone crouching towards the ground.

Clayton made his way out of court, followed by the faithful Hunter, and was soon surrounded by half a score of policemen. Hunter was left to watch the door of the court, because he was well acquainted with Lax, and because should Lax come across Hunter, "God help Mr. Lax!" as Clayton expressed himself. And others were sent by twos and threes through the city to catch this man if it were possible, or to obtain tidings respecting him. "A man cannot bury himself under the ground," said Clayton; "we have always this pull upon them, that they cannot make themselves invisible." But in this case it almost did appear that Mr. Lax had the power.

Though Pat Carroll was not at once set at liberty his trial was brought to an end. It was felt to be impossible to send the case to the jury when the only two witnesses belonging to the Crown had been murdered. The prisoner was remanded, or sent back to gaol, so that the Crown might look for more evidence if more might chance to be found, and everybody else connected in the matter was sent home. A dark gloom settled itself on Galway, and men were heard to whisper among themselves that the Queen's laws were no longer in force. And there was a rowdy readiness to oppose all force, the force of the police for instance, and the force of the military. There were men there who seemed to think that now had come the good time when they might knock anyone on the head at their leisure. It did not come quite to this, as the police were still combined, and their enemies were not so. But such men as Captain Clayton began to look as though they doubted what would become of it. "If he thinks he is big enough to catch a hold of Terry Lax and keep him, he'll precious soon find his mistake." This was said by Con Heffernan of Captain Clayton.

CHAPTER XXXII.

MR. O'MAHONY AS MEMBER OF PARLIAMENT.

FRANK JONES had travelled backwards and forwards between Morony Castle and the North more than once since these things were doing, and had met the new member for Cavan together with Rachel on the very evening on which poor Florian had been murdered. It was not till the next morning that the news had become generally known. "I am sorry to hear, Frank," said Rachel, "that you are all doing so badly at Morony Castle."

"Badly enough."

"Are you fetching all these people down from here to do the work the men there ought to do? How are the men there to get their wages?"

"That is the essence of boycotting," said Frank. "The men there won't get their wages, and can only live by robbing the governor and men like him of their rents. And in that way they can't live long. Everything will be disturbed and ruined."

"It seems to me," said Rachel, "that the whole country is coming to an end."

"Your father is Member of Parliament now, and of course he will set it all to rights."

"He will at any rate do his best to do so," said Rachel, "and will rob no man in the doing it. What do you mean to do with yourself?"

"Stick to the ship till it sinks, and then go down with it."

"And your sisters?"

"They are of the same way of thinking, I take it. They are not good at inventing any way of getting out of their troubles; but they know how to endure."

"Now, Frank," said she, "shall I give you a bit of advice?"

"Oh yes! I like advice."

"You wanted to kiss me just now."

"That was natural at any rate."

"No, it wasn't;——because you and I are two. When a

young man and a young woman are two they shouldn't kiss any more. That is logic."

"I don't know about logic."

"At any rate it is something of the same sort. It is the kind of thing everybody believes in if they want to go right. You and I want to go right, don't we?"

"I believe so."

"Of course we do," and she took hold of his arm and shook him. "It would break your heart if you didn't think I was going right, and why shouldn't I be as anxious about you? Now for my piece of advice. I am going to make a lot of money."

"I am glad to hear it."

"Come and share it with me. I would have shared yours if you had made a lot. You must call me Madame de Iona, or some such name as that. The name does not matter, but the money will be all there. Won't it be grand to be able to help your father and your sisters! Only you men are so beastly proud. Isn't it honest money,—money that has come by singing?"

"Certainly it is."

"And if the wife earns it instead of the husband;—isn't that honest? And then you know," she said, looking up into his face, "you can kiss me right away. Isn't that an inducement?"

The offer was an inducement, but the conversation only ended in a squabble. She rebuked him for his dishonesty, in taking the kiss without acceding to the penalty, and he declared that according to his view of the case, he could not become the fainéant husband of a rich opera singer. "And yet you would ask me to become the fainéante wife of a wealthy landowner. And because, under the stress of the times, you are not wealthy you choose to reject the girl altogether who has given you her heart. Go away. You are no good. When a man stands up on his hind legs and pretends to be proud he never is any good."

Then Mr. O'Mahony came in and had a political discussion with Frank Jones. "Yes," said the Member of Parliament, "I mean to put my shoulder to the wheel, and do the very best that can be done. I cannot believe but what a man in earnest will find out the truth. Politics are not such a hopeless muddle but what some gleam of light may be made to shine through."

"There are such things as leaders," said Frank.

Then Mr. O'Mahony stood up and laid his hand upon his heart. "You remember what Van Artevelde said —'They shall murder me ere make me go the way that is not my way, for an inch.' I say the same."

"What will Mr. Parnell do with such a follower?"

"Mr. Parnell is also an honest man," cried Mr. O'Mahony. "Two honest men looking for light together will never fall out. I at any rate have some little gift of utterance. Perhaps I can persuade a man, or two men. At any rate I will try."

"But how are we to get back to London, father?" said Rachel. "I don't think it becomes an honest Member of Parliament to take money out of a common fund. You will have to remain here in pawn till I go and sing you out." But Rachel had enough left of Lord Castlewell's money to carry them back to London, on condition that they did not stop on the road, and to this condition she was forced to bring her father.

Early on the following morning before they started the news reached Cavan of poor Florian's death. "Oh God! My brother!" exclaimed Frank; but it was all that he did say. He was a man who, like his father, had become embittered by the circumstances of the times. Mr. Jones had bought his property, now thirty years since, with what was then called a parliamentary title. He had paid hard money for it, and had induced his friends to lend their money to assist the purchase, for which he was responsible. Much of the land he had been enabled to keep in his own hands, but on none of the tenants' had he raised the rent. Now there had come forth a law, not from the hand of the Land-leaguers, but from the Government, who, it was believed, would protect those who did their duty by the country. Under this law commissioners were to be appointed,—or sub-commissioners,—men supposed to be not of great mark in the country, who were to reduce the rent according to their ideas of justice. If a man paid ten pounds, —or had engaged to pay ten,—let him take his pen and write down seven or eight as the sub-commissioner should decide. As the outside landlords, the friends of Mr. Jones, must have five pounds out of the original ten, that which was coming to Mr. Jones himself would be about halved. And the condition of Mr. Jones, under the system of boycotting which he was undergoing, was hard to endure. Now Frank was the eldest son, and the property of Castle Morony and Ballintubber was entailed upon him. He was brought up in his early youth to feel that he was to fill that situation, which, of all others, is the most attractive. He was to have been the eldest son of a man of unembarrassed property. Now he was offered to be taken to London as the travelling husband—or upper servant, as it might be—of an opera singer. Then, while he was in this condition, there came to him the news that his brother had been murdered; and he must go home to give what assistance was in his power to his poor, ill-used sisters. It is not to be wondered at that he was embittered. He had been spending some hours of the last day in reading the clauses of the Bill under which the sub-commissioners were to show him what mercy they might think right. As he left Cavan the following morning, his curses were more deep against the Government than against the Land-league.

Mr. Mahony and his daughter got back to Cecil Street in September in a very impecunious state. He soon began to understand that the position of Member of Parliament was more difficult and dangerous than that of a lecturer. The police had interfered with him; but the police had in truth done him no harm, nor had they wanted anything from him. But as Member of Parliament for Cavan the attacks made on his purse were very numerous. And throughout September, when the glory of Parliament was just newly settled upon his shoulders, sundry calls were made upon him for obedience which were distasteful to him. He was wanted over in Ireland. Mr. O'Mahony was an outspoken, frank man, who did not at all like to be troubled with secrets. "I haven't got any money to come over to Ireland just at present. They took what I had away from me in County Cavan during the election. I don't suppose I shall have any to speak of till after Christmas, and then it won't be much. If you have anything for a man to do in London it will be more within my reach." It was thus he wrote to some brother Member of Parliament who had summoned him to a grand meeting at the Rotunda. He was wanted to address the people on the honesty of the principle of paying no rent. "For the matter of that," he wrote to another brother member, "I don't see the honesty. Why are we to take the property from Jack and give it to Bill? Bill would sell it and spend the money, and no good would then have been done to the country. I should have to argue the matter out with you or someone else before I could speak about it at the Rotunda." Then, there arose a doubt whether Mr. O'Mahony was the proper member for Cavan. He settled himself down in Cecil Street and began to write a book about rent. When he began his book he hated rent from his very soul. The difficulty he saw was this: what should you do with the property when you took it away from the landlords? He quite saw his way to taking it away; if only a new order would come from heaven for the creation of a special set of farmers who should be wedded to their land by some celestial matrimony, and should clearly be in possession of it without the perpetration of any injustice. He did not quite see his way to this by his own lights, and therefore he went to the British Museum. When a man wants to write a book full of unassailable facts, he always goes to the British Museum. In this way Mr. O'Mahony purposed to spend his autumn instead of speaking at the Rotunda, because it suited him to live in London rather than in Dublin.

Cecil Street in September is not the most cheerful place in the world. While Rachel had been singing at "The Embankment," with the occasional excitement of a quarrel with Mr. Moss, it had been all very well; but now while her father was studying statistics at the British Museum, she had nothing to do but to practise her singing. "I mean to do something, you know, towards earning that £200 which you have lent me." This she said to Lord Castlewell, who had come up to London to have his teeth looked after. This was the excuse he gave for being in London at this unfashionable season. "I have to sing from breakfast to dinner without stopping one minute, so you may go back to the dentist at once. I haven't time even to see what he has done."

"I have to propose that you and your father shall come and dine with me down at Richmond to-day. There is old Mrs. Peacock, who used to sing bouffe parts at the Queen's Theatre. She is a most respectable old party, and she shall come if you will let her."

"For papa to flirt with?" said Rachel.

"Not at all. With a party of four there is never any flirting. It is all solid sense. I want to have some serious conversation about that £200. Mrs. Peacock will be able to give me her opinion."

"She won't be able to lend me the money?"

"I'm afraid she isn't a good doctor for that disease. But you must dine somewhere, and do say you will come."

But Rachel was determined not to come,—at any rate not to say that she would come without consulting her father. So she explained that the Member of Parliament was hard at work at the British Museum, writing a book against the payment of rents, and that she could not go without consulting him. But Lord Castlewell made that very easy. "I'll go and see," said he, "how a man looks when he is writing a book on such a subject; and I'll be back and tell you all about it. I'll drive you down in my phaeton,—of course if your father consents. If he wants to bring his book with him, the groom shall carry it in a box."

"And what about Mrs. Peacock?"

"There won't be any trouble about her, because she lives at Richmond. You needn't be a bit afraid for your father's sake, because she is over sixty." Then he started off, and came back in half an hour, saying that Mr. O'Mahony had expressed himself quite satisfied to do as he was told.

"The deceit of the world, the flesh, and the devil, get the better of one on every side," said Rachel, when she was left to herself. "Who would have thought of the noble lord spinning off to the British Museum on such an errand as that! But he will give papa a good dinner, and I shan't be any the worse. A man must be very bad before he can do a woman an injury if she is determined not to be injured."

Lord Castlewell drove the two down to Richmond, and very pleasant the drive was. The conversation consisted of quizzing Mr. O'Mahony about his book, as to which he was already beginning to be a little out of heart. But he bore the quizzing well, and was thoroughly good-humoured as he saw the lord and his daughter sitting on the front seat before him. "I am a Land-leaguing Home-Ruler, you know, my lord, of the most advanced description. The Speaker has never turned me out of the House of Commons, only because I have never sat there. Your character will be lost for ever." Lord Castlewell declared that his character would be made for ever, as he had the great prima donna of the next season at his left hand.

The dinner went off very pleasantly. Old Mrs. Peacock declared that she had never known a prima donna before to be the daughter of a Member of Parliament. She felt that great honour was done to the profession.

"Why," said Lord Castlewell, "he is writing a book to prove that nobody should pay any rent!"

"Oh!" said Mrs. Peacock, "that would be terrible. A landlord wouldn't be a landlord if he didn't get any rent;—or hardly." Then Mr. O'Mahony went to work to explain that a landlord was, of his very name and nature, an abomination before the Lord.

"And yet you want houses to live in," said Lord Castlewell.

When they were in the middle of their dinners they were all surprised by the approach of Mr. Mahomet M. Moss. He was dressed up to a degree of beauty which Rachel thought that she had never seen equalled. His shirt-front was full of little worked holes. His studs were gold and turquoise, and those at his wrists were double studs, also gold and turquoise. The tie of his cravat was a thing marvellous to behold. His waistcoat was new for the occasion, and apparently all over marvellously fine needlework. It might, all the same, have been done by a sewing-machine. The breadth of the satin lappets of his dress-coat were most expansive. And his hair must have taken two artists the whole afternoon to accomplish. It was evident to see that he felt himself to be quite the lord's equal by the strength of his personal adornment. "Well, yes," he said, "I have brought Madame Tacchi down here to show her what we can do in the way of a suburban dinner. Madame Tacchi is about to take the place which Miss O'Mahony has vacated at 'The Embankment.' Ah, my lord, you behaved very shabbily to us there."

"If Madame Tacchi," said the lord, "can sing at all like Miss O'Mahony, we shall have her away very soon. Is Madame Tacchi in sight, so that I can see her?"

Then Mr. Moss indicated the table at which the lady sat, and with the lady was Madame Socani.

"They are a bad lot," said Lord Castlewell, as soon as Moss had withdrawn. "I know them, and they are a bad lot, particularly that woman who is with them. It is a marvel to me how you got among them."

Lord Castlewell had now become very intimate with the O'Mahonys; and by what he said showed also his intimacy with Mrs. Peacock.

"They are Americans," said O'Mahony.

"And so are you," said the lord. "There can be good Americans and bad Americans. You don't mean to say that you think worse of an American than of an Englishman."

"I think higher of an Englishman than of an American, and lower also. If I meet an American where a gentleman ought to be, I entertain a doubt; if I meet him where a labourer ought to be, I feel very confident. I suppose that the manager of a theatre ought to be a gentleman."

"I don't quite understand it all," said Mrs. Peacock.

"Nor anybody else," said Rachel. "Father does fly so very high in the air when he talks about people."

After that the lord drove Miss O'Mahony and her father back to Cecil Street, and they all agreed that they had had a very pleasant evening.

CHAPTER XXXIII.

CAPTAIN CLAYTON'S LOVE-MAKING.

THE household at Castle Morony was very sad for some time after the trial. They had hardly begun to feel the death of Florian while the excitement existed as they felt it afterwards. Mr. Jones, his father, seemed to regard the lost boy as though he had been his favourite child. It was not many months since he had refused to allow him to eat in his presence, and had been persuaded by such a stranger as was Captain Clayton, to treat him with some show of affection. When he had driven him into Ballyglunin, he had been stern and harsh to him to the very last. And now he was obliterated with sorrow because he had been robbed of his Florian. The two girls had sorrows of their own; though neither of them would permit her sorrow to create any quarrel between her and her sister. And Frank, who since his return from the North had toiled like a labourer on the property—only doing double a labourer's work—had sorrow, too, of his own. It was understood that he had altogether separated himself from Rachel O'Mahony. The cause of his separation was singular in its nature.

It was now November, and Rachel had already achieved a singularly rapid success at Covent Garden. She still lived in Cecil Street, but there was no lack of money. Indeed, her name had risen into such repute that some Irish people began to think that her father was the proper man for Cavan, simply because she was a great singer. It cannot be said, however, that this was the case among the men who were regarded as the leaders of the party, as they still doubted O'Mahony's obedience. But money at any rate poured into Rachel's lap, and with the money that which was quite as objectionable to poor Frank. He had begun by asserting that he did not wish to live idle on the earnings of a singer; and, therefore, as the singer had said, "he and she were obliged to be two." As she explained to her father, she was badly treated. She was very anxious to be true to her lover; but she did not like living without some lover to whom she might be true. "You see, as I am placed I am exposed to the Mosses. I do want to have a husband to protect me." Then a lover had come forward. Lord Castlewell had absolutely professed to make her the future Marchioness of Beaulieu. Of this there must be more hereafter; but Frank heard of it, and tore his hair in despair.

And there was another misery at Castle Morony. It reached Mr. Jones's ears that Peter was anxious to give warning. It certainly was the case that Peter was of great use to them and that Mr. Jones had rebuked him more than once as having made a great favour of his services. The fact was that Peter, if discharged, would hardly know where to look for another place where he could be equally at home and equally comfortable. And he was treated by the family generally with all that confidence which his faithfulness seemed to deserve. But he was nervous and ill-at-ease under his master's rebukes; and at last there came an event which seemed to harrow up his own soul, and instigated him to run away from County Galway altogether.

"Miss Edith, Miss Edith," he said, "come in here thin and see what I have got to show you." Then, with an air of great mystery, he drew his young mistress into the pantry. "Look at that now! Was ever the like of that seen since the mortial world began?" Then he took out from a dirty envelope a dirty sheet of paper, and exposed it to her eyes. On the top of it was a rude coffin. "Don't it make yer hair stand on end, and yer very flesh creep, Miss Edith, to look at the likes o' that?" And below the coffin there was a ruder skull and two crossbones. "Them's intended for what I'm to be. I understand their language well enough. Look here," and he turned the envelope round and showed that it was addressed to Peter

McGrew, butler, Morony Castle. "They know me well enough all the country round." The letter was as follows:

"Mr. Peter McGrew,

"If you're not out of that before the end of the month, but stay there doing things for them infernal blackguards, your goose is cooked. So now you know all about it.

"From yours,
"Moonlight."

Edith attempted to laugh at this letter, but Peter made her understand that it was no laughing matter.

"I've a married darter in Dublin who won't see her father shot down that way if she knows it."

"You had better take it to papa, then, and give him warning," said Edith.

But this Peter declined to do on the spur of the moment, seeming to be equally afraid of his master and of Captain Moonlight.

"If I'd the Captain here, he'd tell me what I ought to do." The Captain was always Captain Clayton.

"He is coming here to-morrow, and I will show him the letter," said Edith. But she did not on that account scruple to tell her father at once.

"He can go if he likes it," said Mr. Jones, and that was all that Mr. Jones said on the subject.

This was the third visit that the Captain had paid to Morony Castle since the terrible events of the late trial. And it must be understood that he had not spoken a word to either of the two girls since the moment in which he had ventured to squeeze Edith's hand with a tighter grasp than he had given to her sister. They, between them, had discussed him and his character often; but had come to no understanding respecting him.

Ada had declared that Edith should be his, and had in some degree recovered from the paroxysm of sorrow which had first oppressed her. But Edith had refused altogether to look at the matter in that light. "It was quite out of the question," she said, "and so Captain Clayton would feel it. If you don't hold your tongue, Ada," she said, "I shall think you're a brute."

But Ada had not held her tongue, and had declared that if no one else were to know it—no one but Edith and the Captain himself—she would not be made miserable by it.

"What is it?" she said. "I thought him the best, and he is the best. I thought that he thought that I was the best; and I wasn't. It shall be as I say."

After this manner were the discussions held between them; but of these Captain Clayton heard never a word.

When he came he would seem to be full of the flood-gates, and of Lax the murderer. He had two men with him now, Hunter and another. But no further attempt was made to shoot him in the neighbourhood of Headford. "Lax finds it too hot," he said, "since that day in the court house, and has gone away for the present. I nearly know where he is; but there is no good catching him till I get some sort of evidence against him, and if I locked him up as a 'suspect,' he would become a martyr and a hero in the eyes of the whole party. The worst of it is that though twenty men swore that they had seen it, no Galway jury would convict him." But nevertheless he was indefatigable in following up the murderer of poor Florian. "As for the murder in the court house," he said, "I do believe that though it was done in the presence of an immense crowd no one actually saw it. I have the pistol, but what is that? The pistol was dropped on the floor of the court house."

On this occasion Edith brought him poor Peter's letter. As it happened they two were then alone together. But she had taught herself not to expect any allusion to his love. "He is a stupid fellow," said the Captain.

"But he has been faithful. And you can't expect him to look at these things as you do."

"Of course he finds it to be a great compliment. To have a special letter addressed to him by some special Captain Moonlight is to bring him into the history of his country."

"I suppose he will go."

"Then let him go. I would not on any account ask him to stay. If he comes to me I shall tell him simply that he is a fool. Pat Carroll's people want to bother your father, and he would be bothered if he were to lose his man-servant. There is no doubt of that. If Peter desires to bother him let him go. Then he has another idea that he wants to achieve a character for fidelity. He must choose between the two. But I wouldn't on any account ask him for a favour."

Then Edith having heard the Captain's advice was preparing to leave the room when Captain Clayton stopped her. "Edith," he said.

"Well, Captain Clayton."

"Some months ago,—before these sad things had occurred,—I told you what I thought of you, and I asked you for a favour."

"There was a mistake made between us all,—a mistake which does not admit of being put to rights. It was unfortunate, but those misfortunes will occur. There is no more to be said about it."

"Is the happiness of two people to be thus sacrificed, when nothing is done for the benefit of one?"

"What two?" she asked brusquely.

"You and I."

"My happiness will not be sacrificed, Captain Clayton," she said. What right had he to tell that her happiness was in question? The woman spoke,—the essence of feminine self, putting itself forward to defend feminine rights generally against male assumption. Could any man be justified in asserting that a woman loved him till she had told him so? It was evident no doubt,—so she told herself. It was true at least. As the word goes she worshipped the very ground he stood upon. He was her hero. She had been made to think and to feel that he was so by this mistake which had occurred between the three. She had known it before, but it was burned in upon her now. Yet he should not be allowed to assume it. And the one thing necessary for her peace of mind in life would be that she should do her duty by Ada. She had been a fool. She had instigated Ada to believe this thing in which there was no truth. The loss of all ecstasy of happiness must be the penalty which she would pay. And yet she thought of him. Must he pay a similar penalty for her blunder? Surely this would be hard! Surely this would be cruel! But then she did not believe that man ever paid such penalty as that of which she was thinking. He would have the work of his life. It would be the work of her life to remember what she might have been had she not been a fool.

"If so," he said after a pause, "then there is an end of it all," and he looked at her as though he absolutely believed her words, —as though he had not known that her assertion had been mere feminine pretext! She could not endure that he at any rate should not know the sacrifice which she would have to make. But he was very hard to her. He would not even allow her the usual right of defending her sex by falsehood. "If so, there is an end of it all," he repeated, holding out his hand as though to bid her farewell.

She believed him, and gave him her hand. "Good-bye, Captain Clayton," she said.

"Never again," he said to her very gruffly, but still with such a look across his eyes as irradiated his whole face. "This hand shall never again be your own to do as you please with it."

"Who says so?" and she struggled as though to pull her hand away, but he held her as though in truth her hand had gone from her for ever.

"I say so, who am its legitimate owner. Now I bid you tell me the truth, or rather I defy you to go on with the lie. Do you not love me?"

"It is a question which I shall not answer."

"Then," said he, "from a woman to a man it is answered. You cannot make me over to another. I will not be transferred."

"I can do nothing with you, Captain Clayton, nor can you with me. I know you are very strong of course." Then he loosened her hand, and as he did so Ada came into the room.

"I have asked her to be my wife," said the Captain, putting his hand upon Edith's arm.

"Let it be so," said Ada. "I have nothing to say against it."

"But I have," said Edith. "I have much to say against it. We can all live without being married, I suppose. Captain Clayton has plenty to do without the trouble of a wife. And so have you and I. Could we leave our father? And have we forgotten so soon poor Florian? This is no time for marriages. Only think, papa would not have the means to get us decent clothes. As far as I am concerned, Captain Clayton, let there be an end of all this." Then she stalked out of the room.

"Ada, you are not angry with me," said Captain Clayton, coming up to her.

"Oh, no! How could I be angry?"

"I have not time to do as other men do. I do not know that I ever said a word to her; and yet, God knows, that I have loved her dearly enough. She is hot-tempered now, and there are feelings in her heart which fight against me. You will say a word in my favour."

"Indeed, indeed I will."

"There shall be nothing wrong between you and me. If she becomes my wife, you shall be my dearest sister. And I think she will at last. I know,—I do know that she loves me. Poor Florian is dead and gone. All his short troubles are over. We have still got our lives to lead. And why should we not lead them as may best suit us? She talks about your father's present want of money. I would be proud to marry your sister standing as she is now down in the kitchen. But if I did marry her I should have ample means to keep her as would become your father's daughter." Then he took his leave and went back to Galway.

CHAPTER XXXIV.

LORD CASTLEWELL'S LOVE-MAKING.

IT was explained in the last chapter that Frank Jones was not in a happy condition because of the success of the lady whom he loved. Rachel, as Christmas drew nigh, was more and more talked about in London, and became more and more the darling of all musical people. She had been twelve months now on the London boards, and had fully justified the opinion expressed of her by Messrs. Moss and Le Gros. There were those who declared that she sang as no woman of her age had ever sung before. And there had got abroad about her certain stories, which were true enough in the main, but which were all the more curious because of their truth; and yet they were not true altogether. It was known that she was a daughter of a Land-leaguing Member of Parliament, and that she had been engaged to marry the son of a boycotted landlord. Mr. Jones' sorrows, and the death of his poor son, and the murder of the sinner who was to have been the witness at the trial of his brother, were all known and commented on in the London press; and so also was the peculiar vigour of Mr. O'Mahony's politics. Nothing, it was said, could be severed more entirely than were Mr. Jones and Mr. O'Mahony. The enmity was so deep that all ideas of marriage were out of the question. It was, no doubt, true that the gentleman was penniless and the lady rolling in wealth; but this was a matter so grievous that so poor a thing as money could not be allowed to prevail. And then Mr. Moss was talked about as a dragon of iniquity,—which, indeed, was true enough,—and was represented as having caused contracts to be executed which would bind poor Rachel to himself, both as to voice and beauty. But Lord Castlewell had seen her, and had heard her; and Mr. Moss, with all his abominations, was sent down to the bottom of the nethermost pit. The fortune of "The Embankment" was made by the number of visitors who were sent there to see and to hear this wicked fiend; but it all redounded to the honour and glory of Rachel.

But Rachel was to be seen a *fêted* guest at all semi-musical houses. Whispers about town were heard that that musical swell, Lord Castlewell, had been caught at last. And in the midst of all this, Mr. O'Mahony came in for his share of popularity. There was something so peculiar in the connection which bound a violent Land-leaguing Member of Parliament with the prima donna of the day. They were father and daughter, but they looked more like husband and wife, and it always seemed that Rachel had her own way. Mr. O'Mahony had quite achieved a character for himself before the time had come in which he was enabled to open his mouth in the House of Commons. And some people went so far as to declare that he was about to be the new leader of the party.

It certainly was true that about this time Lord Castlewell did make an offer to Rachel O'Mahony.

"That I should have come to this!" she said to the lord when the lord had expressed his wishes.

"You deserve it all," said the gallant lord.

"I think I do. But that you should have seen it,—that you should have come to understand that if I would be your wife I would sing every note out of my body,—to do you good if it

were possible. How have you been enlightened so far as to see
that this is the way in which you may best make yourself
happy?"

Lord Castlewell did not quite like this; but he knew that
his wished-for bride was an unintelligible little person, to whom
much must be yielded as to her own way. He had not given
way to this idea before he had seen how well she had taken her
place among the people with whom he lived. He was forty
years old, and it was time that he should marry. His father
was a very proud personage, to whom he never spoke much.
He, however, would be of opinion that any bride whom his son
might choose would be, by the very fact, raised to the top of the
peerage. His mother was a religious woman, to whom any
matrimony for her son would be an achievement. Now, of the
proposed bride he had learned all manner of good things. She
had come out of Mr. Moss's furnace absolutely unscorched ; so
much unscorched as to scorn the idea of having been touched
by the flames. She was thankful to Lord Castlewell for what
he had done, and expressed her thanks in a manner that was
not grateful to him. She was not in the least put about or confused, or indeed surprised, because the heir of a marquis had
made an offer to her—a singing girl ; but she let him understand
that she quite thought that she had done a good thing. "It
would be so much better for him than going on as he has
gone," she said to her father. And Lord Castlewell knew very
well what were her sentiments.

It cannot be said that he repented of his offer. Indeed
he pressed her for an answer more than once or twice. But her
conduct to him was certainly very aggravating. This matter of
her marriage with an earl was an affair of great moment.
Indeed all London was alive with the subject. But she had not
time to give him an answer because it was necessary that she
should study a part for the theatre. This was hard upon an
earl, and was made no better by the fact that the earl was forty.
"No, my lord earl," she said laughing, "the time for that has
not come yet. You must give me a few days to think of it."
This she said when he expressed a not unnatural desire to give
her a kiss.

But though she apparently made light of the matter to him,
and astonished even her father by her treatment of him, yet she
thought of it with a very anxious mind. She was quite alive to
the glories of the position offered to her, and was not at all
alive to its inconveniences. People would assert that she had
caught the lover who had intended her for other purposes.
"That was of course out of the question," she said to herself.
And she felt sure that she could make as good a countess as
the best of them. With her father as Member of Parliament,
and her husband an earl, she would have done very well with

herself. She would have escaped from that brute Moss, and would have been subjected to less that was disagreeable in the encounter than might have been expected. She must lose the public singing which was attractive to her, and must become the wife of an old man. It was thus in truth that she looked at the noble lord. "There would be an end," she said, "and for ever, of 'Love's young dream.'" The dream had been very pleasant to her. She had thoroughly liked her Frank. He was handsome, fresh, full of passion, and a little violent when his temper lay in that direction. But he had been generous, and she was sure of him that he had loved her thoroughly. After all, was not "Love's young dream" the best?

An answer was at any rate due to Lord Castlewell. But she made up her mind that before she could give the answer, she would write to Frank himself. "My lord," she said very gravely to her suitor, "it has become my lot in life to be engaged to marry the son of that Mr. Jones of whom you have heard in the west of Ireland."

"I am aware of it," said Lord Castlewell gravely.

"It has been necessary that I should tell you myself. Now, I cannot say whether, in all honour, that engagement has been dissolved."

"I thought there was no doubt about it," said the lord.

"It is as I tell you. I must write to Mr. Jones. Hearts cannot be wrenched asunder without some effort in the wrenching. For the great honour you have done me I am greatly thankful."

"Let all that pass," said the lord.

"Not so. It has to be spoken of. As I stand at present I have been repudiated by Mr. Jones."

"Do you mean to ask him to take you back again?"

"I do not know how the letter will be worded, because it has not been yet written. My object is to tell him of the honour which Lord Castlewell proposes to me. And I have not thought it quite honest to your lordship to do this without acquainting you."

Then that interview was over, and Lord Castlewell went away no doubt disgusted. He had not intended to be treated in this way by a singing girl, when he proposed to make her his countess. But with the disgust there was a strengthened feeling of admiration for her conduct. She looked much more like the countess than the singing girl when she spoke to him. And there certainly never came a time in which he could tell her to go back and sing and marry Mr. Moss. Therefore the few days necessary for an answer went by, and then she gave him her reply. "My lord," she said, "if you wish it still, it shall be so."

The time for "Love's young dream" had not gone by for Lord Castlewell. "I do wish it still," he said in a tone of renewed joy.

"Then you shall have all that you wish." Thereupon she put her little hands on his arm, and leant her face against his breast. Then there was a long embrace, but after the embrace she had a little speech to make. "You ought to know, Lord Castlewell, how much I think of you and your high position. A man, they say, trusts much of his honour into the hands of his wife. Whatever you trust to me shall be guarded as my very soul. You shall be to me the one man whom I am bound to worship. I will worship you with all my heart, with all my body, with all my soul, and with all my strength. Your wishes shall be my wishes. I only hope that an odd stray wish of mine may occasionally be yours." Then she smiled so sweetly that as she looked up into his face he was more enamoured of her than ever.

But now we must go back for a moment, and read the correspondence which took place between Rachel O'Mahony and Frank Jones. Rachel's letter ran as follows:

"MY DEAR FRANK,

"I am afraid I must trouble you once again with my affairs; though, indeed, after what last took place between us it ought not to be necessary. Lord Castlewell has proposed to make me his wife; and, to tell you the truth, looking forward into the world, I do not wish to throw over all its pleasures because your honour, whom I have loved, does not wish to accept the wages of a singing girl. But the place is open to you still,—the wages, and the singing girl, and all. Write me a line, and say how it is to be.

"Yours as you would have me to be,
"RACHEL O'MAHONY."

This letter Frank Jones showed to no one. Had he allowed it to be seen by his sister Edith, she would probably have told him that no man ever received a sweeter love-letter from the girl whom he loved. "The place is open to you still,—the wages, the singing girl, and all." The girl had made nothing of this new and noble lover, except to assure his rival that he, the rival, should be postponed to him, the lover, if he, the lover, would write but one word to say that it should be so. But Frank was bad at reading such words. He got it into his head that the girl had merely written to ask the permission of her former suitor to marry this new lordly lover, and, though he did love the girl, with a passion which the girl could never feel for the lord, he wrote back and refused the offer.

"My dear Rachel,

"It is, I suppose, best as it is. We are sinking lower and lower daily. My father is beginning to feel that we shall never see another rent day at Castle Morony. It is not fitting that I should think of joining my fallen fortunes to yours, which are soaring so high. And poor Florian is gone. We are at the present moment still struck to the ground because of Florian. As for you, and the lord who admires you, you have my permission to become his wife. I have long heard that he is your declared admirer. You have before you a glorious future, and I shall always hear with satisfaction of your career.

"Yours, with many memories of the past,
"Francis Jones."

It was not a letter which would have put such a girl as Rachel O'Mahony into good heart unless she had in truth wished to get his agreement to her lordly marriage. "This twice I have thrown myself at his head and he has rejected me." Then she abided Lord Castlewell's coming, and the scene between them took place as above described. The marriage was at once declared as a settled thing. "Now, my dear, you must name the day," said Lord Castlewell, as full of joy as though he were going to marry a duke's daughter.

"I have got to finish my engagement," said Rachel; "I am bound down to the end of May. When June comes you shan't find a girl who will be in a greater hurry. Do you think that I do not wish to become a countess?"

He told her that he would contrive to get her engagement broken. "Covent Garden is not going to quarrel with me about my wife, I'm sure," he said.

"Ah! but my own one," said Rachel, "we will do it all *selon les règles*. I am in a hurry, but we won't let the world know it. I, the future Countess of Castlewell; I, the future Marchioness of Beaulieu, will keep my terms and my allotted times like any candle-snuffer. What do you think Moss will say?"

"What can it signify what Mr. Moss may say?"

"Ah! but my own man, it does signify. Mr. Moss shall know that through it all I have done my duty. Madame Socani will tell lies, but she shall feel in her heart that she has once in her life come across a woman who, when she has signed a bit of paper, intends to remain true to the paper signed. And, my lord, there is still £100 due to you from my father."

"Gammon!" said the lord.

"I could pay it by a cheque on the bank, to be sure, but let us go on to the end of May. I want to see how all the young women will behave when they hear of it." And so some early day in June was fixed for the wedding.

Among others who heard of it were, of course, Mr. Moss and Madame Socani. They heard of it, but of course did not believe it. It was too bright to be believed. When Madame Socani was assured that Rachel had taken the money,—she and her father between them,—she declared, with great apparent satisfaction, that Rachel must be given up as lost. "As to that wicked old man, her father——"

"He's not so very old," said Moss.

"She's no chicken, and he's old enough to be her father. That is, if he is her father. I have known that girl on the stage any day these ten years."

"No, you've not; not yet five. I don't quite know how it is." And Mr. Moss endeavoured to think of it all in such a manner as to make it yet possible that he might marry her. What might not they two do together in the musical world?

"You don't mean to say you'd take her yet?" said Madame Socani, with scorn.

"When I take her you'll be glad enough to join us; that is, if we will have you." Then Madame Socani ground her teeth together, and turned up her nose with redoubled scorn.

But it was soon borne in upon Mr. Moss that the marriage was to be a marriage, and he was in truth very angry. He had been able to endure M. Le Gros' success in carrying away Miss O'Mahony from "The Embankment." Miss O'Mahony might come back again under that or any other name. He—and she —had a musical future before them which might still be made to run in accordance with his wishes. Then he had learned with sincere sorrow that she was throwing herself into the lord's hands, borrowing money of him. But there might be a way out of this which would still allow him to carry out his project. But now he heard that a real marriage was intended, and he was very angry. Not even Madame Socani was more capable of spite than Mr. Moss, though he was better able to hide his rage. Even now, when Christmas-time had come, he would hardly believe the truth, and when the marriage was not instantly carried out, new hopes came to him—that Lord Castlewell would not at last make himself such a fool. He inquired here and there in the musical world and the theatrical world, and could not arrive at what he believed to be positive truth. Then Christmas passed by, and Miss O'Mahony recommenced her singing at Covent Garden. Three times a week the house was filled, and at last a fourth night was added, for which the salary paid to Rachel was very much increased.

"I don't see that the salary matters very much," said Lord Castlewell, when the matter was discussed.

"Oh, but, my lord, it does matter!" She always called him my lord now, with a little emphasis laid on the "my." "They have made father a Member of Parliament, but he does not earn anything. What I can earn up to the last fatal day he shall have, if you will let me give it to him."

They were very bright days for Rachel, because she had all the triumph of success,—success gained by her own efforts.

"I can never do as much as this when I am your countess," she said to her future lord. "I shall dwell in marble halls, as people say, but I shall never cram a house so full as to be able to see, when I look up from the stage, that there is not a place for another man's head; and when my throat gave way the other day I could read all the disappointment in the public papers. I shall become your wife, my lord."

"I hope so."

"And if you will love me I shall be very happy for long, long years."

"I will love you."

"But there will be no passion of ecstasy such as this. Father says that Home-Rule won't be passed because the people will be thinking of my singing. Of course it is all vanity, but there is an enjoyment in it."

But all this was wormwood to Mr. Moss. He had put out his hand so as to clutch this girl now two years since, understanding all her singing qualities, and then in truth loving her. She had taken a positive hatred to him, and had rejected him at every turn of her life. But he had not at all regarded that. He had managed to connect her with his theatre, and had perceived that her voice had become more and more sweet in its tones, and more and more rich in its melody. He had still hoped that he would make her his wife. Madame Socani's abominable proposal had come from an assurance on her part that he could have all that he wished for without paying so dear for it. There had doubtless been some whispering between them over the matter, but the order for the proposal had not come from him. Madame Socani had judged of Rachel as she might have judged of herself. But all that had come to absolute failure. He felt now that he should be paying by no means too dear by marrying the girl. It would be a great triumph to marry her; but he was told that this absurd earl wished to triumph in the same manner.

He set afloat all manner of reports, which, in truth, wounded Lord Castlewell sorely. Lord Castlewell had given her money, and had then failed in his object. So said Mr. Moss. Lord Castlewell had promised marriage, never intending it. Lord Castlewell had postponed the marriage because as the moment drew nearer he would not sacrifice himself. If the lady had a friend, it would be the friend's duty to cudgel the lord, so villainous had been the noble lord's conduct. But yet, in truth, who could have expected that the noble lord would have married the singing girl? Was not his character known? Did anybody in his senses expect that the noble lord would marry Miss Rachel O'Mahony?

"If I have a friend, is my friend to cudgel you, my lord?" she said, clinging on his arm in her usual manner. "My friend is papa, who thinks that you are a very decent fellow, considering your misfortune in being a lord at all. I know where all these words come from;—it is Mahomet M. Moss. There is nothing for it but to live them down with absolute silence."

"Nothing," he replied. "They are a nuisance, but we can do nothing."

But Lord Castlewell did in truth feel what was said about him. Was he not going to pay too dearly for his whistle? No doubt Rachel was all that she ought to be. She was honest, industrious, and high-spirited; and, according to his thinking, she sang more divinely than any woman of her time. And he so thought of her that he knew that she must be his countess or be nothing at all to him. To think of her in any other light would be an abomination to him. But yet, was it worth his while to make her Marchioness of Beaulieu? He could only get rid of his present engagement by some absolute change in his mode of life. For instance, he must shut himself up in a castle and devote himself entirely to a religious life. He must explain to her that circumstances would not admit his marrying, and must offer to pay her any sum of money that she or her father might think fit to name. If he wished to escape, this must be his way; but as he looked at her when she came off the stage, where he always attended her, he assured himself that he did not wish to escape.

CHAPTER XXXV.

MR. O'MAHONY'S APOLOGY.

TIME went on and Parliament met. Mr. O'Mahony went before the Speaker's table and was sworn in. He was introduced by two brother Land-leaguers, and really did take his place with some enthusiasm. He wanted to speak on the first day, but was judiciously kept silent by his colleagues. He expressed an idea that, until Ireland's wrongs had been redressed, there ought not to be a moment devoted to any other subject, and became very violent in his expressions of this opinion. But he was not long kept dumb. Great things were expected from his powers of speech, and, though he had to be brought to silence ignominiously on three or four occasions, still, at last some power of speech was permitted to him.

There were those among his own special brethren who greatly admired him and praised him; but with others of the same class there was a shaking of the head and many doubts. With the House generally, I fear, laughter prevailed rather than true admiration. Mr. O'Mahony, no doubt, could speak well in a debating society or a music hall. Words came from his tongue sweeter than honey. But just at the beginning of the session, the Speaker was bound to put a limit even to Irish eloquence, and in this case was able to do so. As Mr. O'Mahony contrived to get upon his feet very frequently, either in asking a question or in endeavouring to animadvert on the answer given, there was something of a tussle between him and the authority in the chair. It did not take much above a week to make the Speaker thoroughly tired of this new member, and threats were used towards him of a nature which his joint Milesian and American nature could not stand. He was told of dreadful things which could be done to him. Though as yet he could not be turned out of the House, for the state of the young session had not as yet admitted of that new mode of torture, still, he could be named. "Let him name me. My name is Mr. O'Mahony." And Mr. O'Mahony was not a man who could be happy when he was quarrelling with all around him. He was soon worked into a violent passion, in which he made himself ridiculous, but when he had subsided, and the storm was passed, he knew he had misbehaved, and was unhappy. And, as he was thoroughly honest, he could not be got to obey his leaders in everything. He wanted to abolish the Irish landlords, but he was desirous of abolishing them after some special plan of his own, and could hardly be got to work efficiently in harness together with others.

"Don't you think your father is making an ass of himself,—just a little, you know?"

This was said by Lord Castlewell to Rachel when the session was not yet a fortnight old, and made Rachel very unhappy. She did think that her father was making an ass of himself, but she did not like to be told of it. And much as she liked music herself, dear as was her own profession to her, still she felt that, to be a Member of Parliament, and to have achieved the power of making speeches there, was better than to run after opera singers. She loved the man who was going to marry her very well,—or rather, she intended to do so.

He was not to her "Love's young dream." But she intended that his lordship should become love's old reality. She felt that this would not become the case, if love's old reality were to tell her often that her father was an ass. Lord Castlewell's father was, she thought, making an ass of himself. She heard on different sides that he was a foolish, pompous old peer, who could hardly say bo to a goose; but it would not, she thought, become her to tell her future husband her own opinion on that matter. She saw no reason why he should be less reticent in his opinion as to her father. Of course he was older, and perhaps she did not think of that as much as she ought to have done. She ought also to have remembered that he was an earl, and she but a singing girl, and that something was due to him for the honour he was doing her. But of this she would take no account. She was to be his wife, and a wife ought to be equal to the husband. Such at least was her American view of the matter. In fact, her ideas on the matter ran as follows: My future husband is not entitled to call my father an ass because he is a lord, seeing that my father is a Member of Parliament. Nor is he entitled to call him so because he is an ass, because the same thing is true of his own father. And thus there came to be discord in her mind.

"I suppose all Parliament people make asses of themselves sometimes, Lords as well as Commons. I don't see how a man is to go on talking for ever about laws and land-leagues, and those sort of things without doing so. It is all bosh to me. And so I should think it must be to you, as you don't do it. But I do not think that father is worse than anybody else; and I think that his words are sometimes very beautiful."

"Why, my dear, there is not a man about London who is not laughing at him."

"I saw in *The Times* the other day that he is considered a very true and a very honest man. Of course they said that he talked nonsense sometimes; but if you put the honesty against the nonsense, he will be as good as anybody else."

"I don't think you understand, my dear. Honesty is not what they want."

"Oh!"

"But what they don't want especially is nonsense."

"Poor papa! But he doesn't mean to consult them as to what they want. His idea is that if everybody can be got to be honest this question may be settled among them. But it must be talked about, and he, at any rate, is eloquent. I have heard it said that there was not a more eloquent man in New York. I think he has got as many good gifts as anyone else."

In this way there rose some bad feeling. Lord Castlewell did think that there was something wanting in the manner in which he was treated by his bride. He was sure that he loved her, but he was sure also that when a lord marries a singing girl he ought to expect some special observance. And the fact that the singing girl's father was a Member of Parliament was much less to him than to her. He, indeed, would have been glad to have the father abolished altogether. But she had become very proud of her father since he had become a Member of Parliament. Her ideas of the British Constitution were rather vague ; but she thought that a Member of Parliament was at least as good as a lord who was not a peer. He had his wealth; but she was sure that he was too proud to think of that.

Just at this period, when the session was beginning, Rachel began to doubt the wisdom of what she was doing. The lord was, in truth, good enough for her. He was nearly double her age, but she had determined to disregard that. He was plain, but that was of no moment. He had run after twenty different women, but she could condone all that, because he had come at last to run after her. For his wealth she cared nothing,—or less than nothing, because by remaining single she could command wealth of her own ;—wealth which she could control herself, and keep at her own banker's, which she suspected would not be the case with Lord Castlewell's money. But she had found the necessity of someone to lean upon when Frank Jones had told her that he would not marry her, and she had feared Mr. Moss so much that she had begun to think that he would, in truth, frighten her into doing some horrible thing. As Frank had deserted her, it would be better that she should marry somebody. Lord Castlewell had come, and she had felt that the Fates were very good to her. She learned from the words of everybody around,—from her new friends at Covent Garden, and from her old enemies at "The Embankment," and from her father himself, that she was the luckiest singing girl at this moment known in Europe. "By G——, she'll get him !" such had been the exclamation made with horror by Mr. Moss, and the echo of it had found its way to her ears. The more Mr. Moss was annoyed, the greater ought to have been her delight. But,—but was she in truth delighted ? As she came to think of the reality she asked herself what were the pleasures which were promised to her. Did she not feel that a week spent with Frank Jones in some little cottage would be worth a twelvemonth of golden splendour in the " marble halls " which Lord Castlewell was supposed to own? And why had Frank deserted her ? Simply because he would not come with her, and share her money. Frank, she told herself, was, in truth, a gallant fellow. She did love Frank. She acknowledged so much to herself again and again. And yet she was about to marry Lord Castlewell, simply because her doing so would be the severest possible blow to her old enemy, Mr. Moss.

Then she asked herself what would be best for her. She had made for herself a great reputation, and she did not scruple to tell herself that this had come from her singing. She thought very much of her singing, but very little of her beauty. A sort of prettiness did belong to her ; a tiny prettiness which had sufficed to catch Frank Jones. She had laughed about her prettiness and her littleness a score of times with Ada and

Edith, and also with Frank himself. There had been the three
girls who called themselves "Beauty and the Beast" and the
"Small young woman." The reader will understand that it had
not been Ada who had chosen those names; but then Ada was
not given to be witty. Her prettiness, such as it was, had
sufficed, and Frank had loved her dearly. Then had come her
great triumph, and she knew not only that she could sing, but
that the world had recognised her singing. "I am a great
woman, as women go," she had said to herself. But her singing
was to come to an end for ever and ever on the 1st of May next.
She would be the Countess of Castlewell, and in process of time
would be the Marchioness of Beaulieu. But she never again
would be a great woman. She was selling all that for the
"marble halls."

Was she wise in what she was doing? She had lain awake
one long morning striving to answer the question for herself.
"If nobody else should come, of course I should be an ugly old
maid," she said to herself; "but then Frank might perhaps
come again,—Frank might come again,—if Mr. Moss did not
intervene in the meantime." But at last she acknowledged
to herself that she had given the lord a promise. She would
keep her promise, but she could not bring herself to exult at the
prospect. She must take care, however, that the lord should
not triumph over her. The lord had called her father an ass.
She certainly would say a rough word or two if he abused her
father again.

This was the time of the "suspects." Mr. O'Mahony had
already taken an opportunity of expressing an opinion in the
House of Commons that every honest man, every patriotic man,
every generous man, every man in fact who was worth his salt,
was in Ireland locked up as a "suspect," and in saying so
managed to utter very bitter words indeed respecting him who
had the locking up of these gentlemen. Poor Mr. O'Mahony
had no idea that he might have used with propriety as to this
gentleman all the epithets of which he believed the "suspects"
to be worthy; but instead of doing so he called him a "disreputable jailer." It is not pleasant to be called a disreputable jailer
in the presence of all the best of one's fellow citizens, but the
man so called in this instance only smiled. Mr. O'Mahony had
certainly made himself ridiculous, and the whole House were
loud in their clamours at the words used. But that did not
suffice. The Speaker reprimanded Mr. O'Mahony and desired
him to recall the language and apologise for it. Then there
arose a loud debate, during which the member of the Government who had been assailed declared that Mr. O'Mahony had
not as yet been quite long enough in the House to learn the
little details of Parliamentary language; Mr. O'Mahony would
no doubt soften down his eloquence in course of time. But the

Speaker would not be content with this, and was about to order the sinner to be carried away by the Sergeant-at-Arms, when a friend on his right and a friend on his left, and a friend behind him, all whispered into his ear how easy it is to apologise in the House of Commons. "You needn't say he isn't a 'disreputable jailer,' but only call him a 'distasteful warder';—anything will do." This came from the gentleman at Mr. O'Mahony's back, and the order for his immediate expulsion was ringing in his ears. He had been told that he was ridiculous, and could feel that it would be absurd to be carried somewhere into the dungeons. And the man whom he certainly detested at the present moment worse than any other scoundrel on the earth, had made a good-natured apology on his behalf. If he were carried away now, he could never come back again without a more serious apology. Then,—farewell to all power of attacking the jailer. He did as the man whispered into his ears, and begged to substitute "distasteful warder" for the words which had wounded so cruelly the feelings of the right honourable gentleman. Then he looked round the House, showing that he thought that he had misbehaved himself. After that, during Mr. O'Mahony's career as a Member of Parliament, which lasted only for the session, he lost his self-respect altogether. He had been driven to withdraw the true wrath of his eloquence from him "at whose brow," as he told Rachel the next morning, "he had hurled his words with a force that had been found to be intolerable."

Mr. O'Mahony had undoubtedly made himself an ass again on this second, third, and perhaps tenth occasion. This was not the ass he had made himself on the occasion to which Lord Castlewell had referred. But yet he was a thoroughly honest, patriotic man, desirous only of the good of his country, and wishing for nothing for himself. Is it not possible that as much may be said for others who from day to day so violently excite our spleen, as to make us feel that special Irishmen selected for special constituencies are not worthy to be ranked with men? You shall take the whole House of Commons, indifferent as to the side on which they sit,—some six hundred and thirty out of the number,—and will find in conversation that the nature of the animal, the absurdity, the selfishness, the absence of all good qualities, are taken for granted as matters admitting of no dispute. But here was Mr. O'Mahony, as hot a Home-Ruler and Land-leaguer as any of them, who was undoubtedly a gentleman,—though an American gentleman. Can it be possible that we are wrong in our opinions respecting the others of the set?

Rachel heard it all the next day, and, living as she did among Italians and French, and theatrical Americans, and English swells, could not endeavour to make the apology which I have just made for the Irish Brigade generally. She knew that her father had made an ass of himself. All the asinine proportions of the affair had been so explained to her as to leave no doubt on her mind as to the matter. But the more she was sure of it, the more resolved she became that Lord Castlewell should not call her father an ass. She might do so,—and undoubtedly would after her own fashion,—but no such privilege should be allowed to him.

"Oh! father, father," she said to him the next morning, "don't you think you've made a goose of yourself?"

"Yes, I do."

"Then, don't do it any more."

"Yes, I shall. It isn't so very easy for a man not to make a goose of himself in that place. You've got to sit by and do nothing for a year or two. It is very difficult. A man cannot afford to waste his time in that manner. There is all Ireland to be regenerated, and I have to learn the exact words which the prudery of the House of Commons will admit. Of course I have made a goose of myself; but the question is whether I did not make a knave of myself in apologising for language which was undoubtedly true. Only think that a man so brutal, so entirely without feelings, without generosity, without any touch of sentiment, should be empowered by the Queen of England to lock up, not only every Irishman, but every American also, and to keep them there just as long as he pleases! And he revels in it. I do believe that he never eats a good breakfast unless half-a-dozen new 'suspects' are reported by the early police in the morning; and I am not to call such a man a 'disreputable jailer.' I may call him a 'distasteful warder.' It's a disgrace to a man to sit in such a House and in such company. Of course I was a goose, but I was only a goose according to the practices of that special duck-pond." Mr. O'Mahony, as he said this, walked about angrily, with his hands in his breeches' pockets, and told himself that no honest man could draw the breath of life comfortably except in New York.

"I don't know much about it, father," said Rachel, "but I think you'd better cut and run. Your twenty men will never do any good here. Everybody hates them who has got any money, and their only friends are just men as Mr. Pat Carroll, of Ballintubber."

Then, later in the day, Lord Castlewell called to drive his bride in the Park. He had so far overcome family objections as to have induced his sister, Lady Augusta Montmorency, to accompany him. Lady Augusta had been already introduced to Rachel, but had not been much prepossessed. Lady Augusta was very proud of her family, was a religious woman, and was anything but contented with her brother's manner of life. But it was no doubt better that he should marry Rachel than not be married at all; and therefore Lady Augusta had allowed herself to be brought to accompany the singing girl upon this occasion. She was, in truth, an uncommonly good young woman; not beautiful, not clever, but most truly anxious for the welfare of her brother. It had been represented to her that her brother was over head and ears in love with the young lady, and looking at the matter all round, she had thought it best to move a little from her dignity so as to take her sister-in-law coldly by the hand. It need hardly be said that Rachel did not like being taken coldly by the hand, and, with her general hot mode of expression, would have declared that she hated Augusta Montmorency. Now, the two entered the room together, and Rachel kissed Lady Augusta, while she gave only her hand to Lord Castlewell. But there was something in her manner on such occasions which was intended to show affection,—and did show it very plainly. In old days she could decline to kiss Frank in a manner that would set Frank all on fire. It was as much as to say—of course you've a right to it, but on this occasion I don't mean to give it to you. But Lord Castlewell was not imaginative, and did not think of all this. Rachel had intended him to think of it.

"Oh, my goodness!" began the lord, "what a mess your father did make of it last night!" And he frowned as he spoke.

Rachel, as an intended bride—about to be a bride in two or three months—did not like to be frowned at by the man who was to marry her. "That's as people may think, my lord," she said.

"You don't mean to say that you don't think he did make a mess of it?"

"Of course he abused that horrid man. Everybody is abusing him."

"As for that, I'm not going to defend the man." For Lord Castlewell, though by no means a strong politician, was a Tory, and unfortunately found himself agreeing with Rachel in abusing the members of the Government.

"Then why do you say that father made a mess of it?"

"Everybody is talking about it. He has made himself ridiculous before the whole town."

"What! Lord Castlewell!" exclaimed Rachel.

"I do believe your father is the best fellow going; but he ought not to touch politics. He made a great mistake in getting into the House. It is a source of misery to everyone connected with him."

"Or about to be connected with him," said Lady Augusta, who had not been appeased by the flavour of Rachel's kiss.

"There's time enough to think about it yet," said Rachel.

"No, there's not," said Lord Castlewell, who intended to express in rather a gallant manner his intention of going on with the marriage.

"But I can assure you there is," said Rachel, "ample time. There shall be no time for going on with it, if my father is to be abused. As it happens, you don't agree with my father in politics. I, as a woman, should have to call myself as belonging to your party, if we be ever married. I do not know what that party is, and care very little, as I am not a politician myself. And I suppose if we were married, you would take upon yourself to abuse my father for his politics, as he might abuse you. But while he is my father, and you are not my husband, I will not bear it. No, thank you, Lady Augusta, I will not drive out to-day. 'Them's my sentiments,' as people say; and perhaps your brother had better think them over while there's time enough." So saying, she did pertinaciously refuse to be driven by the noble lord on that occasion.

CHAPTER XXXVI.

RACHEL WRITES ABOUT HER LOVERS.

WHAT a dear fellow is Frank Jones! That was Rachel's first idea when Lord Castlewell left her. It was an idea she had driven from out of her mind with all the strength of which she was capable from the moment in which his lordship had been accepted. "He never shall be dear to me again," she had said, thinking of what would be due to her husband; and she had disturbed herself, not without some success, in expelling Frank Jones from her heart. It was not right that the future Lady Castlewell should be in love with Frank Jones. But now she could think about Frank Jones as she pleased. What a dear fellow is Frank Jones! Now, it certainly was the case that Lord Castlewell was not a dear fellow at all. He was many degrees better than Mr. Moss, but for a dear fellow!—She only knew one. And she did tell herself now that the world could hardly be a happy world to her without one dear fellow,—at any rate, to think of.

But he had positively refused to marry her! But yet she did not in the least doubt his love. "I'm a little bit of a thing," she said to herself; "but then he likes little bits of things. At any rate, he likes one."

And then she had thought ever so often over the cause which had induced Frank to leave her. "Why shouldn't he take my money, since it is here to be taken? It is all a man's beastly pride!" But then again she contradicted the assertion to herself. It was a man's pride, but by no means beastly. "If I were a man," she went on saying, "I don't think I should like to pay for my coat and waistcoat with money which a woman had earned; and I should like it the less, because things at home, in my own house, were out of order." And then again she thought of it all. "I should be an idiot to do that. Everybody would say so. What! to give up my whole career for a young man's love,—merely that I might have his arm around my waist? I to do it, who am the greatest singer of my day, and who can, if I please, be Countess of Castlewell to-morrow! That were losing the world for love, indeed! Can any man's love be worth it? And I am going on to become such a singer as the world does not possess another like me. I know it. I feel it daily in the increasing sweetness of the music made. I see it in the wakeful eagerness of men's ears, waiting for some charm of sound,—some wonderful charm,—which they hardly dare to expect, but which always comes at last. I see it in the eyes of the women, who are hardly satisfied that another should be so great. It comes in the worship of the people about the theatre, who have to tell me that I am their god, and keep the strings of the sack from which money shall be poured forth upon them. I know it is coming, and yet I am to marry the stupid earl because I have promised him. And he thinks, too, that his reflected honours will be more to me than all the fame that I can earn for myself. To go down to his castle, and to be dumb for ever, and perhaps to be mother of some hideous little imp who shall be the coming marquis. Everything to be abandoned for that,—even Frank Jones. But Frank Jones is not to be had! Oh, Frank Jones, Frank Jones! If you could come and live in such a marble hall as I could provide for you! It should have all that we want, but nothing more. But it could not have that self-respect which it is a man's first duty in life to achieve." But the thought that she had arrived at was this, —that with all her best courtesy she would tell the Earl of Castlewell to look for a bride elsewhere.

But she would do nothing in a hurry. The lord had been very civil to her, and she, on her part, would be as civil to the lord as circumstances admitted. And she had an idea in her mind that she could not at a moment's notice dismiss this lord and be as she was before. Her engagement with the lord was known to all the musical world. The Mosses and Socanis spent their mornings, noons, and nights in talking about it,—as she well knew. And she was not quite sure that the lord had given her such a palpable cause for quarrelling as to justify her in throwing him over. And when she had as it were thrown him over in her mind, she began to think of other causes for regret. After all it was something to be Countess of Castlewell. She felt that she could play the part well, in spite of all Lady Augusta's coldness. She would soon live the Lady Augusta down into a terrible mediocrity. And then again, there would be dreams of Frank Jones. Frank Jones had been utterly banished. But if an elderly gentleman is desirous that his future wife shall think of no Frank Jones, he had better not begin by calling the father of that young lady a ridiculous ass.

She was much disturbed in mind, and resolved that she would seek counsel from her old correspondent, Frank's sister.

"Dearest Edith," she began, "I know you will let me write to you in my troubles. I am in such a twitter of mind in consequence of my various lovers that I do not know where to turn; nor do I quite know whom I am to call lover number one. Therefore I write to you to ask advice. Dear old Frank used to be lover number one. Of course I ought to call him now Mr. Francis Jones, because another lover is really lover number one. I am engaged to marry, as you are well aware, no less a person than the Earl of Castlewell; and, if all things were to go prosperously with me, I should in a short time be the Marchioness of Beaulieu. Did you ever think of the glory of being an absolutely live marchioness? It is so overwhelming as to be almost too much for me. I think that I should not cower before my position, but that I should, on the other hand, endeavour to soar so high that I should be consumed by my own flames. Then there is lover number three—Mr. Moss—who, I do believe, loves me with the truest affection of them all. I have found him out at last. He wishes to be the legal owner of all the salaries which the singer of La Beata may possibly earn; and he feels that, in spite of all that has come and gone, it is yet possible. Of all the men who ever forgave, Mr. Moss is the most forgiving.

"Now, which am I to take of these three? Of course, if you are the honest girl I take you to be, you will write back word that one, at any rate, is not in the running. Mr. Francis Jones has no longer the honour. But what if I am sure that he loves me; and what, again, if I am sure that he is the only one I love? Let this be quite—quite between ourselves. I am beginning to think that because of Frank Jones I cannot marry that gorgeous earl. What if Frank Jones has spoiled me altogether? Would you wish to see me on this account delivered over to Mr. Mahomet Moss as a donkey between two bundles of hay?

"Tell me what you think of it. He won't take my money. But suppose I earn my money for another season or two? Would not your Irish brutalities be then over; and my father's eloquence, and the eccentricities of the other gentlemen? And would not your brother and your father have in some way settled their affairs? Surely a little money won't then be amiss, though it may have come from the industry of a hard-worked young woman.

"Of course I am asking for mercy, because I am absolutely

devoted to a certain young man. You need not tell him that in so many words; but I do not see why I am to be ashamed of my devotion,—seeing that I was not ashamed of my engagement, and boasted of it to all the world. And I have done nothing since to be ashamed of.

"You have never told me a word of your young man; but the birds of the air are more communicative than some friends. A bird of the air has told me of you, and of Ada also, and had made me understand that from Ada has come all that sweetness which was to be expected from her. But from you has not come that compliance with your fate in life which circumstances have demanded.

"Your affectionate friend,
"RACHEL O'MAHONY."

It could not but be the case that Edith should be gratified by the receipt of such a letter as this. Frank was now at home, and was terribly down in the mouth. Boycotting had lost all its novelty at Morony Castle. His sisters had begun to feel that it was a pleasant thing to have their butter made for them, and pleasant also not to be introduced to a leg of mutton till it appeared upon the table. Frank, too, had become very tired of the work which fell to his lot, though he had been relieved in the heaviest labours of the farm by "Emergency" men, who had been sent to him from various parts of Ireland. But he was thoroughly depressed in heart, as also was his father. Months had passed by since Pat Carroll had stood in the dock at Galway ready for his trial. He was now, in March, still kept in Galway jail under remand from the magistrates. A great clamour was made in the county upon the subject. Florian's murder had stirred all those who were against the League to feel that the Government should be supported. But there had been a mystery attached to that other murder, perpetrated in the court, which had acted strongly on the other side,—on behalf of the League. The murder of Terry Carroll at the moment in which he was about to give evidence,—false evidence, as the Leaguers said,—against his brother was a great triumph to them. It was used as an argument why Pat Carroll should be no longer confined, while Florian's death had been a reason why he never should be released at all. All this kept the memory of Florian's death, and the constant thought of it, still fresh in the minds of them all at Morony Castle, together with the poverty which had fallen upon them, had made the two men weary of their misfortunes. Under such misfortunes, when continued, men do become more weary than women. But Edith thought there would be something in the constancy of Rachel's love to cheer her brother, and therefore the letter made her contented, if not happy.

For herself, she said to herself no love could cheer her. Captain Clayton still hung about Tuam and Headford, but his presence in the neighbourhood was always to be attributed to the evidence of which he was in search as to Florian's death. It seemed now with him that the one great object of his heart was the unravelling of that murder. "It was no mystery," as he said over and over again in Edith's hearing. He knew very well who had fired the rifle. He could see, in his mind's eye, the slight form of the crouching wretch as he too surely took his aim from the temporary barricade. The passion had become so strong with him of bringing the man to justice that he almost felt, that between him and his God he could swear to having seen it. And yet he knew that it was not so. To have the hanging of that man would be to him a privilege only next to that of possessing Edith Jones. And he was a sanguine man, and did believe that in process of time both privileges would be vouchsafed to him.

But Edith was less sanguine. She could not admit to herself the possibility that there should be successful love between her and her hero. His presence there in the neighbourhood of her home was stained by constant references to her brother's blood. And then, though there was no chance for Ada, Ada's former hopes militated altogether against Edith. "He had better go away and just leave us to ourselves," she said to herself. But yet neither was she nor was Ada sunk so low in heart as her father and her brother.

"Frank," she said to her brother, "whom do you think this letter is from?" and she held up in her hand Rachel's epistle.

"I care not at all, unless it be from that most improbable of all creatures, a tenant coming to pay his rent."

"Nothing quite so beautiful as that."

"Or from someone who has evidence to give about some of these murders that are going on?"—A Mr. Morris from the other side of the lake, in County Mayo, had just been killed, and the minds of men were now disturbed with this new horror. —"Anybody can kill anybody who has a taste in that direction. What a country for a man with his family to pitch upon and live in! And that all this should have been kept under so long by policemen and right-thinking individuals, and then burst out like a subterranean fire all over the country, because the hope has been given them of getting their land for nothing! In order to indulge in wholesale robbery they are willing at a moment's notice to undertake wholesale murder."

After listening to words such as these, Edith found it impossible to introduce Rachel's letter on the spur of the moment.

CHAPTER XXXVII.

RACHEL IS ILL.

RACHEL, before the end of March, received the following letter from her friend, but she received it in bed. The whole world of Covent Garden Theatre had been thrown into panic-stricken dismay by the fact that Miss O'Mahony had something the matter with her throat. This was the second attack, the first having been so short as to have caused no trepidations in the world of music; but this was supposed to be sterner in its nature, and to have caused already great alarm. Before March was over it was published to the world at large that Miss O'Mahony would not be able to sing during the forthcoming week.

In this catastrophe her lordly lover was of course the most sedulous of attendants. In truth he was so, though when we last met him and his bride together he had made himself very disagreeable. Rachel had then answered him in such language as to make her think it impossible that he should not quarrel with her; but still here he was, constant at her chamber door. Whether his constancy was due to his position about the theatre or to his ardour as a lover, she did not know; but in either case it troubled her somewhat, and interfered with her renewed dreams about Frank. Then came the following letter from Frank's sister:

"DEAR RACHEL,

"I am not very much surprised, though I was a little, that you should have accepted Lord Castlewell; but I had not quite known the ins and outs of it, not having been there to see. Frank says that the separation had certainly come from him, because he could not bring himself to burden your prosperity with the heavy load of his misfortunes. Poor fellow! They are very heavy. They would have made you both miserable for awhile, unless you could have agreed to postpone your marriage. Why should it not have been postponed?

"But Lord Castlewell came in the way, and I supposed him naturally to be as beautiful and gracious as he is gorgeous and rich. But though you say nothing about him there does creep out from your letter some kind of idea that he is not quite so beautiful in your eyes as was poor Frank. Remember that poor Frank has to wear two blue shirts a week and no more, in order to save the washing! How many does Lord Castlewell wear? How many will he wear when he is a marquis?

"But at any rate it does seem to be the case that you and the earl are not as happy together as your best friends could wish. We had understood that the earl was ready to expire for love at the sound of every note. Has he slackened in his admiration so as to postpone his expiring to the close of every song? Or why is it that Frank should be allowed again to come up and trouble your dreams?

"You are so fond of joking that it is almost impossible for a poor steady-going boycotted young woman to follow you to the end. Of course I understand that what you say about Mr. Moss is altogether a joke. But then what you say about Frank is, I am sure, not a joke. If you love him the best, as I am sure you do—so very much the best as to disregard the marble halls—I advise you, in the gentlest manner possible, to tell the marble halls that they are not wanted. It cannot be right to marry one man when you say that you love another as you do Frank. Of course he will wait if you like to wait. All I can say is, that no man loves a girl better than he loves you.

"We are very much down in the world at the present. We have literally no money. Papa's relatives have given their money to him to invest, and he has laid it out on the property here. Nobody was thought to have done so well as he till lately; but now they cannot get their interest, and, of course, they are impatient. Commissioners have sat in the neighbourhood, and have reduced the rents all round. But they can't reduce what doesn't exist. There are tenants who I suppose will pay. Pat Carroll could certainly have done so. But then papa's share in the property will be reduced almost to nothing. He will not get above five shillings out of every twenty shillings of rent, such as it was supposed to be when he bought it. I don't understand all this, and I am sure I cannot make you do so.

"I have nothing to tell about my young man, as you call him, except that he cannot be mine. I fancy that girls are not fond of writing about their young men when they don't belong to them. Frank, at any rate, is yours, if you will take him; and you can write about him with an open heart. I cannot do so. Think of poor Florian and his horrid death. Is this a time for marriage,—if it were otherwise possible,—which it is not?

"God bless you, dear Rachel. Let me hear from you again soon. I have said nothing to Frank as yet. I attempted it this morning, but was stopped. You can imagine that he, poor fellow, is not very happy.—Yours very affectionately,
"EDITH JONES."

Rachel read the letter on her sick bed, and as soon as it was read Lord Castlewell came to her. There was always a nurse there, but Lord Castlewell was supposed to be able to see the patient, and on one occasion had been accompanied by his sister. It was all done in the most proper form imaginable, much to Rachel's disgust. Incapable as she was in her present state of carrying on any argument, she was desirous of explaining to Lord Castlewell that he was not to hold himself as bound to marry her. "If you think that father is an ass, you had better say so outright, and let there be an end of it." She wished to speak to him after this fashion. But she could not say it in the presence of the nurse and of Lady Augusta. But Lord Castlewell's conduct to herself made her more anxious than ever to say something of the kind. He was very civil, even tender, in his inquiries, but he was awfully frigid. She could tell from his manner that that last speech of hers was rankling in his bosom as the frigid words fell from his lips. He was waiting for some recovery,—a partial recovery would be better than a whole one,—and then he would speak his mind. She wanted to speak her mind first, but she could hardly do so with her throat in its present condition.

She had no other friend than her father, no other friend to take her part with her lovers. And she had, too, fallen into such a state that she could not say much to him. According to the orders of the physician, she was not to interest herself at all about anything.

"I wonder whether the man was ever engaged to two or three lovers at once," she said to herself, alluding to the doctor. "He knows at any rate of Lord Castlewell, and does he think that I am not to trouble myself about him?"

She had a tablet under her pillow, which she took out and wrote on it certain instructions. "Dear father, C. and I quarrelled before I was ill at all, and now he comes here just as though nothing had happened. He said you made an ass of yourself in the House of Commons. I won't have it, and mean to tell him so; but I can't talk. Won't you tell him from me that I shall expect him to beg my pardon, and that I shall never hear anything of the kind again. It must come to this. Your own R." This was handed to Mr. O'Mahony by Rachel that very day before he went down to the House of Commons.

"But, my dear!" he said. Rachel only shook her head. "I can hardly say all this about myself. I don't care twopence whether he thinks me an ass or not."

"But I do," said Rachel on the tablet.

"He is an earl, and has wonderful privileges, as well as a great deal of money."

"Marble halls and impudence," said Rachel on the tablet. Then Mr. O'Mahony, feeling that he ought to leave her in peace, made her a promise, and went his way. At Covent Garden that evening he met the noble lord, having searched for him in vain at Westminster. He was much more likely to find Lord Castlewell among the singers of the day, than with the peers; but of these things Mr. O'Mahony hardly understood all the particulars.

"Well, O'Mahony, how is your charming daughter?"

"My daughter is not inclined to be charming at all. I do hope she may be getting better, but at present she is bothering her head about you."

"It is natural that she should think of me a little sometimes," said the flattered lord.

"She has written me a message which she says that I am to deliver. Now mind, I don't care about it the least in the world." Here the lord looked very grave. "She says that you called me an ass. Well, I am to you, and you're an ass to me. I am sure you won't take it as any insult, neither do I. She wants you to promise that you won't call me an ass any more. Of course it would follow that I shouldn't be able to call you one. We should both be hampered, and the truth would suffer. But as she is ill, perhaps it would be better that you should say that you didn't mean it."

But this was not at all Lord Castlewell's view of the matter. Though he had been very glib with his tongue in calling O'Mahony an ass, he did not at all like the compliment as paid back to him by his father-in-law. And there was something which he did not quite understand in the assertion that the truth would suffer. All the world was certain that Mr. O'Mahony was an ass. He had been turned out of the House of Commons only yesterday for saying that the Speaker was quite wrong, and sticking to it. There was not the slightest doubt in the world about it. But his lordship knew his gamut, which was all that he pretended to know, and never interfered with matters of which he was ignorant. He was treated with the greatest respect at Covent Garden, and nobody ever suspected him of being an ass. And then he had it in his mind to speak very seriously to Rachel as soon as she might be well enough to hear him. "You have spoken to me in a manner, my dear, which I am sure you did not intend." He had all the words ready prepared on a bit of paper in his pocket-book. And he was by no means sure but that the little quarrel might even yet become permanent. He had discussed it frequently with Lady Augusta, and Lady Augusta rather wished that it might become permanent. And Lord Castlewell was not quite sure that he did not wish it also. The young lady had a way of speaking about her own people which was not to be borne. And now she had been guilty of the gross indecency of sending a message to him by her own father,—the very man whom he called an ass. And the man in return only laughed and called him an ass.

But Lord Castlewell knew the proprieties of life. Here was this—girl whom he had proposed to marry, a sad invalid at the moment. The doctor had, in fact, given him but a sad account of the case. "She has strained her voice continually till it threatens to leave her," said the doctor; "I do not say that it will be so, but it may. Her best chance will be to abandon all professional exertions till next year." Then the doctor told him that he had not as yet taken upon himself to hint anything of all this to Miss O'Mahony.

Lord Castlewell was puzzled in the extreme. If the lady lost her voice and so became penniless and without a profession; and if he in such case were to throw her over, and leave her unmarried, what would the world say of him? Would it be possible then to make the world understand that he had deserted her, not on account of her illness, but because she had not liked to hear her father called an ass? And had not Rachel already begun the battle in a manner intended to show that she meant to be the victor? Could it be possible that she herself was desirous of backing out? There was no knowing the extent of the impudence to which these Americans would not go! No doubt she had, by the use of intemperate language on the occasion when she would not be driven out in the carriage, given him ample cause for a breach. To tell the truth, he had thought then that a breach would be expedient. But she had fallen ill, and it was incumbent on him to be tender and gentle. Then, from her very sick bed, she had sent him this impudent message.

And it had been delivered so impudently! "The truth would suffer!" He was sure that there was a meaning in the words intended to signify that he, Lord Castlewell, was and must be an ass at all times. Then he asked himself whether he was an ass because he did not quite understand O'Mahony's argument. Why did the truth suffer? As to his being an ass, —O'Mahony being an ass,—he was sure that there was no doubt about that. All the world said so. The House of Commons knew it,—and the newspapers. He had been turned out of the House for saying the Speaker was wrong, and not apologising for having uttered such words. And he, Lord Castlewell, had so expressed himself only to the woman who was about to be his wife. Then she had had the incredible folly to tell her father, and the father had told him that under certain circumstances the "truth must suffer." He did not quite understand it, but was sure that Mr. O'Mahony had meant to say that they were two fools together.

He was not at all ashamed of marrying a singing girl. It was the thing he would be sure to do. And he thought of some singing girls before his time, and of his time also, whom it would be an honour for such as him to marry. But he would degrade himself—so he felt—by the connection with an advanced Land-leaguing Member of Parliament. He looked round the lot of them, and he assured himself that there was not one from whose loins an English nobleman could choose a wife without disgrace. It was most unfortunate,—so he told himself. The man had not become Member of Parliament till quite the other day. He had not even opened his mouth in Parliament till the engagement had been made. And now, among them all, this O'Mahony was the biggest ass. And yet Lord Castlewell found himself quite unable to hold his own with the Irish member when the Irish member was brought to attack him. He certainly would have made Rachel's conduct a fair excuse for breaking with her,—only that she was ill.

If he could have known the state of Rachel's mind there might have been an end to his troubles. She had now, at length, been made thoroughly wretched by hearing the truth from the doctor,—or what the doctor believed to be the truth. "Miss O'Mahony, I had better tell you, your voice has gone, at any rate for a year."

"For a year!" The hoarse, angry, rusty whisper came forth from her, and in spite of its hoarseness and rustiness was audible enough.

"I fear so. For heaven's sake don't talk; use your tablet." Rachel drew the tablet from under her pillow and dashed it across the room. The doctor picked it up, and, with a kind smile and a little caressing motion of his hand, put it again back under the pillow. Rachel buried her head amidst the bedclothes and sobbed bitterly. "Try to make yourself happy in remembering how you have succeeded," said the doctor.

"It won't be back just the same," she wrote on her tablet.

"It is in God's hands," said the doctor. There came not another word from Rachel, either by her tablet or by any struggle at speech. The doctor, having made what attempts at comfort he could, went his way. Then her father, who had been in and out constantly, came to his daughter. He had not been present when she threw the tablet away, but he knew what the doctor had said to her.

"My pet," he said. But she made no attempt to answer him. A year! At her time of life a year is an eternity. And then this doctor had only told her that her voice was in God's hands. She could talk to herself without any effort. "When they say that they always condemn you. When the doctor tells you that you are in God's hands he means the Devil's."

She had been so near the gods and goddesses, and now she was no more than any other poor woman. She might be less, as her face had begun to wither with her voice. She had all but succeeded; as for her face, as for the mere look of her, let it go. She told herself that she cared nothing for her appearance. What was Lord Castlewell to her,—what even was Frank's love? To stand on the boards of the theatre and become conscious of the intense silence of the crowd before her, —so intense because the tone of her voice was the one thing desired by all the world. And then to open her mouth and to let the music go forth and to see the ears all erect, as she fancied she could, so that not a sound should be lost,—should not be harvested by the hungry hearers! That was to be a very god! As she told herself of all her regrets, there was not a passing sorrow given to Lord Castlewell. And what of the other man? "Oh, Frank, dear Frank, you will know it all now. There need be no more taking money." But she did take some comfort at last in that promise of God's hands. When she had come, as it were, to the bitterest moment of her grief, she told herself that, though it might be even at the end of a whole year, there was something to be hoped.

CHAPTER XXXVIII.

LORD CASTLEWELL IS MUCH TROUBLED.

WHEN her father had been with her half-an-hour, and was beginning to think that he could escape and go down to the House,—and he had a rod in pickle for the Speaker's back, such a rod that the Speaker's back should be sore for the rest of the session—Rachel began her lengthened conversation with him. In the last half-hour she had made up her mind as to what she would say. But the conversation was so long and intricate, being necessarily carried on by means of her tablet, that poor O'Mahony's rod was losing all its pickle. "Father, you must go and see Lord Castlewell at once."

"I think, my dear, he understood me altogether when I saw him before, and he seemed to agree with me. I told him I didn't mind being called an ass, but that you were so absurd as to dislike it. In fact, I gave him to understand that we were three asses; but I don't think he'll say it again."

"It isn't about that at all," said the tablet.

"What else do you want?"

Then Rachel went to work and wrote her demand with what deliberation she could assume.

"You must go and tell him that I don't want to marry him at all. He has been very kind, and you mustn't tell him that he's an ass any more. But it won't do. He has proposed to marry me because he has wanted a singing girl; and I think I should have done for him,—only I can't sing."

Then the father replied, having put himself into such a position on the bed as to read the tablet while Rachel was filling it: "But that'll all come right in a very short time."

"It can't, and it won't. The doctor says a year; but he

knows nothing about it, and says it's in God's hands. He means by that it's as bad as it can be."

"But, my dear——"

"I tell you it must be so."

"But you are engaged. He would never be so base a man as to take your word at such a moment as this. Of course he couldn't do it. If you had had small-pox, or anything horrible like that, he would not have been justified."

"I am as ugly as ever I can be," said the tablet, "and as poor a creature." Then she stopped her pencil for a moment.

"Of course he's engaged to you. Why, my dear, I'd have to cowhide him if he said a word of the kind."

"Oh, no!" said the tablet, with frantic energy.

"But you see if I wouldn't! You see if I don't! I suppose they think a lord isn't to be cowhided in this country. I guess I'll let 'em know the difference."

"But I don't love him," said the tablet.

"Goodness gracious me!"

"I don't. When he spoke of you in that way I began to think of it, and I found I hated him. I do hate him like poison, and I want you to tell him so."

"That will be very disagreeable," said the father.

"Never mind the disagreeables. You tell him so. I tell you he won't be the worst pleased of the lot of us. He wanted a singer, and not a Land-leaguer's daughter; now he hasn't got the singer, but has got the Land-leaguer's daughter. And I'll tell you something else. I want——"

"What do you want?" asked the father, when her hand for a moment ceased to scrawl.

"I want," she said, "Frank Jones. Now you know all about it."

Then she hid her face beneath the bed-clothes, and refused to write another word.

He went on talking to her till he had forgotten the Speaker and the rod in pickle. He besought her to think better of it; and if not that, just at present to postpone any action in the matter. He explained to her how very disagreeable it would be to him to have to go to the lord with such a message as she now proposed. But she only enhanced the vehemence of her order by shaking her head as her face lay buried in the pillow.

"Let it wait for one fortnight," said the father.

"No!" said the girl, using her own voice for the effort.

Then the father slowly took himself off, and making his way to the House of Commons, renewed his passion as he went, and had himself again turned out before he had been half-an-hour in the house.

The earl was sitting alone after breakfast two or three days subsequently, thinking in truth of his difficulty with Rachel. It had come to be manifest to him that he must marry the girl unless something terrible should occur to her. "She might die," he said to himself very sadly, trying to think of cases in which singers had died from neglected throats. And it did make him very sad. He could not think of the perishing of that magnificent treble without great grief; and, after his fashion, he did love her personally. He did not know that he could ever love anyone very much better. He had certainly thought that it would be a good thing that his father and mother and sister should go and live in foreign lands,—in order, in short, that they might never more be heard of to trouble him,—but he did not even contemplate their deaths, so sweet-minded was he. But in the first fury of his love he had thought how nice it would be to be left with his singing girl, and no one to trouble him. Now there came across him an idea that something was due to the Marquis of Beaulieu,—something, that is, to his own future position; and what could he do with a singing girl for his wife who could not sing?

He was unhappy as he thought of it all, and would ever and again, as he meditated, be stirred up to mild anger when he remembered that he had been told that "the truth would suffer." He had intended, at any rate, that his singing girl should be submissive and obedient while in his hands. But here had been an outbreak of passion! And here was this confounded O'Mahony ready to make a fool of himself at a moment's notice before all the world. At that moment the door was opened and Mr. O'Mahony was shown into the room.

"Oh! dear," exclaimed the lord, "how do you do, Mr. O'Mahony? I hope I see you well."

"Pretty well. But upon my word, I don't know how to tell you what I've got to say."

"Has anything gone wrong with Rachel?"

"Not with her illness,—which, however, does not seem to improve. The poor girl! But you'll say she's gone mad."

"What do you mean by that?"

"I really hardly know how I ought to break it. You must have learned by this time that Rachel is a girl determined to have her own way."

"Well; well; well!"

"And, upon my word, when I think of myself, I feel that I have nothing to do but what she bids me."

"It's more than you do for the Speaker, Mr. O'Mahony."

"Yes, it is; I admit that. But Rachel, though she is inclined to be tyrannical, is not such a downright positive old blue-bottle nincoompoop as that white-wigged king of kings. Rachel is bad; but even you can't say that she is bad enough to be Speaker of the House of Commons. My belief is, that he'll come to be locked up yet."

"We have all the highest opinion of him."

"It's because you like to be sat upon. You don't want to be allowed to say bo to a goose. I have often heard in my own country——"

"But you call yourself an Irishman, Mr. O'Mahony."

"Never did so in my life. They called me so over there when they wanted to return me to hold my tongue in that House of Torment; but I guess it will puzzle the best Englishman going to find out whether I'm an American or an Irishman. They did something over there to make me an American; but they did nothing to unmake me as an Irishman. And there I am, member for Cavan; and it will go hard with me if I don't break that Speaker's heart before I've done with him. What! I ain't to say that he goes wrong when he never goes right by any chance?"

"Have you come here this morning, Mr. O'Mahony, to abuse the Speaker?"

"By no means. It was you who threw the Speaker in my teeth."

Lord Castlewell did acknowledge to himself his own imprudence.

"I came here to tell you about my daughter, and upon my word I shall find it more difficult than anything I may have to say to the Speaker. I have the most profound contempt for the Speaker."

"Perhaps he returns it."

"I don't believe he does, or he wouldn't make so much of me as to turn me out of the House. When a man finds it necessary to remove an enemy, let the cause be what it may, he cannot be said to despise that enemy. Now, I wouldn't give a puff of breath to turn him out of the House. In truth, I despise him too much."

"He is to be pitied," said the lord, with a gentle touch of irony.

"I'll tell you what, Lord Castlewell——"

"Don't go on about the Speaker, Mr. O'Mahony,—pray don't."

"You always begin,—but I won't. I didn't come here to speak about him at all. And the Chairman of Committees is positively worse. You know there's a creature called Chairman of Committees?"

"Now, Mr. O'Mahony, I really must beg that you will fight your political battles anywhere but here. I'm not a politician. How is your charming daughter this morning?"

"She is anything but charming. I hardly know what to make of her, but I find that I am always obliged to do what she tells me." There was another allusion to the Speaker on the lord's tongue, but he restrained himself. "She has sent me here to say that she wants the marriage to be broken off."

"Good Heavens!"

"She does. She says that you intend to marry her because she's a singing girl;—and now she can't sing."

"Not exactly that," said the lord.

"And she thinks she oughtn't to have accepted you at all,— that's the truth." The lord's face became very long. "I think myself that it was a little too hurried. I don't suppose you quite knew your own minds."

"If Miss O'Mahony repents——"

"Well, Miss O'Mahony does repent. She has got something into her head that I can't quite explain. She thought that she'd do for a countess very well as long as she was on the boards of a theatre. But now that she's to be relegated to private life she begins to feel that she ought to look after someone about her own age."

"Oh, indeed! Is this her message?"

"Well; yes. It is her message. I shouldn't in such a matter invent it all if she hadn't sent me. I don't know, now I think of it, that she did say anything about her own age. But yet she did," remarked Mr. O'Mahony, calling to mind the assertion made by Rachel that she wanted Frank Jones. Frank Jones was about her own age, whereas the lord was as old as her father.

"Upon my word, I am much obliged to Miss O'Mahony."

"She certainly has meant to be as courteous as she knows how," said Mr. O'Mahony.

"Perhaps on your side of the water they have different ideas of courtesy. The young lady sends me word that now she means to retire from the stage she finds I am too old for her."

"Not that at all," said Mr. O'Mahony. But he said it in an apologetic tone, as though admitting the truth.

Lord Castlewell, as he sat there for a few moments, acknowledged to himself that Rachel possessed certain traits of character which had something fine about them, from whatever side of the water she had come. He was a reasonable man, and he considered that there was a way made for him to escape from this trouble which was not to have been expected. Had Rachel been an English girl, or an Italian, or a Norwegian, he would hardly have been let off so easily. As he was an earl, and about to be a marquis, and as he was a rich man, such suitors are not generally given up in a hurry. This young lady had sent word to him that she had lost her voice permanently and was therefore obliged to surrender that high title, that noble name, and those golden hopes which had glistened before her eyes. No doubt he had offered to marry her because of her singing;—that is, he would not have so offered had she not have been a singer. But he could not have departed from his engagement simply because she had become dumb. He quite understood that Mr. O'Mahony would have been there with his cowhide, and though he was by no means a coward he did not wish to encounter the American Member of the House of Commons in all his rage. In fact, he had been governed in his previous ideas by a feeling of propriety; but propriety certainly did not demand him to marry a young lady who had sent to tell him that he was too old. And this irate member of the House of Commons had come to bring him the message!

"What am I expected to suggest now?" said Lord Castlewell, after awhile.

"Just your affectionate blessing, and you're very sorry," said Mr. O'Mahony, with a shrug. "That's the kind of thing, I should say."

He couldn't send her his affectionate blessing, and he couldn't say he was very sorry. Had the young lady been about to marry his son,—had there been such a son,—he could have blessed her; and he felt that his own personal dignity did not admit of an expression of sorrow.

Was he to let the young lady off altogether? There was something nearly akin,—very nearly akin,—to true love in his bosom as he thought of this. The girl was ill, and no doubt weak, and had been made miserable by the loss of her voice. The doctor had told him that her voice, for all singing purposes, had probably gone for ever. But her beauty remained;—had not so faded, at least, as to have given any token of permanent decay. And that peculiarly bright eye was there; and the wit of the words which had captivated him. The very smallness of her stature, with its perfect symmetry, had also gone far to enrapture him.

No doubt, he was forty. He did not openly pretend even to be less. And where was the young lady, singer or no singer, who if disengaged, would reject the heir to a marquisate because he was forty? And he did not believe that Rachel had sent him any message in which allusion was made to his age. That had been added by the stupid father, who was, without doubt, the biggest fool that either America or Ireland had ever produced. Now that the matter had been brought before him in such bald terms, he was by no means sure that he was desirous of accepting the girl's offer to release him. And the father evidently had no desire to catch him. He must acknowledge that Mr. O'Mahony was an honest fool.

"It's very hard to know what I'm to say." Here Mr. O'Mahony shook his head. "I think that, perhaps, I had better come and call upon her."

"You mustn't speak a word! And, if you're to be considered as no longer engaged, perhaps there might be—you know—something—well, something of delicacy in the matter!"

Mr. O'Mahony felt at the moment that he ought to protect the interests of Frank Jones.

"I understand. At any rate I am not disposed to send her my blessing at present as a final step. An engagement to be married is a very serious step in life."

But her father remembered that she had told him that she wanted Frank Jones. Should he tell the lord the exact truth, and explain all about Frank Jones? It would be the honest thing to do. And yet he felt that his girl should have another chance. This lord was not much to his taste; but still, for a lord, he had his good points.

"I think we had better leave it for the present," said the lord. "I feel that in the midst of all your eloquence I do not quite catch Miss O'Mahony's meaning."

O'Mahony felt that this lord was as bad a lord as any of them. He would like to force the lord to meet him at some debating club where there was no wretched Speaker and there force him to give an answer on any of the burning questions which now excited the two countries.

"Very well. I will explain to Rachel as soon as I can that the matter is still left in abeyance. Of course we feel the honour done us by your lordship in not desiring to accept at once her decision. Her condition is no doubt sad. But I suppose she may expect to hear once more from yourself in a short time."

So Mr. O'Mahony took his leave, and as he went to Cecil Street endeavoured in his own mind to investigate the character of Lord Castlewell. That he was a fool there could be no doubt, a fool with whom he would not be forced to live in the constant intercourse of married life for any money that could be offered to him. He was a man who, without singing himself, cared for nothing but the second-hand life of a theatre. But then he, Mr. O'Mahony, was not a young woman, and was not expected to marry Lord Castlewell. But he had told himself over and over again that Lord Castlewell had been "caught." He was a great lord rolling in money, and Rachel had "caught" him. He had not quite approved of Rachel's conduct, but the lord had been fair game for a woman. What the deuce was he to think now of the lord who would not be let off?

"I wonder whether it can be love for her," said he to himself; "such love as I used to feel."

Then he sighed heavily as he went home.

CHAPTER XXXIX.

CAPTAIN CLAYTON'S FIRST TRIUMPH.

It was now April, and this April was a sad month in Ireland. I do not know why the deaths of two such men as were then murdered should touch the heart with a deeper sorrow than is felt for the fate of others whose lot is lower in life; why the poor widow, who has lost her husband while doing his duty amidst outrages and unmanly revenges, is not to be so much thought of as the sweet lady who has been robbed of her all in the same fashion. But so it is with human nature. We know how a people will weep for their Sovereign, and it was with such tears as that, with tears as sincere as those shed for the best of kings, that Lord Frederick Cavendish and Mr. Burke were lamented. In April these two men had fallen, hacked to death in front of the Viceregal Lodge. By whom they were killed, as I write now, no one knows, and as regards Lord Frederick one can hardly guess the reason. He had come over to Ireland on that very day, to take the place which his luckier predecessor had just vacated, and had as yet done no service, and excited no vengeance in Ireland. He had only attended an opening pageant;—because with him had come a new Lord Lieutenant, —not new indeed to the office, but new in his return. An accident had brought the two together on the day, but Lord Frederick was altogether a stranger, and yet he had been selected. Such had been his fate, and such also the fate of Mr. Burke, who, next to him in official rank, may possibly have been in truth the doomed one. They were both dealt with horribly on that April morning,—and all Ireland was grieving. All Ireland was repudiating the crime, and saying that this horror had surely been done by American hands. Even the murderers native to Ireland seemed to be thoroughly ashamed of this deed.

It would be needless here to tell,—or to attempt to tell,—how one Lord-Lieutenant had made way for another, and one Chief Secretary for another Chief Secretary. It would be trying to do too much. In the pages of a novel the novelist can hardly do more than indicate the sources of the troubles which have fallen upon the country, and can hardly venture to deal with the names and characters of those who have been concerned. For myself, I do most cordially agree with the policy of him in whose place Lord Frederick had this day suffered,—as far as his conduct in Ireland can be read from that which he did and from that which he spoke. As far as he had agreed with the Government in their measure for interfering with the price paid or land in the country,—for putting up a new law devised by themselves in lieu of that time-honoured law by which property has ever been protected in England,—I disagree. Of my disagreement no one will take notice;—but my story cannot be written without expressing it.

But down at Morony Castle, mingled with their sorrows, there was a joy and a triumph; not loud indeed, not sounded with trumpets, not as yet perfect, not quite assured even in the mind of one man; but yet assuring in the mind of that man,—and indeed of one other,—almost to conviction. That man was Captain Yorke Clayton, and that other man was only poor Hunter, the wounded policeman. For such triumph as was theirs a victim is needed; and in this case the victim, the hoped-for victim, was Mr. Lax.

Nothing had ever been made out in regard to the murder of Terry Carroll in the Court House at Galway. Irish mysteries are coming to be unriddled now, but there will be no unriddling of that. Yorke Clayton, together with Hunter and all the police of County Galway, could do nothing in regard to that mystery. They had struggled their very best, and, from the nature of the crime, had found themselves almost obliged to discover the perpetrator. The press of the two countries, the newspapers in other respects so hostile to each other, had united in declaring that the police were bound to know all about it. The police had determined to know nothing about it, because the Government did not dare to bring forward such evidence. This was the Irish Land-league view; and though it contained an accusation against the Government for having contrived the murder itself, it was all the better on that account. The English papers simply said that the Galway police must be fast asleep. This man had been murdered when in the very hands of the officers of justice. The judge had seen the shots fired. The victim fell into the hands of four policemen. The pistol was found at his feet. It was done in daylight, and all Galway was looking on. The kind of things that were said by one set of newspapers and another drove Yorke Clayton almost out of his wits. He had to maintain a show of good humour, and he did maintain it gallantly. "My hero is a hero still," whispered Edith to her own pillow. But, in truth, nothing could be done as to that Galway case. Mr. Lax was still in custody, and was advised by counsel not to give any account of himself at that time. It was indecent on the part of the prosecution that he should be asked to do so. So said the lawyers on his side, but it was clear that nobody in the court and nobody in Galway could be got to say that he or she had seen him do it. And yet Yorke Clayton had himself seen the hip of the stooping man. "I suppose I couldn't swear to it," he said to himself; and it would be hard to see how he could swear to the man without forswearing himself.

R

But while this lamentable failure was going on, success reached him from another side. He didn't care a straw what the newspapers said of him, so long as he could hang Mr. Lax. His triumph in that respect would drown all other failures. Mr. Lax was still in custody, and many insolent petitions had been made on his behalf in order that he might be set free. "Did the Crown intend to pretend that they had any shadow of evidence against him as to the shooting of Terry Carroll?"

"No;—but there was another murder committed a day or two before. Poor young Florian Jones had been murdered. Even presuming that Lax's hand cannot be seen visible in the matter of Terry Carroll, there is, we think, something to connect him with the other murder. The two, no doubt, were committed in the same interest. The Crown is not prepared to allow Lax to escape from its hands quite yet." Then there were many words on the subject going on just at the time at which Lax especially wanted his freedom, and at which, to tell the truth, Yorke Clayton was near the end of his tether in regard to poor Florian.

In the beginning of his inquiry as to the Ballyglunin murder, he entertained an idea that Lax, after firing the shot, had been seen by that wicked car-driver, who had boycotted Mr. Jones in his great need. The reader will probably have forgotten that Mr. Jones had required to be driven home to Morony Castle from Ballyglunin station, and had been refused the accommodation by a wicked old Land-leaguer, who had joined the conspiracy formed in the neighbourhood against Mr. Jones. He had done so, either in fear of his neighbours, or else in a true patriot spirit—because he had gone without any supper, as had also his horses, on the occasion. The man's name was Teddy Mooney, the father of Kit Mooney who stopped the hunting at Moytubber. And he certainly was patriotic. From day to day he went on refusing fares,—for the boycotted personages were after all more capable of paying fares than the boycotting hero of doing without them,—suffering much himself from want of victuals, and more on behalf of his poor animal. He saw his son Kit more than once or twice in those days, and Kit appeared to be the stancher patriot of the two. Kit was a baker, and did earn wages; but he utterly refused to subsidise the patriotism of his father. "If ye can't do that for the ould counthry," said Kit, "ye ain't half the man I took ye for." But he refused him a gallon of oats for his horse.

It was not at once that the old man gave way. He went on boycotting individuals till he hadn't a pair of breeches left to sit upon, and the non-boycotted tradesmen of the little towns around declined to sit upon his car, because the poor horse, fed upon roadside grasses, refused to be urged into a trot. "Tare and ages, man, what's the good of it? Ain't we a-cutting the noses off our own faces, and that with the money so scarce that I haven't seen the sight of a half-crown these two weeks." It was thus that he declared his purpose of going back to the common unpatriotic ways of mankind, to an old pal, whom he had known all his days. He did do so, but found, alas! that his trade had perished in the meanwhile or forced itself into other channels.

The result was that Teddy Mooney became very bitter in spirit, and was for a while an Orangeman, and almost a Protestant. The evil things that had been done to him were terrible to his spirit. He had been threatened with eviction from ten acres of ground because he couldn't pay his rent; or, as he said, because he had declined to drive a maid-servant to the house of another gentleman who was also boycotted. This had not been true, but it had served to embitter Teddy Mooney. And now, at last, he had determined to belong to the other side.

When an Irishman does make up his mind to serve the other side he is very much determined. There is but the meditation of two minutes between Land-leaguing and Orangeism, between boycotting landlords and thorough devotion to the dear old landlord. When Kit Mooney had first laid down the law to his father, how he ought to assist in boycotting all the enemies of the Land-league, no one saw his way clearer than did Teddy Mooney. "I wouldn't mind doing without a bit or a sup," he said, when his son explained to him that he might have to suffer a little for the cause. "Not a bit or a sup when the ould counthry wants it." He had since had a few words with his son Kit, and was now quite on the other side of the question. He was told that somebody had threatened to cut off his old mare's tail because he had driven Phil D'Arcy. Since that he had become a martyr as well as an Orangeman, and was disposed to go any length "for the gintl'men." This had come all about by degrees—had been coming about since poor Florian's murder; and at last he wrote a letter to Yorke Clayton, or got someone else to write it:

"Yer Honour,—It was Lax as dropped Master Flory. Divil a doubt about it. There's one as can tell more about it as is on the road from Ballyglunin all round. This comes from a well-wisher to the ould cause. For Musther Clayton."

When Captain Clayton received this he at once knew from whom it had come. The Land-leaguing car-driver, who had turned gentlemen's friend, was sufficiently well known to history to have been talked about. Clayton, therefore, did not lose much time in going down to Ballyglunin station and requiring to be driven yet once again from thence to Carnlough. "And now, Mr. Teddy Mooney," he said, after they had travelled together a mile or two from Ballyglunin, and had come almost to the spot at which the poor boy had been shot, "tell me what you know about Mr. Lax's movements in this part of the world." He had never come there before since the fatal day without having three policemen with him, but now he was alone. Such a man as Teddy Mooney would be most unwilling to open his mouth in the presence of two or more persons.

"O Lord, Captain, how you come on a poor fellow all unawares!"

"Stop a moment, Mr. Mooney," and the car stopped. "Whereabouts was it the young gentleman perished?"

"Them's the very shot-holes," said Teddy, pointing up to the temporary embrasure, which had indeed been knocked down half a score of times since the murder, and had been as often replaced by the diligent care of Mr. Blake and Captain Clayton.

"Just so. They are the shot-holes. And which way did the murderer run?" Teddy pointed with his whip away to the east, over the ground on which the man had made his escape. "And where did you first see him?"

"See him!" ejaculated Teddy. It became horrible to his imagination as he thought that he was about to tell of such a deed.

"Of course, we know you did see him; but I want to know the exact spot."

"It was over there, nigh to widow Dolan's cottage."

"It wasn't the widow who saw him, I think?"

"Faix, it was the widow thin, with her own eyes. I hardly know'd him. And yet I did know him, for I'd seen him once travelling from Ballinasloe with Pat Carroll. And Lax is a man as when you've once seen him you've seen him for allays. But she knowed him well. Her husband was one of the boys when the Fenians were up. If he didn't go into the widow Dolan's cabin my name's not Teddy Mooney."

"And who else was there?"

"There was no one else; but only her darter, a slip of a girl o' fifteen, come up while Lax was there. I know she come up, because I saw her coming jist as I passed the door."

Captain Clayton entered into very friendly relations with Teddy Mooney on that occasion, trying to make him understand, without any absolute promises, that all the luck and all the rewards,—in fact, all the bacon and oats,—lay on the dish to which Mr. Lax did not belong. Under these influences Teddy did become communicative—though he lied most awfully. That did not in the least shock Captain Clayton, who certainly would have believed nothing had the truth been told him without hesitation. At last it came out that the car-driver was sure as to the personality of Lax,—had seen him again and again since he had first made his acquaintance in Carroll's company, and could swear to having seen him in the widow's cabin. He knew also that the widow and her daughter were intimate with Lax. He had not seen the shot fired. This he said in an assured tone, but Captain Clayton had known that before. He did not expect to find anyone who had seen the shot fired, except Mr. Jones and Peter. As to Peter he had his suspicions. Mr. Jones was certain that Peter had told the truth in declaring that he had seen no one; but the Captain had argued the matter out with him. "A fellow of that kind is in a very hard position. You must remember that for the truth itself he cares nothing. He finds a charm rather in the romantic beauty of a lie. Lax is to him a lovely object, even though he be aware that he and Lax be on different sides. And then he thoroughly believes in Lax; thinks that Lax possesses some mysterious power of knowing what is in his mind, and of punishing him for his enmity. All the want of evidence in this country comes from belief in the marvellous. The people think that their very thoughts are known to men who make their name conspicuous, and dare not say a word which they suppose that it is desired they shall withhold. In this case Peter no doubt is on our side, and would gladly hang Lax with his own hand if he were sure he would be safe. But Lax is a mysterious tyrant, who in his imagination can slaughter him any day; whereas he knows that he shall encounter no harm from you. He and poor Florian were sitting on the car with their backs turned to the embrasure; and Peter's attention was given to the driving of the car,—so that there was no ground for thinking that he had seen the murderer. All the circumstances of the moment ran the other way. But still it was possible."

And Captain Clayton was of opinion that Peter was beginning to be moved from the determined know-nothingness of his primary evidence. He had seen the flash. And then, as his master had run up the bank, he didn't know whether he hadn't caught the flying figure of a man.

"I had the poor boy's head on my knees, Captain Clayton; and how is a poor man to look much about him then?"

In this condition stood Captain Clayton's mind in regard to Peter, when he heard, for the first time, a word about the widow Dolan and the widow Dolan's daughter.

The woman swore by all her gods that she knew nothing of Lax. But then she had already fallen into the difficulty of having been selected as capable of giving evidence. It generally happens that no one first person will be found even to indicate others, so that there is no finding a beginning to the case. But when a witness has been indicated, the witness must speak.

"The big blackguard!" exclaimed Mrs. Dolan, when she

heard of the evil that had been brought her; "to have the imperence to mention my name!"

It was felt, all the country through, to be an impertinence, —for anybody to drag anybody else into the mess of troubles which was sure to arise from an enforced connection with a law court. Most unwillingly the circumstances were drawn from Mrs. Dolan, and with extreme difficulty also from that ingenious young lady her daughter. But, still, it was made to appear that Lax had taken refuge in their cottage, and had gone down from thence to a little brook, where he effected the cleansing of his pistol. The young lady had done all in her power to keep her mother silent, but the mother had at last been tempted to speak of the weapon which Lax had used.

Now there was no further question of letting Lax go loose from prison! That very irate barrister, Mr. O'Donnell, who was accustomed to speak of all the Land-league criminals as patriotic lambs,—whose lamblike qualities were exceeded only by their patriotism,—did not dare to intimate such a wish any further. But he did urge, with all that benevolence for which he was conspicuous, that the trial should come on at that immediate spring assizes. A rumour had, however, already reached the ears of Captain Clayton, and others in his position, that a great alteration was to be effected in the law. This, together with Mrs. Dolan's evidence, might enable him to hang Mr. Lax. Therefore the trial was postponed;—not, indeed, with outspoken reference as to the new measure, but with much confidence in its resources.

It would be useless here to refer to that Bill which was to have been passed for trying certain prisoners in Ireland without the intervention of a jury, and of the alteration which took place in it empowering the Government to alter the venue, and to submit such cases to a selected judge, to selected juries, to selected counties. The Irish judges had remonstrated against the first measure, and the second was to be first tried, so that should it fail the judges might yet be called upon to act.

Such was the law under which criminals were tried in 1882, and the first capital convictions were made under which the country began to breathe freely. But the tidings of the law had got abroad beforehand, and gave a hope of triumph to such men as Captain Clayton. Let a man undertake what duty he will in life, if he be a good man he will desire success; and if he be a brave man he will long for victory. The presence of such a man as Lax in the country was an eyesore to Captain Clayton, which it was his primary duty to remove. And it was a triumph to him now that the time had come in which he might remove him. Three times had Mr. Lax fired at the Captain's head, and three times had the Captain escaped. "I think he has done with his guns and his pistols now," said Captain Clayton, in his triumph.

CHAPTER XL.

YORKE CLAYTON AGAIN MAKES LOVE.

"I AM not quite sure about Peter yet," said Clayton to Mr. Jones. "But if we could look into his very soul I am afraid he could not do much for us."

"I never believed in Peter as a witness," replied Mr. Jones.

"I should like to know exactly what he did see:—whether it was a limb or a bit of his coat. But I think that young lady crept out and saw him cleaning his pistol. And I think that the old lady had a glimpse of the mask. I think that they can be made to say so."

"I saw the mask myself, and the muzzle of the rifle;—and I saw the man running as plainly as I see you."

"That will all be wanted, Mr. Jones. But I trust that we may have to summon you to Dublin. As things are at present, if Lax had been seen in broad daylight firing at the poor boy by a dozen farmers it would do no good in County Galway. There is Miss Edith out there. She is awfully anxious about this wretch who destroyed her brother. I will go and tell her." So Captain Clayton rushed out, anxious for another cause for triumph.

Mr. Jones had heard of his suit, and had heard also that the suit was made to Edith and not to Ada. "There is not one in a dozen who would have taken Edith," said he to himself,—"unless it be one who saw her with my eyes." But yet he did not approve of the marriage. "They were poverty stricken," he said, and Clayton went about from day to day with his life in his hand. "A brave man," he said to himself; "but singularly foolhardy,—unless it be that he wants to die." He had not been called upon for his consent, for Edith had never yielded. She, too, had said that it was impossible. "If Ada would have suited, it might have been possible, but not between Yorke and me." They had both come now to call him by his Christian name; and they to him were Ada and Edith; but with their father he had never quite reached the familiarity of a Christian name.

Mr. Jones had, in truth, been so saddened by the circumstances of the last two years that he could not endure the idea of marriages in his family. "Of course, if you choose, my dear, you can do as you like," he used to say to Edith.

"But I don't choose."

"What there are left of us should, I think, remain together. I suppose they cannot turn me out of this house. The Prime Minister will hardly bring in a Bill that the estates bought this last hundred years shall belong to the owners of the next century. He can do so, of course, as things go now. There are no longer any lords to stop him, and the House of Commons, who want their seats, will do anything he bids them. It's the First Lieutenant who looks after Ireland, who has ideas of justice with which the angels of light have certainly not filled his mind. That we should get nothing from our purchased property this century, and give it up in the course of the next, is in strict accordance with his thinking. We can depend upon nothing. My brother-in-law can, of course, sell me out any day, and would not stop for a moment. Everybody has to get his own, except an Irish landlord. But I think we should fare ill all together. Your brother is behaving nobly, and I don't think we ought to desert him. Of course you can do as you please."

Then the squire pottered on, wretched in heart; or, rather, down in the mouth, as we say, and gave his advice to his younger daughter, not, in truth, knowing how her heart stood. But a man, when he undertakes to advise another, should not be down in the mouth himself. *Equam memento rebus in arduis servare mentem, non secus ac bonis.* If not, your thoughts will be too strongly coloured by your own misfortunes to allow of your advising others.

All this Edith knew,—except the Latin. The meaning of it had been brought home to her by her own light. "Poor papa is so hipped," she said to herself, "that he thinks that nobody will ever be happy again." But still she resolved that she would not marry Yorke Clayton. There had been a mistake, and she had made it,—a miserable blunder for which she was responsible. She did not quite analyse the matter in her own mind, or look into the thoughts of Ada, or of Yorke himself,—the hero of her pillow; but she continued to tell herself that the proper order of things would not admit it. Ada, she knew, wished it. Yorke longed for her, more strongly even than for Lax, the murderer. For herself, when she would allow her thoughts to stray for a moment in that direction, all the bright azure tints of heaven were open to her. But she had made a mistake, and she did not deserve it. She had been a blind fool, and blind fools deserved no azure tints of heaven.

If she could have had her own way she would still have married Ada to Yorke Clayton. When Ada told her that she had got over her foolish love, it was the mere babble of unselfishness. Feel a passion for such a man as Yorke Clayton, look into the depth of his blue eyes, and fancy for herself a partnership with the spirit hidden away within, and then get over it! Edith was guilty here of the folly of judging of her sister as herself. And as for Yorke himself;—a man, she said, always satisfies himself with that which is lovely and beautiful. And with Ada he would have such other gifts as so strong a man as

Yorke always desires in his wife. In temper she was perfect; in unselfishness she was excellent. In all those ways of giving aid, which some women possess and some not at all,—but which, when possessed, go so far to make the comfort of a house,—she was supreme. If a bedroom were untidy, her eye saw it at once. If a thing had to be done at the stroke of noon, she would remember that other things could not be done at the same time. If a man liked his egg half-boiled, she would bear it in her mind for ever. She would know the proper day for making this marmalade and that preserve; and she would never lose her good looks for a moment when she was doing these things. With her little dusting-brush at her girdle, no eyes that knew anything would ever take her for aught but a lady. She was just the wife for Yorke Clayton.

So Edith argued it in her own bosom, adding other wondrous mistakes to that first mistake she had made. In thinking of it all she counted herself for nothing, and made believe that she was ugly in all eyes. She would not allow the man to see as his fancy led him; and could not bring herself to think that if now the man should change his mind and offer his hand to Ada, it would be impossible that Ada should accept it. Nor did she perceive that Ada had not suffered as she had suffered.

"I wanted to catch you just for one moment," said Yorke Clayton, running out so as to catch his prey. She had half wished to fly from him, and had half told herself that any such flight was foolish.

"What is it, Yorke?" she said.

"I think,—I do think that I have at last got Lax upon the hip."

"You are so bloody-minded about Lax."

"What! Are you going to turn round and be merciful?" He was her hero, and she certainly felt no mercy towards the murderer of her brother; no mercy towards him who she now thought had planned all the injury done to her father; no mercy towards him who had thrice fired at her beloved. This wretched man had struggled to get the blood of him who was all the world to her; and had been urged on to his black deeds by no thought, by no feeling, that was not in itself as vile as hell! Lax was to her a viper so noxious as to be beyond the pale of all mercy. To crush him beneath the heel of her boot, so as to make an end of him, as of any other poisonous animal, was the best mercy to all other human beings. But she had said the word at the spur of the moment, because she had been instigated by her feelings to gainsay her hero, and to contradict him, so that he might think that he was no hero of hers. She looked at him for the moment, and said nothing, though he held her by the arm. "If you say I am to spare him, I will spare him."

"No," she answered, "because of your duty."

"Have I followed this man simply as a duty? Have I lain awake thinking of it till I have given to the pursuit such an amount of energy as no duty can require? Thrice he has endeavoured to kill me, firing at me in the dark, getting at me from behind hedges, as no one who has anything of the spirit of man in his bosom will do when he strives to destroy his enemy. All that has been nothing. I am a policeman in search of him, and am the natural enemy of a murderer. Of course in the ordinary way I would not have spared him; but the ordinary way would have sufficed. Had he escaped me I could have laughed at all that. But he took that poor lad's life!" Here he looked sadly into her face, and she could see that there was a tear within his eye. "That was much, but that was not all. That lad was your brother, him whom you so dearly loved. He shot down the poor child before his father's face, simply because he had said that he would tell the truth. When you wept, when you tore your hair, when you flung yourself in sorrow upon the body, I told myself that either he or I must die. And now you bid me be merciful." Then the big tears dropped down his cheeks, and he began to wail himself,—hardly like a man.

And what did Edith do? She stood and looked at him for a few moments; then extricated herself from the hold he still had of her, and flung herself into his arms. He put down his face and kissed her forehead and her cheeks; but she put up her mouth and kissed his lips. Not once or twice was that kiss given; but there they stood closely pressed to each other in a long embrace. "My hero," she said; "my hero." It had all come at last,—the double triumph; and there was, he felt, no happier man in all Ireland than he. He thought, at least, that the double battle had been now won. But even yet it was not so. "Captain Clayton," she began.

"Why Captain? Why Clayton?"

"My brother Yorke," and she pressed both his hands in hers. "You can understand that I have been carried away by my feelings, to thank you as a sister may thank a brother."

"I will not have it," he exclaimed fiercely. "You are no sister, nor can I ever be your brother. You are my very own now, and for ever." And he rushed at her again as though to envelop her in his arms, and to crush her against his bosom.

"No!" she exclaimed, avoiding him with the activity of a young fawn; "not again. I had to beg your pardon, and it was so I did it."

"Twenty times you have offended me, and twenty times you must repeat your forgiveness."

"No, no, it must not be so. I was wrong to say that you were bloody-minded. I cannot tell why I said so. I would not for worlds have you altered in anything ;—except," she said, "in your love for me."

"But have you told me nothing?"

"I have called you my hero,—and so you are."

"Nay, Edith, it is more than that. It is not for me to remind you, but it is more than that."

She stood there blushing before him, over her cheeks and up to her forehead; but yet did not turn away her face.

"How am I to tell you why it is more than that? You cannot tell me," she replied.

"But, Edith——"

"You cannot tell me. There are moments for some of us the feelings of which can never be whispered. You shall be my hero and my brother if you will; or my hero and my friend; or, if not that, my hero and my enemy."

"Never!"

"No, my enemy you cannot be; for him who is about to revenge my brother's death no name less sweet than dearest friend will suffice. My hero and my dearest friend!"

Then she took him by the hand, and turned away from the walk, and, escaping by a narrow path, was seen no more till she met him at dinner with her father and her brother and her sister.

"By God! she shall be mine!" said Clayton. "She must be mine!"

And then he went within, and, finding Hunter, read the details of the evidence for the trial of Mr. Lax in Dublin, as prepared by the proper officers in Galway city.

CHAPTER XLI.

THE STATE OF IRELAND.

IT will be well that they who are interested only in the sensational incidents of our story to skip this chapter and go on to other parts of our tale which may be more in accordance with their taste. It is necessary that this one chapter shall be written in which the accidents that occurred in the lives of our three heroines shall be made subordinate to the political circumstances of the day. This chapter should have been introductory and initiative; but the facts as stated will suit better to the telling of my story if they be told here. There can be no doubt that Ireland has been and still is in a most precarious condition, that life has been altogether unsafe there, and that property has been jeopardised in a degree unknown for many years in the British Islands. It is, I think, the general opinion that these evils have been occasioned by the influx into Ireland of a feeling which I will not call American, but which has been engendered in America by Irish jealousy, and warmed into hatred by distance from English rule. As far as politics are regarded, Ireland has been the vassal of England as Poland has been of those masters under which she has been made to serve. She was subjected to much ill-usage, and though she has readily accepted the language, the civilisation, and the customs of England, and has in fact grown rich by adopting them, the memories of former hardships have clung to her, and have made her ready to receive willingly the teachings of those whose only object it has been to undermine the prestige of the British Empire. In no respect has she more readily taken to her bosom English practices than in that of the letting and the hiring of land. In various countries, such as Italy, Russia, France, and the United States, systems have grown up different from that which has prevailed in England. Whether the English system or any other may be the best is not now the question. But in answering that question it is material to know that Ireland has accepted and, at any rate for two centuries, has followed that system. The landlord has been to his tenants a beneficent or, occasionally, a hard master, and the tenants have acknowledged themselves as dependent, generally with much affection, though not unfrequently with loud complaint. It has been the same in England. Questions of tenant-right, of leases, and of the cruelty of evictions have from time to time cropped up in Ireland. But rents were readily paid up to 1878 and 1879; though abatements were asked for,—as was the case also in England; and there were men ready to tell the Irish from time to time, since the days of O'Connell downwards, that they were ill-treated in being kept out of their "ould" properties by the rightful owners.

Then the American revolt, growing out of Smith O'Brien's logic and physical force, gave birth to Fenianism. The true Fenian I take to be one desirous of opposing British power, by using a fulcrum placed on American soil. Smith O'Brien's logic consisted in his assertion that if his country wished to hammer the British Crown, they could only do it by using hammers. Smith O'Brien achieved little beyond his own exile;— but his words, acting upon his followers, produced Fenianism. That died away, but the spirit remained in America; and when English tenants began to clamour for temporary abatements in their rent, the clamours were heard on the other side of the water, and assisted the views of those American-Irish who had revivified Ribandism and had given birth to the cry of Home Rule.

During the time that this was going on, a long unflagging series of beneficial Acts of Parliament, and of consequently ameliorated circumstances, had befallen the country. I was told the other day by an Irish Judge, whose name stands conspicuous among those who are known for their wisdom and their patriotism, by a Roman Catholic Judge too, that in studying the latter laws of the two countries, the laws affecting England and Ireland in reference to each other, he knew no law by which England was specially favoured, though he knew various laws redounding to the benefit of Ireland. When the cry for some relief to suffering Ireland came up, at the time of the Duchess of Marlborough's Fund, it was alleged in proof of Ireland's poor condition that there was not work by which the labourers could earn wages. I have known Ireland for more than forty years,—say from 1842 to 1882. In 1842 we paid five shillings a week for the entire work of a man. As far as I can learn, we now pay, on an average, nine shillings for the same. The question is not whether five shillings was sufficient, or whether nine be insufficient, but that the normal increase through the country has been and can be proved to be such as is here declared.

I will refer to the banks, which can now be found established in any little town, almost in any village, through the country. Fifty years ago they were very much rarer. Banks do not spring up without money to support them. The increase of wages,—and the banks also in an indirect manner,—have come from that decrease in the population which followed the potato famine of 1846. The famine and its results were terrible while they lasted; but they left behind them an amended state of things. When man has failed to rule the world rightly, God will step in, and will cause famines, and plagues, and pestilence —even poverty itself—with His own Right Arm. But the cure was effected, and the country was on its road to a fair amount of prosperity, when the tocsin was sounded in America, and Home Rule became the cry.

Ireland has lain as it were between two rich countries England, her near neighbour, abounds in coal and iron, and has by means of these possessions become rich among the nations. America, very much the more distant, has by her unexampled agricultural resources put herself in the way to equal England. It is necessary,—necessary at any rate for England's safety,—that Ireland should belong to her. This is here stated as a fact, and I add my own opinion that it is equally necessary for Ireland's welfare. But on this subject there has arisen a feud which is now being fought out by all the weapons of rebellion on one side, and on the other by the force of a dominating Government, restrained, as it is found to be, by the self-imposed bonds of a democratic legislature. But there is the feud, and the battle, and the roaring of the cannons is heard afar off.

I now purpose to describe in a very few words the nature of

the warfare. It may be said that the existence of Ireland as a province of England depends on the tenure of the land. If the land were to be taken altogether from the present owners, and divided in perpetuity among any possible number of tenants, so as to be the property of each tenant, without payment of any rent, all England's sense of justice would be outraged, the English power of governing would be destroyed, and all that could then be done by England would be to give a refuge to the present owners till the time should come for righting themselves, and they should be enabled to make some further attempt for the recovery of their possessions. This would probably arrive, if not sooner, from the annihilation of the new proprietors under the hands of their fellow-countrymen to whom none of the spoil had been awarded. But English statesmen,—a small portion, that is, of English statesmen,—have wished in their philanthropy to devise some measure which might satisfy the present tenants of the land, giving them a portion of the spoil; and might leave the landlords contented,—not indeed with their lot, which they would feel to be one of cruel deprivation, but with the feeling that something had at any rate been left to them. A compromise would be thus effected between the two classes whose interests have always been opposed to each other since the world began,—between the owners of property and those who have owned none.

The statesmen in question have now come into power by means of their philanthropy, their undoubted genius, and great gifts of eloquence. They have almost talked the world out of its power of sober judgment. I hold that they have so succeeded in talking to the present House of Commons. And when the House of Commons has been so talked into any wise or foolish decision, the House of Lords and the whole legislating machinery of the country is bound to follow.

But how should their compromises be effected? It does not suit the present writer to name any individual statesman. He neither wishes to assist in raising a friend to the gods, or to lend his little aid in crushing an enemy. But to the Liberal statesmen of the day, men in speaking well of whom—at a great distance—he has spent a long life, he is now bound to express himself as opposed. We all remember the manner after which the Coercion Bill of 1881 was passed. The hoarse shrieks with which a score of Irish members ran out of the House crying "Privilege," when their voices had been stopped by the salutary but certainly unconstitutional word of the Speaker, is still ringing in our ears. Then the Government and the Irish score were at daggers-drawn with each other. To sit for thirty-six hours endeavouring to pass a clause was then held by all men to be an odious bondage. But when these clauses had thus roughly been made to be the law, the sugar-plum was to follow by which all Ireland was to be appeased. The second Bill of 1881 was passed, which, with various additions, has given rise to Judge O'Hagan's Land Court. That, with its various sub-commissioners, is now engaged in settling at what rate land shall be let in Ireland.

That Judge O'Hagan and his fellow commissioners are well qualified to perform their task,—as well qualified, that is, by kindness, by legal knowledge and general sagacity as any men can be,—I have heard no one deny. In the performance of most difficult duties they have hitherto encountered no censure. But they have, I think, been taxed to perform duties beyond the reach of any mortal wisdom. They are expected to do that which all the world has hitherto failed in doing,—to do that against which the commonest proverbs of ancient and modern wisdom have raised their voice. There is no proverb more common than that of "*caveat emptor.*" It is Judge O'Hagan's business to do for the poorer party in each bargain made between a landlord and a tenant that against which the above proverb warns him. The landlord has declared that the tenant shall not have the land unless he will pay £10 a year for it. The tenant agrees. Then comes Judge O'Hagan and tells the two contracting parties to take up their pens quickly and write down £8 as the fair rent payable for the land. And it was with the object of doing this, of reducing every £10 by some percentage, twenty per cent. or otherwise, that this commission was appointed. The Government had taken upon itself to say that the greed of Irish landlords had been too greedy, and the softness of Irish tenants too soft, and that therefore Parliament must interfere. Parliament has interfered, and £8 is to be written down for a term of years in lieu of £10, and the land is to become the possession of the tenant instead of the landlord as long as he may pay this reduced rent. In fact all the bonds which have bound the landlord to his land are to be annihilated. So also are the bonds which bind the tenant, who will sell the property so acquired when he shall have found that that for which he pays £8 per annum shall have become worth £10 in the market.

It is useless to argue with the commissioners, or with the Government, as to the inexpediency of such an attempt to alter the laws for governing the world, which have forced themselves on the world's acceptance. Many such attempts have been made to alter these laws. The Romans said that twelve per cent. should be the interest for money. A feeling long prevailed in England that legitimate interest should not exceed five per cent. It is now acknowledged that money is worth what it will fetch; and the interests of the young, the foolish, and the reckless, who are tempted to pay too much for it, are protected only by public opinion. The usurer is hated, and the hands of the honest men are against him. That suffices to give the borrower such protection as is needed. So it is with landlords and tenants. Injury is no doubt done, and injustice is enabled to prevail here and there. But it is the lesser injury, the lesser injustice, which cannot be prevented in the long run by any attempt to escape the law of "*caveat emptor*."

It is, however, vain to talk to benevolent commissioners, or to a Government working by eloquence and guided by philanthropy, regardless of political economy. "Would you have the heart," asks the benevolent commissioner, "to evict the poor man from his small holding on which he has lived all his life, where his only sympathies lie, and send him abroad to a distant land, where his solitary tie will be that of labour?" The benevolent commissioner thus expresses with great talk and with something also of the eloquence of his employers the feeling which prevails on that side of the question. But that which he deprecates is just what I could do; and having seen many Irishmen both in America and in Ireland, I know that the American Irishman is the happiest man of the two. He eats more; and in much eating the happiness of mankind depends greatly. He is better clothed, better sheltered, and better instructed. Though his women wail when he departs, he sends home money to fetch them. This may be for the profit of America. There are many who think that it must therefore be to the injury of England. The question now is whether the pathetic remonstrance of the tear-laden commissioner should be allowed to prevail. I say that the tenant who undertakes to pay for land that which the land will not enable him to pay had better go,—under whatever pressure.

Let us see how many details, how many improbabilities, will have to be met before the benevolence of the commissioner can be made to prevail. The reductions made on the rent average something between twenty and twenty-five per cent. Let us take them at twenty. If a tenant has to be evicted for a demand of £10, will he be able to live in comfort if he pay only £8? Shall one tenant live in comfort on a farm, the rent of which has been reduced him from £100 to £80, and another, the reduction having been from £20 to £16? In either case, if a tenant shall do well with two children, how shall he do with six or eight? A true teetotaller can certainly pay double the rent which may be extracted from a man who drinks. Shall the normal tenant earn wages beyond what he gets from the land under his own tillage? Shall the idle man be made equal to the industrious,—or can this be done, or should it be done, by any philanthropy? Statesmen sitting together in a cabinet may resolve that they will set the world right by eloquence and benevolence combined; but the practices to which the world have been brought by long experience will avail more than eloquence and benevolence. Statesmen may decree that land shall be let at a certain rate, and the decree will prevail for a time. It may prevail long enough to put out of gear the present affairs of the Irish world with which these statesmen will have tampered. But the long experience will come back, and bargains will again be made between man and man, though the intervening injuries will be heartbreaking.

But the benevolence of the Government and its commissioners will not have gone far. The Land Law of 1881 has, as I now write, been at work for twelve months, and the results hitherto accomplished have been very small. It may be doubted whether a single reluctant tenant,—a single tenant who would have been unwilling to leave his holding,—has been preserved from American exile by having his £10 or £20 or £30 of rent reduced to £8 or £16 or £24. The commissioners work slowly, having all the skill of the lawyers, on one side or the other, against them. It is piteous to see the hopelessness of three sub-commissioners in the midst of a crowd of Irish attorneys. And the law, as it exists at present, can be made to act only on holdings possessed by tenants for one year. And the skill of the lawyers is used in proving on the part of the landlords that the land is held by firm leases, and cannot, therefore, be subjected to the law; and then by proving, on behalf of the tenants, that the existing leases are illegal, and should be broken. The possession of a lease, which used to be regarded as a safeguard and permanent blessing to the tenant, is now held to be cruelly detrimental to him, as preventing the lowering of his rent, and the immediate creation for him of a tenancy for ever. It is not to be supposed that the sub-commissioners can walk over the land and straightway reduce the rents, though the lands would certainly be subject to such reduction did not the law interfere. In a majority of cases,—a majority as far as all Ireland is concerned,—a feeling of honesty does prevail between landlord and tenant, which makes them both willing to subject themselves to the new law without the interference of attorneys, and many are preparing themselves for such an arrangement. The landlord is willing to lose twenty per cent. in fear of something worse, and the tenant is willing to take it, hardly daring to hope for anything better. Such is the best condition which the law has ventured to anticipate. But in either case this is to be done as tempering the wind to the shorn lamb. The landlord is anxious if possible to save for himself and those who may come after him something of the reality of his property, and the tenant feels that, though something of the nobility of property has been promised to him by the Land-leaguers, he may after all make the best bargain by so far submitting himself to his shorn landlord.

But on estates where the commissioners are allowed their full swing, the whole nature of the property in the land will be altered. The present tenant, paying a tax of £8 per annum which will be subjected to no reduction and on which no abatement can be made, in lieu of a £10 rent, will be the owner. The small man will be infinitely more subject to disturbance than at present, because the tax must be paid. The landlord will feel no mercy for him, seeing that the bonds between them which demanded mercy have been abrogated. The extra £2 or £4 or £6 will not enable the tenant to live the life of ease which he will have promised himself. If his interest has been made to be worth anything,—and it will be worth something, seeing that it has been worth something, and is saleable under its present condition,—it will be sold, and the emigration will continue. There are cruel cases at present. There will be cases not less cruel under the *régime* which the new law is expected to produce. But the new law will be felt to have been unjust as having tampered with the rights of property, and having demanded from the owners of property its sale or other terms than those of mutual contract.

But the time selected for the measure was most inappropriate. If good in itself, it was bad at the time it was passed. Home Rule coming across to us from America had taken the guise of rebellion. I have met gentlemen who, as Home-Rulers, have simply desired to obtain for their country an increase of power in the management of their own affairs. These men have been loyal and patriotic, and it might perhaps be well to meet their views. The Channel no doubt does make a difference between Liverpool and Dublin. But the latter-day Home-Rulers, of whom I speak, brought their politics, their aspirations, and their money from New York, and boldly made use of the means which the British Constitution afforded them to upset the British Constitution as established in Ireland. That they should not succeed in doing this is the determination of all, at any rate on this side of the Channel. It is still, I believe, the desire of most thinking men on the Irish side. But parliamentary votes are not given only to thinking men; and consequently a body of members has appeared in the House, energetic and now well trained, who have resolved by the clamour of their voices to put an end to the British power of governing the country. These members are but a minority among those whom Ireland sends to Parliament; but they have learned what a minority can effect by unbridled audacity. England is still writhing in her attempt to invent some mode of controlling them. But long before any such mode had been adopted,—had been adopted or even planned,—the Government in 1881 brought out their plan for securing to the tenants fair rents, fixity of tenure, and freedom of sale.

As to the first, it will, of course, be admitted by all men that rents should be fair, as also should be the price at which a horse is sold. It is, however, beyond the power of Parliament to settle the terms which shall be fair. "*Caveat emptor*" is the only rule by which fair rents may be reached. By fixity of tenure is meant such a holding of the land as shall enable the tenant to obtain an adequate return for his labour and his capital, and to this is added a romantic and consequently a most unjust idea that it may be well to settle this question on behalf of the tenant by granting him such a term as shall leave no doubt. Let him have the land for ever as long as he will pay a stipulated sum, which shall be considerably less than the landlord's demand. That idea I call romantic, and therefore unjust. But, even though the beauty of the romance be held sufficient to atone for the injustice, this was not the poetical re-arrangement of all the circumstances of land tenure in Ireland. Freedom of sale is necessarily annexed to fixity of tenure. If a man is to have the possession of land in perpetuity, surely he should be allowed to sell it. Whether he be allowed or not, he will contrive to do so. Freedom of sale means, I take it, that the so-called landlord shall have no power of putting a veto on the transaction. We cannot here go into the whole question as it existed in Ulster before 1870; but the freedom of sale intended is such, I think, as I have defined it.

Whether these concessions be good or bad, this was, at any rate, no time for granting them. They seem to me to amount to wholesale confiscation. But supposing me to be wrong in that, can I be wrong in thinking that a period of declared rebellion is not a time for concessions? When the Land Bill was passed the Land-league was in full power; boycotting had become the recognised weapon of an illegal association; and the Home-Rulers of the day,—the party, that is, who represented the Land-league,—were already in such possession of large portions of the country as to prevent the possibility of carrying out the laws.

At this moment the Government brought forward its romantic theory as to the manipulation of land, and, before that theory was at work, commenced its benevolent intentions by locking up all those who were supposed to be guilty of an intention to carry out the Government project further than the Government would carry it out itself. It is held, as a rule, in politics that coercion and concession cannot be applied together. Ireland was in mutiny under the guidance of a mutinous party in the House of Commons, and at that moment a commission was put in operation, under which it was the intention of the Government to transfer the soil of the country at a reduced price to the very men among whom the mutineers are to be found. How do the tidings of such a commission operate upon the ears of Irishmen at large? He is told that under the fear of the Land-league his rent is to be reduced to an extent which is left to his imagination; and then, that he is to be freed altogether from the incubus of a landlord! He is, in fact, made to understand that his cherished Land-league has become all-powerful. And yet he hears that odious men, whom he recognises only as tyrants, are filling the jails through the country with all his dearest friends. Demanding concessions, and the continued increase of them, and having learned the way to seize upon them when they are not given, he will not stand coercion. Abated rent soon becomes no rent. When it is left to the payer of the rent to decide on which system he will act, it is probable that the no-rent theory will prevail.

So it was in 1882. Tenants were harassed by needy landlords, and when they were served with forms of ejectment the landlords were simply murdered, either in their own persons or in that of their servants. Men finding their power, and beginning to learn how much might be exacted from a yielding Government, hardly knew how to moderate their aspirations. When they found that the expected results did not come at once, they resorted to revenge. Why should these tyrants keep them out from the good things which their American friends had promised them, and which were so close within their grasp? And their anger turned not only against their landlords, but against those who might seem in any way to be fighting on the landlords' side. Did a neighbour occupy a field from which a Land-leaguing tenant had been evicted, let the tails of that neighbour's cattle be cut off, or the legs broken of his beasts of burden, or his sheep have their throats cut. Or if the injured one have some scruples of conscience, let the oppressor simply be boycotted, and put out of all intercourse with his brother men. Let no well-intentioned Land-leaguing neighbour buy from him a ton of hay, or sell to him a loaf of bread.

But as a last resource, if all others fail, let the sinner be murdered. We all know, alas! in how many cases the sentence has been pronounced and the judgment given, and the punishment executed.

Such have been the results of the Land Law passed in 1881. And under the curse so engendered the country is now labouring. It cannot be denied that the promoters of the Land Laws are weak, and that the disciples of the Land-league are strong. In order that the truth of this may be seen and made apparent, the present story is told

CHAPTER XLII.

LORD CASTLEWELL'S FAREWELL.

POOR Mr. O'Mahony had enemies on every side. There had come up lately a state of things which must be very common in political life. The hatreds which sound so real when you read the mere words, which look so true when you see their scornful attitudes, on which for the time you are inclined to pin your faith so implicitly, amount to nothing. The Right Honourable A. has to do business with the Honourable B., and can best carry it on by loud expressions and strong arguments such as will be palatable to readers of newspapers; but they do not hate each other as the readers of the papers hate them, and are ready enough to come to terms, if coming to terms is required. Each of them respects the other, though each of them is very careful to hide his respect. We can fancy that the Right Honourable A. and the Honourable B. in their moments of confidential intercourse laugh in their joint sleeves at the antipathies of the public. In the present instance it was alleged that the Right Honourable A. and the Honourable B. had come to some truce together, and had ceased for a while to hit each other hard knocks. Such a truce was supposed to be a feather in the cap of the Honourable B., as he was leader of a poor party of no more than twenty; and the Right Honourable A. had in this matter the whole House at his back. But for the nonce each had come off his high horse, and for the moment there was peace between them.

But Mr. O'Mahony would have no peace. He understood nothing of compromises. He really believed that the Right Honourable gentleman was the fiend which the others had only called him. To him it was a compact with the very devil. Now the leader of his party, knowing better what he was about, and understanding somewhat of the manner in which politics are at present carried on, felt himself embarrassed by the honesty of such a follower as Mr. O'Mahony. Mr. O'Mahony, when he was asked whether he wished to lead or was willing to serve, declared that he would neither lead nor serve. What he wanted was the "good of Ireland." And he was sure that that was not to be obtained by friendship with Her Majesty's Government. This was in itself very well, but he was soon informed that it was not as a free-lance that he had been elected member for Cavan. "That is between me and my constituency," said Mr. O'Mahony, standing up with his head thrown back, and his right hand on his heart. But the constituency soon gave him to understand that he was not the man they had taken him to be.

He, too, had begun to find that to spend his daughter's money in acting patriotism in the House of Commons was not a fine rôle in life. He earned nothing and he did nothing. Unless he could bind himself hand and foot to his party he had not even a spark of delegated power. He was not allowed to speak when he desired, and was called upon to sit upon those weary benches hour after hour, and night after night, only pretending to effect those things which he and his brother members knew could not be done. He was not allowed to be wrathful with true indignation, not for a moment; but he was expected to be there from question time through the long watches of the night—taking, indeed, his turn for rest and food—always ready with some mock indignation by which his very soul was fretted; and no one paid him the slightest respect, though he was, indeed, by no means the least respectable of his party. He would have done true work had it been given him to do. But at the present moment his own party did not believe in him. There was no need at present for independent wrathful eloquence. There seldom is need in the House of Commons for independent eloquence. The few men who have acquired for themselves at last the power of expressing it, not to empty benches, not amidst coughings and hootings, and loud conversation, have had to make their way to that point either by long efficient service or by great gifts of pachydermatousness. Mr. O'Mahony had never served anyone for an hour, and was as thin-skinned as a young girl; and, though his daughter had handed him all her money, so that he might draw upon it as he pleased, he told himself, and told her also, that his doing so was mean. "You're welcome to every dollar, father, only it doesn't seem to make you happy."

"I should be happy to starve for the country, if starving would do anything."

"I don't see that one ever does any good by starving as long as there is bread to eat. This isn't a romantic sort of thing, this payment of rents; but we ought to try and find out what a man really owes."

"No man owes a cent to any landlord on behalf of rent."

"But how is a man to get the land?" she said. "Over in our country a rough pioneering fellow goes and buys it, and then he sells it, and of course the man who buys it hasn't to pay rent. But I cannot see how any fellow here can have a right to the land for nothing." Then Mr. O'Mahony reminded his daughter that she was ill and should not exert herself.

It was now far advanced in May, and Mr. O'Mahony had resolved to make one crushing eloquent speech in the House of Commons and then to retire to the United States. But he had already learned that even this could not be effected without the overcoming of many difficulties. In himself, in his eloquence, in the supply of words, he trusted altogether; but there was the opportunity to be bought, and the Speaker's eye to be found,—he regarded this Speaker's eye as the most false of all luminaries,—and the empty benches to be encountered, and then drowsy reporters to be stirred up; and then on the next morning,—if any next morning should come for such a report,—there would not be a tithe of what he had spoken to be read by any man, and, in truth, very little of what he could speak would be worthy of reading. His words would be honest and indignant and fine-sounding, but the hearer would be sure to say, " What a fool is that Mr. O'Mahony!" At any rate, he understood so much of all this that he was determined to accept the Chiltern Hundreds and flee away as soon as his speech should be made.

It was far advanced in May, and poor Rachel was still very ill. She was so ill that all hope had abandoned her either as to her profession or as to either of her lovers. But there was some spirit in her still, as when she would discuss with her father her future projects. "Let me go back," she said, "and sing little songs for children in that milder climate. The climate is mild down in the South, and there I may, perhaps, find some fragment of my voice." But he who was becoming so despondent both for himself and for his country, still had hopes as to his daughter. Her engagement with Lord Castlewell was not even yet broken. Lord Castlewell had gone out of town at a most unusual period,—at a time when the theatres always knew him, and had been away on the exact day which had been fixed for their marriage. Rachel had done all that lay in herself to disturb the marriage, but Lord Castlewell had held to it, urged by feelings which he had found it difficult to analyse. Rachel had in her sickness determined to have done with him altogether, but latterly she had had no communication with him. She had spoken of him to her father as though he were a being simply to be forgotten. "He has gone away, and, as far as he is concerned, there is an end of me. It could not have finished better." But her mind still referred to Frank Jones, and from him she had received hardly a word of love. Further words of love she could not send him. During her illness many letters, or little notes rather, had been written to Castle Morony on her behalf by her father, and to these there had come replies. Frank was so anxious to hear of her well-doing. Frank had not cared so much for her voice as for her general health. Frank was so sorry to hear of her weakness. It had all been read to her, but as it had been read she had only shaken her head; and her father had not carried the dream on any further. To his thinking she was still engaged to the lord, and it would be better for her that she should marry the lord. The lord no doubt was a fool, and filled the most foolish place in the world, —that of a silly fainéant earl. But he would do no harm to his daughter, and the girl would learn to like the kind of life which would be hers. . At present she was very, very ill, but still there was hope for recovery.

By the treasury of the theatre she had been treated munificently. Her engagement had been almost up to the day fixed for her marriage, and the money which would have become due to her under it had been paid in full. She had sent back the latter payments, but they had been returned to her with the affectionate respects of the managers. Since she had put her foot upon these boards she had found herself to be popular with all around her. That, she had told herself, had been due to the lord who was to become her husband. But Rachel had become, and was likely to become, the means of earning money for them, and they were grateful. To tell the truth, Lord Castlewell had had nothing to do with it.

But gradually there came upon them the conviction that her voice was gone, and then the payment of the money ceased. She, and the doctor, and her father, had discussed it together, and they had agreed to settle that it must be so.

"Yes," said the girl, smiling, "it is bitter. All my hopes! And such hopes! It is as though I were dead, and yet were left alive. If it had been small-pox, or anything in that way, I could have borne it. But this thing, this terrible misfortune!"

Then she laughed, and then burst out sobbing with loud tears, and hid her face.

"You will be married, and still be happy," said the doctor.

"Married! Rubbish! So much you know about it. Am I ever to get strong in my limbs again, so as to be able to cross the water and go back to my own country?"

Here the doctor assured her that she would be able to go back to her own country, if it were needed.

"Father," she said, as soon as the doctor had left her, "let there be an end to all this about Lord Castlewell. I will not marry him."

"But, my dear!"

"I will not marry him. There are two reasons why I should not. I do not love him, and he does not love me. There are two other reasons. I do not want to marry him, and he does not want to marry me."

"But he says he does."

"That is his goodness. He is very good. I do not know why a man should be so good who has had so bad a bringing up. Think of me,—how good I ought to be, as compared with him. I haven't done anything naughty in all my life worse than tear my frock, or scold poor Frank; and yet I find it harder to give him up, merely because of the grandeur, than he does to marry me, the poor singing girl, who can never sing again. No! My good looks are gone, such as they were.

I can feel it, even with my fingers. You had better take me back to the States at once."

"Good-bye, Rachel," said the lord, coming into her room the day but one after this. Her father was not with her, as she had elected to be alone when she would bid her adieu to her intended husband.

"This is very good of you to come to me."

"Of course I came."

"Because you were good. You need not have come unless you had wished it. I had so spoken to you as to justify you in staying away. My voice is gone, and I can only squeak at you in this broken treble."

"Your voice would not have mattered at all."

"Ah, but it has mattered to me. What made you want to marry me?"

"Your beauty quite as much as your voice," said the lord.

"And that has gone too. Everything I had has gone. It is melancholy! No, my lord," she said, interrupting him when he attempted to contradict her, "there is not a word more to be said about it. Voice and beauty, such as it was, and the little wit, are all gone. I did believe in my voice myself, and therefore I felt myself fitting to marry you. I could have left a name behind me if my voice had remained. But, in truth, my lord, it was not fitting. I did not love you."

"That, indeed!"

"As far as I know myself, I did not love you. You have heard me speak of Frank Jones,—a man who can only wear two clean shirts a week because he has been so boycotted by those wretched Irish as to be able to afford no more. I would take him with one shirt to-morrow, if I could get him. One does not know why one loves a person. Of course he's handsome, and strong, and brave. I don't think that has done it, but I just got the fancy into my head, and there it is still. And he with his two shirts, working every day himself with his own hands to earn something for his father, would not marry me because I was a singing girl and took wages. He would not have another shirt to be washed with my money. Oh, that the chance were given to me to go and wash it for him with my own hands!"

Lord Castlewell sat through the interview somewhat distraught, as well he might be; but when it was over, and he had taken his leave and kissed her forehead, as he went home in his cab, he told himself that he had got through that little adventure very well.

CHAPTER XLIII.

MR. MOSS IS FINALLY ANSWERED.

SOME days after the scene last recorded Rachel was sitting in her bedroom, partly dressed, but she was, as she was wont to declare to her father, as weak as a cat with only one life. She had in the morning gone through a good deal of work. She had in the first place counted her money. She had something over £600 at the bank, and she had always supplied her father with what he had wanted. She had told her future husband that she must sing one month in the year so as to earn what would be necessary for the support of the Member of Parliament, and singularly enough her father had yielded. But now the six hundred and odd pounds was all that was left to take them both back to the United States. "I think I shall be able to lecture there," Mr. O'Mahony had said. "Wait till I express my opinion about queens, and lords, and the Speaker! I think I shall be able to say a word or two about the Speaker!—and the Chairman of Committees. A poor little creature who can hardly say bo to a goose unless he had got all the men to back him. I don't want to abuse the Queen, because I believe she does her work like a lady; but if I don't lay it on hot on the Speaker of the British House of Commons, my name is not Gerald O'Mahony."

"You forget your old enemy, the Secretary."

"Him we used to call Buckshot? I'm not so sure about him. At any rate he has had a downfall. When a man's had a downfall I don't care about lecturing against him. But I don't think it probable that the Speaker will have a downfall, and then I can have my fling."

Rachel had dismissed her brougham, and she had written to Edith Jones. That, no doubt, had been the greatest effort of the morning. We need not give here the body of her letter, but it may be understood that she simply declared at length the nature of the prospect before her. There was not a word of Frank Jones in it. She had done that before, and Frank Jones had not responded. She intended to go with her father direct from Liverpool to New York, and her letter was full chiefly of affectionate farewells. To Edith and to Ada and to their father there were a thousand written kisses sent. But there was not a kiss for Frank. There was not a word for Frank, so that any reader of the letter, knowing there was a Frank in the family, would have missed the mention of him, and asked why it was so. It was very, very bitter to poor Rachel this writing to Morony Castle without an allusion to the man; but, as she had said, he had been right not to come and live on her wages, and he certainly was right not to say a word as to their loss, when neither of them had wages on which to live. It would have suited in the United States, but she knew that it would not suit here in the old country, and therefore when the letter was written she was sitting worn-out, jaded and unhappy in her own bedroom.

The lodging was still in Cecil Street, from which spot she and her father had determined not to move themselves till after the marriage, and had now resolved to remain there till Rachel should be well enough for her journey to New York. As she sat there the servant, whom in her later richer days she had taken to herself, came to her and announced a visitor. Mr. Moss was in the sitting-room. "Mr. Moss here!" The girl declared that he was in the sitting-room, and in answer to further inquiries alleged that he was alone. How he had got there the girl could not say. Probably somebody had received a small bribe. Mr. O'Mahony was not in,—nor was anybody in. Rachel told the girl to be ready when she was ready to accompany her into the parlour, and thus resolving that she would see Mr. Moss she sent him a message to this effect. Then she went to work and perfected her dressing very slowly.

When she had completed the work she altered her purpose, and determined that she would see Mr. Moss alone. "You be in the little room close at hand," she said, "and have the door ajar, so that you can come to me if I call. I have no reason to suspect this man, and yet I do suspect him." So saying, she put on her best manners, as it might be those she had learned from the earl when he was to be her husband, and walked into the room. She had often told herself, since the old days, as she had now told the maid, that no real ground for suspicion existed; and yet she knew that she did suspect the man.

Rachel was pale and wan, and moved very slowly as though with haughty gesture. Mr. Moss, no doubt, had reason for knowing that the marriage with Lord Castlewell was at an end. The story had been told about among the theatres. Lord Castlewell did not mean to marry Miss O'Mahony; or else the other and stranger story, Miss O'Mahony did not mean to marry Lord Castlewell. Though few believed that story, it was often told. Theatrical people generally told it to one another as a poetical tale. The young lady had lost her voice and her beauty. The young lady was looking very old and could never sing again. It was absolutely impossible that in such circumstances she should decline to marry the lord if he were willing. But it was more than probable that he should decline to marry her. The theatrical world had been much astonished by Lord Castlewell's folly, and now rejoiced generally over his escape. But that he should still want to marry the young lady, and that she should refuse,—that was quite impossible.

But Mr. Moss was somewhat different from the theatrical world in general. He kept himself to himself, and kept his opinion very much in the dark. Madame Socani spoke to him often about Rachel, and expressed her loud opinion that Lord Castlewell had never been in earnest. And she was of opinion that Rachel's voice had never had any staying property. Madame Socani had once belittled Rachel's voice, and now her triumph was very great. In answer to all this Mr. Moss almost said nothing. Once he did turn round and curse the woman violently, but that was all. Then, when the news had, he thought, been made certain, either in one direction or the other, he came and called on the young lady.

"Well, Mr. Moss," said the young lady, with a smile that was intended to be most contemptible and gracious.

"I have been so extremely sorry to hear of your illness, my dear young lady."

Her grandeur departed from her all at once. To be called this man's "dear young lady" was insufferable. And grandeur did not come easily to her, though wit and sarcasm did.

"Your dear young lady, as you please to call her, has had a bad time of it."

"In memory of the old days I called you so, Miss O'Mahony. You and I used to be thrown much together."

"You and I will never be thrown together again, as my singing is all over."

"It may be so and it may not."

"It is over, at any rate as far as the London theatres go,— as far as you and I go."

"I hope not."

"I tell you it is. I am going back to New York at once, and do not think I shall sing another note as long as I live. I'm going to learn to cook dishes for papa, and we mean to settle down together."

"I hope not," he repeated.

"Very well; but at any rate I must say good-bye to you. I am very weak, and cannot do much in the talking line."

Then she got up and stood before him, as though determined to wish him good-bye. She was in truth weak, but she was minded to stand there till he should have gone.

"My dear Miss O'Mahony, if you would sit down for a moment, I have a proposition to make to you. I think that it is one to which you may be induced to listen."

Then she did sit down, knowing that she would want the strength which rest would give her. The conversation with Mr. Moss might probably be prolonged. He also sat down at a little distance, and held his shining new hat dangling between his knees. It was part of her quarrel with him that he had always on a new hat.

"Your marriage with Lord Castlewell, I believe, is off."

"Just so."

"And also your marriage with Mr. Jones?"

"No doubt. All my marriages are off. I don't mean to be married at all. I tell you I'm going home to keep house for my father."

"Keep house for me," said Mr. Moss.

"I would rather keep house for the devil," said Rachel, rising from her chair in wrath.

"Vy?—vy?"—Mr. Moss was reduced by his eagerness and enthusiasm to his primitive mode of speaking—"Vat is it that you shall want of a man but that he shall love you truly? I come here ready to marry you, and to take my chance in all things. You say your voice has gone. I am here ready to take the risk. Lord Castlewell will not have you, but I will take you." Now he had risen from his chair, and was standing close to her; but she was so surprised at his manner and at his words that she did not answer him at all. "That lord cared for you not at all, but I care. That Mr. Jones, who was to have been your husband, he is gone; but I am not gone. Mr. Jones!" then he threw into his voice a tone of insufferable contempt.

This Rachel could not stand.

"You shall not talk to me about Mr. Jones."

"I talk to you as a man who means vat he is saying. I will marry you to-morrow."

"I would sooner throw myself into that river," she said, pointing down to the Thames.

"You have nothing, if I understand right,—nothing! You have had a run for a few months, and have spent all your money. I have got £10,000! You have lost your voice,—I have got mine. You have no theatre,—I have one of my own. I am ready to take a house and furnish it just as you please. You are living here in these poor, wretched lodgings. Why do I do that?" And he put up both his hands.

"You never will do it," said Rachel.

"Because I love you." Then he threw away his new hat, and fell on his knees before her. "I will risk it all,—because I love you! If your voice comes back,—well! If it do not come back, you will be my wife, and I shall do my best to keep you like a lady."

Here Rachel leant back in her chair, and shut her eyes. In truth she was weak, and was hardly able to carry on the battle after her old fashion. And she had to bethink herself whether the man was making this offer in true faith. If so, there was something noble in it; and, though she still hated the man, as a woman may hate her lover, she would in such case be bound not to insult him more than she could help. A softer feeling than usual came upon her, and she felt that he would be sufficiently punished if she could turn him instantly out of the room. She did not now feel disposed "to stick a knife into him," as she had told her father when describing Mr. Moss. But he was at her knees, and the whole thing was abominable.

"Rachel, say the word, and be mine at once."

"You do not understand how I hate you!" she exclaimed.

"Rachel, come to my arms!"

Then he got up as though to clasp the girl in his embrace. She ran from him, and immediately called the girl whom she had desired to remain in the next room with the door open. But the door was not open, and the girl, though she was in the room, did not answer. Probably the bribe which Mr. Moss had given was to her feeling rather larger than ordinary.

"My darling, my charmer, my own one, come to my arms!"

And he did succeed in getting his hand round on to Rachel's waist, and getting his lips close to her head. She did save her face so that Mr. Moss could not kiss her, but she was knocked into a heap by his violence, and by her own weakness. He still had hold of her as she rose to her feet, and, though he had become acquainted with her weapon before, he certainly did not fear it now. A sick woman, who had just come from her bed, was not likely to have a dagger with her. When she got up she was still more in his power. She was astray, scrambling here and there, so as to be forced to guard against her own awkwardness. Whatever may be the position in which a woman may find herself, whatever battle she may have to carry on, she has first to protect herself from unseemly attitudes. Before she could do anything she had first to stand upon her legs, and gather her dress around her.

"My own one, my life, come to me!" he exclaimed, again attempting to get her into his embrace.

But he had the knife stuck into him. She had known that he would do it, and now he had done it.

"You fool, you," she said; "it has been your own doing."

He fell on the sofa, and clasped his side, where the weapon had struck him. She rang the bell violently, and, when the girl came, desired her to go at once for a surgeon. Then she fainted.

"I never was such a fool as to faint before," she told Frank afterwards. "I never counted on fainting. If a girl faints, of course she loses all her chance. It was because I was ill. But poor Mr. Moss had the worst of it."

Rachel, from the moment in which she fainted, never saw Mr. Moss any more. Madame Socani came to visit her, and told her father, when she failed to see her, that Mr. Moss had only three days to live. Rachel was again in bed, and could only lift up her hands in despair. But to her father, and to Frank Jones, she spoke with something like good humour.

"I knew it would come," she said to her father. "There was something about his eye which told me that an attempt would be made. He would not believe of a woman that she could have a will of her own. By treating her like an animal he thought he would have his own way. I don't imagine he will treat me in that way again." And then she spoke of him to Frank. "I suppose he does like me?"

"He likes your singing,—at so much a month."

"That's all done now. At any rate, he cannot but know that it is an extreme chance. He must fancy that he really likes me. A man has to be forgiven a good deal for that. But a man must be made to understand that if a woman won't have him, she won't! I think Mr. Moss understands it now."

CHAPTER XLIV.

FRANK JONES COMES BACK AGAIN.

THESE last words had been spoken after the coming of Frank Jones, but something has to be said of the manner of his coming, and of the reasons which brought him, and something also which occurred before he came. It could not be that Mr. Moss should be wounded after so desperate a fashion and that not a word should be said about it.

Of what happened at the time of the wounding Rachel knew nothing. She had been very brave and high in courage till the thing was done, but as soon as it was done she sent for the servant and fainted away. She knew nothing of what had occurred till she had been removed out of the room on one side and he on the other. She did not hear, therefore, of the suggestion made by Mr. Moss that some vital part of him had been reached.

He did bleed profusely, but under the aid of the doctor and Mr. O'Mahony, who was soon on the scene, he recovered himself more quickly than poor Rachel, who was indeed somewhat neglected till the hero of the tragedy had been sent away. He behaved with sufficient courage at last, though he had begun by declaring that his days were numbered. At any rate he had said when he found the power of ordinary speech, "Don't let a word be whispered about it to Miss O'Mahony; she isn't like other people." Then he was taken back to his private lodging, and confided to the care of Madame Socani, where we will for the present leave him. Soon after the occurrence,—a day or two after it,—Frank Jones appeared suddenly on the scene. Of course it appeared that he had come to mourn the probable death of Mr. Moss. But he had in truth heard nothing of the fatal encounter till he had arrived in Cecil Street, and then could hardly make out what had occurred amidst the confused utterances.

"Frank Jones!" she exclaimed. "Father, what has brought him here?" and she blushed up over her face and head to the very roots of her hair. "Come up, of course he must come up. When a man has come all the way from Castle Morony he must be allowed to come up. Why should you wish to keep him down in the area?" Then Frank Jones soon made his appearance within the chamber.

It was midsummer, and Rachel occupied a room in the lowest house in the street, looking right away upon the river, and her easy-chair had been brought up to the window at which she sat, and looked out on the tide of river life as it flowed by. She was covered at present with a dressing gown, as sweet and fresh as the morning air. On her head she wore a small net of the finest golden filigree, and her tiny feet were thrust into a pair of bright blue slippers bordered with swansdown. "Am I to come back?" her obedient father had asked. But he had been told not to come back, not quite at present. "It is not that I want your absence," she had said, "but he may. He can tell me with less hesitation that he is going to set up a pig-killing establishment in South Australia than he could probably you and me together." So the father simply slapped him on the back, and bade him walk upstairs till he would find No. 15 on the second landing. "Of course you have heard," he said, as Frank was going, "of what she has been and done to Mahomet M. Moss?"

"Not a word," said Frank. "What has she done?"

"Plunged a dagger into him," said Mr. O'Mahony,—in a manner which showed to Frank that he was not much afraid of the consequences of the accident. "You go up and no doubt she will tell you all about it." Then Frank went up, and was soon admitted into Rachel's room.

"Oh, Frank!" she said, "how are you? What on earth has brought you here?" Then he at once began to ask questions about poor Moss, and Rachel of course to answer them. "Well, yes; how was I to help it? I told him from the time that I was a little girl, long before I knew you, that something of this kind would occur if he would not behave himself."

"And he didn't?" asked Frank, with some little pardonable curiosity.

"No, he did not. Whether he wanted me or my voice, thinking that it would come back again, I cannot tell, but he did want something. There was a woman who brought messages from him, and even she wanted something. Then his ideas ran higher."

"He meant to marry you," said Frank.

"I suppose he did,—at last. I am very much obliged to him, but it did not suit. Then,—to make a short story of it, Frank, I will tell you the whole truth. He took hold of me. I cannot bear to be taken hold of; you know that yourself."

He could only remember how often he had sat with her down among the willows at the lake side with his arm round her waist, and she had never seemed to be impatient under the operation.

"And though he has such a beautiful shiny hat he is horribly awkward. He nearly knocked me down and fell on me, by way of embracing me."

Frank thought that he had never been driven to such straits as that.

"To be knocked down and trampled on by a beast like that! There are circumstances in which a girl must protect herself, when other circumstances have brought her into danger. In those days—yesterday, that is, or a week ago—I was a poor singing girl. I was at every man's disposal, and had to look after myself. There are so many white bears about, ready to eat you, if you do not look after yourself. He tried to eat me, and he was wounded. You do not blame me, Frank."

"No, indeed; not for that."

"What do you blame me for?"

"I cannot think you right," he answered with almost majestic sternness, "to have accepted the offer of Lord Castlewell."

"You blame me for that."

He nodded his head at her.

"What would you have had me do?"

"Marry a man when you love him, but not when you don't."

"Oh, Frank! I couldn't. How was I to marry a man when I loved him,—I who had been so treated? But, sir," she said, remembering herself, "you have no right to say I did not love Lord Castlewell. You have no business to inquire into that matter. Nobody blames you, or can, or shall, in that affair,—not in my hearing. You behaved as gentlemen do behave; gentlemen who cannot act otherwise, because it is born in their bones and their flesh. I—I have not behaved quite so well. Open confession is good for the soul. Frank, I have not behaved quite so well. You may inquire about it. I did not love Lord Castlewell, and I told him so. He came to me when my singing was all gone, and generously renewed his offer. Had I not known that in his heart of hearts he did not wish it,—that the two things were gone for which he had wooed me, —my voice, which was grand, and my prettiness, which was but a little thing, I should have taken his second offer, because

T

it would be well to let him have what he wanted. It was not so; and therefore I sent him away, well pleased."

"But why did you accept him?"

"Oh, Frank! do not be too hard. How am I to tell you—you, of all men, what my reasons were? I was alone in the world; alone with such dangers before me as that which Mr. Moss brought with him. And then my profession had become a reality, and this lord would assist me. Do all the girls refuse the lords who come and ask them?"

Then he stood close over her, and shook his head.

"But I should have done so," she continued after a pause. "I recognise it now; and let there be an end of it. There is a something which does make a woman unfit for matrimony." And the tears coursed themselves down her wan cheeks. "Now it has all been said that need be said, and let there be an end of it. I have talked too much about myself. What has brought you to London?"

"Just a young woman," he whispered slowly.

A pang shot through her heart; and yet not quite a pang, for with it there was a rush of joy, which was not, however, perfect joy, because she felt that it must be disappointed.

"Bother your young woman!" she said; "who cares for your young woman? How are you going on in Galway?"

"Sadly enough, to tell the truth."

"No rents?"

He shook his head.

"Nothing but murders and floods?"

"The same damnable old story running on from day to day."

"And have the girls no servants yet?"

"Not a servant; except old Peter, who is not quite as faithful as he should be."

"And,—and what about that valiant gay young gentleman, Captain Clayton?"

"Everything goes amiss in love as well as war," said Frank. "Between the three of them, I hardly know what they want."

"I think I know."

"Very likely. Everything goes so astray with all of us, so that the wanting it is sufficient reason for not getting it."

"Is that all you have come to tell me?"

"I suppose it is."

"Then you might have stayed away."

"I may as well go, perhaps."

"Go? no! I am not so full of new friends that I can afford to throw away my old like that. Of course you may not go, as you call it! Do you suppose I do not care to hear about those girls whom I love,—pretty nearly with all my heart? Why don't you tell me about them, and your father? You come here, but you talk of nothing but going. You ain't half nice."

"Can I come in yet?" This belonged to a voice behind the door, which was the property of Mr. O'Mahony.

"Not quite yet, father. Mr. Jones is telling me about them all at Morony Castle."

"I should have thought I might have heard that," said Mr. O'Mahony.

"The girls have special messages to send," said Rachel.

"I'll come back in another ten minutes," said Mr. O'Mahony. "I shall not wait longer than that."

"Only their love," said Frank; upon which Rachel looked as though she thought that Frank Jones was certainly an ass.

"Of course I want to hear their love," said Rachel. "Dear Ada, and dear Edith! Why don't you tell me their love?"

"My poor sick girl," he said, laying his hand upon her shoulder, and looking into her eyes.

"Never mind my sickness. I know I am as thin and as wan as an ogre. Nevertheless, I care for their love."

"Rachel, do you care for mine?"

"I haven't got it! Oh, Frank, why don't you speak to me? You have spoken a word, just a word, and all the blood is coming back to my veins already."

"Dearest, dearest, dearest Rachel."

"Now you have spoken; now you have told me of your sisters and your father. Now I know it all! Now my father may come in."

"Do you love me, then?"

"Love you! That question you know to be unnecessary. Love you! Why I spend every day and every night in loving you! But, Frank, you wouldn't have me when I was going to be rich. I ought not to have you now that I am to be poor." But by this time she was in his arms and he was kissing her, till, as she had said, the blood was once again running in her veins. "Oh, Frank, what a tyrant you are! Did I not tell you to let poor father come into the room? You have said everything now. There cannot be another word to say, Frank. Frank, Frank! I have found it out at last. I cannot live without you."

"But how are you to live with me? There is no money."

"Bother money. Wealth is sordid. Washing stockings over a tub is the only life for me,—so long as I have you to come back to me."

"And your health?"

"I tell you it is done. I was merely sick of the Jones complaint. Oh, Heavens! how I can hate people, and how I can love them!" Then she threw herself on the sofa, absolutely worn out by the violence of her emotions.

Mr. O'Mahony was commissioned, and set down by his girl's side to comfort her. But she wanted no comforting. "So you and Frank have made it up, have you?" said Mr. O'Mahony.

"We have never quarrelled so far as I am concerned," said Frank. "The moment I heard Lord Castlewell was dismissed, I came back."

"Yes," said she, raising herself half up on the sofa. "Do you know his story, father? It is rather a nice story for a girl to hear of her own lover, and to feel that it is true. When I was about to make I don't know how many thousand dollars a year by my singing, he would not come and take his share of it. Then I have to think of my own disgrace. But it enhances his glory. Because he was gone, I brought myself to accept this lord."

"Now, Rachel, you shall not exert yourself," said Frank.

"I will, sir," she replied, holding him by the hand. "I will tell my story. He had retreated from the stain, and the lord had come in his place. But he was here always," and she pressed his hand to her side. "He could not be got rid of. Then I lost my voice, and was 'utterly dished,' as the theatrical people say. Then the lord went,—behaving better than I did however,—and I was alone. Oh, what bitter moments there came then,—long enough for the post to go to Ireland and to return! And now he is here. Once more at my feet again, old man, once more! And then he talks to me of money! What is money to me? I have got such a comforting portion that I care not at all for money." Then she all but fainted once again, and Frank and her father both knelt over her caressing her.

It was a long time before Frank left her, her father going in and out of the room as it pleased him the while. Then he declared that he must go down to the House, assuring Frank that one blackguard there was worse than another, but saying that he would see them to the end as long as his time lasted. Rachel insisted that Frank should go with him.

"I am just getting up from my death-bed," she said, laughing, "and you want me to go on like any other man's young woman. I can think about you without talking to you." And so saying she dismissed him.

On the next morning, when he came again, she discussed with him the future arrangements of his life and hers.

"Of course you must stay with your father," she said. "You do not want to marry me at once, I suppose. And of course it is impossible if you do. I shall go to the States with father as soon as this Parliament affair is over. He is turned out of the House so often that he will be off before long for good and all. But there is the mail still running, and remember that what I say is true. I shall be ready and willing to be made Mrs. Frank Jones as soon as you will come and fetch me, and will tell me that you are able to provide me just with a crust and a blanket in County Galway. Whatever little you will do with, I will do with less."

Then she sat upon his knee, and embraced him and kissed him, and swore to him that no other Lord Castlewell who came should interfere with his rights.

"And as for Mr. Moss," she added, "I do not think that he will ever appear again to trouble your little game."

CHAPTER XLV.

MR. ROBERT MORRIS.

ONE morning, a little later in the summer, about the beginning of August, all Galway were terrified by the tidings of another murder. Mr. Morris had been killed,—had been "dropped," as the language of the country now went, from behind a wall built by the roadside. It had been done at about five in the afternoon, in full daylight; and, as was surmised by the police, with the consciousness of many of the peasantry around. He had been walking along the road from Cong to his own house, and had been "dropped," and left for dead by the roadside. Dead, indeed, he was when found. Not a word more would have been said about it, but for the intervention of the police, who were on the spot within three hours of the occurrence. A little girl had been coming into Cong, and had told the news. The little girl was living at Cong, and was supposed to be in no way connected with the murder.

"It's some of them boys this side of Clonbur," said one of the men of Cong.

No one thought it necessary after that to give any further explanation of the circumstances.

Mr. Robert Morris was somewhat of an oddity in his way; but he was a man who only a few months since was most unlikely to have fallen a victim to popular anger. He was about forty years of age, and had lived altogether at Minas Cottage, five or six miles from Cong, as you pass up the head of Lough Corrib, on the road to Maum. He was unmarried, and lived quite alone in a small house, trusting to the attentions of two old domestics and their daughter. He kept a horse and a car and a couple of cows and a few cocks and hens; but otherwise he lived alone. He was a man of property, and had, indeed, come from a family very long established in the county. People said of him that he had £500 a year; but he would have been very glad to have seen the half of it paid to his agent; for Mr. Morris, of Minas Cottage, had his agent as well as any other gentleman. He was a magistrate for the two counties, Galway and Mayo, and attended sessions both at Cong and at Clonbur. But when there he did little but agree with some more active magistrate; and what else he did with himself no one could tell of him.

But it was said in respect to him that he was a benevolent gentleman; and but a year or two since very many in the neighbourhood would have declared him to be especially the poor man's friend. With £500 a year he could have done much; with half that income he could do something to assist them, and something he still did. He had his foibles and fancies, but such as they were they did not tread on the corns of any of his poorer neighbours. He was proud of his birth, proud of his family, proud of having owned, either in his own hands or those of his forefathers, the same few acres,—and many more also, for his forefathers before him had terribly diminished the property. There was a story that his great-great-grandfather had lived in a palatial residence in County Kilkenny. All this he would tell freely, and would remark that to such an extent had the family been reduced by the extravagance of his forefathers. "But the name and the blood they can never touch," he would remark. They would not ask as to his successor, because they valued him too highly, and because Mr. Morris would never have admitted that the time had come when it was too late to bring a bride home to the western halls of his forefathers. But the rumour went that Minas Cottage would go in the female line to a second cousin, who had married a cloth merchant in Galway city, to whom nor to her husband did Mr. Morris ever speak. There might be something absurd in this, but there was nothing injurious to his neighbours, and nothing that would be likely to displease the poorer of them.

But Mr. Morris had been made the subject of various requests from his tenants. They had long since wanted and had received a considerable abatement in their rent. Hence had come the straitened limits of £250 a year. They had then offered the "Griffith's valuation." To explain the "Griffith's valuation" a chapter must be written, and as no one would read the explanation if given here it shall be withheld. Indeed, the whole circumstances of Mr. Morris's property were too intricate to require, or to admit, elucidation here. He was so driven that if he were to keep anything for himself he must do so by means of the sheriff's officer, and hence it had come to pass that he had been shot down like a mad dog by the roadside.

County Galway was tolerably well used to murders by this

time, but yet seemed to be specially astonished by the assassination of Mr. Morris. The innocence of the man ; for the dealings of the sheriff's officer were hardly known beyond the townland which was concerned! And then the taciturnity of the county side when the murder had been effected! It was not such a deed as was the slaughtering of poor Florian Jones, or the killing of Terry Carroll in the Court House. They had been more startling, more alarming, more awful for the tradesmen, and such like, to talk of among themselves, but the feeling of mystery there had been connected with the secret capacity of one individual. Everyone, in fact, knew that those murders had been done by Lax. And all felt that for the doing of murders Lax was irrepressible. But over there in the neighbourhood of Clonbur, or in the village of Cong, Lax had never appeared. There was no one in the place to whom the police could attribute any Lax-like properties. In that respect, the slaughtering of Mr. Morris had something in it more terrible even than those other murders. It seemed as though murder were becoming the ordinary popular mode by which the people should redress themselves,—as though the idea of murder had recommended itself easily to their intellects. And then they had quietly submitted—all of them—to taciturnity. They who were not concerned in the special case, the adjustment that is of Mr. Morris's rent, accepted his murder with perfect quiescence, as did those who were aggrieved. Nobody had seen anything. Nobody had heard anything. Nobody had known anything. Such were the only replies that were given to the police. If Mr. Morris, then why not another—and another—till the whole country would be depopulated? In Mr. Morris's case a landlord had been chosen; but in other localities agents and sheriffs' officers,—and even those keepers on a property which a gentleman is supposed to employ,—were falling to the right and to the left. But of Mr. Morris and his death nothing was heard.

Yorke Clayton of course went down there, for this, too, was in his district, and Hunter went with him, anxious, if possible, to learn something. They saw every tenant on the property; and, indeed, they were not over numerous. There was not one as to whom they could obtain evidence that he was ever ferocious by character. "They've got to think that they have the right to it all. The poor creatures are not so bad as them that is teaching them. If I think as the farm is my own, of course I don't like to be made to pay rent for it." That was the explanation of the circumstances, as given by Mrs. Davies, of the hotel at Clonbur. And it was evident that she thought it to be sufficient. The meaning of it, according to Captain Clayton's reading, was this : " If you allow such doctrines to be preached abroad by Members of Parliament and Land-league leaders,—to be preached as a doctrine fit for the people,—then you cannot be surprised if the people do as they are taught and hold their tongues afterwards."

This Mr. Morris had been the first cousin of our poor old friend Black Tom Daly.

"Good God!" he exclaimed, as soon as he read the news, sitting in his parlour at Daly's Bridge; "there is Bob Morris gone now."

"Bob Morris, of Minas Cottage!" exclaimed Peter Bodkin, who had ridden over to give Tom Daly some comfort in his solitude, if it might be possible.

"By George! yes; Bob Morris! Did you know him?"

"I don't think he ever came out hunting."

"Hunting, indeed! How should he, when he hadn't a horse that he could ride upon? And Bob knew nothing of sport. The better for him, seeing the way that things are going now. No, he never was out hunting, poor fellow! But for downright innocence and kindness and gentleness of heart, there is no one left like him. And now they have murdered him! What is to be the end of it? There is Persse telling me to hold on by the hounds, when I couldn't keep a hound in the kennels at Ahaseragh if it were ever so."

"Times will mend," said Peter.

"And Raheeny Gorse fired so as to drive every fox out of the country! Persse is wrong, and I am wrong to stay at his bidding. The very nature of mankind has altered in the old country. There are not the same hearts within their bosoms. To burn a gorse over a fox's head! There is a damnable cruelty in it of which men were not guilty,—by G——! they were not capable,—a year or two ago. These ruffians from America have come and told them that they shall pay no rent, and their minds have been so filled with the picture that its magnificence has overcome them. They used to tell us that money is the root of all evil; it proves to be true now. The idea that they should pay no rent has been too much for them; and they have become fiends under the feelings which have been roused. Only last year they were mourning over a poor fox like a Christian,—a poor fox that had been caught in a trap, —and now they would not leave a fox in the country, because the gentlemen, they think, are fond of them. The gentlemen are their enemies, and therefore they will spite them. They will drive every gentleman out of the country, and where will they be then?" Here Tom Daly sat quiet for a while, looking silent through the open window, while Peter sat by him feeling the occasion to be too solemn for speech. After a while Tom continued his ejaculations. "Gladstone! Gladstone! There are those who think that man to be great and good; but how can he be great and good if he lets loose such spirits among us?

They tell me that he's a very amiable man in his own family, and goes to church regular ; but he must be the most ignorant human being that ever took upon himself to make laws for a people. He can understand nothing about money, nothing about property, nothing about rents ! I suppose he thinks it fair to take away one man's means and give them to another, simply because one is a gentleman and the other not ! A fair rent ! There's nothing I hate so much in my very soul as the idea of a fair rent. A fair rent means half that a man pays now ; but in a few years' time it will mean again whatever the new landlord may choose to ask. And fixity of tenure ! Every man is to get what doesn't belong to him, and if a man has anything he's to be turned out ; that is fixity of tenure. And freedom of sale ! A man is to be allowed to sell what isn't his own. He thinks that when he has thrown half an eye over a country he can improve it by altering all the wisdom of ages. A man talks and talks, and others listen to him till they flatter him that another God Almighty has been sent upon earth." It was thus that Tom Daly expressed himself as to the Prime Minister of the day ; but Tom was a benighted Tory, and had thought nothing of these subjects till they were driven into his mind by the strange mortality of the foxes around him.

Poor Mr. Morris was buried, and there was an end of him. The cloth merchant's wife in Galway got the property ; and, as far as we can hear at present, is not likely to do as well with it as her husband is with his bales of goods. No man perhaps more insignificant than Mr. Robert Morris could have departed. He did nothing, and his figure, as he walked about between Cong and Clonbur, could be well spared. But his murder had given rise to feelings through the country which were full of mischief and full of awe. He had lived most inoffensively, and yet he had gone simply because it had occurred to some poor ignorant tenant, who had held perhaps ten or fifteen acres of land, out of which he had lived upon the potatoes grown from two or three of them, that things would go better with him if he had not a landlord to hurry him for rent ! Then the tenant had turned in his mind the best means of putting his landlord out of the way, and had told himself that it was an easy thing to do. He had not, of his own, much capacity for the use of firearms ; but he had four pound ten, which should have gone to the payment of his rent, and of this four pound ten, fifteen shillings secured the services of some handy man out of the next parish. He had heard the question of murder freely discussed among his neighbours, and by listening to others had learned the general opinion that there was no danger in it. So he came to a decision, and Mr. Morris was murdered.

So far the question was solved between this tenant and this landlord ; but each one of the neighbours, as he thought of it, felt himself bound to secrecy *pro bono publico.* There was a certain comfort in this, and poor Bob Morris's death seemed likely to be passed over with an easy freedom from suspicion. Any man might be got rid of silently, and there need be no injurious results. But men among themselves began to talk somewhat too freely, and an awe grew among them as this man and that man were named as objectionable. And the men so named were not all landlords or even agents. This man was a sheriff's officer, and that a gamekeeper. The sheriffs' officers and gamekeepers were not all murdered, but they were named, and a feeling of terror crept cold round the hearts of those who heard the names. Who was to be the keeper of the list and decide finally as to the victims? Then suddenly a man went, and no one knew why he went. He was making a fence between two fields, and it was whispered that he had been cautioned not to make the fence. At any rate he had been stoned to death, and though there must have been three at least at the work, no one knew who had stoned him. Men began to whisper among each other, and women also, and at last it was whispered to them that they had better not whisper at all. Then they began to feel that not only was secrecy to be exacted from them, but they were not to be admitted to any participation in the secrecy.

And with such of the gentry as were left there had grown up precautions which could not but fill the minds of the peasantry with a vague sense of fear. They went about with rifles in their hands, and were always accompanied by police. They had thick shutters made to their windows, and barred themselves within their houses. Those who but a few months since had been the natural friends of the people, now appeared everywhere in arms against them. If it was necessary that there should be intercourse between them, that intercourse took place by means of a policeman. A further attempt at murder had been made in the neighbourhood, and was so talked of that it seemed that all kindly feeling had been severed. Men began to creep about and keep out of the way lest they should be suspected; and, indeed, it was the fact that there was hardly an able-bodied man in three parishes to whom some suspicion did not attach itself.

And thus the women would ask for fresh murders, and would feel disappointed when none were reported to them, craving, as it were, for blood. And all this had come to pass certainly within the space of two years! A sweeter-tempered people than had existed there had been found nowhere; nor a people more ignorant, and possessing less of the comforts of civilisation. But no evil was to be expected from them, no harm came from them—beyond a few simple lies, which were only harmful as acting upon their own character. As Tom Daly had said, these very men were not capable of it a few months ago. The tuition had come from America! That, no doubt, was true; but it had come by Irish hearts and Irish voices, by Irish longings and Irish ambition. Nothing could be more false than to attribute the evil to America, unless that becomes American which has once touched American soil. But there does grow up in New York, or thereabouts, a mixture of Irish poverty with American wealth, which calls itself "Democrat," and forms as bad a composition as any that I know from which either to replenish or to create a people.

A very little of it goes unfortunately a long way. It is like gin made of vitriol when mingled with water. A small modicum of gin, though it does not add much spirit to the water, will damnably defile a large quantity. And this gin has in it a something of flavour which will altogether deceive an uneducated palate. There is an alcoholic afflatus which mounts to the brain and surrounds the heart and permeates the veins, which for the moment is believed to be true gin. But it makes itself known in the morning, and after a few mornings tells its own tale too well. These "democrats" could never do us the mischief. They are not sufficient, either in intellect or in number; but there are men among us who have taught themselves to believe that the infuriated gin drinker is the true holder of a new gospel.

CHAPTER XLVI.

CONG.

IN those days Captain Clayton spent much of his time at Cong, and Frank Jones was often with him. Frank, however, had returned from London a much altered man. Rachel had knocked under to him. It was thus that he spoke of it to himself. I do not think that she spoke of it to herself exactly in the same way. She knew her own constancy, and felt that she was to be rewarded.

"Nothing, I think, would ever have made me marry Lord Castlewell."

It was thus she talked to her father while he was awaiting the period of his dismissal.

"I dare say not," said he. "Of course he is a poor weak creature. But he would have been very good to you, and there would have been an end to all your discomforts."

Rachel turned up her nose. An end to all her discomforts! Her father knew nothing of what would comfort her and what would discomfort.

She was utterly discomforted in that her voice was gone from her. She would lie and sob on her bed half the morning, and would feel herself to be inconsolable. Then she would think of Frank, and tell herself that there was some consolation in store even for her. Had her voice been left to her she would have found it to be very difficult to escape from the Castlewell difficulty. She would have escaped, she thought, though the heavens might have been brought down over her head. When the time had come for appearing at the altar, she would have got into the first train and disappeared, or have gone to bed and refused to leave it. She would have summoned Frank at the last moment, and would submit to be called the worst behaved young woman that had ever appeared on the London boards. Now she was saved from that; but,—but at what a cost!

"I might have been the greatest woman of the day, and now I must be content to make his tea and toast."

Then she began to consider whether it was good that any girl should be the greatest woman of the day.

"I don't suppose the Queen has so much the best of it with a pack of troubles on her hands."

But Frank in the meantime had gone back to Galway, and Mr. Robert Morris had been murdered. Soon after the death of Mr. Morris the man had been killed as he was mending the ditch, and Captain Clayton found that the tone of the people was varied in the answers which they made to his inquiries. They were astounded, and, as it were, struck dumb with surprise. Nobody knew anything, nobody had heard anything, nobody had seen anything. They were as much in the dark about poor Pat Gilligan as they had been as to Mr. Robert Morris. They spoke of Pat as though he had been slaughtered by a direct blow from heaven; but they trembled, and were evidently uncomfortable.

"That woman knows something about it," said Hunter to his master, shaking his head.

"No doubt she knows a good deal about it; but it is not because she knows that she is bewildered and bedevilled in her intellect. She is beginning to be afraid that the country is one in which even she herself cannot live in safety."

And the men looked to be dumbfoundered and sheepfaced. They kept out of Captain Clayton's way, and answered him as little as possible. "What's the good of axing when ye knows that I knows nothing?" This was the answer of one man, and was a fair sample of the answers of many; but they were given in such a tone that Clayton was beginning to think that the evil was about to work its own cure.

"Frank," he said one day when he was walking with his friend in the gloom of the evening, "this state of things is too horrible to endure." The faithful Hunter followed them, and another policeman, for the Captain was never allowed to stir two steps without the accompaniment of a brace of guards.

"Much too horrible to be endured," said Frank. "My idea is that a man, in order to make the best of himself, should run away from it. Life in the United States has no such horrors as these. Though we're apt to say that all this comes from America, I don't see American hands in it."

"You see American money."

"American money in the shape of dollar bills; but they have all been sent by Irish people. The United States is a large place, and there is room there, I think, for an honest man."

"I'll never be frightened out of my own country," said Clayton. "Nor do I think there is occasion. These abominable reprobates are not going to prevail in the end."

"They have prevailed with poor Tom Daly. He was a man who worked as hard as anyone to find amusement,—and employment too. He never wronged anyone. He was even so honest as to charge a fair price for his horses. And there he is, left high and dry, without a horse or a hound that he can venture to keep about his own place. And simply because the majority of the people have chosen that there shall be no more hunting; and they have proved themselves to be able to have their own way. It is impossible that poor Daly should hunt if they will not permit him, and they carry their orders so far that he cannot even keep a hound in his kennels because they do not choose to allow it."

"And this you think will be continued always?" asked Clayton.

"For all that I can see it may go on for ever. My father has had those water-gates mended on the meadows though he could ill afford it. I have told him that they may go again to-morrow. There is no reason to judge that they should not do so. The only two men,—or the man, rather, and the boy,—who have been punished for the last attempt were those who endeavoured to tell of it. See what has come of that!"

"All that is true."

"Will it not be better to go to America, to go to Africa, to go to Asia, or to Russia even, than to live in a country like this, where the law can afford you no protection, and where the lawgivers only injure you?"

"I know nothing about the lawgivers," said Clayton, "but I have to say a word or two about the law. Do you think this kind of thing is going to remain?"

"It does remain, and every day becomes worse."

"An evil will always become worse till it begins to die away. I think I see the end of things approaching. Evil-doers are afraid of each other, and these poor fellows here live in mortal agony lest some Lax of the moment should be turned loose at their own throats. I don't think that Lax is an institution that will remain for ever in the country. This present Lax we have fast locked up. Law at present, at any rate, has so much of power that it is able to lock up a Lax,—when it can catch him. As for this present man, I do hope that the law will find itself powerful enough to fasten a rope round his neck. No Galway jury would find him guilty, and that is bad enough. But the lawgivers have done this for us, that we may try him before a Dublin jury, and there are hopes. When Lax has been well hung out of the world I can turn round and take a moment for my own happiness."

Yorke Clayton, as he said this, was alluding to his love affair with Edith Jones. He had now conquered all the family with one exception. Even the father had assented that it should be so, though tardily and with sundry misgivings. The one person was Edith herself, and it had come to be acknowledged by all around her that she loved Yorke Clayton. As she herself never now denied it, it was admitted on all sides at Morony Castle that the Captain was certainly the favoured lover. But Edith still held out, and had gone so far as to tell the Captain that he could not be allowed to come to the Castle unless he would desist.

"I never shall desist," he had replied. "As to that you may take my word." Then Edith had of course loved him so much the more.

"I don't think this kind of thing will go on," he continued, still addressing Frank Jones. "The people are so fickle that they cannot be constant even to anything evil. It is quite on the cards that Black Tom Daly should next year be the most popular master of hounds in all Ireland, and that Mr. Kit Mooney should not be allowed to show his face within reach of Moytubber Gorse on hunting mornings."

"They'd have burned the gorse before they have come round to that state of feeling. Look at Raheeny."

"It isn't so easy to destroy anything," said the philosophic Clayton. "If the foxes are frightened out of Raheeny or Moytubber, they will go somewhere else. And even if poor Tom Daly were to run away from County Galway, as you're talking of doing, the county would find another master."

"Not like Tom Daly," said Frank Jones, enthusiastically.

"There are as good fish in the sea as ever were caught. Tom Daly is a first-class man, I admit ; and he had no more obedient slave than myself when I used to get out hunting two or three days in the session. But he is a desponding man, and cannot look forward to better times. For myself, I own that my hopes are fixed. Hang Lax, and then the millennium !"

"I will quite agree as to the hanging of Lax," said Frank ;

"but for any millennium, I want something more strong than Irish feeling. You'll excuse me, old fellow."

"Oh, certainly! Of course, I'm an Irishman myself, and might have been a Lax instead of a policeman, if chance had got hold of me in time. As it is, I've a sort of feeling that the policeman is going to have the best of it all through Ireland." Then there came a sudden sound as of a sharp thud, and Yorke Clayton fell as it were dead at Frank Jones's feet.

This occurred at a corner of the road, from which a little boreen or lane ran up the side of the mountain between walls about three feet high. But here some benevolent enterprising gentleman, wishing to bring water through Lower Lough Cong to Lough Corrib, had caused the beginnings of a canal to be built, which had, however, after the expenditure of large sums of money, come to nothing. But the ground, or rather rock, had so been moved and excavated as to make it practicable for some men engaged, as had been this man, to drop at once out of sight. Hunter was at once upon his track, with the other policeman, both of whom fired at him. But as they acknowledged afterwards, they had barely seen the skirt of his coat in the gloom of the evening. The whole spot up and behind the corner of the road was so honeycombed by the works of the intended canal as to afford hiding-places and retreats for a score of murderers. Here, as was afterwards ascertained, there was but one, and that one had apparently sufficed.

Frank Jones had remained on the road with his friend, and had raised him in his arms when he fell. "They have done for me this time," Clayton had said, but had said no more. He had in truth fainted, but Frank Jones, in his ignorance, had thought that he was dead. It turned out afterwards that the bullet had struck his ribs in the front of his body, and, having been turned by the bone, had passed round to his back, and had there buried itself in the flesh. It needs not that we dwell with any length on this part of our tale, but may say at once that the medical skill of Cong sufficed to extract the bullet on the next morning.

After a while one of the two policemen came back to the road, and assisted Frank Jones to carry up poor Clayton to the inn. Hunter, though still maimed by his wound, stuck to the pursuit, assisted by two other policemen from Cong, who soon appeared upon the scene. But the man escaped, and his flight was soon covered by the darkness of night. It had been eight o'clock before the party had left the inn, and had wandered with great imprudence further than they had intended. At least, so it was said after the occurrence; though, had nothing happened they would have reached their homes before night had in truth set in. But men said of Clayton that he had become so hardened by the practices of his life, and by the failure of all attempts hitherto made against him, that he had become incredulous of harm.

"They have got me at last," he said to Frank the next morning. "Thank God it was not you instead of me. I have been thinking of it as I lay here in the night, and have blamed myself greatly. It is my business and not yours." And then again further on in the day he sent a message to Edith. "Tell her from me that it is all over now, but that had I lived she would have had to be my wife."

But from that time forth he did in truth get better, though we in these pages can never again be allowed to see him as an active working man. It was his fault,—as the Galway doctor said, his egregious sin,—to spend the most of his time in lying on a couch out in the garden at Morony Castle, and talking of the fate of Mr. Lax. The remainder of his hours he devoted to the acceptance of little sick-room favours from his hostess,—I would say from his two hostesses, were it not that he soon came to terms with Ada, under which Ada was not to attend to him with any particular care. "If I could catch that fellow," he said to Ada, alluding to the man who had intended to murder him, "I would have no harm done to him. He should be let free at once; for I could not possibly have got such an opportunity by any other means."

But poor Edith, the while, felt herself to be badly used. She and Ada had often talked of the terrible perils to which Yorke Clayton was subjected, and, as the reader may remember, had discussed the propriety of a man so situated allowing himself to become familiar with any girl. But now Captain Clayton was declared to be safe by everybody. The doctors united in saying that his constitution would carry him through a cannon-ball. But Edith felt that all the danger had fallen to her lot.

In the meantime the search for the double murderers,— unless indeed one murderer had been busy in both cases,—was carried vainly along. The horror of poor Mr. Morris's fate had almost disappeared under the awe occasioned by the attack on Captain Clayton. It was astonishing to see how entirely Mr. Morris, with all his family and his old acres, and with Minas Cottage,—which, to the knowledge of the entire population of Cong, was his own peculiar property,—was lost to notice under the attack that had been made with so much audacity on Captain Yorke Clayton. He, as one of four, all armed to the teeth, was attacked by one individual, and attacked successfully. There were those who said at first that the bars of Galway Gaol must have been broken, and that Lax the omnipotent, Lax the omnipresent, had escaped. And it certainly was the case that many were in ignorance as to who the murderer had been. Probably all were ignorant,—all of those who were in truth well acquainted with the person of Mr. Morris's murderer. And in the minds of the people generally the awe became greater than ever. To them it was evident that anybody could murder anybody ; and evident also that it was permitted to them to do so by this new law which had sprung up of late in the country, almost enjoining them to exercise this peculiar mode of retaliation. The bravest thought that they were about to have their revenge against their old masters, and determined that the revenge should be a bloody one. But the more cowardly, and very much the more numerous on that account, feared that, poor as they were, they might be the victims. No man among them could be much poorer than Pat Gilligan, and he had been chosen as one to be murdered, for some reason known only to the murderer.

A new and terrible aristocracy was growing up among them,—the aristocracy of hidden firearms. There was but little said among them, even by the husband to the wife, or by the father to the son ; because the husband feared his wife, and the father his own child. There had been a feeling of old among them that they were being ground down by the old aristocracy. There must ever be such an idea on the part of those who do not have enough to eat in regard to their betters, who have more than plenty. It cannot be but that want should engender such feeling. But now the dread of the new aristocracy was becoming worse than that of the old. In the dull, dim minds of these poor people there arose, gradually indeed but quickly, a conviction that the new aristocracy might be worse even than the old ; and that law, as administered by Government, might be less tyrannical than the law of those who had no law to govern them. So the people sat silent at their hearths, or crawled miserably about their potato patches, speaking not at all of the life around them.

When a week was over, tidings came to them that Captain Clayton, though he had been shot right through the body,— though the bullet had gone in at his breast and come out at his back, as the report went,—was still alive, and likely to live. "He's a-spending every hour of his blessed life a-making love to a young lady who is a-nursing him." This was the report brought up to Cong by the steward of the lake steamer, and was received as a new miracle by the Cong people. The fates had decreed that Captain Clayton should not fall by any bullet fired by Lax, the Land-leaguer ; for, though Lax, the Landleaguer, was himself fast in prison when the attempt was made, such became more than ever the creed of the people when it was understood that Captain Clayton, with his own flesh and blood, was at this moment making love to Mr. Jones's youngest daughter at Morony Castle.

U

CHAPTER XLVII.

KERRYCULLION.

Captain Clayton was thoroughly enjoying life, now perhaps, for the first time since he had had a bullet driven through his body. It had come to pass that everything, almost everything, was done for him by the hands of Edith. And yet Ada was willing to do everything that was required; but she declared always that what she did was of no avail. "Unless you take it to him, you know he won't eat it," she would still say. No doubt this was absurd, because the sick man's appetite was very good, considering that a hole had been made from his front to his back within the last month. It was still September, the weather was as warm as summer, and he insisted on lying out in the garden with his rugs around him, and enjoying the service of all his slaves. But among his slaves Edith was the one whom the other slaves found it most difficult to understand.

"I will go on," she said to her father, "and do everything for him while he is an invalid. But, when he is well enough to be moved, either he or I must go out of this."

Her father simply said that he did not understand it; but then he was one of the other slaves.

"Edith," said the Captain, one day, speaking from his rugs on the bank upon the lawn, "just say that one word, 'I yield.' It will have to be said sooner or later."

"I will not say it, Captain Clayton," said Edith with a firm voice.

"So you have gone back to the Captain," said he.

"I will go back further than that, if you continue to annoy me. It shall be nothing but plain 'sir,' as hard as you please. You might as well let go my hand; you know that I do not take it away violently, because of your wound."

"I know—I know—I know that a girl's hand is the sweetest thing in all creation if she likes you, and leaves it with you willingly." Then there was a little pull, but it was only very little.

"Of course, I don't want to hurt you," said Edith.

"And, therefore, it feels as though you loved me. Of course it does. Your hand says one thing and your voice another. Which way does your heart go?"

"Right against you," said Edith. But she could not help blushing at the lie as she told it. "My conscience is altogether against you, and I advise you to attend more to that than to anything else." But still he held her hand, and still she let him hold it.

At that moment Hunter appeared upon the scene, and Edith regained her hand. But had the Captain held the hand, Hunter would not have seen it. Hunter was full of his own news; and, as he told it, very dreadful the story was. "There has been a murder worse than any that have happened yet, just the other side of the lake," and he pointed away to the mountains, and to that part of Lough Corrib which is just above Cong.

"Another murder?" said Edith.

"Oh, miss, no other murder ever told of had any horror in it equal to this! I don't know how the governor will keep himself quiet there, with such an affair as this to be looked after. There are six of them down,—or at any rate five."

"When a doubt creeps in, one can always disbelieve as much as one pleases."

"You can hardly disbelieve this, sir, as I have just heard the story from Sergeant Malcolm. There were six in the house, and five have been carried out dead. One has been taken to Cong, and he is as good as dead. Their names are Kelly. An old man and an old woman, and another woman and three children. The old woman was very old, and the man appears to have been her son."

"Have they got nobody?" asked Clayton.

"It appears not, sir. But there is a rumour about the place that there were many of them in it."

"Looking after one another," said Clayton, "so that none should escape his share of the guilt."

"It may be so. But there were many in it, sir. I can't tell much of the circumstances, except the fact that there are the five bodies lying dead." And Hunter, with some touch of dramatic effect and true pathos, pointed again to the mountains which he had indicated as the spot where this last murder was committed.

It was soon settled among them that Hunter should go off to the scene of action, Cong, or wherever else his services might be required, and that he should take special care to keep his master acquainted with all details as they came to light. For us, we may give here the details as they did reach the Captain's ears in the course of the next few days.

Hunter's story had only been too true. The six persons had been murdered, barring one child, who had been taken into Cong in a state which was supposed hardly to admit of his prolonged life. The others, who now lay dead at a shebeen house in the neighbourhood, consisted of an old woman and her son, and his wife and a grown daughter, and a son. All these had been killed in various ways,—had been shot with rifles, and stoned with rocks, and made away with, after any fashion that might come most readily to the hands of brutes devoid of light, of mercy, of conscience, and apparently of fear. It must have been a terrible sight to see, for those who had first broken in upon the scene of desolation. In the course of the next morning it had become known to the police, and it was soon rumoured throughout England and Ireland that there had been ten murderers engaged in the bloody fray. It must have been as Captain Clayton had surmised; one with another intent upon destroying that wretched family,—or perhaps only one among its number,—had insisted that others should accompany him. A man who had been one of their number was less likely to tell if he had a hand in it himself. And so there were ten of them. It might be that one among the number of the murdered had seen the murder of Mr. Morris, or of Pat Gilligan, or the attempted murder of Captain Clayton. And that one was not sure not to tell,—had perhaps shown by some sign and indication that to tell the truth about the deed was in his breast,—or in hers! Some woman living there might have spoken such a word to a friend less cautious in that than were the neighbours in general. Then we can hear, or fancy that we can hear, the muttered reasons of those who sought to rule amidst that bloody community. They were a family of the Kellys,—these poor doomed creatures,—but amidst those who whispered together, amidst those who were forced to come into the whispering, there were many of the same family; or, at any rate, of the same name. For the Kellys were a tribe who had been strong in the land for many years. Though each of the ten feared to be of the bloody party, each did not like not to be of it, for so the power would have come out of their hands. They wished to be among the leading aristocrats, though still they feared. And thus they came together, dreading each other, hating each other at last; each aware that he was about to put his very life within the other's power, and each trying to think, as far as thoughts would come to his dim mind, that to him might come some possibility of escape by betraying his comrades.

But a miracle had occurred,—that which must have seemed to be a miracle when they first heard it, and to the wretches themselves, when its fatal truth was made known to them. While in the dead of night they were carrying out this most inhuman massacre there were other eyes watching them; six other eyes were looking at them, and seeing what they did perhaps more plainly than they would see themselves! Think of the scene! There were six persons doomed, and ten who had agreed to doom them; and three others looking on from behind a wall, so near as to enable them to see it all, under the fitful light of the stars! Nineteen of them engaged round one small cabin, of whom five were to die that night;—and as to ten others, it cannot but be hoped that the whole ten may pay the penalty due to the offended feelings of an entire nation!

It may be that it shall be proved that some among the ten

had not struck a fatal blow. Or it may fail to be proved that some among the ten have done so. It will go hard with any man to adjudge ten men to death for one deed of murder ; and it is very hard for that one to remember always that the doom he is to give is the only means in our power to stop the downward path of crime among us. It may be that some among the ten shall be spared, and it may be that he or they who spare them shall have done right.

But such was not the feeling of Captain Yorke Clayton, as he discussed the matter, day after day, with Hunter, or with Frank Jones, upon the lawn at Castle Morony. "It would be the grandest sight to see,—ten of them hanging in a row."

"The saddest sight the world could show," said Frank.

"Sad enough, that the world should want it. But if you had been employed as I have for the last few years, you would not think it sad to have achieved it. If the judge and the jury will do their work as it should be done there will be an end to this kind of thing for many years to come. Think of the country we are living in now! Think of your father's condition, and of the injury which has been done to him and to your sisters, and to yourself. If that could be prevented and atoned for, and set right by the hanging in one row of ten such miscreants as those, would it not be a noble deed done? These ten are frightful to you because there are ten at once,—ten in the same village,—ten nearly of the same name ! People would call it a bloody assize where so many are doomed. But they scruple to call the country bloody where so many are murdered day after day. It is the honest who are murdered ; but would it not be well to rid the world of these ruffians? And, remember, that these ten would not have been ten, if some one or two had been dealt with for the first offence. And if the ten were now all spared, whose life would be safe in such a Golgotha ? I say that, to those who desire to have their country once more human, once more fit for an honest man to live in, these ten men hanging in a row will be a goodly sight."

There must have been a feeling in the minds of these three men that some terrible step must be taken to put an end to the power of this aristocracy, before life in the country would be again possible. When they had come together to watch their friends and neighbours, and see what the ten were about to do, there must have been some determination in their hearts to tell the story of that which would be enacted. Why should these ten have all the power in their own hands ? Why should these questions of life and death be remitted to them, to the exclusion of those other three ? And if this family of Kellys were doomed, why should there not be other families of other Kellys,—why not their own families ? And if Kerrycullion were made to swim in blood,—for that was the name of the townland in which these Kellys lived,—why not any other homestead round the place in which four or five victims may have hidden themselves? So the three, with mutual whisperings among themselves, with many fears and with much trembling, having obtained some tidings of what was to be done, agreed to follow and to see. It was whispered about that one of the family, the poor man's wife, probably, had seen the attack made upon poor Pat Gilligan, and may, or may not, have uttered some threat of vengeance; may have shown some sign that the murder ought to be made known to someone. Was not Pat Gilligan her sister's husband's brother's child? And he was not one of the other, the rich aristocracy, against whom all men's hands were justly raised. Some such word had probably passed the unfortunate woman's lips, and the ten men had risen against her. The ten men, each protecting each other, had sworn among themselves that so villainous a practice, so glaring an evil as this, of telling aught to the other aristocracy, must be brought to an end.

But then the three interfered, and it was likely that the other, the rich aristocracy, should now know all about it. It was not to save the lives of those unfortunate women and children that they went. There would be danger in that. And though the women and children were, at any rate, their near neighbours, why should they attempt to interfere and incur manifest dangers on their account? But they would creep along and see, and then they could tell; or should they be disturbed in their employment, they could escape amidst the darkness of the night. There could be no escape for those poor wretches, stripped in their bed; none for that aged woman, who could not take herself away from among the guns and rocks of her pursuers; none for those poor children; none, indeed, for the father of the family, upon whom the ten would come in his lair. If his wife had threatened to tell, he must pay for his wife's garrulity. Pat Gilligan had suffered for some such offence, and it was but just that she and he and they should suffer also. But the three might have to suffer, also, in their turns, if they consented to subject themselves to so bloody an aristocracy. And therefore they stalked forth at night and went up to Kerrycullion, at the heels of the other party, and saw it all. Now, one after another, the six were killed, or all but killed, and then the three went back to their homes, resolved that they would have recourse to the other aristocracy.

Between Galway and Cong and Kerrycullion, Hunter was kept going in these days so as to obtain always the latest information for his master. For, though the neighbourhood of Morony Castle was now supposed to be quiet, and though the Captain was not at the moment on active service, Hunter was still allowed to remain with him. And, indeed, Captain Clayton's opinion was esteemed so highly, that, though he could do nothing, he was in truth on active service. "They are sticking to their story, all through?" he asked Hunter, or rather communicated the fact to Hunter for his benefit.

"Oh, yes! sir; they stick to their story. There is no doubt about them now. They can't go back."

"And that boy can talk now?"

"Yes, sir; he can talk a little."

"And what he says agrees with the three men? There will be no more murders in that county, Hunter, or in County Galway either. When they have once learned to think it possible that one man may tell of another, there will be an end to that little game. But they must hang them of course."

"Oh, yes! sir," said Hunter. "I'd hang them myself; the whole ten of them, rather than keep them waiting."

"The trial is to be in Dublin. Before that day comes we shall find what they do about Lax. I don't suppose they will want me; or if they did, for the matter of that, I could go myself as well as ever."

"You could do nothing of the kind, Captain Clayton," said Edith, who was sitting there. "It is absurd to hear you talk in such a way."

"I don't suppose he could just go up to Dublin, miss," said Hunter.

"Not for life and death?" roared the sick man.

"I suppose you could for life and death," said Hunter,—with a little caution.

"For his own death he could," said Edith. "But it's the death of other people that he is thinking of now."

"And you, what are you thinking of?"

"To tell the truth, just at this moment I was thinking of yours. You are here under our keeping, and as long as you remain so, we are bound to do what we can to keep you from killing yourself; you ought to be in your bed."

"Tucked up all round,—and you ought to be giving me gruel." Then Hunter simpered and went away. He generally did go away when the love-scenes began.

"You could give one something which would cure me instantly."

"No, I could not! There are no such instant cures known in the medical world for a man who has had a hole right through him."

"That bullet will certainly be immortal."

"But you will not if you talk of going up to Dublin."

"Edith, a kiss would cure me."

"Captain Clayton, you are in circumstances which should prevent you from alluding to any such thing. I am here to nurse you, and I should not be insulted."

"That is true," he said. "And if it be an insult to tell you what a kiss would do for me, I withdraw the word. But the feeling it would convey, that you had in truth given yourself to me, that you were really, really my own, would I think cure me, though a dozen bullets had gone through me."

Then when Ada had come down, Edith went to her bedroom, and kissed the pillow, instead of him. Oh, if it might be granted to her to go to him, and frankly to confess, that she was all, all his own! And she felt, as days went on, she would have to yield, though honour still told her that she should never do so.

CHAPTER XLVIII.

THE NEW ARISTOCRACY FAILS.

FROM this moment the mystery of the new aristocracy began to fade away, and get itself abolished. Men and women began to feel that there might be something worse in store for them than the old course of policemen, juries, and judges. It had seemed, at first, as though these evil things could be brought to an end, and silenced altogether as far as their blessed country was concerned. A time was coming in which everyone was to do as he pleased, without any fear that another should tell of him. Though a man should be seen in the broad daylight cutting the tails off half a score of oxen it would be recognised in the neighbourhood as no more than a fair act of vengeance, and nothing should be told of the deed, let the policemen busy themselves as they might. And the beauty of the system consisted in the fact that the fear of telling was brought home to the minds of all men, women, and children. Though it was certain that a woman had seen a cow's tail mangled, though it could be proved beyond all doubt that she was in the field when the deed was done, yet if she held her peace no punishment would await her. The policemen and the magistrate could do nothing to her. But Thady O'Leary, the man who had cut a cow's tail off, could certainly punish her. If nothing else were done she could be boycotted, or, in other words, not allowed to buy or sell the necessaries of life. Or she could herself be murdered, as had happened to Pat Gilligan. The whole thing had seemed to run so smoothly!

But now there had come, or would soon come, a change o'er the spirit of the dream. The murder of Pat Gilligan, though it had made one in the necessary sequence of events, one act in the course of the drama which, as a whole, had appeared to be so perfect, seemed to them all to have about it something terrible. No one knew what offence Pat Gilligan had given, or why he had been condemned. Each man began to tremble as he thought that he too might be a Pat Gilligan, and each woman that she might be a Mrs. Kelly. It was better to go back to the police and the magistrates than this!

I do not know that we need lean too heavily on the stupidity of the country's side in not having perceived that this would be so. The country's side is very slow in perceiving the course which things will take. These ten murderers had been brought together, each from fear of the others; and they must have felt that though they were ten,—a number so great when they considered the employment on which they were engaged as to cause horror to the minds of all of them,—the ten could not include all who should have been included. Had the other three been taken in, if that were possible, how much better it would have been! But the desire for murder had not gone so far,—its beauty had not been so perfectly acknowledged as to make it even yet possible to comprise a whole parish in destroying one family.

Then the three had seen that the whole scheme, the mystery of the thing, the very plan upon which it was founded, must be broken down and thrown to the winds. And we can imagine that, when the idea first came upon the minds of those three, that the entire family of the Kellys was to be sacrificed to stop the tongue of one talkative old woman, a horror must have fallen upon them as they recognised the duty which was incumbent on them. The duty of saving those six unfortunates they did not recognise. They could not screw themselves up to the necessary pitch of courage to enable them to enter in among loaded pistols and black-visaged murderers. The two women and the children had to die, though the three men were so close to them; so close as to have been certainly able to save them, or some of them, had they rushed into the cabin and created the confusion of another advent. To this they could not bring themselves, for are not the murderers armed? But an awful horror must have crept round their minds as they thought of the self-imposed task they had undertaken. They waited until the murders had been completed, and then they went back home and told the police.

From this moment the mystery by which murders in County Galway and elsewhere were for a short period protected was over in Ireland. Men have not seen, as yet, how much more lovely it is to tell frankly all that has been done, to give openly such evidence as a man may have to police magistrates and justices of the peace, than to keep anything wrapped within his own bosom. The charm of such outspoken truth does not reconcile itself at once to the untrained mind; but the fact of the loveliness does gradually creep in, and the hideous ugliness of the other venture. On the minds of those men of Kerrycullion something of the ugliness and something of the loveliness must have made itself apparent. And when this had been done it was not probable that a return to the utter ugliness of the lie should be possible. Whether the ten be hanged,—to the intense satisfaction of Hunter and his master,—or some fewer number, such as may suffice the mitigated desire for revenge which at present is burning in the breasts of men, the thing will have been done, and the mystery with all its beauty will have passed away.

At Castle Morony the beginning of the passing away of the mystery was hailed with great delight. It took place in this wise. A little girl who had been brought up there in the kitchen, and had reached the age of fifteen under the eyes of Ada and Edith,—a slip of a girl, whose feet our two girls had begun to trammel with shoes and stockings, and who was old enough to be proud of the finery though she could not bear the confinement,—had gone under the system of boycotting, when all the other servants had gone also. Peter, who was very stern in his discipline to the younger people, had caught hold of her before she went, and had brought her to Mr. Jones, recommending that at any rate her dress should be stripped from her back, and her shoes and stockings from her feet. "If you war to wallop her, sir, into the bargain, it would be a good deed done," Peter had said to his master.

"Why should I wallop her for leaving my service?"

"She ain't guv' no notice," said the indignant Peter.

"And if I were to wallop you because you had taken it into your stupid head to leave me at a moment's notice, should I be justified in doing so?"

"There is differences," said Peter, drawing himself up.

"You are stronger, you mean, and Feemy Carroll is weak. Let her go her own gait as she pleases. How am I to take upon myself to say that she is not right to go? And for the shoes and stockings, let them go with her, and the dress also, if I am supposed to have any property in it. Fancy a Land-leaguer in Parliament asking an indignant question as to my detaining forcibly an unwilling female servant. Let them all go; the sooner we learn to serve ourselves the better for us. I suppose you will go too before long."

This had been unkind, and Peter had made a speech in which he had said so. But the little affair had taken place in the beginning of the boycotting disarrangements, and Mr. Jones had been bitter in spirit. Now the girls had shown how deftly they could do the work, and had begun to talk pleasantly how well they could manage to save the wages and the food. "It's my food you'll have to save, and my wages," said Captain

Clayton. But this had been before he had a hole driven through him, and he was only awed by a frown.

But now news was brought in that Feemy had crept in at the back door. "Drat her impcrence," said Peter, who brought in the news. "It's like her ways to come when she can't get a morsel of wholesome food elsewhere."

Then Ada and Edith had rushed off to lay hold of the delinquent, who had indeed left a feeling in the hearts of her mistresses of some love for her little foibles. "Oh! Feemy, so you've come back again," said Ada, "and you've grown so big!" But Feemy cowered and said not a word. "What have you been doing all the time?" said Edith. "Miss Ada and I have had to clean out all the pots and all the pans, and all the gridirons, though for the matter of that there has been very little to cook on them." Then Ada asked the girl whether she intended to come back to her old place.

"If I'm let," said the girl, bursting into tears.

"Where are the shoes and stockings?" said Ada.

But the girl only wept.

"Of course you shall come back, shoes or no shoes. I suppose times have been too hard with you at home to think much of shoes or stockings. Since your poor cousin was shot in jail,"—for Feemy was a cousin of the tribe of Carrolls,—" I fear it hasn't gone very well with you all." But to this Feemy had only answered by renewed sobs. She had, however, from that moment taken up her residence as of yore in the old house, and had gone about her business just as though no boycotting edict had been pronounced against Castle Morony.

And gradually the other servants had returned, falling back into their places almost without a word spoken. One boy, who had in former days looked after the cows, absolutely did come and drive them in to be milked one morning without saying a word.

"And who are you, you young deevil?" said Peter to him.

"I'm just Larry O'Brien."

"And what business have you here?" said Peter. "How many months ago is it since last year you took yourself off without even a word said to man or woman? Who wants you back again now, I wonder?"

The boy, who had grown half-way to a man since he had taken his departure, made no further answer, but went on with the milking of his cows.

And the old cook came back again from Galway, though she came after the writing of a letter which must have taken her long to compose, and the saying of many words.

"Honoured Miss," the letter went, "I've been at Peter Corcoran's doing work any time these twelve months. And glad I've been to find a hole to creep into. But Peter Corcoran's house isn't like Castle Morony, and so I've told him scores of times. But Peter is one of them Land-leaguers, and is like to be bruk', horse, foot, and dragoons, bekaise he wouldn't serve the gentry. May the deevil go along with him, and with his pollytiks. Sure you know, miss, they wouldn't let me stay at Castle Morony. Wasn't one side in pollitiks the same as another to an old woman like me, who only wants to 'arn her bit and her sup? I don't care the vally of a tobacco-pipe for none of them now. So if the squire would take me back again, may God bless him for iver and iver, say I." Then this letter was signed Judy Corcoran,—for she too was of the family of the Corcorans,—and became the matter for many arrangements, in the course of which she once more was put into office as cook at Castle Morony.

Then Edith wrote the following letter to her friend Rachel, who still remained in London, partly because of her health and partly because her father had not yet quite settled his political affairs. But that shall be explained in another chapter.

"DEAREST RACHEL,

"Here we are beginning to see daylight, after having been buried in Cimmerian darkness for the best part of two years. I never thought how possible it would be to get along without servants to look after us, and how much of the pleasures of life might come without any of its comforts. Ada and I for many months have made every bed that has been slept in in the house, till we have come to think that the making of beds is the proper employment for ladies. And every bit of food has been cooked by us, till that too has become ladylike in our eyes. And it has been done for papa, who has, I think, liked his bed and his dinner all the better, because they have passed through his daughters' hands. But, dear papa! I'm afraid he has not borne the Cimmerian darkness as well as have we, who have been young enough to look forward to the return of something better.

"What am I to say to you about Frank, who will not talk much of your perfections, though he is always thinking of them? I believe he writes to you constantly, though what he says, or of what nature it is, I can only guess. I presume he does not send many messages to Lord Castlewell, who, however, as far as I can see, has behaved beautifully. What more can a girl want than to have a lord to fall in love with her, and to give her up just as her inclination may declare itself?

"What I write for now, specially, is to add a word to what I presume Frank may have said in one of his letters. Papa says that neither you nor Mr. O'Mahony are to think of leaving this side of the water without coming down to Castle Morony. We have got a cook now, and a cow-boy.

What more can you want? And old Peter is here still, always talking about the infinite things which he has done for the Jones family. Joking apart, you must of course come and see us again once before you start for New York. Is Frank to go with you? That is a question to which we can get no answer at all from Frank himself.

"In your last you asked me about my affairs. Dear girl, I have no affairs. I am in such a position that it is impossible for me to have what you would call affairs. Between you and Frank everything is settled. Between me and the man to whom you allude there is nothing settled, except that there is no ground for settlement. He must go one way and I another. It is very sad, you will say. I, however, have done it for myself, and I must bear the burden.

"Yours always lovingly,
"EDITH."

CHAPTER XLIX.

IT is not to be supposed that Mr. Jones succumbed altogether to the difficulties which circumstances had placed in his way. His feelings had been much hurt both by those who had chosen to call themselves his enemies and by his friends, and under such usage he became somewhat sullen. Having suffered a grievous misfortune he had become violent with his children, and had been more severely hurt by the death of the poor boy who had been murdered than he had confessed. But he had still struggled on, saying but little to anybody till at last he had taken Frank into his confidence, when Frank had returned from London with his marriage engagement dissolved. And the re-engagement had not at all interfered with the renewed intimacy between Frank and his father, because the girl was absolved from her singing. The father had feared the son would go away from him, and lead an idle life, enjoying the luxuries which her rich salary would purchase. Frank had shared his father's feelings in this respect, but still the squire had had his misgivings. All that was now set to rights by the absolute destruction of poor Rachel's voice.

Poor Mr. Jones had indeed received comfort from other sources more material than this. His relatives had put their heads together, and had agreed to bear some part of the loss which had fallen upon the estate; not the loss, that is, from the submerged meadows, which was indeed Mr. Jones's own private concern, but from the injury done to him by the commissioners. Indeed, as things went on, that injury appeared to be less ex-

tensive than had been imagined, though the injustice, as it
struck Mr. Jones's mind, was not less egregious. Where there
was a shred of a lease the sub-commissioners were powerless,
and though attempts had been made to break the leases they
had failed ; and men were beginning to say that the new law
would be comparatively powerless because it would do so little.
The advocates for the law pointed out that, taking the land of
Ireland all through, not five per cent., and again others not two
per cent., would be affected by it. Whether it had been worth
while to disturb the sanctity of contracts for so small a result
is another question ; but our Mr. Jones certainly did feel the
comfort that came to him from the fact. Certain fragments
of land had been reduced by the sub-commissioners after
ponderous sittings, very beneficial to the lawyers, but which
Mr. Jones had found to be grievously costly to him. He
had thus agreed to other reductions without the lawyers,
and felt those also to be very grievous, seeing that since
he had purchased the property with a Parliamentary title
he had raised nothing. There was no satisfaction to him
when he was told that a Parliamentary title meant nothing,
because a following Parliament could undo what a preceding
Parliament hàd done. But as the arrangements went on he
came to find that no large proportion of the estates would be
affected, and that gradually the rents would be paid. They had
not been paid as yet, but such he was told was the coming
prospect. Pat Carroll had risen up as a great authority at
Ballintubber, and had refused to pay a shilling. He had also
destroyed those eighty acres of meadow-land which had sat so
near Mr. Jones's heart. It had been found impossible to punish
him, but the impossibility was to be traced to that poor boy's
delinquency. As the owner of the property turned it all over
within his own bosom, he told himself that it was so. It was
that that had grieved him most, that which still sat heavy on
his heart. But the boy was gone, and Pat Carroll was in prison,
and Pat Carroll's brother had been murdered in Galway court-
house. Lax, too, was in prison, and Yorke Clayton swore by
all his gods that he should be hanged. It was likely that he
would be hanged, and Yorke Clayton might find his comfort in
that. And now had come up this terrible affair at Kerrycullion,
from which it was probable that the whole mystery of the new
aristocracy would be abandoned. Mr. Jones, as he thought of
it all, whispered to himself that if he would still hold up his
head, life might yet be possible at Castle Morony. "It will
only be for myself,—only for myself and Ada," he said, still
mourning greatly over his fate. "And Ada will go, too. The
beauty of the flock wlll never be left to remain here with her
father." But in truth his regrets were chiefly for Edith. If
that bloodthirsty Captain would have made himself satisfied
with Ada, he might still have been happy.

In these days he would walk down frequently to the meadows and see the work which the men were doing. He had greatly enlarged them, having borrowed money for the purpose from the Government Land Commissioners, and was once again allowing new hopes to spring in his heart. Though he was a man so silent, and appearing to be so apathetic, he was intent enough on his own purposes when they became clear before his eyes. From his first coming into this country his purport had been to do good, as far as the radius of his circle went, to all whom it included. The necessity of living was no doubt the same with him as with others,—and of living well. He must do something for himself and his children. But together with this was the desire, nearly equally strong, of being a benefactor to those around him. He had declared to himself when he bought the property that with this object would he settle himself down upon it, and he had not departed from it. He had brought up his children with this purpose; and they had learned to feel, one and all, that it was among the pleasures and the duties of their life. Then had come Pat Carroll, and everything had been embittered for him. All Ballintubber and all Morony had seemed to turn against him. When he found that Pat Carroll was disposed to be hostile to him, he made the man a liberal offer to take himself off to America. But Mr. Jones, in those days, had heard nothing of Lax, and was unaware that Lax was a dominant spirit under whom he was doomed to suffer.

"I did not know you so well then," said Captain Clayton to Mr. Jones, now some weeks hence, "or I could have told you that Pat Carroll is nobody. Pat Carroll is considered nobody, because he has not been to New York. Mr. Lax has travelled, and Mr. Lax is somebody. Mr. Lax settled himself in County Mayo, and thus he allowed his influence to spread itself among us over here in County Galway. Mr. Lax is a great man, but I rather think that he will have to be hanged in Galway jail before a month has passed over his head."

Mr. Jones usually took his son with him when he walked about among the meadows, and he again expressed his wishes to him as though Frank hereafter were to have the management of everything. But on one occasion, towards the latter half of the afternoon, he went alone. There were different wooden barriers, having sluice gates passing between them, over which he would walk, and at present there were sheep on the upper meadows, on which the luxuriant grass had begun to grow in the early summer. He was looking at his sheep now, and thinking to himself that he could find a market for them in spite of all that the boycotters could do to prevent him. But in one corner, where the meadows ceased, and Pat Carroll's land began, he met an old man whom he had known well in former years, named Con Heffernan. It was absolutely the case that he, the landlord, did not at the present moment know who occupied Pat Carroll's land, though he did know that he had received no rent for the last three years. And he knew also that Con Heffernan was a friend of Carroll's, or, as he believed, a distant cousin. And he knew also that Con was supposed to have been one of those who had assisted at the destruction of the sluice gates.

"Well, Con, how are you?" he said.

"Why thin, yer honour, I'm only puirly. It's bad times as is on us now, indeed and indeed."

"Whose fault is that?" said the squire.

"Not yer honour's. I will allys say that for your honour. You never did nothing to none of us."

"You had land on the estate till some twelve months since, and then you were evicted for five gales of rent."

"That's thrue, too, yer honour."

"You ought to be a rich man now, seeing that you have got two-and-a-half years' rent in your pocket, and I ought to be poor, seeing that I've got none of it."

"Is it puir for yer honour, and is it rich for the like of me?"

"What have you done with the money, Con,—the five gales of rent?"

"'Deed, yer honour, and I don't be just knowing anything about it."

"I suppose the Land-leaguers have had some of it?"

"I suppose they have, thin; the black divil run away with them for Laaguers!"

"Have you quarrelled with the League, Con?"

"I have quarrelled with a'most of the things which is a-going at the present moment."

"I'm sorry for that, as quarrels with old friends are always bad."

"The Laague, then, isn't any such old friend of mine. I niver heerd of the Laague, not till nigh three years ago. What with Faynians, and Moonlighters, and Home-Rulers, and now with thim Laaguers, they don't lave a por boy any pace."

* * * * *

POSTSCRIPT.

In a preliminary note to the first volume I stated why this last written novel of my father's was never completed. He had intended that Yorke Clayton should marry Edith Jones, that Frank Jones should marry Rachel O'Mahony, and that Lax should be hanged for the murder of Florian Jones; but no other coming incident, or further unravelling of the story, is known.—H.M.T.

THE END.

CHARLES DICKENS AND EVANS, CRYSTAL PALACE PRESS.

[March, 1884.

CHATTO & WINDUS'S
LIST OF BOOKS.

* * * * * * * * *

ut.—The Fellah: An Egyptian Novel. By EDMOND ABOUT. Translated by Sir RANDAL ROBERTS. Post 8vo, illustrated boards, 2s.; cloth limp, 2s. 6d.

ams (W. Davenport), Works by:

Dictionary of the Drama. Being a comprehensive Guide to the Plays, Playwrights, Players, and Playhouses of the United Kingdom and America, from the Earliest to the Present Times. Crown 8vo, halfbound, 12s. 6d.

atter-Day Lyrics. Edited by W. DAVENPORT ADAMS. Post 8vo, cloth limp, 2s. 6d.

ulps and Quiddities. Selected by W. DAVENPORT ADAMS. Post 8vo, cloth limp, 2s. 6d.

vertising, A History of, from Earliest Times. Illustrated by Anecdotes, Curious Specimens, and Notices of Successful Advertisers. By HENRY SAMPSON. Crown 8vo, with Coloured Frontispiece and Illustrations, cloth gilt, 7s. 6d.

ony Column (The) of "The mes," from 1800 to 1870. Edited, with an Introduction, by ALICE CLAY. Post 8vo, cloth limp, 2s. 6d.

le (Hamilton), Works by:

rr of Carrlyon. Post 8vo, illustrated boards, 2s.

nfidences. Post 8vo, illustrated boards, 2s.

Alexander (Mrs.).—Maid, Wife, or Widow? A Romance. By Mrs. ALEXANDER. Post 8vo, illustrate boards, 2s.; cr. 8vo, cloth extra, 3s. 6d.

Allen (Grant), Works by:

Colin Clout's Calendar. Crown 8vo, cloth extra, 6s.

The Evolutionist at Large. Crown 8vo, cloth extra, 6s.

Vignettes from Nature. Crown 8vo, cloth extra, 6s.

Architectural Styles, A Handbook of. Translated from the German of A. ROSENGARTEN, by W. COLLETT-SANDARS. Crown 8vo, cloth extra, with 639 Illustrations, 7s. 6d.

Art (The) of Amusing: A Collection of Graceful Arts, Games, Tricks, Puzzles, and Charades. By FRANK BELLEW. With 300 Illustrations. C 8vo, cloth extra, 4s. 6d.

Artemus Ward:

Artemus Ward's Works: The Work of CHARLES FARRER BROWNE, better known as ARTEMUS WARD. With Portrait and Facsimile. Crown 8vo cloth extra, 7s. 6d.

Artemus Ward's Lecture on the Mormons. With 32 Illustrations. Edited, with Preface, by EDWARD P. HINGSTON. Crown 8vo, 6d.

The Genial Showman: Life and Adventures of Artemus Ward. By EDWARD P. HINGSTON. With a Frontispiece. Crown 8vo, cloth extra, 3s. 6d.

Ashton (John), Works by:
A History of the Chap-Books of the Eighteenth Century. With nearly 400 Illusts., engraved in facsimile of the originals. Cr. 8vo, cl. ex., 7s. 6d.
Social Life in the Reign of Queen Anne. From Original Sources. With nearly 100 Illusts. Cr.8vo,cl.ex.,7s.6d.
Humour, Wit, and Satire of the Seventeenth Century. With nearly 100 Illusts. Cr. 8vo, cl. extra, 7s. 6d.
English Caricature and Satire on Napoleon the First. With 120 Illustrations from the Originals. Two Vols., demy 8vo, 28s. [*In preparation.*

Bacteria.—A Synopsis of the Bacteria and Yeast Fungi and Allied Species. By W. B. GROVE, B.A. With over 100 Illustrations. Cr. 8vo, cloth extra, 3s. 6d. [*In preparation.*

Balzac's " Comedie Humaine " and its Author. With Translations by H. H. WALKER. Post 8vo, cl. limp, 2s. 6d.

Bankers, A Handbook of London; together with Lists of Bankers from 1677. By F. G. HILTON PRICE. Crown 8vo, cloth extra, 7s. 6d.

Bardsley (Rev. C.W.), Works by:
English Surnames: Their Sources and Significations. Cr.8vo,cl. extra, 7s.6d.
Curiosities of Puritan Nomenclature. Crown 8vo, cloth extra, 7s. 6d.

Bartholomew Fair, Memoirs of. By HENRY MORLEY. With 100 Illusts. Crown 8vo, cloth extra, 7s. 6d.

Beauchamp. — Grantley Grange: A Novel. By SHELSLEY BEAUCHAMP. Post 8vo, illust. bds., 2s.

Beautiful Pictures by British Artists: A Gathering of Favourites from our Picture Galleries. In Two Series. All engraved on Steel in the highest style of Art. Edited, with Notices of the Artists, by SYDNEY ARMYTAGE, M.A. Imperial 4to, cloth extra, gilt and gilt edges, 21s. per Vol.

Bechstein.— As Pretty as Seven, and other German Stories. Collected by LUDWIG BECHSTEIN. With Additional Tales by the Brothers GRIMM, and 100 Illusts. by RICHTER. Small 4to, green and gold, 6s. 6d.; gilt edges, 7s. 6d.

Beerbohm.— Wanderings in Patagonia; or, Life among the Ostrich Hunters. By JULIUS BEERBOHM. With Illusts. Crown 8vo, cloth extra, 3s. 6d.

Belgravia for 1884.
Shilling Monthly, Illustrated MACNAB.—Two Serial Stories are appearing in this Magazine: ' Lover's Creed," by Mrs. C HOEY; and " The Wearing of Green," by the Author of " Lov Debt."
⁎ *Now ready, the Volume for N*   BER, 1883, *to* FEBRUARY, 1884, *cloth gilt edges,* 7s. 6d.; *Cases for bi Vols.,* 2s. *each.*

Belgravia Holiday Num With Stories by JAMES PAYN, ROBINSON, J. ARBUTHNOT WI and others. Demy 8vo, with Ill tions, 1s. [*Prepa*

Bennett (W.C.,LL.D.),Works
A Ballad History of England. 8vo, cloth limp, 2s.
Songs for Sailors. Post 8vo, limp, 2s.

Besant (Walter) and Ja Rice, Novels by. Post 8vo, boards, 2s. each; cloth limp, 2 each; or crown 8vo, cloth 3s. 6d. each.
Ready-Money Mortiboy.
With Harp and Crown.
This Son of Vulcan.
My Little Girl.
The Case of Mr. Lucraft.
The Golden Butterfly.
By Celia's Arbour.
The Monks of Thelema.
'Twas in Trafalgar's Bay.
The Seamy Side.
The Ten Years' Tenant.
The Chaplain of the Fleet.

Besant (Walter), Novels b
All Sorts and Conditions of An Impossible Story. With Illu tions by FRED. BARNARD. C. 8vo, cloth extra, 3s. 6d.; post illustrated boards, 2s.
The Captains' Room, &c. Frontispiece by E. J. WHEF Crown 8vo, cloth extra, 3s. 6d.; 8vo, illustrated boards, 2s.
All in a Garden Fair. Three crown 8vo.
Dorothy Forster. Three Vols., c 8vo. [*Sho*

Betham-Edwards (M.), No by. Crown 8vo, cloth extra, 3s each.; post 8vo, illust. bds., 2s.
Felicia. | Kitty.

Bewick (Thomas) & his Pupils. By AUSTIN DOBSON. With 100 Illustrations. Square 8vo, cloth extra, 10s. 6d. [*Preparing.*

Birthday Books:—
The Starry Heavens: A Poetical Birthday Book. Square 8vo, handsomely bound in cloth, 2s. 6d.
Birthday Flowers: Their Language and Legends. By W. J. GORDON. Beautifully Illustrated in Colours by VIOLA BOUGHTON. In illuminated cover, crown 4to, 6s.
The Lowell Birthday Book. With Illusts., small 8vo, cloth extra, 4s. 6d.

Bishop.—Old Mexico and her Lost Provinces. By WILLIAM HENRY BISHOP. With 120 Illustrations. Demy 8vo, cloth extra, 10s. 6d.

Blackburn's (Henry) Art Handbooks. Demy 8vo, Illustrated, uniform in size for binding.
Academy Notes, separate years, from 1875 to 1883, each 1s.
Academy Notes, 1884. With Illustrations. 1s. [*Preparing.*
Academy Notes, 1875-79. Complete in One Vol., with nearly 600 Illusts. in Facsimile. Demy 8vo, cloth limp, 6s.
Grosvenor Notes, 1877. 6d.
Grosvenor Notes, separate years, from 1878 to 1883, each 1s.
Grosvenor Notes, 1884. With Illustrations. 1s. [*Preparing.*
Grosvenor Notes, 1877-82. With upwards of 300 Illustrations. Demy 8vo, cloth limp, 6s.
Pictures at South Kensington. With 70 Illustrations. 1s.
The English Pictures at the National Gallery. 114 Illustrations. 1s.
The Old Masters at the National Gallery. 128 Illustrations. 1s. 6d.
A Complete Illustrated Catalogue to the National Gallery. With Notes by H. BLACKBURN, and 242 Illusts. Demy 8vo, cloth limp, 3s.
The Paris Salon, 1884. With over 300 Illusts. Edited by F. G. DUMAS. Demy 8vo, 3s. [*Preparing.*
The Art Annual, 1883-4. Edited by F. G. DUMAS. With 300 full-page Illustrations. Demy 8vo, 5s.

Boccaccio's Decameron; or, Ten Days' Entertainment. Translated into English, with an Introduction by THOMAS WRIGHT, F.S.A. With Portrait, and STOTHARD's beautiful Copperplates. Cr. 8vo, cloth extra, gilt, 7s. 6d.

Blake (William): Etchings from his Works. By W. B. SCOTT. With descriptive Text. Folio, half-bound boards, India Proofs, 21s.

Bowers'(G.) Hunting Sketches:
Canters in Crampshire. Oblong 4to, half-bound boards, 21s.
Leaves from a Hunting Journal. Coloured in facsimile of the originals. Oblong 4to, half-bound, 21s.

Boyle (Frederick), Works by:
Camp Notes: Stories of Sport and Adventure in Asia, Africa, and America. Crown 8vo, cloth extra, 3s. 6d.; post 8vo, illustrated bds., 2s.
Savage Life. Crown 8vo, cloth extra, 3s. 6d.; post 8vo, illustrated bds., 2s.

Brand's Observations on Popular Antiquities, chiefly Illustrating the Origin of our Vulgar Customs, Ceremonies, and Superstitions. With the Additions of Sir HENRY ELLIS. Crown 8vo, cloth extra, gilt, with numerous Illustrations, 7s. 6d.

Bret Harte, Works by:
Bret Harte's Collected Works. Arranged and Revised by the Author. Complete in Five Vols., crown 8vo, cloth extra, 6s. each.
 Vol. I. COMPLETE POETICAL AND DRAMATIC WORKS. With Steel Portrait, and Introduction by Author.
 Vol. II. EARLIER PAPERS—LUCK OF ROARING CAMP, and other Sketches—BOHEMIAN PAPERS—SPANISH AND AMERICAN LEGENDS.
 Vol. III. TALES OF THE ARGONAUTS—EASTERN SKETCHES.
 Vol. IV. GABRIEL CONROY.
 Vol. V. STORIES — CONDENSED NOVELS, &c.
The Select Works of Bret Harte, in Prose and Poetry. With Introductory Essay by J. M. BELLEW, Portrait of the Author, and 50 Illustrations. Crown 8vo, cloth extra, 7s. 6d.
Gabriel Conroy: A Novel. Post 8vo, illustrated boards, 2s.
An Heiress of Red Dog, and other Stories. Post 8vo, illustrated boards, 2s.; cloth limp, 2s. 6d.
The Twins of Table Mountain. Fcap. 8vo, picture cover, 1s.; crown 8vo, cloth extra, 3s. 6d.
Luck of Roaring Camp, and other Sketches. Post 8vo, illust. bds., 2s.
Jeff Briggs's Love Story. Fcap 8vo, picture cover, 1s.; cloth extra, 2s. 6d.
Flip. Post 8vo, illustrated boards, 2s.; cloth limp, 2s. 6d.
Californian Stories (including THE TWINS OF TABLE MOUNTAIN, JEFF BRIGGS'S LOVE STORY, &c.) Post 8vo, illustrated boards, 2s.

Brewer (Rev. Dr.), Works by:

The Reader's Handbook of Allusions, References, Plots, and Stories. Third Edition, revised throughout, with a New Appendix, containing a COMPLETE ENGLISH BIBLIOGRAPHY. Cr. 8vo, 1,400 pp., cloth extra, 7s. 6d.

A Dictionary of Miracles: Imitative, Realistic, and Dogmatic. Crown 8vo, cloth extra, 7s. 6d. [*Immediately*.

Brewster (Sir David), Works by:

More Worlds than One: The Creed of the Philosopher and the Hope of the Christian. With Plates. Post 8vo, cloth extra, 4s. 6d.

The Martyrs of Science: Lives of GALILEO, TYCHO BRAHE, and KEPLER. With Portraits. Post 8vo, cloth extra, 4s. 6d.

Letters on Natural Magic. A New Edition, with numerous Illustrations, and Chapters on the Being and Faculties of Man, and Additional Phenomena of Natural Magic, by J. A. SMITH. Post 8vo, cloth extra, 4s. 6d.

Brillat-Savarin.—Gastronomy

as a Fine Art. By BRILLAT-SAVARIN. Translated by R. E. ANDERSON, M.A. Post 8vo, cloth limp, 2s. 6d.

Browning.—The Pied Piper of

Hamelin. By ROBERT BROWNING. Illust. by GEORGE CARLINE. Large 4to, illuminated cover, 1s. [*In preparation*.

Burnett (Mrs.), Novels by:

Surly Tim, and other Stories. Post 8vo, illustrated boards, 2s.

Kathleen Mavourneen. Fcap. 8vo, picture cover, 1s.

Lindsay's Luck. Fcap. 8vo, picture cover, 1s.

Pretty Polly Pemberton. Fcap. 8vo picture cover, 1s.

Burton (Captain), Works by:

To the Gold Coast for Gold: A Personal Narrative. By RICHARD F. BURTON and VERNEY LOVETT CAMERON. With Maps and Frontispiece. Two Vols., crown 8vo, cloth extra, 21s.

The Book of the Sword: Being a History of the Sword and its Use in all Countries, from the Earliest Times. By RICHARD F. BURTON. With over 400 Illustrations. Square 8vo, cloth extra, 32s.

Buchanan'

Ballads of With a HUGHES.

Selected Po With Fro Crown 8vc

Undertone London Pc extra, 6s.

The Book o extra, 6s.

White Rose Crown 8vc

Idylls and Crown 8vc

St. Abe and of Salt La piece by 8vo, cloth

The Hebrid Land of I brides. SMALL.

A Poet's from the BUCHANA

The Shado mance. 3s. 6d.; p

A Child of a Frontis extra, 3s. 6

God and th Illustratio Crown 8v 8vo, illust

The Mart Romance. COOPER. post 8vo,

Love Me fo piece by cloth extr trated boa

Annan Wa Vols., cro

The New At Vols., cro

Foxglove Vols., cro

Robert Buc cal Work trait. Cr

Burton (R

The Anat New Edi and enric Classical extra, 7s.

Melanchol Abridgme TON'S A Post 8vo,

Bunyan's Pilgrim's Progress.
Edited by Rev. T. Scott. With 17 Steel Plates by Stothard, engraved by Goodall, and numerous Woodcuts. Crown 8vo, cloth extra, gilt, 7s. 6d.

Byron (Lord):
Byron's Letters and Journals. With Notices of his Life. By Thomas Moore. A Reprint of the Original Edition, newly revised, with Twelve full-page Plates. Crown 8vo, cloth extra, gilt, 7s. 6d.
Byron's Don Juan. Complete in One Vol., post 8vo, cloth limp, 2s.

Cameron (Commander) and Captain Burton.—To the Gold Coast for Gold: A Personal Narrative. By Richard F. Burton and Verney Lovett Cameron. With Frontispiece and Maps. Two Vols., crown 8vo, cloth extra, 21s.

Cameron (Mrs. H. Lovett), Novels by:
Juliet's Guardian. Post 8vo, illustrated boards, 2s.; crown 8vo, cloth extra, 3s. 6d.
Deceivers Ever. Post 8vo, illustrated boards, 2s.; crown 8vo, cloth extra, 3s. 6d.

Campbell.—White and Black: Travels in the United States. By Sir George Campbell, M.P. Demy 8vo, cloth extra, 14s.

Carlyle (Thomas):
Thomas Carlyle: Letters and Recollections. By Moncure D. Conway, M.A. Crown 8vo, cloth extra, with Illustrations, 6s.
On the Choice of Books. By Thomas Carlyle. With a Life of the Author by R. H. Shepherd. New and Revised Edition, post 8vo, cloth extra, Illustrated, 1s. 6d.
The Correspondence of Thomas Carlyle and Ralph Waldo Emerson, 1834 to 1872. Edited by Charles Eliot Norton. With Portraits. Two Vols., own 8vo, cloth extra, 24s.

Chapman's (George) Works:
Vol. I. contains the Plays complete, including the doubtful ones. Vol. II., the Poems and Minor Translations, with an Introductory Essay by Algernon Charles Swinburne. Vol. III., the Translations of the Iliad and Odyssey. Three Vols., crown 8vo, cloth extra, 18s.; or separately, 6s. each.

Chatto & Jackson.—A Treatise on Wood Engraving, Historical and Practical. By Wm. Andrew Chatto and John Jackson. With an Additional Chapter by Henry G. Bohn; and 450 fine Illustrations. A Reprint of the last Revised Edition. Large 4to, half-bound, 28s.

Chaucer:
Chaucer for Children: A Golden Key. By Mrs. H. R. Haweis. With Eight Coloured Pictures and numerous Woodcuts by the Author. New Ed., small 4to, cloth extra, 6s.
Chaucer for Schools. By Mrs. H. R. Haweis. Demy 8vo, cloth limp, 2s.6d.

City (The) of Dream: A Poem. Fcap. 8vo, cloth extra, 6s. [*In the press.*

Cobban.—The Cure of Souls: A Story. By J. Maclaren Cobban. Post 8vo, illustrated boards, 2s.

Collins (C. Allston).—The Bar Sinister: A Story. By C. Allston Collins. Post 8vo, illustrated boards, 2s.

Collins (Mortimer & Frances), Novels by:
Sweet and Twenty. Post 8vo, illustrated boards, 2s.
Frances. Post 8vo, illust. bds., 2s.
Blacksmith and Scholar. Post 8vo, illustrated boards, 2s.; crown 8vo cloth extra, 3s. 6d.
The Village Comedy. Post 8vo, illus'. boards, 2s.; cr. 8vo, cloth extra, 3s. 6d
You Play Me False. Post 8vo, illust. boards, 2s.; cr. 8vo, cloth extra, 3s. 6d.

Collins (Mortimer), Novels by:
Sweet Anne Page. Post 8vo, illustrated boards, 2s.; crown 8vo, cloth extra, 3s. 6d.
Transmigration. Post 8vo, illustrated boards, 2s.; crown 8vo, cloth extra, 3s. 6d.
From Midnight to Midnight. Post 8vo, illustrated boards, 2s.; crown 8vo, cloth extra, 3s. 6d.
A Fight with Fortune. Post 8vo, illustrated boards, 2s.

Colman's Humorous Works: "Broad Grins," "My Nightgown and Slippers," and other Humorous Works, Prose and Poetical, of George Colman. With Life by G. B. Buckstone, and Frontispiece by Hogarth. Crown 8vo, cloth extra, gilt, 7s. 6d.

Collins (Wilkie), Novels by.
Each post 8vo, illustrated boards, 2s; cloth limp, 2s. 6d.; or crown 8vo, cloth extra, Illustrated, 3s. 6d.

Antonina. Illust. by A. Concanen.
Basil. Illustrated by Sir John Gilbert and J. Mahoney.
Hide and Seek. Illustrated by Sir John Gilbert and J. Mahoney.
The Dead Secret. Illustrated by Sir John Gilbert and A. Concanen.
Queen of Hearts Illustrated by Sir John Gilbert and A. Concanen.
My Miscellanies. With Illustrations by A. Concanen, and a Steel-plate Portrait of Wilkie Collins.
The Woman in White. With Illustrations by Sir John Gilbert and F. A. Fraser.
The Moonstone. With Illustrations by G. Du Maurier and F. A. Fraser.
Man and Wife. Illust. by W. Small.
Poor Miss Finch. Illustrated by G. Du Maurier and Edward Hughes.
Miss or Mrs.? With Illustrations by S. L. Fildes and Henry Woods.
The New Magdalen. Illustrated by G. Du Maurier and C. S. Rands.
The Frozen Deep. Illustrated by G. Du Maurier and J. Mahoney.
The Law and the Lady. Illustrated by S. L. Fildes and Sydney Hall.
The Two Destinies.
The Haunted Hotel. Illustrated by Arthur Hopkins.
The Fallen Leaves.
Jezebel's Daughter.
The Black Robe.

Heart and Science: A Story of the Present Time. New and Cheaper Edition. Crown 8vo, cloth extra, 3s. 6d.

Convalescent Cookery: A Family Handbook. By Catherine Ryan. Post 8vo, cloth limp, 2s. 6d.

Conway (Moncure D.), Works by:

Demonology and Devil-Lore. Two Vols., royal 8vo, with 65 Illusts., 28s.
A Necklace of Stories. Illustrated by W. J. Hennessy. Square 8vo, cloth extra, 6s.
The Wandering Jew. Crown 8vo, cloth extra, 6s.
Thomas Carlyle: Letters and Recollections. With Illustrations. Crown 8vo, cloth extra, 6s.

Cook (Dutt
Hours with
Steel Plate
Cheaper Ed
Nights at t
English St
Edition. C
Leo: A Nov
boards, 2s.
Paul Foster
illustrated
cloth extra,

Copyright.
English and
Literary an
Sidney Jer
Temple, Esq.
8vo, cloth lin

Cornwall.—
of the Wes
Drolls, Trad
of Old Cornw
by Robert
Revised Edi
Two Steel
George Cr
cloth extra, 7

Creasy.—M
Etonians: v
History of
Edward Cr
Fifteen Decis
Crown 8vo,
Portraits, 7s.

Cruikshan
The Comic
Two Seri
to 1843;
1853. A
Humour o
hew, Alb
Robert I
Woodcuts
Cruikshan
Crown 8vo
volumes, 7

The Life of
Blanchar
"The Lif
With 84
Cheaper E
ditional Pl
compiled I
cloth extra

Robinson C
Edition, w
Steel Plat
shank. Cr
100 Large
printed or
India pro
price 36s.

CHATTO & WINDUS, PICCADILLY. 7

Cussans.—Handbook of Heraldry; with Instructions for Tracing Pedigrees and Deciphering Ancient MSS., &c. By JOHN E. CUSSANS. Entirely New and Revised Edition, illustrated with over 400 Woodcuts and Coloured Plates. Crown 8vo, cloth extra, 7s. 6d.

Cyples.—Hearts of Gold: A Novel. By WILLIAM CYPLES. Crown 8vo, cloth extra, 3s. 6d.

Daniel.— Merrie England in the Olden Time. By GEORGE DANIEL. With Illustrations by ROBT. CRUIKSHANK. Crown 8vo, cloth extra, 3s. 6d.

Daudet.—Port Salvation; or, The Evangelist. By ALPHONSE DAUDET. Translated by C. HARRY MELTZER. With Portrait of the Author. Crown 8vo, cloth extra, 3s. 6d.

Davenant. — What shall my Son be? Hints for Parents on the Choice of a Profession or Trade for their Sons. By FRANCIS DAVENANT, M.A. Post 8vo, cloth limp, 2s. 6d.

Davies (Dr. N. E.), Works by:
One Thousand Medical Maxims. Crown 8vo, 1s.; cloth, 1s. 6d.
Nursery Hints: A Mother's Guide. Crown 8vo, 1s.; cloth, 1s. 6d.

Davies' (Sir John) Complete Poetical Works, including Psalms I. to L. in Verse, and other hitherto Unpublished MSS., for the first time Collected and Edited, with Memorial-Introduction and Notes, by the Rev. A. B. GROSART, D.D. Two Vols., crown 8vo, cloth boards, 12s.

De Maistre.—A Journey Round My Room. By XAVIER DE MAISTRE. Translated by HENRY ATTWELL. Post 8vo, cloth limp, 2s. 6d.

De Mille.—A Castle in Spain. A Novel. By JAMES DE MILLE. With a Frontispiece. Crown 8vo, cloth extra, 3s. 6d.

Derwent (Leith), Novels by:
Our Lady of Tears. Cr. 8vo, cloth extra, 3s. 6d.; post 8vo, illust. bds., 2s.
Circe's Lovers. Crown 8vo, cloth extra, 3s. 6d.

Dickens (Charles), Novels by:
Post 8vo, illustrated boards, 2s. each.
Sketches by Boz. | Nicholas Nickleby.
Pickwick Papers. | Oliver Twist.

The Speeches of Charles Dickens. (*Mayfair Library*.) Post 8vo, cloth limp, 2s. 6d.

The Speeches of Charles Dickens, 1841-1870. With a New Bibliography, revised and enlarged. Edited and Prefaced by RICHARD HERNE SHEPHERD. Crown 8vo, cloth extra, 6s.

About England with Dickens. By ALFRED RIMMER. With 57 Illustrations by C. A. VANDERHOOF, ALFRED RIMMER, and others. Sq. 8vo, cloth extra, 10s. 6d.

Dictionaries:

A Dictionary of Miracles: Imitative, Realistic, and Dogmatic. By the Rev. E. C. BREWER, LL.D. Crown 8vo, cloth extra, 7s. 6d. [*Immediately.*

A Dictionary of the Drama: Being a comprehensive Guide to the Plays, Playwrights, Players, and Playhouses of the United Kingdom and America, from the Earliest to the Present Times. By W. DAVENPORT ADAMS. A thick volume, crown 8vo, half-bound, 12s. 6d. [*In preparation.*

Familiar Allusions: A Handbook of Miscellaneous Information; including the Names of Celebrated Statues, Paintings, Palaces, Country Seats, Ruins, Churches, Ships, Streets, Clubs, Natural Curiosities, and the like. By WM. A. WHEELER and CHARLES G. WHEELER. Demy 8vo, cloth extra, 7s. 6d.

The Reader's Handbook of Allusions, References, Plots, and Stories. By the Rev. E. C. BREWER, LL.D. Third Edition, revised throughout, with a New Appendix, containing a Complete English Bibliography. Crown 8vo, 1,400 pages, cloth extra, 7s. 6d.

Short Sayings of Great Men. With Historical and Explanatory Notes. By SAMUEL A. BENT, M.A. Demy 8vo, cloth extra, 7s. 6d.

The Slang Dictionary: Etymological, Historical, and Anecdotal. Crown 8vo, cloth extra, 6s. 6d.

Words, Facts, and Phrases: A Dictionary of Curious, Quaint, and Out-of-the-Way Matters. By ELIEZER EDWARDS. Crown 8vo, half-bound, 12s. 6d.

Dobson (W. T.), Works by:
Literary Frivolities, Fancies, Follies, and Frolics. Post 8vo, cloth limp, 2s. 6d.
Poetical Ingenuities and Eccentricities. Post 8vo, cloth limp, 2s. 6d.

Doran.—Memories of our Great Towns; with Anecdotic Gleanings concerning their Worthies and their Oddities. By Dr. JOHN DORAN, F.S.A. With 38 Illustrations. New and Cheaper Edition, crown 8vo, cloth extra, 7s. 6d.

Drama, A Dictionary of the. Being a comprehensive Guide to the Plays, Playwrights, Players, and Playhouses of the United Kingdom and America, from the Earliest to the Present Times. By W. DAVENPORT ADAMS. (Uniform with BREWER'S "Reader's Handbook.") Crown 8vo, half-bound, 12s. 6d. [*In preparation.*]

Dramatists, The Old. Crown 8vo, cloth extra, with Vignette Portraits, 6s. per Vol.
Ben Jonson's Works. With Notes Critical and Explanatory, and a Biographical Memoir by WM. GIFFORD. Edited by Colonel CUNNINGHAM. Three Vols.
Chapman's Works. Complete in Three Vols. Vol. I. contains the Plays complete, including the doubtful ones; Vol. II., the Poems and Minor Translations, with an Introductory Essay by ALGERNON CHAS. SWINBURNE; Vol. III., the Translations of the Iliad and Odyssey.
Marlowe's Works. Including his Translations. Edited, with Notes and Introduction, by Col. CUNNINGHAM. One Vol.
Massinger's Plays. From the Text of WILLIAM GIFFORD. Edited by Col. CUNNINGHAM. One Vol.

Dyer.—The Folk-Lore of Plants. By T. F. THISELTON DYER, M.A., &c. Crown 8vo, cloth extra, 7s. 6d. [*In preparation.*]

Edwardes (Mrs. A.), Novels by:
A Point of Honour. Post 8vo, illustrated boards, 2s.
Archie Lovell. Post 8vo, illust. bds., 2s.; crown 8vo, cloth extra, 3s. 6d.

Eggleston.—Roxy: A Novel. By EDWARD EGGLESTON. Post 8vo, illust. boards, 2s.; cr. 8vo, cloth extra, 3s. 6d.

Early English Poets. Edited, with Introductions and Annotations, by Rev. A. B. GROSART, D.D. Crown 8vo, cloth boards, 6s. per Volume.
Fletcher's (Giles, B.D.) Complete Poems. One Vol.
Davies' (Sir John) Complete Poetical Works. Two Vols.
Herrick's (Robert) Complete Collected Poems. Three Vols.
Sidney's (Sir Philip) Complete Poetical Works. Three Vols.

Herbert (Lord) of Cherbury's Poems. Edited, with Introduction, by J. CHURTON COLLINS. Crown 8vo, parchment, 8s.

Emanuel.—On Diamonds and Precious Stones: their History, Value, and Properties; with Simple Tests for ascertaining their Reality. By HARRY EMANUEL, F.R.G.S. With numerous Illustrations, tinted and plain. Crown 8vo, cloth extra, gilt, 6s.

Englishman's House, The: A Practical Guide to all interested in Selecting or Building a House, with full Estimates of Cost, Quantities, &c. By C. J. RICHARDSON. Third Edition. With nearly 600 Illustrations. Crown 8vo, cloth extra, 7s. 6d.

Ewald (Alex. Charles, F.S.A.), Works by:
Stories from the State Papers. With an Autotype Facsimile. Crown 8vo, cloth extra, 6s.
The Life and Times of Prince Charles Stuart, Count of Albany, commonly called the Young Pretender. From the State Papers and other Sources. New and Cheaper Edition, with a Portrait, crown 8vo, cloth extra, 7s. 6d.

Eyes, The.—How to Use our Eyes, and How to Preserve Them. By JOHN BROWNING, F.R.A.S., &c. With 37 Illustrations. Crown 8vo, 1s.; cloth 1s. 6d.

Fairholt.—Tobacco: Its History and Associations; with an Account of the Plant and its Manufacture, and its Modes of Use in all Ages and Countries. By F. W. FAIRHOLT, F.S.A. With Coloured Frontispiece and upwards of 100 Illustrations by the Author. Crown 8vo, cloth extra, 6s.

amiliar Allusions: A Handbook of Miscellaneous Information; Including the Names of Celebrated Statues, Paintings, Palaces, Country Seats, Ruins, Churches, Ships, Streets, Clubs, Natural Curiosities, and the like. By WILLIAM A. WHEELER, Author of "Noted Names of Fiction;" and CHARLES G. WHEELER. Demy 8vo, cloth extra, 7s. 6d.

araday (Michael), Works by:
The Chemical History of a Candle: Lectures delivered before a Juvenile Audience at the Royal Institution. Edited by WILLIAM CROOKES, F.C.S. Post 8vo, cloth extra, with numerous Illustrations, 4s. 6d.

On the Various Forces of Nature, and their Relations to each other: Lectures delivered before a Juvenile Audience at the Royal Institution. Edited by WILLIAM CROOKES, F.C.S. Post 8vo, cloth extra, with numerous Illustrations, 4s. 6d.

In-Bec.—The Cupboard Papers: Observations on the Art of Living and Dining. By FIN-BEC. Post 8vo, cloth limp, 2s. 6d.

itzgerald (Percy), Works by:
The Recreations of a Literary Man; or, Does Writing Pay? With Recollections of some Literary Men, and a View of a Literary Man's Working Life. Cr. 8vo, cloth extra, 6s.

The World Behind the Scenes. Crown 8vo, cloth extra, 3s. 6d.

Little Essays: Passages from the Letters of CHARLES LAMB. Post 8vo, cloth limp, 2s. 6d.

Post 8vo, illustrated boards, 2s. each.
Bella Donna. | Never Forgotten.
The Second Mrs. Tillotson.
Polly.
Seventy-five Brooke Street.

etcher's (Giles, B.D.) Complete Poems: Christ's Victorie in Heaven, Christ's Victorie on Earth, Christ's Triumph over Death, and Minor Poems. With Memorial-Introduction and Notes by the Rev. A. B. GROSART, D.D. Cr. 8vo, cloth bds., 6s.

onblanque.—Filthy Lucre: A Novel. By ALBANY DE FONBLANQUE. Post 8vo, illustrated boards, 2s.

rench Literature, History of.
By HENRY VAN LAUN. Complete in 3 Vols., demy 8vo, cl. bds., 7s. 6d. each.

Francillon (R. E.), Novels by:
Crown 8vo, cloth extra, 3s. 6d. each; post 8vo, illust. boards, 2s. each.
Olympia. | Queen Cophetua.
One by One.

Esther's Glove. Fcap. 8vo, picture cover, 1s.
A Real Queen. Three Vols., cr. 8vo.

Frere.—Pandurang Hari; or, Memoirs of a Hindoo. With a Preface by Sir H. BARTLE FRERE, G.C.S.I., &c. Crown 8vo, cloth extra, 3s. 6d.; post 8vo, illustrated boards, 2s.

Friswell.—One of Two: A Novel. By HAIN FRISWELL. Post 8vo, illustrated boards, 2s.

Frost (Thomas), Works by:
Crown 8vo, cloth extra, 3s. 6d. each.
Circus Life and Circus Celebrities.
The Lives of the Conjurers.
The Old Showmen and the Old London Fairs.

Fry.—Royal Guide to the London Charities, 1884-5. By HERBERT FRY. Showing, in alphabetical order, their Name, Date of Foundation, Address, Objects, Annual Income, Chief Officials, &c. Published Annually. Crown 8vo, cloth, 1s. 6d. [*Immediately.*]

Gardening Books:
A Year's Work in Garden and Greenhouse: Practical Advice to Amateur Gardeners as to the Management of the Flower, Fruit, and Frame Garden. By GEORGE GLENNY. Post 8vo, cloth limp, 2s. 6d.

Our Kitchen Garden: The Plants we Grow, and How we Cook Them. By TOM JERROLD, Author of "The Garden that Paid the Rent," &c. Post 8vo, cloth limp, 2s. 6d.

Household Horticulture: A Gossip about Flowers. By TOM and JANE JERROLD. Illustrated. Post 8vo, cloth limp, 2s. 6d.

The Garden that Paid the Rent. By TOM JERROLD. Fcap. 8vo, illustrated cover, 1s.; cloth limp, 1s. 6d.

Garrett.—The Capel Girls: A Novel. By EDWARD GARRETT. Post 8vo, illust. bds., 2s.; cr. 8vo, cl. ex., 3s. 6d.

German Popular Stories. Collected by the Brothers GRIMM, and Translated by EDGAR TAYLOR. Edited, with an Introduction, by JOHN RUSKIN. With 22 Illustrations on Steel by GEORGE CRUIKSHANK. Square 8vo, cloth extra, 6s. 6d. gilt edges, 7s. 6d.

Gentleman's Magazine (The) for 1884. One Shilling Monthly. A New Serial Story, entitled "Philistia," by CECIL POWER, is now appearing. "Science Notes," by W. MATTIEU WILLIAMS, F.R.A.S., and "Table Talk," by SYLVANUS URBAN, are also continued monthly.

⁎ Now ready, the Volume for JULY to DECEMBER, 1883, cloth extra, price 8s. 6d.; Cases for binding, 2s. each.

Gibbon (Charles), Novels by:
Crown 8vo, cloth extra, 3s. 6d. each; post 8vo, illustrated boards, 2s. each.
Robin Gray.
For Lack of Gold.
What will the World Say?
In Honour Bound.
In Love and War.
For the King.
Queen of the Meadow.
In Pastures Green.
The Braes of Yarrow.
The Flower of the Forest.
A Heart's Problem.

Post 8vo, illustrated boards, 2s.
The Dead Heart.

Crown 8vo, cloth extra, 3s. 6d. each.
The Golden Shaft.
Of High Degree.

Fancy-Free. Three Vols., crown 8vo.

Gilbert (William), Novels by:
Post 8vo, illustrated boards, 2s. each.
Dr. Austin's Guests.
The Wizard of the Mountain.
James Duke, Costermonger.

Gilbert (W. S.), Original Plays by: In Two Series, each complete in itself, price 2s. 6d. each.
The FIRST SERIES contains — The Wicked World — Pygmalion and Galatea — Charity — The Princess — The Palace of Truth — Trial by Jury.
The SECOND SERIES contains — Broken Hearts — Engaged — Sweethearts — Gretchen — Dan'l Druce — Tom Cobb — H.M.S. Pinafore — The Sorcerer — The Pirates of Penzance.

Glenny.—A Year's Work in Garden and Greenhouse: Practical Advice to Amateur Gardeners as to the Management of the Flower, Fruit, and Frame Garden. By GEORGE GLENNY. Post 8vo, cloth limp, 2s. 6d.

Godwin.—Lives of the Necromancers. By WILLIAM GODWIN. Post 8vo, cloth limp, 2s.

Golden Library, The:
Square 16mo (Tauchnitz size), cloth limp, 2s. per volume.
Bayard Taylor's Diversions of the Echo Club.
Bennett's (Dr. W. C.) Ballad History of England.
Bennett's (Dr. W. C.) Songs for Sailors.
Byron's Don Juan.
Godwin's (William) Lives of the Necromancers.
Holmes's Autocrat of the Breakfast Table. With an Introduction by G. A. SALA.
Holmes's Professor at the Breakfast Table.
Hood's Whims and Oddities. Complete. All the original Illustrations.
Irving's (Washington) Tales of a Traveller.
Irving's (Washington) Tales of the Alhambra.
Jesse's (Edward) Scenes and Occupations of a Country Life.
Lamb's Essays of Elia. Both Series Complete in One Vol.
Leigh Hunt's Essays: A Tale for a Chimney Corner, and other Pieces. With Portrait, and Introduction by EDMUND OLLIER.
Mallory's (Sir Thomas) Mort d'Arthur: The Stories of King Arthur and of the Knights of the Round Table. Edited by B. MONTGOMERIE RANKING.
Pascal's Provincial Letters. A New Translation, with Historical Introduction and Notes, by T. M'CRIE, D.D.
Pope's Poetical Works. Complete.
Rochefoucauld's Maxims and Moral Reflections. With Notes, and Introductory Essay by SAINTE-BEUVE.
St. Pierre's Paul and Virginia, and The Indian Cottage. Edited, with Life, by the Rev. E. CLARKE.
Shelley's Early Poems, and Queen Mab. With Essay by LEIGH HUNT.
Shelley's Later Poems: Laon and Cythna, &c.
Shelley's Posthumous Poems, the Shelley Papers, &c.
Shelley's Prose Works, including A Refutation of Deism, Zastrozzi, St. Irvyne, &c.
White's Natural History of Selborne. Edited, with Additions, by THOMAS BROWN, F.L.S.

Golden Treasury of Thought, The: An ENCYCLOPÆDIA OF QUOTATIONS from Writers of all Times and Countries. Selected and Edited by THEODORE TAYLOR. Crown 8vo, cloth gilt and gilt edges, 7s. 6d.

Gordon Cumming (C. F.), Works by:
In the Hebrides. With Autotype Facsimile and numerous full-page Illustrations. Demy 8vo, cloth extra, 8s. 6d.

In the Himalayas. With numerous Illustrations. Demy 8vo, cloth extra, 8s. 6d. [*Shortly.*

Graham.—The Professor's Wife: A Story. By LEONARD GRAHAM. Fcap. 8vo, picture cover, 1s.; cloth extra, 2s. 6d.

Greeks and Romans, The Life of the, Described from Antique Monuments. By ERNST GUHL and W. KONER. Translated from the Third German Edition, and Edited by Dr. F. HUEFFER. With 545 Illustrations. New and Cheaper Edition, demy 8vo, cloth extra, 7s. 6d.

Greenwood (James), Works by:
The Wilds of London. Crown 8vo, cloth extra, 3s. 6d.

Low-Life Deeps: An Account of the Strange Fish to be Found There. Crown 8vo, cloth extra, 3s. 6d.

Dick Temple: A Novel. Post 8vo, illustrated boards, 2s.

Guyot.—The Earth and Man; or, Physical Geography in its relation to the History of Mankind. By ARNOLD GUYOT. With Additions by Professors AGASSIZ, PIERCE, and GRAY; 12 Maps and Engravings on Steel, some Coloured, and copious Index. Crown 8vo, cloth extra, gilt, 4s. 6d.

Hair (The): Its Treatment in Health, Weakness, and Disease. Translated from the German of Dr. J. PINCUS. Crown 8vo, 1s.; cloth, 1s. 6d.

Hake (Dr. Thomas Gordon), Poems by:
Maiden Ecstasy. Small 4to, cloth extra, 8s.

New Symbols. Crown 8vo, cloth extra, 6s.

Legends of the Morrow. Crown 8vo, cloth extra, 6s.

The Serpent Play. Crown 8vo, cloth extra, 6s.

Hall.—Sketches of Irish Character. By Mrs. S. C. HALL. With numerous Illustrations on Steel and Wood by MACLISE, GILBERT, HARVEY, and G. CRUIKSHANK. Medium 8vo, cloth extra, gilt, 7s. 6d.

Halliday.—Every-day Papers. By ANDREW HALLIDAY. Post 8vo, illustrated boards, 2s.

Handwriting, The Philosophy of. With over 100 Facsimiles and Explanatory Text. By DON FELIX DE SALAMANCA. Post 8vo, cloth limp, 2s. 6d.

Hanky-Panky: A Collection of Very Easy Tricks, Very Difficult Tricks, White Magic, Sleight of Hand, &c. Edited by W. H. CREMER. With 200 Illustrations. Crown 8vo, cloth extra, 4s. 6d.

Hardy (Lady Duffus).—Paul Wynter's Sacrifice: A Story. By Lady DUFFUS HARDY. Post 8vo, illust. boards, 2s.

Hardy (Thomas).—Under the Greenwood Tree. By THOMAS HARDY, Author of "Far from the Madding Crowd." Crown 8vo, cloth extra, 3s. 6d.; post 8vo, illustrated boards, 2s.

Haweis (Mrs. H. R.), Works by:
The Art of Dress. With numerous Illustrations. Small 8vo, illustrated cover, 1s.; cloth limp, 1s. 6d.

The Art of Beauty. New and Cheaper Edition. Crown 8vo, cloth extra, with Coloured Frontispiece and Illustrations, 6s.

The Art of Decoration. Square 8vo, handsomely bound and profusely Illustrated, 10s. 6d.

Chaucer for Children: A Golden Key. With Eight Coloured Pictures and numerous Woodcuts. New Edition, small 4to, cloth extra, 6s.

Chaucer for Schools. Demy 8vo, cloth limp, 2s. 6d.

Haweis (Rev. H. R.).—American Humorists. Including WASHINGTON IRVING, OLIVER WENDELL HOLMES, JAMES RUSSELL LOWELL, ARTEMUS WARD, MARK TWAIN, and BRET HARTE. By the Rev. H. R. HAWEIS, M.A. Crown 8vo, cloth extra, 6s.

Hawthorne (Julian), Novels by.
Crown 8vo, cloth extra, 3s. 6d. each;
post 8vo, illustrated boards, 2s. each.
  Garth.
  Ellice Quentin.
  Sebastian Strome.
  Prince Saroni's Wife.
  Dust.

Mrs. Gainsborough's Diamonds.
Fcap. 8vo, illustrated cover, 1s.;
cloth extra, 2s. 6d.

Fortune's Fool. Crown 8vo, cloth extra, 3s. 6d.

Beatrix Randolph. With Illustrations by A. FREDERICKS. Crown 8vo, cloth extra, 3s. 6d. [*Preparing.*]

Heath (F. G.).— My Garden
Wild, and What I Grew There. By FRANCIS GEORGE HEATH, Author of "The Fern World," &c. Crown 8vo, cloth extra, 5s.; cloth gilt, and gilt edges, 6s.

Helps (Sir Arthur), Works by:
Animals and their Masters. Post 8vo, cloth limp, 2s. 6d.
Social Pressure. Post 8vo, cloth limp, 2s. 6d.
Ivan de Biron: A Novel. Crown 8vo, cloth extra, 3s. 6d.; post 8vo, illustrated boards, 2s.

Heptalogia (The); or, The
Seven against Sense. A Cap with Seven Bells. Cr. 8vo, cloth extra, 6s.

Herbert.—The Poems of Lord
Herbert of Cherbury. Edited, with an Introduction, by J. CHURTON COLLINS. Crown 8vo, bound in parchment, 8s.

Herrick's (Robert) Hesperides,
Noble Numbers, and Complete Collected Poems. With Memorial-Introduction and Notes by the Rev. A. B. GROSART, D.D., Steel Portrait, Index of First Lines, and Glossarial Index, &c. Three Vols., crown 8vo, cloth boards, 18s.

Hesse-Wartegg (Chevalier
Ernst von), Works by:
Tunis: The Land and the People. With 22 Illustrations. Crown 8vo, cloth extra, 3s. 6d.
The New South-West: Travelling Sketches from Kansas, New Mexico, Arizona, and Northern Mexico. With 100 fine Illustrations and Three Maps. Demy 8vo, cloth extra, 14s. [*In preparation.*]

Hindley (Charles), Works by:
Crown 8vo, cloth extra, 3s. 6d. each.
Tavern Anecdotes and Sayings: Including the Origin of Signs, and Reminiscences connected with Taverns, Coffee Houses, Clubs, &c. With Illustrations.
The Life and Adventures of a Cheap Jack. By One of the Fraternity Edited by CHARLES HINDLEY.

Holmes (O. Wendell), Works by
The Autocrat of the Breakfast Table. Illustrated by J. GORDON THOMSON. Post 8vo, cloth limp, 2s. 6d.; another Edition in smaller type, with an Introduction by G. A. SALA. Post 8vo, cloth limp, 2s.
The Professor at the Breakfast Table; with the Story of Iris. Post 8vo, cloth limp, 2s.

Holmes. — The Science of
Voice Production and Voice Preservation: A Popular Manual for the Use of Speakers and Singers. By GORDON HOLMES, M.D. Crown 8vo, cloth limp, with Illustrations, 2s. 6d.

Hood (Thomas):
Hood's Choice Works, in Prose and Verse. Including the Cream of the Comic Annuals. With Life of the Author, Portrait, and 200 Illustrations. Crown 8vo, cloth extra, 7s. 6d.
Hood's Whims and Oddities. Complete. With all the original Illustrations. Post 8vo, cloth limp, 2s.

Hood (Tom), Works by:
From Nowhere to the North Pole A Noah's Arkæological Narrative With 25 Illustrations by W. BRUNTON and E. C. BARNES. Square crown 8vo, cloth extra, gilt edges, 6s.
A Golden Heart: A Novel. Post 8vo illustrated boards, 2s.

Hook's (Theodore) Choice Humorous Works, including his Ludicrous Adventures, Bons Mots, Puns and Hoaxes. With a New Life of the Author, Portraits, Facsimiles, and Illustrations. Crown 8vo, cloth extra gilt, 7s. 6d.

Hooper.—The House of Raby
A Novel. By Mrs. GEORGE HOOPER Post 8vo, illustrated boards, 2s.

Horne.—Orion : An Epic Poem
in Three Books. By RICHARD HENGIST HORNE. With Photographic Portrait from a Medallion by SUMMERS. Tenth Edition, crown 8vo cloth extra, 7s.

Howell.—Conflicts of Capital and Labour, Historically and Economically considered: Being a History and Review of the Trade Unions of Great Britain, showing their Origin, Progress, Constitution, and Objects, in their Political, Social, Economical, and Industrial Aspects. By GEORGE HOWELL. Cr. 8vo, cloth extra, 7s. 6d.

Hugo. — The Hunchback of Notre Dame. By VICTOR HUGO. Post 8vo, illustrated boards, 2s.

Hunt.—Essays by Leigh Hunt. A Tale for a Chimney Corner, and other Pieces. With Portrait and Introduction by EDMUND OLLIER. Post 8vo, cloth limp, 2s.

Hunt (Mrs. Alfred), Novels by:
Crown 8vo, cloth extra, 3s. 6d. each; post 8vo, illustrated boards, 2s. each.
Thornicroft's Model.
The Leaden Casket.
Self-Condemned.

Ingelow.—Fated to be Free: A Novel. By JEAN INGELOW. Crown 8vo, cloth extra, 3s. 6d.; post 8vo, illustrated boards, 2s.

Irish Wit and Humour, Songs of. Collected and Edited by A. PERCEVAL GRAVES. Post 8vo, cloth limp, 2s. 6d.

Irving (Henry).—The Paradox of Acting. Translated, with Annotations, from Diderot's "Le Paradoxe sur le Comédien," by WALTER HERRIES POLLOCK. With a Preface by HENRY IRVING. Crown 8vo, in parchment, 4s. 6d.

Irving (Washington), Works by:
Post 8vo, cloth limp, 2s. each.
Tales of a Traveller.
Tales of the Alhambra.

James.—Confidence: A Novel. By HENRY JAMES, Jun. Crown 8vo, cloth extra, 3s. 6d.; post 8vo, illustrated boards, 2s.

Janvier.—Practical Keramics for Students. By CATHERINE A. JANVIER. Crown 8vo, cloth extra, 6s.

Jay (Harriett), Novels by. Each Crown 8vo, cloth extra, 3s. 6d.; or post 8vo, illustrated boards, 2s.
The Dark Colleen.
The Queen of Connaught.

Jefferies (Richard), Works by:
Nature near London. Crown 8vo, cloth extra, 6s.
The Life of the Fields. Crown 8vo, cloth extra, 6s. [In the press.

Jennings (H. J.).—Curiosities of Criticism. By HENRY J. JENNINGS. Post 8vo, cloth limp, 2s. 6d.

Jennings (Hargrave). — The Rosicrucians: Their Rites and Mysteries. With Chapters on the Ancient Fire and Serpent Worshippers. By HARGRAVE JENNINGS. With Five full-page Plates and upwards of 300 Illustrations. A New Edition, crown 8vo, cloth extra, 7s. 6d.

Jerrold (Tom), Works by:
The Garden that Paid the Rent. By TOM JERROLD. Fcap. 8vo, illustrated cover, 1s.; cloth limp, 1s. 6d.
Household Horticulture: A Gossip about Flowers. By TOM and JANE JERROLD. Illustrated. Post 8vo, cloth limp, 2s. 6d.
Our Kitchen Garden: The Plants we Grow, and How we Cook Them. By TOM JERROLD. Post 8vo, cloth limp, 2s. 6d.

Jesse.—Scenes and Occupations of a Country Life. By EDWARD JESSE. Post 8vo, cloth limp, 2s.

Jones (Wm., F.S.A.), Works by:
Finger-Ring Lore: Historical, Legendary, and Anecdotal. With over 200 Illustrations. Crown 8vo, cloth extra, 7s. 6d.
Credulities, Past and Present; including the Sea and Seamen, Miners, Talismans, Word and Letter Divination, Exorcising and Blessing of Animals, Birds, Eggs, Luck, &c. With an Etched Frontispiece. Crown 8vo, cloth extra, 7s. 6d.
Crowns and Coronations: A History of Regalia in all Times and Countries. With One Hundred Illustrations. Cr. 8vo, cloth extra, 7s. 6d.

Jonson's (Ben) Works. With Notes Critical and Explanatory, and a Biographical Memoir by WILLIAM GIFFORD. Edited by Colonel CUNNINGHAM. Three Vols., crown 8vo, cloth extra, 18s.; or separately, 6s. each.

Josephus, The Complete Works of. Translated by WHISTON. Containing both "The Antiquities of the Jews" and "The Wars of the Jews." Two Vols., 8vo, with 52 Illustrations and Maps, cloth extra, gilt, 14s.

Kavanagh.—The Pearl Fountain, and other Fairy Stories. By BRIDGET and JULIA KAVANAGH. With Thirty Illustrations by J. MOYR SMITH. Small 8vo, cloth gilt, 6s.

Kempt.—Pencil and Palette: Chapters on Art and Artists. By ROBERT KEMPT. Post 8vo, cloth limp, 2s. 6d.

Kingsley (Henry), Novels by:
Each crown 8vo, cloth extra, 3s. 6d.; or post 8vo, illustrated boards, 2s.
Oakshott Castle. | Number Seventeen

Lamb (Charles):

Mary and Charles Lamb: Their Poems, Letters, and Remains. With Reminiscences and Notes by W. CAREW HAZLITT. With HANCOCK'S Portrait of the Essayist, Facsimiles of the Title-pages of the rare First Editions of Lamb's and Coleridge's Works, and numerous Illustrations. Crown 8vo, cloth extra, 10s. 6d.

Lamb's Complete Works, in Prose and Verse, reprinted from the Original Editions, with many Pieces hitherto unpublished. Edited, with Notes and Introduction, by R. H. SHEPHERD. With Two Portraits and Facsimile of Page of the "Essay on Roast Pig." Cr. 8vo, cloth extra, 7s. 6d.

The Essays of Elia. Complete Edition. Post 8vo, cloth extra, 2s.

Poetry for Children, and Prince Dorus. By CHARLES LAMB. Carefully Reprinted from unique copies. Small 8vo, cloth extra, 5s.

Little Essays: Sketches and Characters. By CHARLES LAMB. Selected from his Letters by PERCY FITZGERALD. Post 8vo, cloth limp, 2s. 6d.

Lane's Arabian Nights, &c.:

The Thousand and One Nights: commonly called, in England, "THE ARABIAN NIGHTS' ENTERTAINMENTS." A New Translation from the Arabic, with copious Notes, by EDWARD WILLIAM LANE. Illustrated by many hundred Engravings on Wood, from Original Designs by WM. HARVEY. A New Edition, from a Copy annotated by the Translator, edited by his Nephew, EDWARD STANLEY POOLE. With a Preface by STANLEY LANE-POOLE. Three Vols., demy 8vo, cloth extra, 7s. 6d. each.

Arabian Society in the Middle Ages: Studies from "The Thousand and One Nights." By EDWARD WILLIAM LANE, Author of "The Modern Egyptians," &c. Edited by STANLEY LANE-POOLE. Cr. 8vo, cloth extra, 6s.

Lares and Penates; or, The Background of Life. By FLORENCE CADDY. Crown 8vo, cloth extra, 6s.

Larwood (Jacob), Works by:

The Story of the London Parks. With Illustrations. Crown 8vo, cloth extra, 3s. 6d.

Clerical Anecdotes. Post 8vo, cloth limp, 2s. 6d.

Forensic Anecdotes. Post 8vo, cloth limp, 2s. 6d.

Theatrical Anecdotes. Post 8vo, cloth limp, 2s. 6d.

Leigh (Henry S.), Works by:

Carols of Cockayne. With numerous Illustrations. Post 8vo, cloth limp, 2s. 6d.

Jeux d'Esprit. Collected and Edited by HENRY S. LEIGH. Post 8vo, cloth limp, 2s. 6d.

Life in London; or, The History of Jerry Hawthorn and Corinthian Tom. With the whole of CRUIKSHANK'S Illustrations, in Colours, after the Originals. Crown 8vo, cloth extra, 7s. 6d.

Linton (E. Lynn), Works by
Post 8vo, cloth limp, 2s. 6d. each.
Witch Stories.
The True Story of Joshua Davidson.
Ourselves Essays on Women.

Crown 8vo, cloth extra, 3s. 6d. each; post 8vo, illustrated boards, 2s. each.
Patricia Kemball.
The Atonement of Leam Dundas.
The World Well Lost.
Under which Lord?
With a Silken Thread.
The Rebel of the Family.
"My Love!"

Ione. Three Vols., crown 8vo.

Locks and Keys.—On the Development and Distribution of Primitive Locks and Keys. By Lieut.-Gen. PITT-RIVERS, F.R.S. With numerous Illustrations. Demy 4to, half Roxburghe, 16s.

ngfellow:

ongfellow's Complete Prose Works. Including "Outre Mer," "Hyperion," "Kavanagh," "The Poets and Poetry of Europe," and "Driftwood." With Portrait and Illustrations by VALENTINE BROMLEY. Crown 8vo, cloth extra, 7s. 6d.

ongfellow's Poetical Works. Carefully Reprinted from the Original Editions. With numerous fine Illustrations on Steel and Wood. Crown 8vo, cloth extra, 7s. 6d.

ucy.—Gideon Fleyce: A Novel. By HENRY W. LUCY. Crown 8vo, cloth extra, 3s. 6d.; post 8vo, illustrated boards, 2s.

usiad (The) of Camoens. Translated into English Spenserian Verse by ROBERT FFRENCH DUFF. Demy 8vo, with Fourteen full-page Plates, cloth boards, 18s.

lcCarthy (Justin, M.P.), Works by:

A History of Our Own Times, from the Accession of Queen Victoria to the General Election of 1880. Four Vols. demy 8vo, cloth extra, 12s. each.—Also a POPULAR EDITION, in Four Vols. crown 8vo, cloth extra, 6s. each.

A Short History of Our Own Times. One Volume, crown 8vo, cloth extra, 6s.

History of the Four Georges. Four Vols. demy 8vo, cloth extra, 12s. each. [Vol. I. *in the press.*

Crown 8vo, cloth extra, 3s. 6d. each; post 8vo, illustrated boards, 2s. each.
  Dear Lady Disdain.
  The Waterdale Neighbours.
  My Enemy's Daughter.
  A Fair Saxon.
  Linley Rochford
  Miss Misanthrope.
  Donna Quixote.
  The Comet of a Season.

Maid of Athens. With 12 Illustrations by F. BARNARD. Three Vols., crown 8vo.

McCarthy (Justin H.), Works by:

Serapion, and other Poems. Crown 8vo, cloth extra, 6s.

An Outline of the History of Ireland, from the Earliest Times to the Present Day. Cr. 8vo, 1s.; cloth, 1s. 6d.

MacDonald (George, LL.D.), Works by:

The Princess and Curdie. With 11 Illustrations by JAMES ALLEN. Small crown 8vo, cloth extra, 5s.

Gutta-Percha Willie, the Working Genius. With 9 Illustrations by ARTHUR HUGHES. Square 8vo, cloth extra, 3s. 6d.

Paul Faber, Surgeon. With a Frontispiece by J. E. MILLAIS. Crown 8vo, cloth extra, 3s. 6d.; post 8vo, illustrated boards, 2s.

Thomas Wingfold, Curate. With a Frontispiece by C. J. STANILAND. Crown 8vo, cloth extra, 3s. 6d.; post 8vo, illustrated boards, 2s.

Macdonell.—Quaker Cousins: A Novel. By AGNES MACDONELL. Crown 8vo, cloth extra, 3s. 6d.; post 8vo, illustrated boards, 2s.

Macgregor. — Pastimes and Players. Notes on Popular Games. By ROBERT MACGREGOR. Post 8vo, cloth limp, 2s. 6d.

Maclise Portrait-Gallery (The) of Illustrious Literary Characters; with Memoirs—Biographical, Critical, Bibliographical, and Anecdotal—illustrative of the Literature of the former half of the Present Century. By WILLIAM BATES, B.A. With 85 Portraits printed on an India Tint. Crown 8vo, cloth extra, 7s. 6d.

Macquoid (Mrs.), Works by:

In the Ardennes. With 50 fine Illustrations by THOMAS R. MACQUOID. Square 8vo, cloth extra, 10s. 6d.

Pictures and Legends from Normandy and Brittany. With numerous Illustrations by THOMAS R. MACQUOID. Square 8vo, cloth gilt, 10s. 6d.

Through Normandy. With 90 Illustrations by T. R. MACQUOID. Square 8vo, cloth extra, 7s. 6d.

Through Brittany. With numerous Illustrations by T. R. MACQUOID. Square 8vo, cloth extra, 7s. 6d.

About Yorkshire. With 67 Illustrations by T. R. MACQUOID, Engraved by SWAIN. Square 8vo, cloth extra, 10s. 6d.

The Evil Eye, and other Stories. Crown 8vo, cloth extra, 3s. 6d.; post 8vo, illustrated boards, 2s.

Lost Rose, and other Stories. Crown 8vo, cloth extra, 3s. 6d.; post 8vo, illustrated boards, 2s.

Mackay.—Interludes and Undertones: or, Music at Twilight. By CHARLES MACKAY, LL.D. Crown 8vo, cloth extra, 6s.

Magician's Own Book (The): Performances with Cups and Balls, Eggs, Hats, Handkerchiefs, &c. All from actual Experience. Edited by W. H. CREMER. With 200 Illustrations. Crown 8vo, cloth extra, 4s. 6d.

Magic No Mystery: Tricks with Cards, Dice, Balls, &c., with fully descriptive Directions; the Art of Secret Writing; Training of Performing Animals, &c. With Coloured Frontispiece and many Illustrations. Crown 8vo, cloth extra, 4s. 6d.

Magna Charta. An exact Facsimile of the Original in the British Museum, printed on fine plate paper, 3 feet by 2 feet, with Arms and Seals emblazoned in Gold and Colours. Price 5s.

Mallock (W. H.), Works by:
The New Republic; or, Culture, Faith and Philosophy in an English Country House. Post 8vo, cloth limp, 2s. 6d.; Cheap Edition, illustrated boards, 2s.
The New Paul and Virginia; or, Positivism on an Island. Post 8vo, cloth limp, 2s. 6d.
Poems. Small 4to, bound in parchment, 8s.
Is Life worth Living? Crown 8vo, cloth extra, 6s.

Mallory's (Sir Thomas) Mort d'Arthur: The Stories of King Arthur and of the Knights of the Round Table. Edited by B. MONTGOMERIE RANKING. Post 8vo, cloth limp, 2s.

Marlowe's Works. Including his Translations. Edited, with Notes and Introduction, by Col. CUNNINGHAM. Crown 8vo, cloth extra, 6s.

Marryat (Florence), Novels by:
Crown 8vo, cloth extra, 3s. 6d. each; or, post 8vo, illustrated boards, 2s.
Open! Sesame!
Written in Fire.

Post 8vo, illustrated boards, 2s. each.
A Harvest of Wild Oats.
A Little Stepson.
Fighting the Air.

Masterman.—Half a Dozen Daughters: A Novel. By J. MASTERMAN. Post 8vo, illustrated boards, 2s.

Mark Twain, Works by:
The Choice Works of Mark Twain. Revised and Corrected throughout by the Author. With Life, Portrait, and numerous Illustrations. Crown 8vo, cloth extra, 7s. 6d.
The Adventures of Tom Sawyer. With 100 Illustrations. Small 8vo, cloth extra, 7s. 6d. CHEAP EDITION, illustrated boards, 2s.
An Idle Excursion, and other Sketches. Post 8vo, illustrated boards, 2s.
The Prince and the Pauper. With nearly 200 Illustrations. Crown 8vo, cloth extra, 7s. 6d.
The Innocents Abroad; or, The New Pilgrim's Progress: Being some Account of the Steamship "Quaker City's" Pleasure Excursion to Europe and the Holy Land. With 234 Illustrations. Crown 8vo, cloth extra, 7s. 6d. CHEAP EDITION (under the title of "MARK TWAIN'S PLEASURE TRIP"), post 8vo, illust. boards, 2s.
A Tramp Abroad. With 314 Illustrations. Crown 8vo, cloth extra, 7s. 6d. Without Illustrations, post 8vo, illustrated boards, 2s.
The Stolen White Elephant, &c. Crown 8vo, cloth extra, 6s.; post 8vo, illustrated boards, 2s.
Life on the Mississippi. With about 300 Original Illustrations. Crown 8vo, cloth extra, 7s. 6d.
The Adventures of Huckleberry Finn. With numerous Illustrations by the Author. Crown 8vo, cloth extra, 7s. 6d. [*Preparing.*

Massinger's Plays. From the Text of WILLIAM GIFFORD. Edited by Col. CUNNINGHAM. Crown 8vo, cloth extra, 6s.

Mayhew.—London Characters and the Humorous Side of London Life. By HENRY MAYHEW. With numerous Illustrations. Crown 8vo, cloth extra, 3s. 6d.

Mayfair Library, The:
Post 8vo, cloth limp, 2s. 6d. per Volume.
A Journey Round My Room. By XAVIER DE MAISTRE. Translated by HENRY ATTWELL.
Latter-Day Lyrics. Edited by W. DAVENPORT ADAMS.
Quips and Quiddities. Selected by W. DAVENPORT ADAMS.
The Agony Column of "The Times," from 1800 to 1870. Edited, with an Introduction, by ALICE CLAY.
Balzac's "Comedie Humaine" and its Author. With Translations by H. H. WALKER.

MAYFAIR LIBRARY, *continued*—
Melancholy Anatomised: A Popular Abridgment of "Burton's Anatomy of Melancholy."
Gastronomy as a Fine Art. By BRILLAT-SAVARIN.
The Speeches of Charles Dickens.
Literary Frivolities, Fancies, Follies, and Frolics. By W. T. DOBSON.
Poetical Ingenuities and Eccentricities. Selected and Edited by W. T. DOBSON.
The Cupboard Papers. By FIN-BEC.
Original Plays by W. S. GILBERT. FIRST SERIES. Containing: The Wicked World — Pygmalion and Galatea—Charity—The Princess—The Palace of Truth—Trial by Jury.
Original Plays by W. S. GILBERT. SECOND SERIES. Containing: Broken Hearts — Engaged — Sweethearts— Gretchen—Dan'l Druce—Tom Cobb —H.M.S. Pinafore—The Sorcerer —The Pirates of Penzance.
Songs of Irish Wit and Humour. Collected and Edited by A. PERCEVAL GRAVES.
Animals and their Masters. By Sir ARTHUR HELPS.
Social Pressure. By Sir A. HELPS.
Curiosities of Criticism. By HENRY J. JENNINGS.
The Autocrat of the Breakfast-Table. By OLIVER WENDELL HOLMES. Illustrated by J. GORDON THOMSON.
Pencil and Palette. By ROBERT KEMPT.
Little Essays: Sketches and Characters. By CHARLES LAMB. Selected from his Letters by PERCY FITZGERALD.
Clerical Anecdotes. By JACOB LARWOOD.
Forensic Anecdotes; or, Humour and Curiosities of the Law and Men of Law. By JACOB LARWOOD.
Theatrical Anecdotes. By JACOB LARWOOD.
Carols of Cockayne. By HENRY S. LEIGH.
Jeux d'Esprit. Edited by HENRY S. LEIGH.
True History of Joshua Davidson. By E. LYNN LINTON.
Witch Stories. By E. LYNN LINTON.
Ourselves: Essays on Women. By E. LYNN LINTON.
Pastimes and Players. By ROBERT MACGREGOR.
The New Paul and Virginia. By W. H. MALLOCK.

MAYFAIR LIBRARY, *continued*—
The New Republic. By W. H. MALLOCK.
Puck on Pegasus. By H. CHOLMONDELEY-PENNELL.
Pegasus Re-Saddled. By H. CHOLMONDELEY-PENNELL. Illustrated by GEORGE DU MAURIER.
Muses of Mayfair. Edited by H. CHOLMONDELEY-PENNELL.
Thoreau: His Life and Aims. By H. A. PAGE.
Puniana. By the Hon. HUGH ROWLEY.
More Puniana. By the Hon. HUGH ROWLEY.
The Philosophy of Handwriting. By DON FELIX DE SALAMANCA.
By Stream and Sea. By WILLIAM SENIOR.
Old Stories Re-told. By WALTER THORNBURY.
Leaves from a Naturalist's Note-Book. By Dr. ANDREW WILSON.

Medicine, Family.—One Thousand Medical Maxims and Surgical Hints, for Infancy, Adult Life, Middle Age, and Old Age. By N. E. DAVIES, Licentiate of the Royal College of Physicians of London. Crown 8vo, 1s.; cloth, 1s. 6d.

Merry Circle (The): A Book of New Intellectual Games and Amusements. By CLARA BELLEW. With numerous Illustrations. Crown 8vo, cloth extra, 4s. 6d.

Middlemass (Jean), Novels by:
Touch and Go. Crown 8vo, cloth extra, 3s.6d.; post 8vo, illust. bds., 2s.
Mr. Dorillion. Post 8vo, illust. bds., 2s.

Miller. — Physiology for the Young; or, The House of Life: Human Physiology, with its application to the Preservation of Health. For use in Classes and Popular Reading. With numerous Illustrations. By Mrs. F. FENWICK MILLER. Small 8vo, cloth limp, 2s. 6d.

Milton (J. L.), Works by:
The Hygiene of the Skin. A Concise Set of Rules for the Management of the Skin; with Directions for Diet, Wines, Soaps, Baths, &c. Small 8vo, 1s.; cloth extra, 1s. 6d
The Bath in Diseases of the Skin. Small 8vo, 1s.; cloth extra, 1s. 6d.
The Laws of Life, and their Relation to Diseases of the Skin. Small 8vo, 1s.; cloth extra, 1s. 6d.

Moncrieff.—The Abdication; or, Time Tries All. An Historical Drama. By W. D. SCOTT-MONCRIEFF. With Seven Etchings by JOHN PETTIE, R.A., W. Q. ORCHARDSON, R.A., J. MACWHIRTER, A.R.A., COLIN HUNTER, R. MACBETH, and TOM GRAHAM. Large 4to, bound in buckram, 21s.

Murray (D. Christie), Novels by. Crown 8vo, cloth extra, 3s. 6d. each; post 8vo, illustrated boards, 2s. each.

A Life's Atonement.
A Model Father.
Joseph's Coat.
Coals of Fire.
By the Gate of the Sea.

Crown 8vo, cloth extra, 3s. 6d. each.

Val Strange: A Story of the Primrose Way.
Hearts.
The Way of the World. Three Vols., crown 8vo.

North Italian Folk. By Mrs. COMYNS CARR. Illust. by RANDOLPH CALDECOTT. Square 8vo, cloth extra, 7s. 6d.

Number Nip (Stories about), the Spirit of the Giant Mountains. Retold for Children by WALTER GRAHAME. With Illustrations by J. MOYR SMITH. Post 8vo, cloth extra, 5s.

Nursery Hints: A Mother's Guide in Health and Disease. By N. E. DAVIES, L.R.C.P. Crown 8vo, 1s.; cloth, 1s. 6d.

Oliphant. — Whiteladies: A Novel. With Illustrations by ARTHUR HOPKINS and HENRY WOODS. Crown 8vo, cloth extra, 3s. 6d.; post 8vo, illustrated boards, 2s.

O'Reilly.—Phœbe's Fortunes: A Novel. With Illustrations by HENRY TUCK. Post 8vo, illustrated boards, 2s.

O'Shaughnessy (Arth.), Works by:

Songs of a Worker. Fcap. 8vo, cloth extra, 7s. 6d.
Music and Moonlight. Fcap. 8vo, cloth extra, 7s. 6d.
Lays of France. Crown 8vo, cloth extra, 10s. 6d.

Ouida, Novels by. Crown 8vo, cloth extra, 5s. each; post 8vo, illustrated boards, 2s. each.

Held in Bondage.	A Dog of Flanders.
Strathmore.	Pascarel.
Chandos.	Signa.
Under Two Flags.	In a Winter City.
Cecil Castlemaine's Gage.	Ariadne.
	Friendship.
Idalia.	Moths.
Tricotrin.	Pipistrello.
Puck.	A Village Commune.
Folle Farine.	
Two Little Wooden Shoes.	Bimbi.
	In Maremma.

Wanda: A Novel. Crown 8vo, cloth extra, 5s.

Frescoes: Dramatic Sketches. Crown 8vo, cloth extra, 10s. 6d.

Bimbi: PRESENTATION EDITION. Sq. 8vo, cloth gilt, cinnamon edges, 7s. 6d.

Princess Napraxine. Three Vols., crown 8vo. [*Shortly.*

Wisdom, Wit, and Pathos. Selected from the Works of OUIDA by F. SYDNEY MORRIS. Small crown 8vo, cloth extra, 5s.

Page (H. A.), Works by:

Thoreau: His Life and Aims: A Study. With a Portrait. Post 8vo, cloth limp, 2s. 6d.

Lights on the Way: Some Tales within a Tale. By the late J. H. ALEXANDER, B.A. Edited by H. A. PAGE. Crown 8vo, cloth extra, 6s.

Pascal's Provincial Letters. A New Translation, with Historical Introduction and Notes, by T. M'CRIE, D.D. Post 8vo, cloth limp, 2s.

Paul Ferroll:

Post 8vo, illustrated boards, 2s. each
Paul Ferroll: A Novel.
Why Paul Ferroll Killed His Wife.

Paul.—Gentle and Simple. By MARGARET AGNES PAUL. With a Frontispiece by HELEN PATERSON. Cr. 8vo, cloth extra, 3s. 6d.; post 8vo, illustrated boards, 2s.

Payn (James), Novels by.
Crown 8vo, cloth extra, 3s. 6d. each;
post 8vo, illustrated boards, 2s. each.

Lost Sir Massingberd.
The Best of Husbands
Walter's Word.
Halves. | Fallen Fortunes.
What He Cost Her.
Less Black than We're Painted.
By Proxy. | High Spirits.
Under One Roof. | Carlyon's Year.
A Confidential Agent.
Some Private Views.
From Exile.
A Grape from Thorn.
For Cash Only.

Post 8vo, illustrated boards, 2s. each.

A Perfect Treasure.
Bentinck's Tutor.
Murphy's Master.
A County Family. | At Her Mercy.
A Woman's Vengeance.
Cecil's Tryst.
The Clyffards of Clyffe.
The Family Scapegrace
The Foster Brothers.
Found Dead.
Gwendoline's Harvest.
Humorous Stories.
Like Father, Like Son.
A Marine Residence.
Married Beneath Him.
  Abbey.
Not Wooed, but Won.
Two Hundred Pounds Reward.

Kit: A Memory. Crown 8vo, cloth extra, 3s. 6d.

The Canon's Ward. Three Vols., crown 8vo.

Pennell (H. Cholmondeley),
Works by: Post 8vo, cloth limp, 2s. 6d. each.

Puck on Pegasus. With Illustrations.
The Muses of Mayfair. Vers de Société, Selected and Edited by H. C. PENNELL.
Pegasus Re-Saddled. With Ten full-page Illusts. by G. DU MAURIER.

Phelps.—Beyond the Gates.
By ELIZABETH STUART PHELPS, Author of "The Gates Ajar." Crown 8vo, cloth extra, 2s. 6d. Published by special arrangement with the Author, and Copyright in England and its Dependencies.

Pirkis.—Trooping with Crows:
A Story. By CATHERINE PIRKIS. Fcap. 8vo, picture cover, 1s.

Planché (J. R.), Works by:
The Cyclopædia of Costume; or, A Dictionary of Dress—Regal, Ecclesiastical, Civil, and Military—from the Earliest Period in England to the Reign of George the Third. Including Notices of Contemporaneous Fashions on the Continent, and a General History of the Costumes of the Principal Countries of Europe. Two Vols., demy 4to, half morocco, profusely Illustrated with Coloured and Plain Plates and Woodcuts, £7 7s. The Vols. may also be had *separately* (each complete in itself) at £3 13s. 6d. each: Vol. I. THE DICTIONARY. Vol. II. A GENERAL HISTORY OF COSTUME IN EUROPE.

The Pursuivant of Arms; or, Heraldry Founded upon Facts. With Coloured Frontispiece and 200 Illustrations. Crown 8vo, cloth extra, 7s. 6d.

Songs and Poems, from 1819 to 1879. Edited, with an Introduction, by his Daughter, Mrs. MACKARNESS. Crown 8vo, cloth extra, 6s.

Play-time: Sayings and Doings
of Babyland. By EDWARD STANFORD. Large 4to, handsomely printed in Colours, 5s.

Plutarch's Lives of Illustrious
Men. Translated from the Greek, with Notes Critical and Historical, and a Life of Plutarch, by JOHN and WILLIAM LANGHORNE. Two Vols., 8vo, cloth extra, with Portraits, 10s. 6d.

Poe (Edgar Allan):—
The Choice Works, in Prose and Poetry, of EDGAR ALLAN POE. With an Introductory Essay by CHARLES BAUDELAIRE, Portrait and Facsimiles. Crown 8vo, cloth extra, 7s. 6d.

The Mystery of Marie Roget, and other Stories. Post 8vo, illustrated boards, 2s.

Pope's Poetical Works. Complete in One Volume. Post 8vo, cloth limp, 2s.

Price (E. C.), Novels by:
Valentina: A Sketch. With a Frontispiece by HAL LUDLOW. Crown 8vo, cloth extra, 3s. 6d.; post 8vo, illustrated boards, 2s.

The Foreigners. Crown 8vo, cloth extra, 3s. 6d. [*Shortly*

Proctor (Richd. A.), Works by:
Flowers of the Sky. With 55 Illustrations. Small crown 8vo, cloth extra, 4s. 6d.
Easy Star Lessons. With Star Maps for Every Night in the Year, Drawings of the Constellations, &c. Crown 8vo, cloth extra, 6s.
Familiar Science Studies. Crown 8vo, cloth extra, 7s. 6d.
Rough Ways made Smooth: A Series of Familiar Essays on Scientific Subjects. Cr. 8vo, cloth extra, 6s.
Our Place among Infinities: A Series of Essays contrasting our Little Abode in Space and Time with the Infinities Around us. Crown 8vo, cloth extra, 6s.
The Expanse of Heaven: A Series of Essays on the Wonders of the Firmament. Cr. 8vo, cloth extra, 6s.
Saturn and its System. New and Revised Edition, with 13 Steel Plates. Demy 8vo, cloth extra, 10s. 6d.
The Great Pyramid: Observatory, Tomb, and Temple. With Illustrations. Crown 8vo, cloth extra, 6s.
Mysteries of Time and Space. With Illustrations. Crown 8vo, cloth extra, 7s. 6d.
Wages and Wants of Science Workers. Crown 8vo, 1s. 6d.

Pyrotechnist's Treasury (The); or, Complete Art of Making Fireworks. By THOMAS KENTISH. With numerous Illustrations. Cr. 8vo, cl. extra, 4s. 6d.

Rabelais' Works. Faithfully Translated from the French, with variorum Notes, and numerous characteristic Illustrations by GUSTAVE DORÉ. Crown 8vo, cloth extra, 7s. 6d.

Rambosson.—Popular Astronomy. By J. RAMBOSSON, Laureate of the Institute of France. Translated by C. B. PITMAN. Crown 8vo, cloth gilt, with numerous Illustrations, and a beautifully executed Chart of Spectra, 7s. 6d.

Reader's Handbook (The) of Allusions, References, Plots, and Stories. By the Rev. Dr. BREWER. Third Edition, revised throughout, with a New Appendix, containing a COMPLETE ENGLISH BIBLIOGRAPHY. Crown 8vo, 1,400 pages, cloth extra, 7s. 6d.

Richardson. — A Ministry of Health, and other Papers. By BENJAMIN WARD RICHARDSON, M.D., &c. Crown 8vo, cloth extra, 6s.

Reade (Charles, D.C.L.), Novels by. Post 8vo, illustrated boards, 2s. each; or crown 8vo, cloth extra, Illustrated, 3s. 6d. each.
Peg Woffington. Illustrated by S. L. FILDES, A.R.A.
Christie Johnstone. Illustrated by WILLIAM SMALL.
It is Never Too Late to Mend. Illustrated by G. J. PINWELL.
The Course of True Love Never did run Smooth. Illustrated by HELEN PATERSON.
The Autobiography of a Thief; Jack of all Trades; and James Lambert. Illustrated by MATT STRETCH.
Love me Little, Love me Long. Illustrated by M. ELLEN EDWARDS.
The Double Marriage. Illustrated by Sir JOHN GILBERT, R.A., and CHARLES KEENE.
The Cloister and the Hearth. Illustrated by CHARLES KEENE.
Hard Cash. Illustrated by F. W. LAWSON.
Griffith Gaunt. Illustrated by S. L. FILDES, A.R.A., and WM. SMALL.
Foul Play. Illustrated by GEORGE DU MAURIER.
Put Yourself in His Place. Illustrated by ROBERT BARNES.
A Terrible Temptation. Illustrated by EDW. HUGHES and A. W. COOPER.
The Wandering Heir. Illustrated by HELEN PATERSON, S. L. FILDES, A.R.A., CHARLES GREEN, and HENRY WOODS, A.R.A.
A Simpleton. Illustrated by KATE CRAUFORD.
A Woman-Hater. Illustrated by THOS. COULDERY.
Readiana. With a Steel Plate Portrait of CHARLES READE.
A New Collection of Stories. In Three Vols., crown 8vo. [Preparing.

Riddell (Mrs. J. H.), Novels by:
Crown 8vo, cloth extra, 3s. 6d. each; post 8vo, illustrated boards, 2s. each.
Her Mother's Darling.
The Prince of Wales's Garden Party.

Rimmer (Alfred), Works by:
Our Old Country Towns. With over 50 Illusts. Sq. 8vo, cloth gilt, 10s. 6d.
Rambles Round Eton and Harrow. 50 Illusts. Sq. 8vo, cloth gilt, 10s. 6d.
About England with Dickens. With 58 Illustrations by ALFRED RIMMER and C. A. VANDERHOOF. Square 8vo, cloth gilt, 10s. 6d.

Robinson (F. W.), Novels by:
Women are Strange. Cr. 8vo, cloth extra, 3s. 6d.; post 8vo, illust. bds., 2s.
The Hands of Justice. Crown 8vo, cloth extra, 3s. 6d.

Robinson (Phil), Works by:
The Poets' Birds. Crown 8vo, cloth extra, 7s. 6d.
The Poets' Beasts. Crown 8vo, cloth extra, 7s. 6d. [*In preparation.*

Robinson Crusoe: A beautiful reproduction of Major's Edition, with 37 Woodcuts and Two Steel Plates by GEORGE CRUIKSHANK, choicely printed. Crown 8vo, cloth extra, 7s. 6d. 100 Large-Paper copies, printed on handmade paper, with India proofs of the Illustrations, price 36s.

Rochefoucauld's Maxims and Moral Reflections. With Notes, and an Introductory Essay by SAINTE-BEUVE. Post 8vo, cloth limp, 2s.

Roll of Battle Abbey, The; or, A List of the Principal Warriors who came over from Normandy with William the Conqueror, and Settled in this Country, A.D. 1066-7. With the principal Arms emblazoned in Gold and Colours. Handsomely printed, price 5s.

Rowley (Hon. Hugh), Works by:
Post 8vo, cloth limp, 2s. 6d. each.
Puniana: Riddles and Jokes. With numerous Illustrations.
More Puniana. Profusely Illustrated.

Russell (Clark).—Round the Galley-Fire. By W. CLARK RUSSELL, Author of "The Wreck of the *Grosvenor.*" Cr. 8vo, cloth extra, 6s.

Sala.—Gaslight and Daylight. By GEORGE AUGUSTUS SALA. Post 8vo, illustrated boards, 2s.

Sanson.—Seven Generations of Executioners: Memoirs of the Sanson Family (1688 to 1847). Edited by HENRY SANSON. Crown 8vo, cloth extra, 3s. 6d.

Saunders (John), Novels by:
Crown 8vo, cloth extra, 3s. 6d. each; post 8vo, illustrated boards, 2s. each.
Bound to the Wheel.
One Against the World.
Guy Waterman.
The Lion in the Path.
The Two Dreamers.

Science Gossip: An Illustrated Medium of Interchange for Students and Lovers of Nature. Edited by J. E. TAYLOR, F.L.S., &c. Devoted to Geology, Botany, Physiology, Chemistry, Zoology, Microscopy, Telescopy, Physiography, &c. Price 4d. Monthly; or 5s. per year, post free. It contains Original Illustrated Articles by the best-known Writers and Workers of the day. A Monthly Summary of Discovery and Progress in every department of Natural Science is given. Large space is devoted to Scientific "Notes and Queries," thus enabling every lover of nature to chronicle his own original observations, or get his special difficulties settled. For active workers and collectors the "Exchange Column" has long proved a well and widely known means of barter and exchange. The column devoted to "Answers to Correspondents" has been found helpful to students requiring personal help in naming specimens, &c. The Volumes of *Science Gossip* for the last eighteen years contain an unbroken History of the advancement of Natural Science within that period. Each Number contains a Coloured Plate and numerous Woodcuts. Vols. I. to XIV. may be had at 7s. 6d. each; and Vols. XV. to XIX. (1883), at 5s. each.

"Secret Out" Series, The:
Crown 8vo, cloth extra, profusely Illustrated, 4s. 6d. each.
The Secret Out: One Thousand Tricks with Cards, and other Recreations; with Entertaining Experiments in Drawing-room or "White Magic." By W. H. CREMER. 300 Engravings.
The Pyrotechnist's Treasury; or, Complete Art of Making Fireworks. By THOMAS KENTISH. With numerous Illustrations.
The Art of Amusing: A Collection of Graceful Arts, Games, Tricks, Puzzles, and Charades. By FRANK BELLEW. With 300 Illustrations.
Hanky-Panky: Very Easy Tricks, Very Difficult Tricks, White Magic, Sleight of Hand. Edited by W. H. CREMER. With 200 Illustrations.
The Merry Circle: A Book of New Intellectual Games and Amusements. By CLARA BELLEW. With many Illustrations.
Magician's Own Book: Performances with Cups and Balls, Eggs, Hats, Handkerchiefs, &c. All from actual Experience. Edited by W. H. CREMER. 200 Illustrations.

The "Secret Out" Series, *continued*—
  Magic No Mystery: Tricks with Cards, Dice, Balls, &c., with fully descriptive Directions; the Art of Secret Writing; Training of Performing Animals, &c. With Coloured Frontispiece and many Illustrations.

Senior (William), Works by:
  Travel and Trout in the Antipodes. Crown 8vo, cloth extra, 6s.
  By Stream and Sea. Post 8vo, cloth limp, 2s. 6d.

Seven Sagas (The) of Prehistoric Man. By JAMES H. STODDART, Author of "The Village Life." Crown 8vo, cloth extra, 6s.

Shakespeare:
  The First Folio Shakespeare.—MR. WILLIAM SHAKESPEARE's Comedies, Histories, and Tragedies. Published according to the true Originall Copies. London, Printed by ISAAC IAGGARD and ED. BLOUNT. 1623.—A Reproduction of the extremely rare original, in reduced facsimile, by a photographic process—ensuring the strictest accuracy in every detail. Small 8vo, half-Roxburghe, 7s. 6d.
  The Lansdowne Shakespeare. Beautifully printed in red and black, in small but very clear type. With engraved facsimile of DROESHOUT'S Portrait. Post 8vo, cloth extra, 7s. 6d.
  Shakespeare for Children: Tales from Shakespeare. By CHARLES and MARY LAMB. With numerous Illustrations, coloured and plain, by J. MOYR SMITH. Crown 4to, cloth gilt, 6s.
  The Handbook of Shakespeare Music. Being an Account of 350 Pieces of Music, set to Words taken from the Plays and Poems of Shakespeare, the compositions ranging from the Elizabethan Age to the Present Time. By ALFRED ROFFE. 4to, half-Roxburghe, 7s.
  A Study of Shakespeare. By ALGERNON CHARLES SWINBURNE. Crown 8vo, cloth extra, 8s.

Shelley's Complete Works, in Four Vols., post 8vo, cloth limp, 8s.; or separately, 2s. each. Vol. I. contains his Early Poems, Queen Mab, &c., with an Introduction by LEIGH HUNT; Vol. II., his Later Poems, Laon and Cythna, &c.; Vol. III., Posthumous Poems, the Shelley Papers, &c.; Vol. IV., his Prose Works, including A Refutation of Deism, Zastrozzi, St. Irvyne, &c.

Sheridan's Complete Works, with Life and Anecdotes. Including his Dramatic Writings, printed from the Original Editions, his Works in Prose and Poetry, Translations, Speeches, Jokes, Puns, &c. With a Collection of Sheridaniana. Crown 8vo, cloth extra, gilt, with 10 full-page Tinted Illustrations, 7s. 6d.

Short Sayings of Great Men. With Historical and Explanatory Notes by SAMUEL A. BENT, M.A. Demy 8vo, cloth extra, 7s. 6d.

Sidney's (Sir Philip) Complete Poetical Works, including all those in "Arcadia." With Portrait, Memorial-Introduction, Essay on the Poetry of Sidney, and Notes, by the Rev. A. B. GROSART, D.D. Three Vols., crown 8vo, cloth boards, 18s.

Signboards: Their History. With Anecdotes of Famous Taverns and Remarkable Characters. By JACOB LARWOOD and JOHN CAMDEN HOTTEN. Crown 8vo, cloth extra, with 100 Illustrations, 7s. 6d.

Sims (G. R.), Works by:
  How the Poor Live. With 60 Illustrations by FRED. BARNARD. Large 4to, 1s.
  Horrible London. Reprinted, with Additions, from the *Daily News*. Large 4to, 6d. [*Shortly.*

Sketchley.—A Match in the Dark. By ARTHUR SKETCHLEY. Post 8vo, illustrated boards, 2s.

Slang Dictionary, The: Etymological, Historical, and Anecdotal. Crown 8vo, cloth extra, gilt, 6s. 6d.

Smith (J. Moyr), Works by:
  The Prince of Argolis: A Story of the Old Greek Fairy Time. By J. MOYR SMITH. Small 8vo, cloth extra, with 130 Illustrations, 3s. 6d.
  Tales of Old Thule. Collected and Illustrated by J. MOYR SMITH. Crown 8vo, cloth gilt, profusely Illustrated, 6s.
  The Wooing of the Water Witch: A Northern Oddity. By EVAN DALDORNE. Illustrated by J. MOYR SMITH. Small 8vo, cloth extra, 6s.

South-West, The New: Travelling Sketches from Kansas, New Mexico, Arizona, and Northern Mexico. By ERNST VON HESSE-WARTEGG. With 100 fine Illustrations and 3 Maps. 8vo, cloth extra, 14s. [*In preparation.*

Spalding.—Elizabethan Demonology: An Essay in Illustration of the Belief in the Existence of Devils, and the Powers possessed by Them. By T. ALFRED SPALDING, LL.B. Crown 8vo, cloth extra, 5s.

Speight.— The Mysteries of Heron Dyke. By T. W. SPEIGHT. With a Frontispiece by M. ELLEN EDWARDS. Crown 8vo, cloth extra, 3s. 6d.; post 8vo, illustrated boards, 2s.

Spenser for Children. By M. H. TOWRY. With Illustrations by WALTER J. MORGAN. Crown 4to, with Coloured Illustrations, cloth gilt, 6s.

Staunton.—Laws and Practice of Chess; Together with an Analysis of the Openings, and a Treatise on End Games. By HOWARD STAUNTON. Edited by ROBERT B. WORMALD. New Edition, small cr. 8vo, cloth extra, 5s.

Sterndale.—The Afghan Knife: A Novel. By ROBERT ARMITAGE STERNDALE. Cr. 8vo, cloth extra, 3s. 6d.; post 8vo, illustrated boards, 2s.

Stevenson (R. Louis), Works by:
Travels with a Donkey in the Cevennes. Frontispiece by WALTER CRANE. Post 8vo, cloth limp, 2s. 6d.
An Inland Voyage. With a Frontispiece by WALTER CRANE. Post 8vo, cloth limp, 2s. 6d.
Virginibus Puerisque, and other Papers. Crown 8vo, cloth extra, 6s.
Familiar Studies of Men and Books. Crown 8vo, cloth extra, 6s.
New Arabian Nights. Crown 8vo, cl. extra, 6s.; post 8vo, illust. bds., 2s.
The Silverado Squatters. With Frontispiece. Cr. 8vo, cloth extra, 6s.

St. John.—A Levantine Family. By BAYLE ST. JOHN. Post 8vo, illustrated boards, 2s.

Stoddard.—Summer Cruising in the South Seas. By CHARLES WARREN STODDARD. Illustrated by WALLIS MACKAY. Crown 8vo, cloth extra, 3s. 6d.

St. Pierre.—Paul and Virginia, and The Indian Cottage. By BERNARDIN DE ST. PIERRE. Edited, with Life, by the Rev. E. CLARKE. Post 8vo, cloth limp, 2s.

Stories from Foreign Novelists. With Notices of their Lives and Writings. By HELEN and ALICE ZIMMERN; and a Frontispiece. Crown 8vo, cloth extra, 3s. 6d.

Strutt's Sports and Pastimes of the People of England; including the Rural and Domestic Recreations, May Games, Mummeries, Shows, Processions, Pageants, and Pompous Spectacles, from the Earliest Period to the Present Time. With 140 Illustrations. Edited by WILLIAM HONE. Crown 8vo, cloth extra, 7s. 6d.

Suburban Homes (The) of London: A Residential Guide to Favourite London Localities, their Society, Celebrities, and Associations. With Notes on their Rental, Rates, and House Accommodation. With a Map of Suburban London. Crown 8vo, cloth extra, 7s. 6d.

Swift's Choice Works, in Prose and Verse. With Memoir, Portrait, and Facsimiles of the Maps in the Original Edition of "Gulliver's Travels." Cr. 8vo, cloth extra, 7s. 6d.

Swinburne (Algernon C.), Works by:
The Queen Mother and Rosamond. Fcap. 8vo, 5s.
Atalanta in Calydon. Crown 8vo, 6s.
Chastelard. A Tragedy. Crown 8vo, 7s.
Poems and Ballads. FIRST SERIES. Fcap. 8vo, 9s. Also in crown 8vo, at same price.
Poems and Ballads. SECOND SERIES. Fcap. 8vo, 9s. Also in crown 8vo, at same price.
Notes on Poems and Reviews. 8vo, 1s.
William Blake: A Critical Essay. With Facsimile Paintings. Demy 8vo, 16s.
Songs before Sunrise. Crown 8vo, 10s. 6d.
Bothwell: A Tragedy. Crown 8vo, 12s. 6d.
George Chapman: An Essay. Crown 8vo, 7s.
Songs of Two Nations. Cr. 8vo, 6s.
Essays and Studies. Crown 8vo, 12s.
Erechtheus: A Tragedy. Crown 8vo, 6s.
Note of an English Republican on the Muscovite Crusade. 8vo, 1s.
A Note on Charlotte Bronte. Crown 8vo, 6s.
A Study of Shakespeare. Crown 8vo, 8s.
Songs of the Springtides. Crown 8vo, 6s.
Studies in Song. Crown 8vo, 7s.

A. C. SWINBURNE'S WORKS, *continued*—
Mary Stuart: A Tragedy. Crown 8vo, 8s.
Tristram of Lyonesse, and other Poems. Crown 8vo, 9s.
A Century of Roundels. Small 4to, cloth extra, 8s.

Syntax's (Dr.) Three Tours: In Search of the Picturesque, in Search of Consolation, and in Search of a Wife. With the whole of ROWLANDSON'S droll page Illustrations in Colours and a Life of the Author by J. C. HOTTEN. Medium 8vo, cl. extra, 7s. 6d.

Taine's History of English Literature. Translated by HENRY VAN LAUN. Four Vols., small 8vo, cloth boards, 30s.—POPULAR EDITION, Two Vols., crown 8vo, cloth extra, 15s.

Taylor (Dr.).—The Sagacity and Morality of Plants: A Sketch of the Life and Conduct of the Vegetable Kingdom. By J. E. TAYLOR, F.L.S., &c. With Coloured Frontispiece and 100 Illustrations. Crown 8vo, cloth extra, 7s. 6d.

Taylor's (Bayard) Diversions of the Echo Club: Burlesques of Modern Writers. Post 8vo, cl. limp, 2s.

Taylor's (Tom) Historical Dramas: "Clancarty," "Jeanne Darc," "'Twixt Axe and Crown," "The Fool's Revenge," "Arkwright's Wife," "Anne Boleyn," "Plot and Passion." One Vol., crown 8vo, cloth extra, 7s. 6d.
⁎ The Plays may also be had separately, at 1s. each.

Thackerayana: Notes and Anecdotes. Illustrated by Hundreds of Sketches by WILLIAM MAKEPEACE THACKERAY, depicting Humorous Incidents in his School-life, and Favourite Characters in the books of his every-day reading. With Coloured Frontispiece. Cr. 8vo, cl. extra, 7s. 6d.

Thomas (Bertha), Novels by. Crown 8vo, cloth extra, 3s. 6d. each; post 8vo, illustrated boards, 2s. each.
Cressida.
Proud Maisie.
The Violin-Player.

Thomson's Seasons and Castle of Indolence. With a Biographical and Critical Introduction by ALLAN CUNNINGHAM, and over 50 fine Illustrations on Steel and Wood. Crown 8vo, cloth extra, gilt edges, 7s. 6d.

Thomas (M.).—A Fight for Life: A Novel. By W. MOY THOMAS. Post 8vo, illustrated boards, 2s.

Thornbury (Walter), Works by
Haunted London. Edited by EDWARD WALFORD, M.A. With Illustrations by F. W. FAIRHOLT, F.S.A. Crown 8vo, cloth extra, 7s. 6d.
The Life and Correspondence of J. M. W. Turner. Founded upon Letters and Papers furnished by his Friends and fellow Academicians. With numerous Illustrations in Colours, facsimiled from Turner's Original Drawings. Crown 8vo, cloth extra, 7s. 6d.
Old Stories Re-told. Post 8vo, cloth limp, 2s. 6d.
Tales for the Marines. Post 8vo, illustrated boards, 2s.

Timbs (John), Works by:
The History of Clubs and Club Life in London. With Anecdotes of its Famous Coffee-houses, Hostelries, and Taverns. With numerous Illustrations. Cr. 8vo, cloth extra, 7s. 6d.
English Eccentrics and Eccentricities: Stories of Wealth and Fashion, Delusions, Impostures, and Fanatic Missions, Strange Sights and Sporting Scenes, Eccentric Artists, Theatrical Folks, Men of Letters, &c. With nearly 50 Illusts. Crown 8vo, cloth extra, 7s. 6d.

Torrens. — The Marquess Wellesley, Architect of Empire. An Historic Portrait. By W. M. TORRENS, M.P. Demy 8vo, cloth extra, 14s.

Trollope (Anthony), Novels by: Crown 8vo, cloth extra, 3s. 6d. each; post 8vo, illustrated boards, 2s. each.
The Way We Live Now.
The American Senator.
Kept in the Dark.
Frau Frohmann.
Marion Fay.

Mr. Scarborough's Family. Crown 8vo, cloth extra, 3s. 6d.
The Land-Leaguers. Crown 8vo, cloth extra, 3s. 6d. [*Shortly*.

Trollope (Frances E.), Novels by
Like Ships upon the Sea. Crown 8vo, cloth extra, 3s. 6d.; post 8vo, illustrated boards, 2s.
Mabel's Progress. Crown 8vo, cloth extra, 3s. 6d.
Anne Furness. Crown 8vo, cloth extra, 3s. 6d.

Trollope (T. A.).—Diamond Cut Diamond, and other Stories. By THOMAS ADOLPHUS TROLLOPE. Crown 8vo, cloth extra, 3s. 6d.; post 8vo, illustrated boards, 2s.

Tytler (Sarah), Novels by:
Crown 8vo, cloth extra, 3s. 6d. each; post 8vo, illustrated boards, 2s. each.
What She Came Through.
The Bride's Pass.

Van Laun.—History of French Literature. By HENRY VAN LAUN. Complete in Three Vols., demy 8vo, cloth boards, 7s. 6d. each.

Villari.—A Double Bond: A Story. By LINDA VILLARI. Fcap. 8vo, picture cover, 1s.

Walcott.—Church Work and Life in English Minsters; and the English Student's Monasticon. By the Rev. MACKENZIE E. C. WALCOTT, B.D. Two Vols., crown 8vo, cloth extra, with Map and Ground-Plans, 14s.

Walford (Edw., M.A.), Works by:
The County Families of the United Kingdom. Containing Notices of the Descent, Birth, Marriage, Education, &c., of more than 12,000 distinguished Heads of Families, their Heirs Apparent or Presumptive, the Offices they hold or have held, their Town and Country Addresses, Clubs, &c. Twenty-fourth Annual Edition, for 1884, cloth, full gilt, 50s. (Shortly.
The Shilling Peerage (1884). Containing an Alphabetical List of the House of Lords, Dates of Creation, Lists of Scotch and Irish Peers, Addresses, &c. 32mo, cloth, 1s. Published annually.
The Shilling Baronetage (1884). Containing an Alphabetical List of the Baronets of the United Kingdom, short Biographical Notices, Dates of Creation, Addresses, &c. 32mo, cloth, 1s. Published annually.
The Shilling Knightage (1884). Containing an Alphabetical List of the Knights of the United Kingdom, short Biographical Notices, Dates of Creation, Addresses, &c. 32mo, cloth, 1s. Published annually.
The Shilling House of Commons (1884). Containing a List of all the Members of the British Parliament, their Town and Country Addresses, &c. 32mo, cloth, 1s. Published annually.

EDW. WALFORD'S WORKS, continued—
The Complete Peerage, Baronetage, Knightage, and House of Commons (1884). In One Volume, royal 32mo, cloth extra, gilt edges, 5s. Published annually.
Haunted London. By WALTER THORNBURY. Edited by EDWARD WALFORD, M.A. With Illustrations by F. W. FAIRHOLT, F.S.A. Crown 8vo, cloth extra, 7s. 6d.

Walton and Cotton's Complete Angler; or, The Contemplative Man's Recreation; being a Discourse of Rivers, Fishponds, Fish and Fishing, written by IZAAK WALTON; and Instructions how to Angle for a Trout or Grayling in a clear Stream, by CHARLES COTTON. With Original Memoirs and Notes by Sir HARRIS NICOLAS, and 61 Copperplate Illustrations. Large crown 8vo, cloth antique, 7s. 6d.

Wanderer's Library, The:
Crown 8vo, cloth extra, 3s. 6d. each.
Wanderings in Patagonia; or, Life among the Ostrich Hunters. By JULIUS BEERBOHM. Illustrated.
Camp Notes: Stories of Sport and Adventure in Asia, Africa, and America. By FREDERICK BOYLE.
Savage Life. By FREDERICK BOYLE.
Merrie England in the Olden Time. By GEORGE DANIEL. With Illustrations by ROBT. CRUIKSHANK.
Circus Life and Circus Celebrities. By THOMAS FROST.
The Lives of the Conjurers. By THOMAS FROST.
The Old Showmen and the Old London Fairs. By THOMAS FROST.
Low-Life Deeps. An Account of the Strange Fish to be found there. By JAMES GREENWOOD.
The Wilds of London. By JAMES GREENWOOD.
Tunis: The Land and the People. By the Chevalier de HESSE-WARTEGG. With 22 Illustrations.
The Life and Adventures of a Cheap Jack. By One of the Fraternity. Edited by CHARLES HINDLEY.
The World Behind the Scenes. By PERCY FITZGERALD.
Tavern Anecdotes and Sayings. Including the Origin of Signs, and Reminiscences connected with Taverns, Coffee Houses, Clubs, &c. By CHARLES HINDLEY. With Illusts.
The Genial Showman: Life and Adventures of Artemus Ward. By E. P. HINGSTON. With a Frontispiece.

The Wanderer's Library, *continued*—

The Story of the London Parks. By Jacob Larwood. With Illustrations.

London Characters. By Henry Mayhew. Illustrated.

Seven Generations of Executioners: Memoirs of the Sanson Family (1688 to 1847). Edited by Henry Sanson.

Summer Cruising in the South Seas. By Charles Warren Stoddard. Illustrated by Wallis Mackay.

Warner.—A Roundabout Journey. By Charles Dudley Warner, Author of "My Summer in a Garden." Crown 8vo, cloth extra, 6s.

Warrants, &c.:—

Warrant to Execute Charles I. An exact Facsimile, with the Fifty-nine Signatures, and corresponding Seals. Carefully printed on paper to imitate the Original, 22 in. by 14 in. Price 2s.

Warrant to Execute Mary Queen of Scots. An exact Facsimile, including the Signature of Queen Elizabeth, and a Facsimile of the Great Seal. Beautifully printed on paper to imitate the Original MS. Price 2s.

Magna Charta. An Exact Facsimile of the Original Document in the British Museum, printed on fine plate paper, nearly 3 feet long by 2 feet wide, with the Arms and Seals emblazoned in Gold and Colours. Price 5s.

The Roll of Battle Abbey; or, A List of the Principal Warriors who came over from Normandy with William the Conqueror, and Settled in this Country, A.D. 1066-7. With the principal Arms emblazoned in Gold and Colours. Price 5s.

Westropp.—Handbook of Pottery and Porcelain; or, History of those Arts from the Earliest Period. By Hodder M. Westropp. With numerous Illustrations, and a List of Marks. Crown 8vo, cloth limp, 4s. 6d.

Whistler v. Ruskin: Art and Art Critics. By J. A. Macneill Whistler. Seventh Edition, square 8vo, 1s.

White's Natural History of Selborne. Edited, with Additions, by Thomas Brown, F.L.S. Post 8vo, cloth limp, 2s.

Williams (W. Mattieu, F.R.A.S.), Works by:

Science Notes. See the Gentleman's Magazine. 1s. Monthly.

Science in Short Chapters. Crown 8vo, cloth extra, 7s. 6d.

A Simple Treatise on Heat. Crown 8vo, cloth limp, with Illusts., 2s. 6d.

Wilson (Dr. Andrew, F.R.S.E.), Works by:

Chapters on Evolution: A Popular History of the Darwinian and Allied Theories of Development. Second Edition. Crown 8vo, cloth extra, with 259 Illustrations, 7s. 6d.

Leaves from a Naturalist's Notebook. Post 8vo, cloth limp, 2s. 6d.

Leisure-Time Studies, chiefly Biological. Second Edition. Crown 8vo, cloth extra, with Illustrations, 6s.

Wilson (C.E.).—Persian Wit and Humour: Being the Sixth Book of the Baharistan of Jami, Translated for the first time from the Original Persian into English Prose and Verse. With Notes by C. E. Wilson, M.R.A.S., Assistant Librarian Royal Academy of Arts. Cr. 8vo, parchment binding, 4s.

Winter (J. S.), Stories by:
Crown 8vo, cloth extra, 3s. 6d. each post 8vo, illustrated boards, 2s. each.

Cavalry Life.

Regimental Legends.

Wood.—Sabina: A Novel. By Lady Wood. Post 8vo, illustrated boards, 2s.

Words, Facts, and Phrases: A Dictionary of Curious, Quaint, and Out-of-the-Way Matters. By Eliezer Edwards. Cr. 8vo, half-bound, 12s. 6d.

Wright (Thomas), Works by:

Caricature History of the Georges. (The House of Hanover.) With 400 Pictures, Caricatures, Squibs, Broadsides, Window Pictures, &c. Crown 8vo, cloth extra, 7s. 6d.

History of Caricature and of the Grotesque in Art, Literature, Sculpture, and Painting. Profusely Illustrated by F. W. Fairholt, F.S.A. Large post 8vo, cloth extra, 7s. 6d.

Yates (Edmund), Novels by:
Post 8vo, illustrated boards 2s. each.

Castaway.

The Forlorn Hope.

Land at Last.

NOVELS BY THE BEST AUTHORS.
At every Library.

Princess Napraxine. By OUIDA. Three Vols. [*Shortly.*
Dorothy Forster. By WALTER BESANT. Three Vols. [*Shortly.*
The New Abelard. By ROBERT BUCHANAN. Three Vols.
Fancy-Free, &c. By CHARLES GIBBON. Three Vols.
Ione. E. LYNN LINTON. Three Vols.
The Way of the World. By D. CHRISTIE MURRAY. Three Vols.

Maid of Athens. By JUSTIN MCCARTHY, M.P. With 12 Illustrations by FRED. BARNARD. Three Vols.
The Canon's Ward. By JAMES PAYN. Three Vols.
A Real Queen. By R. E. FRANCILLON. Three Vols.
A New Collection of Stories by CHARLES READE. Three Vols. [*In preparation.*

THE PICCADILLY NOVELS.
Popular Stories by the Best Authors. LIBRARY EDITIONS, many Illustrated, crown 8vo, cloth extra, 3s. 6d. each.

BY MRS. ALEXANDER.
Maid, Wife, or Widow?

BY W. BESANT & JAMES RICE.
Ready-Money Mortiboy.
My Little Girl.
The Case of Mr. Lucraft.
This Son of Vulcan.
With Harp and Crown.
The Golden Butterfly.
By Celia's Arbour.
The Monks of Thelema.
'Twas in Trafalgar's Bay.
The Seamy Side.
The Ten Years' Tenant.
The Chaplain of the Fleet.

BY WALTER BESANT.
All Sorts and Conditions of Men.
The Captains' Room.

BY ROBERT BUCHANAN.
A Child of Nature.
God and the Man.
The Shadow of the Sword.
The Martyrdom of Madeline.
Love Me for Ever.

BY MRS. H. LOVETT CAMERON.
Deceivers Ever.
Juliet's Guardian.

BY MORTIMER COLLINS.
Sweet Anne Page.
Transmigration.
From Midnight to Midnight.

MORTIMER & FRANCES COLLINS.
Blacksmith and Scholar.
The Village Comedy.
You Play me False.

BY WILKIE COLLINS.
Antonina.
Basil.
Hide and Seek.
The Dead Secret.
Queen of Hearts.
My Miscellanies.
Woman in White.
The Moonstone.
Man and Wife.
Poor Miss Finch.
Miss or Mrs.?
New Magdalen.
The Frozen Deep.
The Law and the Lady.
The Two Destinies
Haunted Hotel
The Fallen Leaves
Jezebel's Daughter
The Black Robe.
Heart and Science

BY DUTTON COOK.
Paul Foster's Daughter

BY WILLIAM CYPLES.
Hearts of Gold.

BY JAMES DE MILLE.
A Castle in Spain.

BY J. LEITH DERWENT.
Our Lady of Tears. | Circe's Lovers.

PICCADILLY NOVELS, *continued—*
BY M. BETHAM-EDWARDS.
Felicia. | Kitty.
BY MRS. ANNIE EDWARDES.
Archie Lovell.
BY R. E. FRANCILLON.
Olympia. | Queen Cophetua.
One by One.
Prefaced by Sir BARTLE FRERE.
Pandurang Hari.
BY EDWARD GARRETT.
The Capel Girls.
BY CHARLES GIBBON.
Robin Gray.
For Lack of Gold.
In Love and War.
What will the World Say?
For the King.
In Honour Bound.
Queen of the Meadow.
In Pastures Green.
The Flower of the Forest.
A Heart's Problem.
The Braes of Yarrow.
The Golden Shaft.
Of High Degree.
BY THOMAS HARDY.
Under the Greenwood Tree.
BY JULIAN HAWTHORNE.
Garth.
Ellice Quentin.
Sebastian Strome.
Prince Saroni's Wife.
Dust.
Fortune's Fool.
BY SIR A. HELPS.
Ivan de Biron.
BY MRS. ALFRED HUNT.
Thornicroft's Model.
The Leaden Casket.
Self-Condemned.
BY JEAN INGELOW.
Fated to be Free.
BY HENRY JAMES, Jun.
Confidence.
BY HARRIETT JAY.
The Queen of Connaught.
The Dark Colleen.
BY HENRY KINGSLEY.
Number Seventeen.
Oakshott Castle.

PICCADILLY NOVELS, *continued—*
BY E. LYNN LINTON.
Patricia Kemball.
Atonement of Leam Dundas.
The World Well Lost.
Under which Lord?
With a Silken Thread.
The Rebel of the Family.
"My Love!"
BY HENRY W. LUCY.
Gideon Fleyce.
BY JUSTIN McCARTHY, M.P.
The Waterdale Neighbours.
My Enemy's Daughter.
Linley Rochford. | A Fair Saxon.
Dear Lady Disdain.
Miss Misanthrope.
Donna Quixote.
The Comet of a Season.
BY GEORGE MAC DONALD, LL.D.
Paul Faber, Surgeon.
Thomas Wingfold, Curate.
BY MRS. MACDONELL.
Quaker Cousins.
BY KATHARINE S. MACQUOID.
Lost Rose. | The Evil Eye.
BY FLORENCE MARRYAT.
Open! Sesame! | Written in Fire.
BY JEAN MIDDLEMASS.
Touch and Go.
BY D. CHRISTIE MURRAY
Life's Atonement. | Coals of Fire.
Joseph's Coat. | Val Strange.
A Model Father. | Hearts.
By the Gate of the Sea.
BY MRS. OLIPHANT.
Whiteladies.
BY MARGARET A. PAUL
Gentle and Simple.
BY JAMES PAYN.
Lost Sir Massingberd. | High Spirits.
Best of Husbands | Under One Roof.
Fallen Fortunes. | Carlyon's Year.
Halves. | A Confidential Agent.
Walter's Word. | From Exile.
What He Cost Her | A Grape from Thorn.
Less Black than We're Painted. | For Cash Only.
By Proxy. | Kit: A Memory

CHATTO & WINDUS, PICCADILLY.

PICCADILLY NOVELS, continued—

BY E. C. PRICE.
Valentina.
The Foreigners.

BY CHARLES READE, D.C.L.
It is Never Too Late to Mend.
Hard Cash. | Peg Woffington.
Christie Johnstone.
Griffith Gaunt.
The Double Marriage.
Love Me Little, Love Me Long.
Foul Play.
The Cloister and the Hearth.
The Course of True Love.
The Autobiography of a Thief.
Put Yourself in His Place.
A Terrible Temptation.
The Wandering Heir. | A Simpleton.
A Woman-Hater. | Readiana.

BY MRS. J. H. RIDDELL.
Her Mother's Darling.
Prince of Wales's Garden-Party.

BY F. W. ROBINSON.
Women are Strange.
The Hands of Justice.

BY JOHN SAUNDERS.
Bound to the Wheel.
Guy Waterman.
One Against the World.
The Lion in the Path.
The Two Dreamers.

PICCADILLY NOVELS, continued—

BY T. W. SPEIGHT.
The Mysteries of Heron Dyke.

BY R. A. STERNDALE.
The Afghan Knife.

BY BERTHA THOMAS.
Proud Maisie. | Cressida.
The Violin-Player.

BY ANTHONY TROLLOPE.
The Way we Live Now.
The American Senator.
Frau Frohmann.
Marion Fay.
Kept in the Dark.
Mr. Scarborough's Family.
The Land-Leaguers.

BY FRANCES E. TROLLOPE.
Like Ships upon the Sea.
Anne Furness.
Mabel's Progress.

BY T. A. TROLLOPE.
Diamond Cut Diamond.

By IVAN TURGENIEFF and Others.
Stories from Foreign Novelists.

BY SARAH TYTLER
What She Came Through.
The Bride's Pass.

BY J. S. WINTER.
Cavalry Life.
Regimental Legends.

CHEAP EDITIONS OF POPULAR NOVELS.
Post 8vo, illustrated boards, 2s. each.

BY EDMOND ABOUT.
The Fellah.

BY HAMILTON AÏDÉ.
Carr of Carrlyon. | Confidences.

BY MRS. ALEXANDER.
Maid, Wife, or Widow?

BY SHELSLEY BEAUCHAMP.
Grantley Grange.

BY W. BESANT & JAMES RICE.
Ready-Money Mortiboy.
With Harp and Crown.
This Son of Vulcan.
My Little Girl.
The Case of Mr. Lucraft.
The Golden Butterfly.

BY BESANT AND RICE, continued—
By Celia's Arbour.
The Monks of Thelema.
'Twas in Trafalgar's Bay.
The Seamy Side.
The Ten Years' Tenant.
The Chaplain of the Fleet.
All Sorts and Conditions of Men.
The Captains' Room.

BY FREDERICK BOYLE.
Camp Notes. | Savage Life.

BY BRET HARTE.
An Heiress of Red Dog.
The Luck of Roaring Camp.
Californian Stories.
Gabriel Conroy. | Flip

CHEAP POPULAR NOVELS, *continued—*
BY ROBERT BUCHANAN.
The Shadow of the Sword.
A Child of Nature.
God and the Man.
The Martyrdom of Madeline.
Love Me for Ever.
BY MRS. BURNETT.
Surly Tim.
BY MRS. LOVETT CAMERON.
Deceivers Ever. | Juliet's Guardian.
BY MACLAREN COBBAN.
The Cure of Souls.
BY C. ALLSTON COLLINS.
The Bar Sinister.
BY WILKIE COLLINS.

Antonina.	Miss or Mrs.?
Basil.	The New Magdalen.
Hide and Seek.	
The Dead Secret.	The Frozen Deep.
Queen of Hearts.	Law and the Lady.
My Miscellanies.	The Two Destinies
Woman in White.	Haunted Hotel.
The Moonstone.	The Fallen Leaves.
Man and Wife.	Jezebel's Daughter
Poor Miss Finch.	The Black Robe.

BY MORTIMER COLLINS.
Sweet Anne Page.
Transmigration.
From Midnight to Midnight.
A Fight with Fortune.
MORTIMER & FRANCES COLLINS.
Sweet and Twenty. | Frances.
Blacksmith and Scholar.
The Village Comedy.
You Play me False.
BY DUTTON COOK.
Leo. | Paul Foster's Daughter.
BY J. LEITH DERWENT.
Ou Lady of Tears.
BY CHARLES DICKENS.
Sketches by Boz.
The Pickwick Papers.
Oliver Twist.
Nicholas Nickleby.
BY MRS. ANNIE EDWARDES.
A Point of Honour. | Archie Lovell.
BY M. BETHAM-EDWARDS.
Felicia. | Kitty.
BY EDWARD EGGLESTON.
Roxy.

CHEAP POPULAR NOVELS, *continued—*
BY PERCY FITZGERALD.
Bella Donna. | Never Forgotten.
The Second Mrs. Tillotson.
Polly.
Seventy-five Brooke Street.
BY ALBANY DE FONBLANQUE.
Filthy Lucre.
BY R. E. FRANCILLON.
Olympia. | Queen Cophetua.
One by One.
Prefaced by Sir H. BARTLE FRERE.
Pandurang Hari.
BY HAIN FRISWELL.
One of Two.
BY EDWARD GARRETT.
The Capel Girls.
BY CHARLES GIBBON.

Robin Gray.	Queen of the Meadow.
For Lack of Gold.	
What will the World Say?	In Pastures Green
	The Flower of the Forest.
In Honour Bound.	
The Dead Heart.	A Heart's Problem
In Love and War.	The Braes of Yarrow.
For the King.	

BY WILLIAM GILBERT.
Dr. Austin's Guests.
The Wizard of the Mountain.
James Duke.
BY JAMES GREENWOOD.
Dick Temple.
BY ANDREW HALLIDAY.
Every-Day Papers.
BY LADY DUFFUS HARDY.
Paul Wynter's Sacrifice.
BY THOMAS HARDY.
Under the Greenwood Tree.
BY JULIAN HAWTHORNE.
Garth. | Sebastian Strome
Ellice Quentin. | Dust.
Prince Saroni's Wife.
BY SIR ARTHUR HELPS.
Ivan de Biron.
BY TOM HOOD.
A Golden Heart.
BY MRS. GEORGE HOOPER.
The House of Raby.
BY VICTOR HUGO.
The Hunchback of Notre Dame.

CHATTO & WINDUS, PICCADILLY. 31

CHEAP POPULAR NOVELS, *continued—*
BY MRS. ALFRED HUNT.
Thornicroft's Model.
The Leaden Casket.
Self-Condemned.

BY JEAN INGELOW.
Fated to be Free.

BY HARRIETT JAY.
The Dark Colleen.
The Queen of Connaught.

BY HENRY KINGSLEY.
Oakshott Castle. | Number Seventeen

BY E. LYNN LINTON.
Patricia Kemball.
The Atonement of Leam Dundas.
The World Well Lost.
Under which Lord?
With a Silken Thread.
The Rebel of the Family.
"My Love!"

BY HENRY W. LUCY.
Gideon Fleyce.

BY JUSTIN McCARTHY, M.P.
Dear Lady Disdain.
The Waterdale Neighbours.
My Enemy's Daughter.
A Fair Saxon.
Linley Rochford.
Miss Misanthrope.
Donna Quixote.
The Comet of a Season.

BY GEORGE MACDONALD.
Paul Faber, Surgeon.
Thomas Wingfold, Curate.

BY MRS. MACDONELL.
Quaker Cousins.

BY KATHARINE S. MACQUOID.
The Evil Eye. | Lost Rose.

BY W. H. MALLOCK.
The New Republic.

BY FLORENCE MARRYAT.
Open! Sesame! | A Little Stepson.
A Harvest of Wild | Fighting the Air.
Oats. | Written in Fire.

BY J. MASTERMAN.
Half-a-dozen Daughters.

BY JEAN MIDDLEMASS.
Touch and Go. | Mr. Dorillion.

CHEAP POPULAR NOVELS, *continued—*
BY D. CHRISTIE MURRAY.
A Life's Atonement.
A Model Father.
Joseph's Coat.
Coals of Fire.
By the Gate of the Sea.

BY MRS. OLIPHANT.
Whiteladies.

BY MRS. ROBERT O'REILLY.
Phœbe's Fortunes.

BY OUIDA.
Held in Bondage.
Strathmore.
Chandos.
Under Two Flags.
Idalia.
Cecil Castlemaine.
Tricotrin.
Puck.
Folle Farine.
A Dog of Flanders.
Pascarel.
TwoLittleWooden Shoes.
Signa.
In a Winter City.
Ariadne.
Friendship.
Moths.
Pipistrello.
A Village Commune.
Bimbi.
In Maremma.

BY MARGARET AGNES PAUL.
Gentle and Simple.

BY JAMES PAYN.
Lost Sir Massingberd.
A Perfect Treasure.
Bentinck's Tutor.
Murphy's Master.
A County Family.
At Her Mercy.
A Woman's Vengeance.
Cecil's Tryst.
Clyffards of Clyffe.
The Family Scapegrace.
Foster Brothers.
Found Dead.
Best of Husbands.
Walter's Word.
Halves.
Fallen Fortunes.
What He Cost Her.
Humorous Stories
Gwendoline's Harvest.
Like Father, Like Son.
A Marine Residence.
Married Beneath Him.
Mirk Abbey.
Not Wooed, but Won.
£200 Reward.
Less Black than We're Painted.
By Proxy.
Under One Roof.
High Spirits.
Carlyon's Year.
A Confidential Agent.
Some Private Views.
From Exile.
A Grape from a Thorn.
For Cash Only.

BY EDGAR A. POE.
The Mystery of Marie Roget.

CHEAP POPULAR NOVELS, *continued*—
BY E. C. PRICE.
Valentina.

BY CHARLES READE.
It is Never Too Late to Mend.
Hard Cash.
Peg Woffington.
Christie Johnstone.
Griffith Gaunt.
Put Yourself in His Place.
The Double Marriage.
Love Me Little, Love Me Long.
Foul Play.
The Cloister and the Hearth.
The Course of True Love.
Autobiography of a Thief.
A Terrible Temptation.
The Wandering Heir.
A Simpleton.
A Woman-Hater.
Readiana.

BY MRS. J. H. RIDDELL.
Her Mother's Darling.
Prince of Wales's Garden Party.

BY F. W. ROBINSON.
Women are Strange.

BY BAYLE ST. JOHN.
A Levantine Family.

BY GEORGE AUGUSTUS SALA.
Gaslight and Daylight.

BY JOHN SAUNDERS.
Bound to the Wheel.
One Against the World.
Guy Waterman.
The Lion in the Path.
Two Dreamers.

BY ARTHUR SKETCHLEY.
A Match in the Dark.

BY T. W. SPEIGHT.
The Mysteries of Heron Dyke.

BY R. A. STERNDALE.
The Afghan Knife.

BY R. LOUIS STEVENSON.
New Arabian Nights.

BY BERTHA THOMAS.
Cressida. | Proud Maisie.
The Violin-Player.

BY W. MOY THOMAS.
A Fight for Life.

CHEAP POPULAR NOVELS, *continued*—
BY WALTER THORNBURY.
Tales for the Marines.

BY T. ADOLPHUS TROLLOPE.
Diamond Cut Diamond.

BY ANTHONY TROLLOPE.
The Way We Live Now.
The American Senator.
Frau Frohmann.
Marion Fay.
Kept in the Dark.

By FRANCES ELEANOR TROLLOPE
Like Ships Upon the Sea.

BY MARK TWAIN.
Tom Sawyer.
An Idle Excursion.
A Pleasure Trip on the Continent of Europe.
A Tramp Abroad.
The Stolen White Elephant.

BY SARAH TYTLER.
What She Came Through.
The Bride's Pass.

BY J. S. WINTER.
Cavalry Life. | Regimental Legends

BY LADY WOOD.
Sabina.

BY EDMUND YATES.
Castaway. | The Forlorn Hope.
Land at Last.

ANONYMOUS.
Paul Ferroll.
Why Paul Ferroll Killed his Wife.

Fcap. 8vo, picture covers, 1s. each.
Jeff Briggs's Love Story. By BRET HARTE.
The Twins of Table Mountain. By BRET HARTE.
Mrs. Gainsborough's Diamonds. By JULIAN HAWTHORNE.
Kathleen Mavourneen. By Author of "That Lass o' Lowrie's."
Lindsay's Luck. By the Author of "That Lass o' Lowrie's."
Pretty Polly Pemberton. By the Author of "That Lass o' Lowrie's."
Trooping with Crows. By Mrs. PIRKIS.
The Professor's Wife. By LEONARD GRAHAM.
A Double Bond. By LINDA VILLARI.
Esther's Glove. By R. E. FRANCILLON.
The Garden that Paid the Rent. By TOM JERROLD.

www.ingramcontent.com/pod-product-compliance
Lightning Source LLC
Chambersburg PA
CBHW032049220426
43664CB00008B/925